When people communicate, they often adapt their interaction styles to one another. For example, they may match each other's behavior, synchronize the timing of behavior, or behave in opposite ways. This volume analyzes these dyadic interaction patterns and builds a case for a new theory of adaptation. Interaction Adaptation Theory draws the soundest principles from previous theories while being responsive to current empirical evidence. To develop this theory the authors summarize a broad range of theories that seek to predict and explain adaptation patterns such as synchrony, mirroring, matching, reciprocity, compensation, convergence, and divergence. These summaries include examination of the evidence supporting each theory, operational issues, statistical analysis procedures, and definitions of terms used, before presenting new data that incorporate these methodological considerations. It concludes by suggesting new research directions that would test the theory in order to bring the research full circle and connect interaction patterns with outcomes.

Interpersonal adaptation

# Interpersonal adaptation
## Dyadic interaction patterns

**Judee K. Burgoon**
*University of Arizona*

**Lesa A. Stern**
*Southern Illinois University – Edwardsville*

**Leesa Dillman**
*University of Nevada, Las Vegas*

CAMBRIDGE
UNIVERSITY PRESS

Published by the Press Syndicate of the University of Cambridge
The Pitt Building, Trumpington Street, Cambridge CB2 1RP
40 West 20th Street, New York, NY 10011-4211, USA
10 Stamford Road, Oakleigh, Melbourne 3166, Australia

First published 1995

Printed in the United States of America

*Library of Congress Cataloging-in-Publication Data*
Burgoon, Judee K.
Interpersonal adaptation : dyadic interaction patterns / Judee K.
Burgoon, Lesa A. Stern, Leesa Dillman.
p. cm.
Includes bibliographical references (p. ) and index.
ISBN 0-521-45120-5 (hc)
1. Interpersonal communication.   2. Adaptability (Psychology)
3. Interpersonal relations.   4. Intimacy (Psychology)   I. Stern,
Lesa A.   II. Dillman, Leesa.   III. Title.
BF637.C45B86 1995
153.6 – dc20                                                  94-43249
                                                                    CIP

A catalog record for this book is available from the British Library.

ISBN 0-521-45120-5 hardback

This book is dedicated to the University of Arizona's
Department of Communication –
to the community of scholars that forms its corpus
and to the ideas and ideals that are its spirit.

# Contents

*List of figures and tables*                                    *page* xiii
*Preface*                                                              xv

**I   Overview**

1   Introduction                                                      3
    The basic patterns                                               4
    The importance of interaction adaptation                         5
    Overview of the chapters                                         8
    A guide to using this volume                                    14

**II   Interaction adaptation theories and models**

2   Biological approaches                                           19
    Interactional synchrony                                         19
        Definitions                                                 20
        Origins and evidence of synchrony                           21
        Functions                                                   23
    Mimicry and mirroring                                           25
        Definitions                                                 25
        Evidence of mimicry and mirroring                           27
    Conclusion                                                      29

3   Arousal and affect approaches                                   30
    Affiliative Conflict Theory                                     30
        The original theory                                         30
        Argyle and Cook's modification                              32
        Empirical support                                           33
        Criticisms of ACT                                           34
        Recent modifications of ACT                                 35
        Summary                                                     37
    Arousal-Labeling Theory                                         38
        Assumptions, propositions, and hypotheses                   38

Empirical support                                          40
Criticisms                                                 42
Summary                                                    43
Markus-Kaplan and Kaplan's Bidimensional Model             43
  Assumptions and propositions                             44
  Criticisms                                               45
  Summary                                                  46
Discrepancy-Arousal Theory                                 46
  Norms, preferences, and experiences to
    expectations to discrepancies                          47
  Discrepancies to arousal to affect                       48
  Affect to behavioral response                            48
  Empirical support                                        49
  Summary                                                  53
Dialectical models                                         54
  Assumptions                                              54
  Empirical support                                        56
  Contributions                                            57
  Criticisms                                               57
  Summary                                                  58
Conclusion                                                 58

4  Social norm approaches                                  60
The norm of reciprocity                                    60
  Empirical support                                        62
Social Exchange Theory and Resource Exchange
    Theory                                                 63
  Reciprocal resource exchange                             63
  Empirical support                                        65
Couple interaction and the "dyadic effect"                 66
  Empirical evidence                                       66
  Criticisms                                               69
  Summary                                                  71
Communication Accommodation Theory                         72
  The original theory                                      72
  Later modifications of CAT                               74
  Empirical support                                        75
  Criticisms                                               77
  Summary                                                  78
Conclusion                                                 79

5　Communication and cognitive approaches　81
　A functional perspective　81
　Emphasis on meaning and interpretation　83
　Patterson's Sequential-Functional Model　84
　　The original theory　84
　　　Antecedent factors　84
　　　Preinteraction mediators　86
　　　Interaction phase　87
　　Recent modifications of SFM　88
　　Empirical support　89
　　Contributions　92
　　Criticisms　92
　　Summary　93
　[ Expectancy Violations Theory　94
　　Assumptions, propositions, and hypotheses　94
　　Application to reciprocity and compensation　97
　　Empirical support　98
　　Summary　104
　[ Cognitive-Valence Theory　105
　　Assumptions, propositions, and hypotheses　105
　　Contributions　108
　　Empirical support　108
　　Criticisms　109
　Motor mimicry revisited　109
　　Empirical support for communicative motor
　　　mimicry　110
　　Contributions and criticisms　110
　　Summary　111
　Conclusion　111

III　Issues in studying interaction adaptation

6　Reconceptualizing interaction adaptation patterns　115
　Previous definitions and conceptualizations　116
　Criteria for distinguishing adaptation patterns　117
　　Directedness and behavioral contingency　117
　　Mutual versus unidirectional influence　120
　　Change versus maintenance　120
　　Magnitude versus direction of change　122
　　Timing and rhythmicity　123
　　Intentionality　124

|  | Behavioral equivalence | 126 |
|  | Proposed definitions | 128 |
|  | Conclusion | 130 |
| 7 | Operationalizing adaptation patterns | 132 |
|  | Exchange principles | 132 |
|  | Directed and contingent responses | 132 |
|  | Change versus maintenance | 135 |
|  | Concatenous responses | 136 |
|  | Contiguous versus lagged responses | 137 |
|  | Directionality versus magnitude | 138 |
|  | Functional orientation and functional equivalence | 138 |
|  | Perceived versus behavioral adaptation | 140 |
|  | Size of measurement unit | 142 |
|  | Observer versus participant perspective | 144 |
|  | Sample composition | 145 |
|  | Conclusion | 146 |
| 8 | Analyzing adaptation patterns | 148 |
|  | Level of measurement | 150 |
|  | Between-dyads versus within-dyads analyses | 152 |
|  | Pearson product-moment correlation | 153 |
|  | Canonical correlation | 156 |
|  | Intraclass correlation | 156 |
|  | Cross-sectional versus longitudinal and serial data | 158 |
|  | Markov chains and lag sequential analysis | 160 |
|  | Time-series models | 161 |
|  | Interrupted time-series models | 163 |
|  | Cross-lagged panel correlation | 165 |
|  | Repeated measures analysis of variance | 166 |
|  | Univariate or multivariate data | 167 |
|  | Single versus multiple statistical approaches | 168 |
|  | Conclusion | 169 |
| **IV** | **Multimethod tests of reciprocity and compensation** | |
| 9 | A first illustration | 173 |
|  | Method | 174 |
|  | Multiple discriminant analysis results | 174 |
|  | Pearson product-moment correlations | 175 |
|  | Baseline interview results | 181 |
|  | Manipulation interview results | 182 |

Summary and interpretations 184
Intraclass correlations 186
  Baseline interview results 186
  Manipulation interview results 187
  Summary and interpretations 187
Individual time-series correlations 188
  Comparisons by dyad and condition 188
  Analysis by channel 196
  Analysis by behavior 196
  Summary and implications 197
Interrupted time series 198
  Summary and implications 202
Repeated measures MANOVAs 203
  Summary and implications 212
Conclusions 212

10 Further illustrations 214
A second multimethod dyadic interaction experiment 214
  Method 215
    Participants, confederates, and observers 215
    Independent variables 216
    Procedure 216
    Manipulation checks 217
    Nonverbal dependent measures 217
  Results 217
    Manipulation and confederate behavior checks 217
    Pearson product-moment correlations and
      intraclass correlations 221
    Repeated measures analyses of variance 224
Discussion 235
  Substantive conclusions 235
  Methodological implications 241
Deception/suspicion experiments 243
Conclusion 247

**V Developing a new interpersonal adaptation theory**

11 The theories revisited 251
The extant theories 251
The research evidence 254
Theory implications 256

Reasons for nonisomorphism between theories and
  empirical data                                         259
Principles guiding Interaction Adaptation Theory         261
Our model: Interaction Adaptation Theory                265
  RED examples                                           274
  rEd examples                                           275
  reD examples                                           276
Conclusion                                               278

12  A research agenda                                    280
Testing our proposed theory                              280
  Assessing required, expected, desired, and actual
    behavior levels                                      280
  An illustration                                        283
  Measurement considerations in assessing
    functional equivalence                               284
  Use of within-dyads versus between-dyads
    analyses                                             285
  Identification of moderators                           285
Linking interaction patterns to outcomes                286
  Effects on communicator evaluation                    287
  Effects on relationship functioning and
    satisfaction                                         292
  Social influence effects                               295
  Linking outcomes to patterns: A preliminary
    assessment                                           297
Conclusion                                               299

*References*                                             303
*Index*                                                  331

# List of figures and tables

**FIGURES**

| | | |
|---|---|---|
| 1.1 | Hierarchical arrangement of theories | 11 |
| 3.1 | Patterson's Arousal-Labeling Theory | 40 |
| 3.2 | Relationships posited in Discrepancy-Arousal Theory | 50 |
| 5.1 | Patterson's Sequential-Functional Model | 90 |
| 5.2 | Expectancy Violations Theory applied to involvement changes | 99 |
| 5.3 | Andersen's Cognitive-Valence Theory | 106 |
| 6.1 | Illustration of different interaction patterns and their associated definitions | 130 |
| 8.1 | Illustration of different adaptation patterns resulting from within-dyad and between-dyad analyses | 153 |
| 8.2 | Illustration of interrupted time-series regression line on criterion of expressiveness | 164 |
| 10.1 | Reciprocity/compensation patterns on global nonverbal measures | 236 |
| 10.2 | Reciprocity/compensation patterns on composite nonverbal measures | 238 |
| 11.1 | Components of Interaction Adaptation Theory | 271 |

**TABLES**

| | | |
|---|---|---|
| 5.1 | Results from the Hale and Burgoon (1984) experiment | 101 |
| 9.1 | Means, Pearson product-moment correlations | 176 |
| 9.2 | Time-series correlations and Fisher-transformed $z$-tests on nonverbal measures | 189 |
| 9.3 | Significant compensation and reciprocity patterns | 192 |

9.4   Interrupted time-series analysis on kinesic/proxemic
      involvement and arousal                                    200
9.5   F-Values for significant effects in repeated measures
      MANOVAs                                                    204
9.6   Means for significant effects in repeated measures
      MANOVAs                                                    206
10.1  Reliabilities on nonverbal measures                       218
10.2  Pearson product-moment correlations and intraclass
      correlations for participant and target                   222
10.3  F-tests for significant communication, main effects,
      trends for time, and communication by time
      interactions on participant behavior                      226
10.4  Confederate and participant means for significant
      communication and time effects                            228
12.1  Relationship of subjects' interaction adaptation
      patterns to their postinteraction ratings of
      confederates                                               300

# Preface

Sometimes a great notion springs up at you. Many of the conclusions in this book arose that way. Other times, an idea sidles up, nudging you time and time again from the periphery. That seems to better fit how this book came about.

The first seed was probably planted at Michigan State University, where the climate, if inhospitable to the body, was highly conducive to interpersonal explorations. There, Judee taught a graduate seminar called Theories of Interpersonal Intimacy. The seed germinated at the University of Arizona, with the aid of the warm desert sun and further graduate seminars, titled Dyadic Interaction Processes and Theories of Intimacy Exchange. But it truly began to take root when the three of us, now working as a research team, realized that no single volume or article could offer us a comprehensive analysis to guide our own theorizing and research in this at once exciting and frustrating area.

And so the book grew, with much nurturing, weeding, and pruning from a host of student "gardeners" – people like Jerry Hale, Dave Buller, Milt Shatzer, Mary Diez, Rodney Reynolds, Lynn Aho, Beth Le Poire, Aileen Buslig, Renee Klingle, Patricia Rockwell, Michael Payne, Jamie Comstock, Cindy White, Pamela Koch, Eusebio Alvaro, Leu Strope, Kristen Burge, Mike Voloudakis, Megan Sheehan, and Carol Hensley – whose penetrating questions, summaries, editings, and critiques provided essential nutrients and to whom we owe a debt of gratitude. Among these students, two deserve special acknowledgment for their special insights, cogent criticisms, and edifying editorial suggestions: To Laura Guerrero and Walid Afifi, we extend our special thanks and appreciation.

Our efforts were buoyed not only by our students and colleagues locally but by many other colleagues here and abroad. Among them was Joe Cappella, long-time fellow gardener toiling in the same fertile interaction and involvement soil, who provided a most helpful review that led us to reexamine our new theory and to tackle once again issues of indeterminacy and falsifiability. Also helpful were David Kenny and Judith Hall, who read earlier versions of article submissions and/or book chapters and who offered invaluable commentaries on the methods we were recommending or employing. Their insights were joined by many other anonymous reviewers on this volume and on various projects related to it. Others due our thanks include Julia Hough, our Cambridge University Press editor, who, in addition to offering her own editorial suggestions, also allowed us time for our thinking to mature. We hope, like good wine, that the additional fermentation and distillation periods have resulted in a richer product. And fellow editor Catherine Max, who extended a most timely invitation to review a sociolinguistics manuscript on mutualities in dialogue that proved to be additionally enriching. Finally, three co-authors on two separate research projects – Beth Le Poire, Robert Rosenthal, and Doug Kelley – contributed significantly to some of the research reported in Chapters 9 and 10.

One would think with so many great minds tending this crop of theories and methods that the harvest by now would be rich. Indeed, the yield has been high – at least in our estimation – but this is a labor-intensive endeavor and much work remains to be done. And so we hope that in the future many others will join the ranks and that, through many seasons, ever-improving strains of interpersonal adaptation theories and methods will spring forth.

*Part I*

---

Overview

---

# 1

## Introduction

Imagine conversations as the erector set of human relationships: They not only create the foundation and frame on which relationships are built but supply the mortar that binds people together. Effective communication permits the smooth meshing of individuals into relationships while awkward communication weakens and erodes these relationships. In every human context – be it home, work, or play – the role of conversation in the negotiation of human relations cannot be overstated.

So how do people accomplish effective communication? One way is through adapting their interaction patterns to one another. Visualize two dancers, so perfectly synchronized that each partner's movement is enmeshed with the other's steps in a fluid and graceful union. When one steps forward the other steps back. They twirl apart then back together. Or one dancer's move is echoed by the other's. This coordination may result from the dancers responding to their partner's actual or anticipated behavior or to both.

Now imagine this same kind of coordination in conversation. People may adapt their communication behavior to one another in a variety of ways. These adaptation patterns undergird human interactions and relationships. Our objectives in this volume are to analyze the nature of these patterns, their possible antecedents and consequences, and their implications for understanding interpersonal communication. In so doing, we will review a broad range of theories that seek to predict and explain interaction patterns, examine the research evidence that has been amassed in their behalf, discuss methodological implications for studying adaptation in interpersonal communication, and present new data that incorporates many of these methodological considerations. We will conclude with our own Interaction Adaptation Theory, which we believe builds upon the soundest principles from previous theories and is responsive to the mounting empirical evidence.

## THE BASIC PATTERNS

The patterns to be considered in this book go by many names – adaptive responses, accommodation, interpersonal coordination, matching, mirroring, convergence, reciprocity, mimicry, compensation, divergence, complementarity, synchrony, dissynchrony. Basically, they refer to whether the interaction behaviors of two or more individuals are "nonrandom, patterned, or synchronized in both timing and form" (Bernieri & Rosenthal, 1991, p. 403) and whether the patterns are similar or dissimilar. For example, if one individual becomes increasingly involved in the conversation, the other may adapt by also becoming more involved or by becoming less involved. Often these patterns are subsumed under the general headings of *mutual influence* or *communication accommodation/nonaccommodation* (see Cappella, 1987; Giles, Coupland, & Coupland, 1991b; Street, 1988). Although "adaptation" and "accommodation" can be used interchangeably, we prefer the former because the latter has special meaning in the context of cognitive information-processing theories and because we do not wish readers to associate our use of the term specifically with Communication Accommodation Theory or with usages implying concessions (e.g., Rusbult, Verette, Whitney, Slovik, & Lipkus, 1991).

An umbrella term for many of these patterns is *behavioral matching,* which refers to one interactant's behavior being much like another's. Behaviors can be highly similar or even identical because two interactants begin a conversation that way or because their behaviors *converge* (become increasingly alike) over time (see Giles, Coupland, & Coupland, 1991a). If the behaviors involved are visual ones and are identical in form (e.g., one person's posture is just like the partner's), the pattern is called *mirroring.* If the behaviors instead reflect some temporal, rhythmic, and smoothly meshed coordination between interactants, the pattern is called *interactional synchrony* (Bernieri & Rosenthal, 1991; Burgoon, Buller, & Woodall, 1989). Mirroring and synchrony reflect *reciprocity.* To reciprocate, as defined by the *American Heritage Dictionary,* is "to show or feel in response or return," "to make a return for something given or done," or "to give or take mutually; to interchange." As a communication principle this translates into shared expectations that people will respond with the same or similar behaviors to the communication exhibited by another. Another type of reciprocity is *motor mimicry,* in which a person reflexively engages in an empathic behavior (e.g., a wince) that is an appropriate response to the partner's current situation and often mimics what the other person is displaying or has displayed during the recounting of an event (Bavelas, Black, Lemery, & Mullett, 1986).

The opposites of matching, mirroring, convergence, synchrony, and reciprocity are complementarity, divergence, dissynchrony, and compensation. *Complementarity* occurs when "the behaviour of each participant differs from, but complements, that of the other" (Hinde, 1979, p. 79); that is, interactants maintain a dissimilar exchange pattern (Street, 1991). *Divergence* is moving toward a more dissimilar pattern, so it entails change on at least one person's part. *Dissynchrony,* as its name implies, is the opposite of synchrony, a noticeable lack of rhythmic coordination between two interactants' communication patterns, like striking a discord. Finally, interpersonal *compensation* (which is distinct from intrapersonal compensation) has been more narrowly defined as a shift in one's own gaze or proximity in a direction opposite that of the partner (Argyle & Dean, 1965) or more broadly as the exchange of opposite approach and avoidance behaviors: "Compensation results when participants respond with dissimilar behaviours or adapt them in opposite directions" (Street & Cappella, 1985, p. 244).

## THE IMPORTANCE OF INTERACTION ADAPTATION

Why are these interpersonal patterns so important to study? One reason is that adaptation is an essential, defining feature of interpersonal communication (Cappella, 1991b). Another is that all of these patterns occur with high regularity within conversations. His review of the substantial body of literature on these patterns led Cappella (1981) to conclude:

> The one incontrovertible conclusion derived from this review is that mutual influence in expressive behaviors is a pervasive feature of social interaction, found across a variety of behaviors. This pervasiveness extends not only across behaviors but across developmental time. Very young infants, in their 1st weeks of life, and their adult caretakers show the kind of compensatory and reciprocal influences that adults exhibit later. I find such evidence striking testimony to the fundamental nature of mutual influence in human social behavior. One must be awed by the flexible yet patterned responses that social actors make to one another. (p. 123)

Yet a third reason is that these patterns are instrumental in defining and maintaining our interpersonal relationships. Beginning at birth, we adapt to caregivers and they to us, and all of our subsequent interpersonal relationships are marked by the ways in which we interact. These interaction patterns generally signify the state of interpersonal relationships (e.g., intimate or nonintimate) and they are critical to the development and maintenance of those relationships. As interaction patterns become habitualized, they can significantly influence relational progress or deterioration. Rubin (1983), for example, in a book aptly titled *Intimate Strangers* characterizes the development of intimacy as a dance of approach and avoidance; if the pulls of avoidance are stronger than the pulls of approach, true intimacy may elude a couple.

Last, our choices of interaction patterns have very real and practical consequences, both for the immediate interaction and for what follows it. Some patterns facilitate smooth, comfortable, and meaningful interaction while others may create cycles of misunderstanding, discomfort, or aggression. Consider the following examples:

- A manager is preparing to visit a new work site. Should she plan to adopt the same informal dress and language as the employees or dress in a suit and use a more formal language style? Which will make her and the employees more comfortable? Which will facilitate her ability to communicate effectively with them? And which will foster their subsequent compliance with her wishes?

- An interrogator wants to determine whether a person being questioned is being truthful or not. Should he be affable and approachable so that his demeanor "disarms" the accused and leads him to be more forthcoming, or should he be intimidating so that the accused becomes submissive and acquiesces to the information requests? Which style will result in greater accuracy in detecting deception?

- A therapist wants a reticent client to become more disclosive. Should she talk a lot, in hopes that the client will respond in kind or should she be silent, in hopes that the client will eventually fill the void by talking? Will one pattern ultimately lead to more successful therapy?

- An applicant for a job is being interviewed by someone who is highly casual in her conversational style. Will he be better liked and increase his probability of being hired if he matches the interviewer's style or if he maintains a more reserved demeanor?

- A woman wants to extinguish the romantic overtures of a fellow employee. Should she be very distant and disinterested or not? Will her behavior cause him to become even more interested and to pursue her more vigorously or will he match her own disinterest and leave her alone?

• A married couple has fallen into a pattern of escalating hostilities and conflict. If the husband now adopts a more appeasing stance in their arguments, will the wife become even more attacking, in response to his submissiveness, or will she also deescalate hostilities? And will the changed interaction pattern affect their satisfaction with, and commitment to, their relationship?

These examples make plain that the types of interaction patterns people enact can influence the immediate success or failure of interpersonal exchanges as well as have extended effects after the interchange is over. They may even have severe and far-reaching macrosocial implications. Consider: Cross-cultural differences in conversational norms may lead to mismatched interaction styles during intercultural encounters. For example, when North Americans want someone to speak up, they often talk louder themselves, hoping for a reciprocity effect. But Middle Easterners think if someone is speaking loudly to them, they are not being deferent enough and so they speak more softly. Several speaking turns between these two may leave the North American shouting and the Middle Easterner mumbling incoherently. Another example: Anglo-American listeners tend to use continuous gaze to signal attentiveness to a speaker, while African-American listeners do so only intermittently and instead use more frequent gaze while talking (Erickson, 1979). This can lead to awkward silences, to Anglo-Americans repeating statements that may appear condescending, and to a generally "out of sync" interaction. (See Burgoon et al., 1989, for additional cross-cultural differences.) The lack of synchronization can give rise to a host of misunderstandings and negative consequences. It is easy to imagine that the ways in which adversaries adopt increasingly similar or dissimilar interaction styles during dispute mediation or collective bargaining may retard or facilitate the prospect of reaching solutions. At a yet more macroscopic level, international conflict can escalate or deescalate through a reciprocal, tit-for-tat pattern of aggressiveness or reciprocal concessions. Thus, an understanding of the nature of different interpersonal interaction patterns may bring greater insights into larger sociopolitical issues.

Perhaps because of their significant ramifications for human communication and human relationships, these kinds of issues have generated prolific research and theorizing about such interaction patterns as matching, accommodation, reciprocity, and compensation. Most of that literature has focused on the patterns themselves or on their antecedents. Consequently, our attention will center there as well. In attempting to bring some coherence to this voluminous material, we will give extensive attention to both the conceptual and methodological issues involved in interaction adaptation. We also present new data that simultaneously serve as concrete illustrations of how interaction adaptation can be studied from different methodological vantage points and shed new light on the nature of adaptation patterns. All of this culminates in our own original theory of the factors prompting different interaction patterns. We conclude by returning to the all important issue of postinteractional consequences, in the belief that a fuller understanding of interpersonal adaptation will emerge from considering preinteractional and postinteractional factors in addition to the interaction itself.

## OVERVIEW OF THE CHAPTERS

We begin in Chapters 2 through 5 by reviewing the existing theories and research. The issue of interpersonal adaptation has spawned a profusion of theories and lines of inquiry, most of which have concerned the ways in which people manage conversational involvement or intimacy (e.g., Cappella, 1979, 1984, 1991b; Cappella & Planalp, 1981; Kenny & La Voie, 1982; Putnam & Jones, 1982; Ross, Cheyne, & Lollis, 1988; VanLear, 1983). However, some research looks at rhythmic patterns and the extent to which parties synchronize their patterns. Other work considers the circumstances under which people converge toward or diverge from one another in their communication style – language, speech patterns, and the like.

Some excellent summaries already available cover many of the bases (e.g., Andersen, 1985; Andersen & Andersen, 1984; Cappella, 1983; Firestone, 1977; Hale & Burgoon, 1984; Patterson, 1973, 1983; Rosenfeld, 1987; Street & Cappella, 1985). These summaries, however, are neither exhaustive nor current, given the continuing accumulation of research findings that has occurred in the last five years. Our objective is therefore to update and synthesize the various models and their empirical support, with an eye toward ultimately advancing our own model.

A quick perusal of the extant theories and explanations can be bewildering. For example, Aiello (1987), Andersen and Andersen (1984), Hale and Burgoon (1984), and O'Connor and Gifford (1988) have proffered variants on the following classes of theories, all of which are discussed in succeeding chapters: (a) reciprocity-based models, (b) intimacy regulation or affiliative conflict theories, (c) expectancy and discrepancy models, (d) arousal-based models, including arousal labeling and arousal valence, (e) functional models, and (f) social cognition or attribution-based models. Others have classified theories according to the types of predictions. Kaplan, Firestone, Klein, and Sodikoff (1983), for example, identified four different types of predictions in the literature: (a) straight reciprocity, in which one person's behavior is matched by the other's, (b) compensation, in which one person's behavior is met with opposite behaviors by the other, (c) attraction mediation, in which people approach each other if their initial attraction is positive and avoid each other if their initial attraction is negative, regardless of what the other does, and (d) attraction transformation, in which people are predicted to reciprocate the approach of attractive others but to compensate the approach of unattractive others. Abele (1986) proposed three alternative predictions specifically for the relationship of gaze to topic intimacy: (a) compensation, in which a person's gaze compensates for topic intimacy throughout the interaction, (b) adaptation, in which gaze is inversely related to topic intimacy at the beginning of an interaction but differences dissipate by the end of the interaction, and (c) sequencing, in which gaze decreases as partner's predictability increases over time. Yet others (e.g., Street & Cappella, 1985) have classified theories according to the primary explanatory mechanisms underlying them. This has commonly resulted in three broad classes – arousal models, cognitive models, and functional models.

Gleaned from all of this literature is a potpourri of factors proposed as instigating or controlling adaptation processes, among them:

1. social attraction and similarity (e.g. Lynn, 1978; Wallbott, forthcoming)
2. social exchange and equity principles (e.g., Roloff & Campion, 1985)
3. norms and obligations (e.g., La Gaipa, 1977; Lynn, 1978)
4. modeling (e.g., Hosman & Tardy, 1980)
5. motor mimicry (e.g., Bavelas, Black, Lemery, & Mullett, 1986)
6. synchrony (e.g., Bullowa, 1975)
7. social control motivations (e.g., Patterson, 1983)
8. self-presentation concerns (e.g., Shaffer & Tomarelli, 1989)
9. attributions of intent (e.g., Street & Cappella, 1985)

10. cognitive biases (e.g., La Gaipa, 1977)
11. reinforcement (e.g., La Gaipa, 1977)
12. individual differences in intimacy predispositions, personality, mood, emotional state, social refractory state, etc. (e.g., Kaplan, 1977)
13. environmental definitions and constraints (e.g., Kaplan, 1977)
14. interaction functions and goals (e.g., Snyder, 1992)
15. relational definitions and stage (e.g., Altman & Taylor, 1973)
16. frame attunement (e.g., Kendon, 1990)

Given the diversity of theories and explanations that have been advanced and the disciplines from which they derive (psychology, communication, sociology, linguistics, anthropology, psychiatry), it is perhaps unsurprising that no single theory has yet emerged as conceptually superior. Empirical efforts to conduct "critical tests" pitting various theories against each other (e.g., Abele, 1986; Hale & Burgoon, 1984; Kaplan et al., 1983; Lynn, 1978) have likewise failed to produce a "winner." When we first approached this literature, then, our intent was to analyze more deeply the assumptions underlying each theory, to identify explicitly each theory's key premises, and to assess the extent of empirical support for each. Our present intent in summarizing this literature is to trace the important lines of thought and inquiry that have been foundational to the extant knowledge about interpersonal adaptation and to extract from each what seem to be the most valid principles. In turn, these principles will be incorporated in the new model we are advancing.

There are numerous ways this material could be organized. The organizational framework we shall follow is our own. Because we come to this body of literature from a communication perspective, it is useful for us to consider the degree to which various models incorporate communication principles and treat interaction patterns as intentional, symbolic activities. Many of the theorists whose work we will cite might disagree with where we have placed their contribution. Our aim is heurism rather than organizational hegemony. Accordingly, we believe the different models and theories can be arrayed along a continuum ranging from, at one extreme, what can be variously labeled as reactive, automatic, nonsymbolic, and/or indicative behavior to, at the other extreme, communicative, mindful, intentional, and/or symbolic behavior. This arrangement is depicted in Figure 1.1.

Without belaboring all that the different terms imply, let it suffice to

Reactive/Automatic/
Nonsymbolic/
Indicative Behavior

I. **BIOLOGICAL MODELS**
   (based on comfort needs, safety, bonding, social
   organization, universal processes)
   **Interactional Synchrony**
   **Motor Mimicry and Mirroring**

II. **AROUSAL AND AFFECT MODELS**
   (addition of psychological needs to above
   factors)
   **Affiliative Conflict Theory**
   **Arousal-Labeling Theory**
   **Bidimensional Model**
   **Discrepancy-Arousal Theory**
   **Dialectical Models**

Biological and Psychological
Needs – Focus on Individual

Habitual
Behavior

III. **SOCIAL NORM MODELS**
   (incorporation of cultural, societal factors,
   ingroup-outgroup relations)
   **Norm of Reciprocity**
   **Social Exchange and Resource Exchange**
   **Theories**
   **The Dyadic Effect**
   **Communication Accommodation Theory**

Social Processes,
Societal Needs – Focus on
Groups

IV. **COMMUNICATION AND COGNITION**
   **MODELS**
   (emphasis on functions, goals, meanings,
   perceptions, attributions)
   **Sequential-Functional Model**
   **Expectancy Violations Theory**
   **Cognitive-Valence Theory**
   **Motor Mimicry Revisited** (Bavelas et al.)

Hybrid Needs and Goals –
Focus on Dyads

Communicative/
Mindful/
Intentional/
Symbolic

Figure 1.1   Hierarchical arrangement of theories.

say that some displays, like those of other species, are innate, evolutionary-based signals that occur automatically without intent or deliberate forethought. They arise as natural, nonarbitrary signals that are nonsymbolic and nonpropositional and, as a consequence, may be more indicative of a person's state of affairs (much as a flushed complexion indicates that a person has a fever) than communicative. At the other extreme are behaviors that are intentional, conscious behaviors that are strategic and symbolic (i.e., rely on a shared, socially constructed coding system). In between are behaviors that are potentially communicative but often operate in a more mindless, habitual manner, perhaps because they are well-practiced ("overlearned") routines that typically facilitate smooth interaction. For example, interactants may unconsciously adjust their speaking tempo to one another so that they can switch speaking turns without talking over each other and experiencing awkward silences. For more detailed analyses of these distinctions, we direct the interested reader to Andersen (1991), Bavelas (1990), Buck (1988, 1991), Burgoon (1994), Ekman and Friesen (1969b), Kellermann (1992), Liska (1987, 1993a–c), and Motley (1990a,b, 1991).

Chapter 2 covers theories that largely fit the innate/reactive/ unintentional end of the continuum in that the behaviors appear to be biologically driven. Such models assume or posit such universal, biologically rooted factors as safety, comfort, bonding, and social organization as driving mechanisms for the observed interaction behavior. Theories or models entailing synchrony or innate mimicry principles are included here (e.g., Bernieri, Reznick, & Rosenthal, 1988; Condon & Ogston, 1967). The attention in these models is almost exclusively nonverbal.

Chapter 3 encompasses models that give arousal and affect a central role. These include Affiliative Conflict Theory, the Arousal-Labeling Model, Discrepancy-Arousal Theory, a bidimensional approach– avoidance model, and dialectic theories or models (e.g., Altman, Vinsel, & Brown, 1981; Argyle & Dean, 1965; Cappella & Greene, 1982, 1984; Markus-Kaplan & Kaplan, 1984). As will be seen, these theories are primarily psychological in their focus, with individual needs such as attachment and privacy providing major impetus for interaction adjustments, most of which are nonverbal in nature.

Chapter 4 examines theories that begin to shift attention to sociological factors such as social norms, social exchange principles, and ingroup/outgroup relations that prompt behavioral change (e.g., Dindia, 1988; Giles et al., 1991a; Gouldner, 1960; Roloff, 1987; Street & Giles, 1982). Here, group influences and learned patterns of behavior become more central. Communication issues begin to play an increasingly significant role, and verbal behavior receives real attention for the first time.

Chapter 5 addresses recent models that incorporate many or all of the aforenamed features as well as acknowledge more explicitly what communication functions are being fulfilled by various conversational patterns. Representative works include Patterson's Sequential-Functional Model, Expectancy Violations Theory, Cognitive Valence Theory, and Motor Mimicry (see, e.g., Andersen, 1985; Bavelas, Black, Chovil, Lemery, & Mullett, 1988; Hale & Burgoon, 1984; Patterson, 1982, 1983).

As we review these theories and models, it will become apparent that many of them invoke the same elements and predictions, with later models building upon rather than repudiating earlier ones. The increase in complexity in later models has brought a concomitant reduction in falsifiability and fewer attempts to subject the theories to empirical verification. Thus, much of the research to be reviewed tests earlier rather than later models. Nevertheless, many of the early studies have implications for later theories and in some cases foreshadow the directions later theorizing has taken. Our reviews of the literature will therefore not be strictly chronological but rather will progress from the simpler, biologically driven models to the more complicated ones incorporating psychological, sociological, and communication elements.

The foundation of prior literature having been laid, Chapter 6 proceeds to discuss various definitional issues that need to be addressed and have so far prevented a clear synthesis of the theories and related literature. Terms such as matching, reciprocity, compensation, convergence, divergence, synchrony, and complementarity are reviewed and their correspondences or differences analyzed. The objective of this analysis is to promote greater uniformity in the vocabulary used to reference interaction adaptation processes as well as to use these definitions to reexamine the extent of empirical support for the different interaction patterns.

Chapter 7 translates these conceptual definition issues into operational ones. If one is to conduct research on matching, reciprocity, and compensation patterns, what are the implications for design and measurement? For example, should perceived or actual reciprocity be measured? And how should lagged behaviors be taken into account? These issues are addressed in detail.

Chapter 8 reviews statistical analysis alternatives that have been commonly employed in testing patterns. Several possible approaches are then illustrated in Chapters 9 and 10 by applying various analysis techniques to different data sets and examining how results complement or contradict one another. These chapters have as their dual purposes illustrating how statistical analysis strategies compare in the kinds of conclusions they yield and presenting substantive conclusions about the degree to which matching, reciprocity, and compensation occur in normal conversation, based on use of multivariate data and multiple analysis methods.

The final two chapters build upon this base by proposing a new theory and suggesting directions for research in testing it. Conceptual, operational, and analytical issues addressed in the preceding chapters establish criteria by which previous research can be judged. In Chapter 11, these criteria are applied in a critique of previous work and an assessment of the viable elements of each. The empirical findings and critique become the foundation for the proposed Interaction Adapation Theory. The theory incorporates biological, psychological, and social factors from previous models in its explanatory calculus while incorporating some communicative factors not acknowledged previously.

Chapter 12 concludes by proposing future research that addresses theoretical issues raised by our own and others' models and offering methodological suggestions for gaining a more comprehensive understanding of adaptation patterns. As part of a future research agenda, we consider the question of how interaction patterns affect postinteractional outcomes. We review what little is known so far about the effects of different patterns on such outcomes as relationship definitions, relational satisfaction, and influence, and we propose further possibilities for considering the link between interaction adaptation patterns and postinteractional consequences.

## A GUIDE TO USING THIS VOLUME

In creating this volume, our objective has been to reach at least two different audiences. The first is advanced students of interpersonal behavior and interpersonal relationships who are most interested in what we already know about interaction patterns. For such readers, probably the most relevant chapters are 2 through 5, which cover the existing theories and research; Chapter 11, which critiques previous theories and offers our own model; and Chapter 12, which examines the effects of these interaction patterns. Chapter 6, on definitional issues, might also be helpful in sorting through the various theories. We believe that principles of interaction adaptation are highly relevant to such diverse contexts as friendship formation, family relations, employment interviews, employer–employee interactions, negotiation and dispute resolution, intercultural encounters, race relations, teacher–student exchanges, therapist–client interchanges, and interactions between health care professionals and their patients. We expect that students with any of these interests will be able to apply the theories and principles to encounters of interest to them.

The second audience we hope to reach is scholars and advanced students interested in conducting research on dyadic or group interaction generally and adaptation patterns specifically. For such readers, the most relevant chapters are Chapters 6 through 10, on how to define, operationalize, and statistically analyze these patterns, and Chapter 12, on possibilities for future research. Because the kind of research that has been conducted to date has emanated from communication scholars, psychologists, sociologists, linguists, anthropologists, family relations scholars, and clinicians, the material included here may be useful to all these disciplines.

In all cases, we have aimed to keep the chapters short so that, like a travel package, readers can select those excursions that are of most interest and skip others. Of course, we hope that many who share our enthusiasm (as well as our exasperation) with this area of study will choose to take the full tour.

*Part II*

---

Interaction adaptation theories and models

---

# 2

## Biological approaches

With this chapter we begin to review theories and models that have been advanced to predict and explain interaction adaptation patterns. We begin with the biologically rooted adaptation patterns of synchrony, mimicry, and mirroring, which are typically performed without awareness or volition. These patterns may be the elemental organizing principles for all social interaction. As such, they are likely prerequisites for matching, convergence, and reciprocity. That is, they may be necessary but not sufficient conditions for reciprocal adaptation.

### INTERACTIONAL SYNCHRONY

Social interaction is rhythmically and hierarchically organized (Bruneau, 1994; Chapple, 1982; Condon & Ogston, 1971). It entails regular *patterns* of behavior in which each interactant's behavior influences the other's behavior (Cappella, 1991a). The dyad rather than single individuals, and dynamic rather than static behaviors, are at the heart of synchrony.

Specifically, interactional synchrony focuses on how individuals coordinate their communication behaviors temporally with those of another conversant to achieve a kind of "goodness of fit" between them. It represents a nonrandom co-occurrence of mutual adaptation (Cappella, 1981). Synchrony and motor mimicry together may be the basis for one person "catching" another's mood, emotion, or behavior pattern. Their influence on human interaction is so compelling that Hatfield, Cacioppo, and Rapson (1994) advanced the following basic proposition in their case for emotional contagion:

> In conversation, people tend automatically and continuously to mimic and synchronize their movements with the facial expressions, voices, postures, movements, and instrumental behaviors of others. (p. 10)

### Definitions

Originally conceptualized by Condon and Ogston (1966, 1967, 1971), synchrony actually occurs at both the intrapersonal and interpersonal levels. *Intrapersonal synchrony,* also known as speaker or self-synchrony, is defined as the coordination of behavior to one's own vocal–verbal stream. Interpersonal or *interactional synchrony* occurs during social interactions and involves behaviors of both the speaker and listener. Condon and Ogston (1971) originally conceptualized interactional synchrony as congruence between a listener's changes in body motion with those of a speaker's vocal–verbal stream. They contended that an interactional synchrony explanation cannot predict what body parts will actually move nor in what direction that movement will occur. Therefore, they believed the key to synchrony is the rhythmicity or cyclical nature of behaviors and the coordination between behavioral "change points" rather than similarities between the behaviors themselves.

More recently, Bernieri and colleagues (Bernieri, Reznick, & Rosenthal, 1988; Bernieri & Rosenthal, 1991) have argued for expanding the concept of synchrony to include three components: *interaction rhythms, simultaneous movement,* and *behavioral meshing.* The rhythmicity component, which is defined as the degree of congruence between the behavioral cycles of two or more people, can be viewed as the metronome to which human communication is set. The coordination of rhythms between two people is believed to arise through the process of *entrainment* (Condon & Ogston, 1966; Kendon, 1990), whereby one person's cycles are "captured" by another's. Like a tuning fork, one person's rhythms become attuned to, or set in motion by, the other's. Relevant to this principle is the concept of a *zeitgeber* or "time giver," which refers to environmental features, day–night cycles, social cues, or another human that creates rhythms to which people synchronize their behavior (Bernieri & Rosenthal, 1991). When two individuals in an interaction exhibit similar temporal patterns in their combined behavior, they are considered "in sync" with each other. The rhythm of their interaction may result from either of the participants or an external source serving as the "time giver."

By measuring the behavioral cycles of each individual in an interaction, and then comparing the two cycles for their congruency, researchers are able to determine the degree of entrainment between two individuals. Early research in this area focused primarily on coordination of body movement to vocalization within or between individuals.

More recent work tends to focus on the rhythms occurring between two interactants' body movements. In other words, vocalizations no longer appear to be the only or even the primary form of *zeitgeber.*

A second component of interactional synchrony is *simultaneous behavior,* which refers to the co-occurrence of two or more movements, gestures, vocalizations, or body positions. In addition to the timing of behavioral changes coinciding between two individuals, this facet of synchrony implicitly incorporates aspects of behavioral matching, postural congruence, mirroring, and motor mimicry (discussed shortly).

A third component is *behavioral meshing,* which is the coordination of two separate individuals' behavioral patterns into a single, unified, and meaningful "whole" (Bernieri & Rosenthal, 1991, p. 413). Much as two dancers adapt to each other's movements, conversants' behaviors and sequences are seen to relate to each other's actions. For example, an auditor may insert head nods and other backchannel cues at appropriate junctures during a speaker's utterances. In short, behaviors come together in some fashion to form a simultaneous or complementary pattern.

Although these previous descriptions imply that synchrony is a speaker–auditor phenomenon, Saine (reported in Burgoon & Saine, 1978, pp. 232–233) proposed two competing models for silences in interactions that imply two different types of synchrony. The *simultaneous or synchronous model* is one in which two interactants engage in simultaneous, similar behavior during a single speaking turn; that is, the auditor's behavior shows some similarities to that of the speaker. The *concatenous model* is one in which two interactants show similarities across two adjacent speaking turns; that is, the similarities are sequential, from speaker to speaker. For example, people may exchange turns in a rapid and apparently effortless manner. Saine proposed that the greater the degree of simultaneous and concatenous similarity, the smaller the likelihood of an "awkward silence" or breakdown in the interaction. He also speculated that such "synchrony" signals support, agreement, solidarity, and attraction. His distinction suggests that the concept of synchrony should be further expanded to incorporate sequential speaker–speaker forms of activity.

## Origins and evidence of synchrony

The phenomenon of synchrony has received widespread support. Though its underlying causes have been contested, most scholars ascribe an innate and biological origin to synchrony (see, e.g., Bruneau,

1994; Bullowa, 1975; Byers, 1976; Cappella, 1981; Hatfield et al., 1994). This conclusion is bolstered by evidence that interactional synchrony may begin in utero, is evident as early as 20 minutes after birth, and even appears between nonhuman primates (chimpanzees) and in response to human speech (Condon, 1980, 1982; Condon & Ogston, 1967). The fact that people can synchronize an incredible number of speech behaviors with staggering speed – often within 1/20 of a second – is further evidence of the reflexive and therefore presumably innate nature of synchrony (Hatfield et al., 1994).

Perhaps because of its assumed biological origins, the majority of studies on synchrony have investigated the rhythmic patterns occurring between infants and their caregivers. Based on the assumption that synchronous behavior reflects an innate need for predictable behavioral rhythms, a number of studies have documented nonrandom patterns of rhythmic behavior very early in life (e.g., Als, Tronick, & Brazelton, 1979; Brazelton, Tronick, Adamson, Als, & Wise, 1975; Bullowa, 1975; Condon & Ogston, 1971; Kempton, 1980). For example, one study of infant–adult interactions found that 61% of body movements were interactionally synchronous (Berghout-Austin & Peery, 1983). Another showed that when one mother failed to maintain consistent microrhythms (i.e., her tempo and kinesic displays were irregular), the infant's engagement decreased significantly (Beebe et al., 1982). In addition to microrhythms – high-frequency periods of only a few seconds or fractions of seconds – adult caretakers may also adapt to macrorhythms – lower frequency periods such as sleep–wake cycles, attention–nonattention cycles, and feeding cycles. These results, beyond implying an innate desire for order and rhythm in human social interaction, confirm systematic variation in interactants' behaviors and bolster the existence of rhythmic behavioral patterns among adults.

Numerous other studies have documented interactional synchrony among adults (see Hatfield et al., 1994, for a summary). One study, for example, found that vocal activity between interaction partners showed high cyclicity (rhymicity), and the coupling of rhythms between two speakers exceeded that between a speaker's vocal activity and own heart rate (Warner, Malloy, Schneider, Knoth, & Wilder, 1987). This underscores that interaction rhythms are highly responsive to social cues and may be more affected by them than by physiological states.

One voice disclaiming the prevalence of synchrony has been McDowall (1978a,b). Based on his own failure to find more than chance rates of synchrony among conversational partners or greater synchrony among friends than strangers, he concluded that previous findings of synchrony were an artifact of measurement or methodology. Gatewood and Rosenwein (1981), however, refuted McDowall. They contended that because McDowall redefined interactional synchrony in a nonstandard, inappropriate way, not only were his results flawed, but any generalizations from McDowall's two studies were irrelevant to the majority of interactional synchrony work based on conceptualizations offered by Condon and Kendon. In a separate rebuttal, Kempton (1980) reinforced the validity of prior research by reviewing the numerous methodological checks that had been undertaken in it. Thus, the presence of interactional synchrony stands largely undisputed.

However, this does not mean that all interactions are automatically characterized by a high degree of synchrony and coordination. Several factors may inhibit or attenuate it. Culture is one factor. For example, although Condon (1982) found evidence of synchrony between people of the same and different subcultures, synchrony was greater between individuals of the same subculture. Erikson and Schultz (1982), who examined dissynchrony, or arrhythmia, similarly found that cultural differences in interaction styles could disrupt interaction timing. People from different cultures may be on different "metronomes" (e.g., New Yorkers use fairly fast-paced speech, whereas those from the deep south of the United States speak slower), making adaptation to one another more difficult.

Individual differences in language, skills, and mental functioning are additional factors affecting synchrony (Chapple, 1982). Condon and Ogston (1966) found that schizophrenics demonstrated far less synchrony than nonschizophrenics, and Condon (1982) reported a lack of synchrony in dyslexic and other learning-disabled people. Street and Cappella (1989) concluded that "the degree to which interactants are able to coordinate and adjust conversational speech behaviors in relation to those of partners is contingent upon certain social, linguistic, and cognitive skills" (p. 500). Together, these studies imply that the general proclivity toward synchrony is modified by cultural, experiential, and other individual processes.

## Functions

Why interactional synchrony is a universal feature of human behavior is a controversial issue. Most explanations point to the functions that synchrony serves. Its early emergence in infancy implies that it fulfills basic survival needs of bonding, physical safety, and comfort (Condon, 1980; Condon & Sander, 1974). Cappella (1991a) contends that it is designed to structure the neonate's environment, to regulate emotional stimulation, and to facilitate social interaction with caretakers. Others see synchrony as laying the foundation for higher-order language and communication skills that are essential to socialization and represent mental well-being (e.g., Condon & Ogston, 1971; Kempton, 1980; Rosenfeld, 1982; Wylie, 1985). It should be noted, however, that the causal ordering of the latter function has been questioned. Street and Cappella (1989) contended that it is the lack of language, social, and cognitive skills that leads to less synchrony rather than the lack of synchrony leading to the absence of skills. That is, covariation between synchrony and other social and communicative skills does not confirm that synchrony functions as a developmental factor.

Synchrony may also function to facilitate or inhibit interaction. Tronick, Als, and Brazelton (1977) suggested that young children may use synchrony strategically to promote interaction and dissynchrony to disengage from interaction. As illustration, Brazelton et al. (1975) observed that when mothers failed to display rhythmic behavior, infants compensated by trying to draw their mothers into interaction, but if their mothers continued to act nonresponsively, the infants ultimately reciprocated the mother's nonresponsiveness. Once the mothers displayed a normal rhythmic involvement pattern with their infants, the infants responded in kind. Als et al. (1979) similarly found that infants utilize gaze to either facilitate or avoid interaction, and Bernieri et al. (1988) found an increase in negative emotional states associated with dissynchronous interactions between adults and infants, implying an emotional function of synchrony.

Adults may likewise use synchrony to regulate interaction as well as to signal such relational messages as interest, involvement, rapport, similarity, and approval (Kendon, 1970). In a study designed to address this issue, Bernieri et al. (1988) examined the difference in synchrony between mothers and their own 14-month-old children, mothers with unfamiliar children, and pseudointeractions artificially derived from split-screen edited versions of the genuine mother–infant interactions. Each version was presented on videotape to a group of judges who provided subjective ratings of synchrony. True mother–infant pairs were found to display significantly more genuine synchrony than pseudosynchrony. That is, genuine mother–infant interactions were rated as more synchronous than tapes of mothers interacting with unfamiliar infants or genuine mother–infant pairs presented in pseudointeraction tapes. Further, mothers in actual interaction with unfamiliar infants showed greater dissynchrony than mothers in pseudointeractions with their own or unfamiliar infants. Bernieri et al. offered two possible reasons for the greater synchrony in true mother–infant interactions. First, mothers may simply be more familiar with the behavioral patterns of their own infants than they are with those of other children and therefore able to anticipate and adjust to their actions more readily. Second, synchrony may be a reflection of the greater rapport and motivation to interact with one's own mother than with a stranger.

Berghout-Austin and Peery (1983) posit another function of synchrony, suggesting that rhythmic interactions may serve a speech-processing function. This conjecture is based on their finding that synchrony occurs both with and without vocalization, though it is more frequent when accompanied by speech. Also supporting the speech-processing explanation is Dittmann's work showing that body movements in interactions tend to follow pauses, regardless of whether they are within-turn or between-turn pauses, and to occur more at "start positions" than at "nonstart positions" (Dittmann, 1974; Dittmann & Llewellyn, 1969). This suggests they are intricately connected to the speech encoding process and may be indicative of difficulty in encoding language.

Kempton (1980) quarrels with a speech-processing explanation, claiming that reactions to speech are too slow to account for interactional synchrony. Speech, however, seems to be tied integrally to synchronous movements. For example, Kendon (1974) studied interactional synchrony among adults in a London pub and found that speaker–listener pairs engaged in alternate mirroring and synchrony. He also found synchrony occurring between observers (i.e., nonparticipants) and a speaker even in the absence of eye contact, suggesting that the rhythm of speech was causing the nonrandom body movement.

In sum, it appears that interactional synchrony originates as an automatic biological force serving basic survival needs such as bonding, physical safety, and comfort. However, it may also function to regulate interaction and facilitate speech processing as well as express relational and emotional states.

## MIMICRY AND MIRRORING

### Definitions

Motor mimicry refers to the tendency to imitate others' nonverbal expressions, particularly expressions such as laughter, pleasure, embarrassment, pain, discomfort, and physical exertion. Traditional theories of motor mimicry consider the process to be an instinctual overt reaction that is appropriate to another person's situation rather than to one's own. Summarizing these earlier theories, Allport (1968) characterized mimicry as "a perceptual motor reaction" (p. 32) or behavioral manifestation of a sympathetic response to another's circumstance that can be equated with empathy. For example, when a person ducks or raises the hands to cover the face while observing a ball being thrown at another person's head, motor mimicry has occurred. Wallbott (in press) discusses various early conceptualizations of motor mimicry that include the notions of a basic "imitation drive" and the "tendency for ideomotoric reactions" (p. 6). Though mimicry implies that empathic processes are operant, Wallbott adds that empathy does not guarantee enactment of mimetic behavioral patterns. Bavelas, Black, Lemery, MacInnis, and Mullett (1986) explain that empathy has both cognitive and affective dimensions. That is, one can cognitively "take on the role of the other" (e.g., Mead, 1934) or one can experience vicariously and portray behaviorally another's emotions.

This conceptualization of motor mimicry requires neither that others be present to witness the display nor that the observer have a prior relationship with the observed. Hence, this form of motor mimicry does not qualify as symbolic or intentional. Later views of motor mimicry investigated by Bavelas and her colleagues emphasize communicative functions and meanings. This modified view of motor mimicry is examined in Chapter 5.

Though mirroring is a term often used interchangeably with mimicry, the two are not identical patterns. Mimicry occurs in response to a stimulus and is often directed toward another person; mirroring is the imitation of another's body movements, or what Scheflen (1964) and Kendon (1990) refer to as postural congruence. Imitation implies that one must observe the partner's behavior before it can be copied. Mimicry differs from mirroring in that one does not have to observe the partner's response, only the stimulus for a response. So a person may wince in response to hearing about another's injury. Similar to biological synchrony, mirroring is posited to serve a bonding or affiliative function and to signal rapport among interactants (e.g., LaFrance, 1979; LaFrance & Ickes, 1981; Trout & Rosenfeld, 1980). In child development literature, it is suggested that mirroring is a process by which infants and young children learn to behave. This is what Bandura (1977) labeled "modeling."

### Evidence of mimicry and mirroring

The traditional view of motor mimicry is dependent on inferences about cognitive and affective responses. Several researchers have found that overt facial responses to emotional experiences may occur instantaneously – sometimes changing as quickly as within one-eighth to one-fifth of a second – and at times imperceptibly (e.g., Cacioppo, Tassinary, & Fridlund, 1990; Haggard & Isaacs, 1966). The rapidity and apparent lack of conscious control associated with mimicry and mirroring reactions have led to the claim that these behaviors reflect innate and empathic responses. For example, Hull (1933) designed a creative experiment in which he unobtrusively videotaped a subject viewing someone else lean forward and backward. The observer's body swayed appropriately with the stimulus person's lean. In another study, O'Toole and Dubin (1968) videotaped mothers spoon feeding their infants and found that mothers tended to make facial expressions mimicking the infants' eating behaviors.

These patterns, however, cannot conclusively be labeled mimicry since there was no objective assessment of the internal empathic experience of the subjects. Instead, an argument can be made that the observed behaviors involve a simple mirroring or modeling process. The mothers in O'Toole and Dubin's (1968) study, for instance, may have been demonstrating tacitly to their children the appropriate mouth position for eating with a spoon.

If the obligation to show an internal empathy response is suspended, then the evidence of mirroring and vocal and facial mimicry is substantial. Studies of this phenomenon tend to focus on one of three areas: facial, vocal, or postural mirroring and mimicry. A number of studies provide evidence that mothers and infants mimic one another's facial and emotional expressions (e.g., Haviland & Lelwica, 1987; O'Toole & Dubin, 1968; Reissland, 1988). Termine and Izard (1988) found, for example, that 9-month-old infants tended to mirror their mothers' expressions of joy and sadness. They also reported that infants may avert gaze in response to their mothers' expressions of sadness. It is possible that these were merely instances of modeling or mirroring, but they may also represent mimicry, that is, appropriately responding to the situation of the mother. In another interesting study, Hsee, Hatfield, Carlson, and Chemtob (1990) demonstrated that students viewing a film of a man telling either a very happy or a very sad story responded with happier facial expressions upon hearing the happy story and sadder facial ex-

pressions when hearing the sad story. Again, suspending the requirement for evidence of actual empathy, these reactions by observers to the
situation of a stranger clearly suggest mimicry was operating.

In addition to the face, larger body parts and muscle groups have been
found to be part of the mirroring and mimicry process (Hatfield &
Rapson, 1990). For example, Berger and Hadley (1975) found that
observers' muscles respond to another's situation as if "to help them
out." Subjects watching a videotape of a stutterer had more EMG activity in the lip region, while those watching a videotape of two arm
wrestlers evidenced more activity in the forearm region. In another
study, LaFrance (1982) observed students in a classroom mimicking the
instructor's posture and arm positions.

There is also evidence of vocal mimicry. For example, Simner (1971)
found that infants respond by crying when they hear another infant
crying, but not when they hear an artificially produced cry. Hatfield et
al. (1994) suggest the infant is responding to another's emotional
distress rather than to noise per se. As with facial mimicry and mirroring, Condon (1982) found that people's mimicry and synchronization
with the speech sounds of others occur very rapidly. Hatfield et al.
(1994) summarize research documenting the considerable number of
vocal characteristics people tend to mimic almost simultaneously.
Among these are speech rate (Street, 1984; Webb, 1972), utterance
durations (Matarazzo, Weitman, Saslow, & Wiens, 1963), response latencies (Cappella & Planalp, 1981; Matarazzo & Wiens, 1972), and
speech accents (Giles & Powesland, 1975).

All of the foregoing research supports a high degree of symmetry and
mutuality in interaction. However, Papousek (in press) rightly notes that
due to the infant's limited linguistic competence, a number of asymmetries necessarily occur. Though it may be instinctual for infants to match
behaviors with their caregivers, concomitant evidence of asymmetrical
patterns suggests that convergence and divergence develop over time,
and matching and complementary patterns of behavior are fine-tuned
early in life. Thus, matching (or reciprocity) evolve rather than being
fully present at the outset of interaction; they are an outcome of, rather
than the impetus for, parent–infant interaction. Extending the argument
for a learning component to matching, Wallbott (in press) contends that
ontogenetically, imitations occur at an automatic level. Later, as a child
develops perspective-taking skills (necessary for mimicry), the process
of imitating another becomes more cognitively based. Wallbott proposes a model explaining how matching and motor mimicry occur

tacitly and establish a sense of similarity with another. As one's cognitive skills develop (particularly the ability to take on the role of the partner), the notion of similarity that derives from basic motor mimicry or matching behaviors influences a sense of liking and attraction for the partner and fosters further interactive congruence and convergence. Thus, matching behavior is both innate and learned and its extent is dependent on the degree of liking and attraction that develop.

Several of these authors further contend that mimicry and mirroring, even if tacitly performed, convey messages of rapport, solidarity, attraction, and warmth to observers and participants. However, Davis (1985) argues that perhaps because of the speed with which mimicry and mirroring occur, these behavioral patterns cannot be "learned" or faked. He claims that people either have this innate knack or they do not, and to try to force it appears "phony." In other words, although communicative messages may be inferred from these behaviors, they appear to be automatic, instinctual responses.

## CONCLUSION

Interactional synchrony, motor mimicry, and mirroring, though similar, can be distinguished from one another. In some literature, these three terms are used interchangeably, contributing to confusion in both conceptual and operational definitions. Abundant evidence has been amassed that these are universal and probably innate response patterns. Some researchers suggest a basic motivation of bonding or rapport underlying each. Others contend that these behavioral patterns serve more complex communicative and speech-processing functions. Irrespective of how many or which functions they serve, these patterns appear to represent a biological substratum to later communication processes and may signify a strong pressure toward adaptation. Further, while these behaviors may be performed without volition or cognition, humans at times use them intentionally to send messages such as affiliation or submission. Finally, culture may set limits on how much or what type of adaptation is acceptable.

# 3

## Arousal and affect approaches

The prior chapter examined those processes that have some biological basis or innate drive as the motivating force behind interactional adaptation. Whereas biological "drives" and forces are also prevalent in the theories reviewed in this chapter, there is a greater emphasis on arousal and psychological needs, elements derived initially from work on general human spatial behavior. Aiello (1987) identifies the needs undergirding spatially based arousal and affect theories as follows:

> Overstimulation models of stress, arousal, and overload suggest that an individual maintains a preferred interaction distance from others in order to avoid excessive arousal, stimulation, and a variety of stressors associated with proximity that is too close. Behavioral constraint models maintain that adequate personal space prevents our behavioral freedom from being threatened. (p. 393)

Although the theories to be presented here by no means focus exclusively on proxemics, they share in common an emphasis on immediacy and intimacy phenomena, with most focusing on nonverbal behavior. Frequently cited theories in this category are Affiliative Conflict Theory, Arousal-Labeling Theory, Bidimensional Theory, Discrepancy-Arousal Theory, and dialectical models.

### AFFILIATIVE CONFLICT THEORY

#### The original theory

Affiliative Conflict Theory (ACT), also referred to as Equilibrium Theory, was first introduced by Argyle and Dean (1965) to account for the functions of gaze and for the role of gaze in relation to other intimacy behaviors during interpersonal encounters. Originally, ACT postulated that people have competing needs or desires for intimacy and autonomy. These set into motion a balancing act between approach and avoidance forces as partners try to negotiate and maintain a comfortable level of intimacy in their interactions.⌉

Intimacy is posited to be a function of eye contact, physical proximity, topic intimacy, amount of smiling, and other pertinent behaviors (Argyle & Dean, 1965). Individuals and dyads seek an equilibrium level – homeostasis – where distance and immediacy behaviors are close enough to meet affiliative needs while allowing enough "space" to achieve privacy and autonomy./ According to ACT, increases or decreases in intimacy disturb the equilibrium level, which produces anxiety. Anxiety, in turn, prompts individuals to adjust one or more intimacy behaviors so as to restore equilibrium. This adjustment process is known as compensation.

⟨The need to balance approach and avoidance forces operates at both the individual and dyadic levels.⟩Intrapersonally, one's own desire for intimacy or autonomy with a partner generates corresponding behaviors that reflect one's preferred level of each of these.⟨Disequilibrium triggers intrapersonal and/or interpersonal compensation. *Intrapersonal compensation* occurs when one individual adjusts for changes in one or more of *own* intimacy behaviors by altering other intimacy behaviors in the opposite direction.⟩If one makes intrapersonal adjustments, the level of intimacy between the two interactants may remain unchanged.

⟨*Interpersonal compensation* (defined generally for now, and defined more precisely in Chapter 6) occurs when one person's change in intimacy is met by corresponding changes in the *partner's* intimacy behaviors.⟩Adjustments may occur on the exact behavior as the partner's, as when decreased eye contact is compensated by another's increased eye contact, or on a different but related behavior, as when increased proximity is offset by decreased eye contact.

Because the focus of this book is on interaction patterns between people, when the term compensation is used, it refers to interpersonal compensation. When *intrapersonal compensation* is discussed, it will be referred to as such. The ongoing operation of both intrapersonal and interpersonal compensation increases the complexity of interaction patterns because either or both types of compensation may happen at any point in time.

ACT becomes even more complex when one considers that approach and avoidance preferences are variable across partners and situations. When two interactants have differing preferred levels of intimacy, they must (consciously or unconsciously) negotiate their differences to arrive at an equilibrium level that is mutually acceptable. In cases where preferences are disparate, such as when one person has a high need for affiliation and the other almost no desire for affiliation, the interaction may be abandoned because of discomfort produced by sustained disequilibrium. Where two people have matched intimacy preferences, such as might occur when both have a high need for affiliation or when intimacy level is dictated by social norms, no such negotiation is necessary.

## Argyle and Cook's modification

In response to numerous tests of ACT (reviewed below) that found only partial support for compensation, Argyle and Cook (1976) modified and extended the original theory. First, they expanded the pool of intimacy behaviors to include form of address, emotional expression, absence of physical barriers, openness of posture, and friendliness. In so doing, they expanded the domain of the theory.

Second, they noted that behavior is largely guided by social norms, which implies that equilibrium levels are determined not only by personal preferences for intimacy and autonomy but also by the environment in which the people interact. For example, a couple may have a mutually strong approach need, but may "constrain" their intimacy behaviors to a socially acceptable level if they are in public. Behaviors that are more under social governance should be manipulated less frequently. For example, self disclosure between friends may be less constrained or rule-governed than eye contact patterns. Compensation should be more likely in those behaviors that are free to vary. Further implications are that the manipulation of strongly rule-governed or scripted behaviors, such as staring or inappropriate intimate touch, may produce great anxiety, leading to strongly reactive, consistent cases of compensation.

Third, the repeated evidence of noncompensatory responses led Argyle and Cook (1976) to acknowledge that reciprocity or matching may occur in response to intimacy changes. For example, unacquainted individuals consistently exhibit reciprocity between gaze and verbal disclosure (Firestone, 1977). In such interactions, other functions such as affinity seeking and information processing may temporarily override approach–avoidance needs. Compensation may be more prevalent in established relationships. Presumably, once a mutually comfortable balance between approach-avoidance forces is established in ongoing relationships, partners should be inclined to maintain it unless and until the balance is upset (perhaps by an external factor), at which point they should compensate so as to restore the dyadic balance.

## Empirical support

ACT spawned a stream of research, spanning several decades, that tested relationships among verbal and nonverbal indices of intimacy. Most early research focused on the nonverbal immediacy behaviors of proximity, lean, orientation, and gaze and on verbal self disclosure (see Aiello, 1987; Cappella, 1981; Firestone, 1977; Patterson, 1973, for summaries). In one of the early reviews, Firestone (1977) concluded that spatial adjustments produce diverse responses:

> Spatial distance, posture, and visual behavior features of dyadic inter-action appear to show complex interdependencies. Both facilitative and inhibitory relationships abound. Clearly, the conclusion that non-verbal approach by one party induces withdrawal by the other is unwarranted. (pp. 40–41)

Yet Cappella (1981) arrived at an opposite conclusion in his review, contending that the research evidence overwhelmingly supports the claim that increased proximity leads to compensatory responses on distancing, gaze, posture, body orientation, bodily activity, verbal out-put, and the like. Of the 36 studies in Cappella's review, 22 studies assessed gaze in response to proximity manipulations, with 12 reporting compensation, 5 reporting nonaccommodation, 5 reporting mixed re-sults, and none reporting only reciprocity. Proximity increases also consistently elicited proxemic compensation by the partner. Addi-tionally, proxemic changes were rarely reciprocated with other imme-diacy behaviors. These results might suggest that physical closeness produces such discomfiture that partners consistently respond by in-creasing physical distance or psychological distance.

Subsequently, however, Aiello (1987) arrived at a more tempered conclusion, contending that compensation is more common in stable than developing relationships and that matching and reciprocity are a frequent occurrence in the latter. He also concluded that comfort-oriented models do not predict observable compensation as long as variations in immediacy behaviors fall within an optimal distance range.

Clearly, the mixed findings and claims in these reviews offer only partial and inconsistent support for ACT. Proximity is the most consis-tent elicitor of compensation, but *at best* it produces frequent, not uni-

versal, compensation primarily on gaze, inasmuch as other corresponding immediacy behaviors often show reciprocity. One might mistakenly
assume from these findings that the converse should be true: Increased
gaze should elicit proxemic compensation. Yet, Cappella's review
(1981) does not offer overwhelming support for this claim. When looking at the bigger picture of gaze effects on other immediacy behaviors,
Cappella indicated that nonaccommodation and reciprocity were the
primary responses, with compensation occurring rather infrequently.
Other intimacy behaviors likewise showed a mix of compensation,
reciprocity, and nonaccommodation.

Moreover, many factors such as gender and personality attributes
have been found to moderate responses (Aiello, 1977a,b, 1987; Argyle
& Ingham, 1972). Males have been found to compensate increased eye
contact, whereas females have shown a curvilinear relationship suggestive of partial compensation and partial reciprocation. By personality,
extroverted and neurotic individuals have displayed more gaze than
introverted and "healthy" people in response to immediacy increases,
perhaps because their comfort threshold for immediacy is greater. Approach forces may have been more operative for extroverts and avoidance forces for introverts.

### Criticisms of ACT

Despite the wealth of studies invoking ACT, very few valid tests have
been conducted. The theory requires that an equilibrium level be established between dyad members prior to a change in intimacy by one
partner. Yet many early studies had subjects look at a photograph of
another person while varying the distance between the subject and the
photo. The subjects' amount of eye contact was measured as distance
from the photograph varied. When confederates were substituted for
photographs, subjects displayed highly unnatural eye contact patterns.
For example, in Argyle and Dean's (1965) experiment, the confederate
continuously stared at the subject throughout the interaction. Additionally, very few studies incorporated a change in net intimacy from
the equilibrium level.

Others have criticized tests of ACT for employing flawed or artificial
methods. For example, Patterson (1983) argues that many studies conducted between 1965 and 1976 artificially induced compensation, as the
typical experiment utilized a subject interacting with a stranger in "a
rather sterile, minimally furnished laboratory room. Under such circum-

stances most of the interpersonal and setting cues are sufficiently negative that the labeling process may easily produce some type of negative affect" (p. 15). This negative affect, according to Patterson (1976, 1983), may have produced the compensatory responses.

Additional criticisms lodged against ACT are that the same studies that found pervasive compensatory patterns also yielded several instances of matching (which are not *explicitly* accounted for by the theory); the multiple factors in the theory make it nonfalsifiable; and the theory lacks explanatory mechanisms for how and why equilibrium levels change (Aiello, 1987).

## Recent modifications of ACT

Based on our description of the theory so far, one might deduce that matching should be the typical response, according to ACT, as long as intimacy behaviors are enacted *within the established equilibrium range.* That is, both people should enact similar degrees of intimacy within the equilibrium range. Thus, matching would be the normative pattern of interaction and compensatory reactions would arise only when intimacy behaviors fall outside the equilibrium range.

Aiello and Thompson (1980), however, in attempting to extend and improve the theory, proposed just the opposite. They suggested that compensation is most likely to occur *within intermediate distance ranges,* which are the presumed preferred distance ranges, and that unsuccessful compensation or extremes of distance should produce excessive discomfort that prompts complete withdrawal from the interaction. Their prediction, then, appears to be the opposite of ACT, which requires moving into a high discomfort zone before compensation is activated. They grounded their new model in the assumption that,

> approach forces will continue to predominate during interaction as long as there is some possibility of relieving some of the discomfort. Once the deviations from the desired level of involvement become too great, avoidant forces are much more likely to predominate, and as a result individuals will be more likely to withdraw from the interaction. (Aiello & Thompson, 1980, p. 403)

The concept of approach forces prevailing until discomfort exceeds some threshold is sensible (and compatible with our own interpretation of ACT). But the argument that approach forces should prevail under normal interaction circumstances leads to a prediction of matching and reciprocity, not compensation, unless one individual first behaves in an avoidant way (something that has to be accounted for) and the other individual then compensates with approach behavior. It seems more reasonable to assume that as long as interaction is operating within the preferred distance range, interaction should be comfortable and therefore not require compensatory activity. And if discomfort is only activated when interaction behaviors become extreme, then discomfort is no longer the trigger for compensation, which puts the Aiello and Thompson model at odds with the basic premise of ACT. Additionally, it seems intuitively more plausible that undesirably low levels of involvement would initially be met with efforts to increase involvement rather than with withdrawal.

Another modification has been offered by Knowles (1980, 1989), who reconceptualized ACT under the rubric of field theory (Lewin, 1951). An important contribution of field theory is that behavior is goal oriented and purposeful, yet not necessarily mindful. Additionally, field theory acknowledges the importance of the environment's impact on human behavior. According to field theory, approach and avoidance gradients draw people together and repel them away from each other. Two different fields operate to create these gradients – force and power fields. Force fields are internal to the individual and are created by that individual's desires, goals, and psychological mechanisms. The need for intimacy might propel an individual toward another. The force of the field is determined by both the valence of the goal and its psychological immediacy. The closer the goal, the more intense the field. On the other hand, power fields are external to the individual, such as presence or absence of other people in the environment and social norms.

Knowles makes two fundamental distinctions about the nature of approach and avoidance gradients. First, the approach gradient is extremely variable because it is intimately tied in with needs and desires. It thus fluctuates with people's internal states. Second, the avoidance gradient is relatively stable, as it has to do with enduring features such as fear of being known and fear of rejection. Knowles (1989) claims that the situation primarily influences avoidance gradients.

Knowles' (1989) reconceptualization of ACT is that people feel discomfort when their internal approach and avoidance gradients are not equal. Therefore, any discrepancy between them produces anxiety. However, the discomfort is greater in more immediate situations than in nonimmediate situations. For example, a discrepancy in approach–avoidance gradients is much more aversive when someone is too close than when too far away, holding the discrepancy between gradients constant. Predicting reciprocity and compensation is thus a matter of knowing the gradients of both partners in an interaction. If both people have a stronger approach than avoidance gradient, then intimacy behaviors should be reciprocated by both partners until the behaviors "match" and satisfy the approach needs.

Knowles allows for constant redefinition of gradients and thus a fluctuating equilibrium level. With this modification to ACT, additional problems are introduced. First, precise predictions are difficult because they are predicated on knowing the approach and avoidance gradients of both people. If gradients fluctuate "from moment to moment" (Knowles, 1989, p. 64), then accurate prediction appears limited to more long-standing goals within stable situations. Second, testing this theory appears virtually impossible, as the gradients may have changed in the interim between measurement and observation. Third, although Knowles's (1989) reconceptualization of ACT provides many new insights, it was specifically designed to predict and explain spatial behavior and may not extend beyond it. At this point, it appears that more definition and extension to the interactional domain is necessary for the model to be fruitful. Similarly, ways in which to measure gradients accurately and from "moment to moment" are necessary before valid testing can take place.

So what can we take away from Knowles's (1989) work? The notion that approach gradients are more variable and internally driven whereas avoidance forces are more stable and situationally driven appears useful for the entire gamut of interaction adaptation patterns. Also intriguing is the notion that equal discrepancies between approach and avoidance gradients do not produce equal discomfort (i.e., more discomfort is felt when the partner is too close than too far away from oneself). Last, the recognition that both approach and avoidance forces are operating at all times in an interaction (with differing intensities) appears valid. Even when we want to be intimate with another, the fear of being too intimate or being rejected (avoidance gradient) may lurk in the background as an influential factor determining behavior.

## Summary

ACT spawned a curriculum of studies on interaction patterns as well as inspired a host of theories to account for these patterns. Its most significant contributions have been the introduction of arousal or discomfort as a primary indicator of behavioral changes, and attention to compensation as one major interaction pattern in interpersonal communication.] The trend over the years in theory development has been to extend the basic tenets of this model by adding elements such as cognitions, expectations, and emotional labels that "fine tune" the predictive and explanatory power of this model. Continued reliance on the basic assumptions and elements of ACT affirms its influential impact and some of the "truths" it has uncovered.

## AROUSAL-LABELING THEORY

Although one might have expected ACT to account for reciprocal patterns, inasmuch as sociological discussion on the norm of reciprocity (e.g., Gouldner, 1960) and Jourard's (1959) psychological research on reciprocal self-disclosure patterns predated ACT, it did not. As has often happened, scholars examining reciprocity were working in isolation from those studying compensation. The former tended to focus on verbal self disclosure and resource exchange, whereas the latter tended to center on nonverbal behaviors. Nevertheless, evidence of microlevel reciprocity of nonverbal intimacy behaviors began to emerge, prompting the need to merge the two lines of inquiry and to import the concept of reciprocity into the nonverbal intimacy domain.

The first theory to include both reciprocal and compensatory patterns of nonverbal intimacy behaviors in dyadic interaction was Patterson's (1976) Arousal-Labeling Theory (ALT). It included the appealing aspects of equilibrium theory while incorporating an explanation for reciprocal responses. The primary components of ALT, which are explicated below, are these:

$$Intimacy \rightarrow arousal \rightarrow affective\ labeling \rightarrow behavioral$$
$$change \qquad\qquad\qquad response$$

### Assumptions, propositions, and hypotheses

ALT assumes that there is an appropriate, or expected, level of intimacy display between conversational partners. Intimacy behaviors falling within this range are comfortable and do not produce anxiety or arousal. ALT retained this central premise from ACT. ALT departs from ACT when changes in intimacy behaviors are enacted. Whereas ACT posits that all intimacy changes exceeding the equilibrium level are met with compensatory responses, ALT suggests that *arousal change* and subsequent cognitive-affective labeling are pivotal in determining whether compensatory, reciprocal, or no behavioral adjustments are made. Thus, ALT explicitly introduces arousal as the key mediating force behind behavioral adjustments.

Patterson's (1976) reliance on Schachter and Singer's (1962) work on the emotional labeling of arousal led him to argue that changes in intimacy behaviors induce undifferentiated arousal in one's partner. However, Patterson (1976, 1983) noted that arousal *change* is the fundamental criterion, rather than stable levels of heightened, moderate, or depressed arousal. ALT suggests that *small* changes in intimacy behaviors by Person A may not elicit a response from Person B. In such cases, behavioral adjustment does not occur because slight variations in intimacy and arousal are either not noticed, or (if noticed) are too small to produce the "sufficient" arousal required to activate the affective-labeling process. This is the only situation in which ALT allows for nonaccommodation.

Once arousal change exceeds the perceptual threshold, the undifferentiated arousal is labeled either positively or negatively. Labeling depends on three factors: level of acquaintance between partners, the setting in which the behaviors occur, and recipient's perceived control over the situation (Patterson, 1976). Arousal may be labeled negatively if a person feels out of control (anxious) about the intimacy change or if it is embarrassing. In these cases, increased intimacy is threatening, anxiety producing, or unwanted. Arousal change is labeled positively if the person likes the intimacy behaviors or is relieved by their display. Patterson (1983) argues that, "If past experience, the situation, and related cues are positive, the individual will develop a positive affective or emotional reaction such as affection, love or comfort . . . [which] should facilitate the reciprocation of involvement" (pp. 14–15). Patterson relies on the premise that intimacy and affection are desirable from people we like.

Negatively experienced arousal, according to ALT, leads to compensation in order to reduce felt anxiety or discomfort. Conversely, Patterson (1976) predicts that reciprocity occurs when arousal is labeled positively (see Figure 3.1). Eliminating negative arousal through compensatory adjustments or gaining more positive arousal through reciprocity are central principles of this theory.

The ALT assumptions and hypotheses can be summarized as follows:

1. *Interactants establish a comfortable level of intimacy.*
2. *Changes in intimacy behaviors lead to arousal change.* Arousal is initially "undifferentiated."

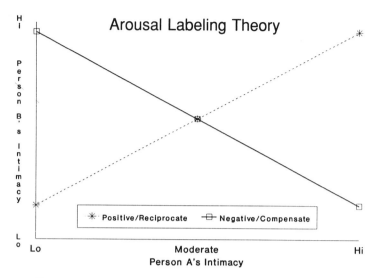

Figure 3.1   Patterson's Arousal-Labeling Theory.

3. *Sufficient arousal change is necessary before the affective labeling process occurs.* If there is insufficient arousal change, then no labeling or reaction occurs.
4. *Undifferentiated arousal change is labeled either positive or negative, depending on relational acquaintance between interactants, the setting, and perceived control over the situation.*
5. *Positive labeling leads to reciprocal responses; negative labeling leads to compensatory responses.*

The most compelling contributions of ALT are the inclusion of both reciprocal and compensatory reactions within a single model and its applicability to both increases and decreases in intimacy behavior. Another strength of ALT is the notion that arousal change, rather than level of arousal, is important to behavioral reactions. Additionally, recognizing that all intimacy changes do not produce sufficient arousal and thus fail to produce behavioral reactions accounts for nonaccommodation patterns.

### Empirical support

Support for ALT is mixed at best. As illustration, Coutts, Schneider, and Montgomery's (1980) test of ALT did not support it. No changes in intimacy behaviors emerged in the positive condition (where ALT predicts reciprocity), and eye gaze and smiles were reciprocated in the negative affect condition (where ALT predicts compensatory responses). Patterson, Jordan, Hogan, and Frerker (1981) also found mixed support in that the same manipulations did not produce uniform results at different times and there was nonaccommodation in conditions where arousal change should have been sufficient to produce labeling and subsequent adjustments. Patterson et al. (1981) concluded that the *meaning* behind the behavior change may influence reactions.

Patterson et al.'s (1981) study uncovered some noteworthy problems with testing ALT. One problem is the assessment of subject's arousal. The three different measures of arousal used in their investigation were uncorrelated with each other, leaving one in a quandary as to which arousal estimate to use. Also, they found neutral ratings associated with one of their conditions and ALT does not allow for neutral arousal valence.

In two more recent studies (Hale & Burgoon, 1984; Iizuka, Mishima, & Matsumoto, 1989), empirical tests failed to support ALT. The mixed results presented in Hale and Burgoon (1984) indicate that some behaviors and measures (e.g., overall involvement, head nods, perceived relational intimacy) showed reciprocity, others (e.g., body orientation) showed compensation, and yet others (eye contact, verbal immediacy) showed reciprocity of increased immediacy and compensation of decreased immediacy. Iizuka et al.'s (1989) test also produced mixed results such that positive labeling produced nonaccommodation while negative labeling produced both reciprocity and compensation. Further, subjects apparently failed to perceive their own arousal (self-report), but behavioral indices produced contrary evidence.

In yet one other example of mixed or contradictory support for ALT, Ickes, Patterson, Rajecki, and Tanford (1982) found that people tended to reciprocate increased involvement behaviors with a disliked other, presumably to "win the other over" to a more positive interaction. In this case, strangers given a negative expectancy of the partner should have, by Patterson's (1976, 1983) account, responded to increased intimacy with decreased intimacy – a compensatory response. Instead, they did the opposite.

Some support for ALT can be deduced from Coutts, Irvine, and Schneider (1977), although this study was designed to test equilibrium theory. They found that after a baseline period (which was intended to establish an equilibrium level), increased gaze led to decreased smiling.

wever, not all behavioral relationships supported ALT. Moreover, a : test of ALT needs to include arousal and nonarousal conditions, :s of the three criteria that determine the affective label, positive and negative affect conditions, and both increased and decreased intimacy conditions. These conditions were not met in this study, nor any study to date.

### Criticisms

Although ALT improves upon equilibrium theory, it also manifests a host of problems. Patterson (1985) concedes that ALT fails to account for the "initiation of behavioural sequences or the motivations for reactive adjustments" (p. 194). Thus, it is limited to behavioral reactions to changes in intimacy. The recognition of communicator goals and messages is lacking in this theory.

Patterson also does not explicate sufficiently how he selected among the multitude of possible factors acquaintance, perceived control, and setting as the crucial ones affecting labeling. Additionally, other than the few case examples offered by Patterson (1976, 1983), how these criteria determine the label is unclear; ALT does not indicate how to label "mixed criteria" instances. Little clarification is made in further writings, perhaps because Patterson (1985) himself eventually abandoned this theory, and introduced a new one, the Sequential-Functional Model.

Patterson argues that cues present in the situation affect the labeling of arousal change. Although not clearly argued in this model, yet made explicit in his Sequential-Functional Model, preinteractional factors embedded in the situation "attach" themselves to emergent arousal change. Thus, the labeling process is partially embedded in the situation before the interaction begins. These situational cues may be appropriate for a static form of labeling rather than moment-to-moment changes in arousal and labeling, making ALT less capable of accounting for many of the dynamic reciprocal and compensatory changes made within an interaction.

Although not necessarily a fatal flaw, ALT may be criticized (similar to Schachter and Singer's, 1962, work on emotions) on the grounds that one cannot confirm the sequential ordering between arousal and labeling. Does arousal precede or follow labeling of situations? Also, the instantaneous nature of many intimacy changes suggests an automatic rather than calculated labeling process.

Because of the role of the arousal-attribution process, an adequate test of ALT is difficult. It might be more useful to forsake the process by which arousal is labeled and argue that the positive or negative label, regardless of how it is derived, is the crucial element on which to focus. One may assess more accurately subjects' positive or negative experience of their arousal than the factors that determined that label.

Other factors, such as arousal *intensity* and *degree* of positive or negative labeling might also influence interaction patterns (Hayduk, 1983). Additionally, although both increases and decreases in intimacy behaviors are accounted for by ALT, the examples of intimacy decreases are strictly from an overly intimate level, such that the decreases are positively labeled and therefore reciprocated in order to move the interaction to a more comfortable level of involvement. There is no account of what should happen in cases where a person decreases involvement and the evaluation is negative. A comprehensive theory should explain reactions to both positive and negative labeling of both increases and decreases in involvement.

Finally, some (e.g., Aiello, 1987; Hayduk, 1983) have noted that ALT may place too much emphasis on cognitions and that its endless feedback loops, with indeterminacy regarding how each arousal change will be labeled, make it more amenable to post hoc explanations than to a priori predictions and verification.

### Summary

Although ALT has not received widespread support, it has made significant contributions to the study of adaptation patterns by incorporating both reciprocal and compensatory patterns of adaptation within a single theory. Additionally, the key role of valencing (although not necessarily of arousal) is retained in current theories.

### MARKUS-KAPLAN AND KAPLAN'S BIDIMENSIONAL MODEL

This model was created to explain outcomes of both physical and psychological interpersonal distancing. Although it has received little attention apart from its initial conception, it provides further insight into dyadic adaptation patterns, specifically with regard to the effects of the communicators' characteristics and internal drive and need states on patterns of behavior.

Markus-Kaplan and Kaplan's (1984) Bidimensional Model (BM) evolved out of two lines of research: research aimed at explaining reciprocity-compensation patterns in interaction and research identifying functions of behavior within interactions. Borrowing the intimacy and social control functions from Patterson's (1982) functional typology, Markus-Kaplan and Kaplan regard *intimacy* as the closeness or "union" between interactants. They consider it a spontaneous reaction to the affect one feels toward an interactional partner. Thus, interpersonal distancing under the intimacy function is the result of "felt positivity" toward the other and not under conscious control. (Patterson, 1982, similarly regards it as indicative behavior.) *Social control,* on the other hand, is regarded as more purposive and mindful behavior toward reaching a goal or influencing one's partner.

### Assumptions and propositions

Markus-Kaplan and Kaplan (1984) argue that previously unidimensional views of reciprocity and compensation and of intimacy and social control functions lead to inadequate explanations of approach and avoidance behavior patterns. Thus, they proposed the BM.

The BM assumes that interaction response patterns are relatively stable and depend upon persistent internal drives and needs, such as fear of abandonment and absorption. Markus-Kaplan and Kaplan therefore suggest that two bipolar dimensions, attachment–detachment and individuation–deindividuation, are underlying dimensions that can better account for stable interpersonal distancing patterns. *Individuation–deindividuation* represents one's "ego strength," that is, the extent to which one holds a clear and distinct self-identity that is separate from the other. *Attachment–detachment* refers to the strength of the relationship; one can be close to or distant from one's partner. Human interaction may be classified into one of four quadrants of behavioral response tendencies that are defined by the attachment–detachment and individuation–deindividuation dimensions: reciprocity, compensation, social control, and intimacy. Reciprocity is defined as "an individuated and attached mode of functioning, compensation as a deindividuated and detached mode, intimacy is defined as a deindividuated and attached style and social control as one that is individuated and detached" (Markus-Kaplan & Kaplan, 1984, p. 315).

Coupling each person's approach or avoidance response mode with the partner's results in predictions such as the following:

1. *Interactions between participants who are individuated and attached produce "mature reciprocity," also a pattern of mutual avoidance and mutual approach.* This interaction is labeled "mature" because individuals are ". . . synchronizing their needs for intimacy and separation" (Markus-Kaplan & Kaplan, 1984, p. 325).
2. *Interactions between a deindividuated, detached person and an individuated, attached partner result in compensation.*
3. *Interactions between two people dominated by intimacy drives produce an "embedded" structure that appears as reciprocal intimacy.* Such individuals sacrifice separation for intimacy. Though the outcome looks like reciprocity, according to our conceptualization it might only be matching because it is a function of individual need states and not necessarily adaptation to the partner.
4. *Interactions between two people dominated by social control drives produce reciprocal avoidance.* Such individuals sacrifice intimacy for individuation.
5. *Interactions between one person dominated by social control needs and a partner pursuing intimacy result in a "rejection–intrusion" pattern.* That is, the intimacy-driven person consistently approaches and the social control-driven person consistently avoids regardless of what the partner does. This pattern may appear to be compensatory, but Markus-Kaplan and Kaplan (1984) argue that because it does not involve an adaptation of either partner directed toward the other, it should be labeled rejection–intrusion rather than compensation.

### Criticisms

Except for its original publication in 1984, the BM has not been embraced as a mainstream model nor tested empirically. Two overriding factors may account for this. First and foremost, the lack of conceptual clarity of this model prevents adoption. There is very little rationale and justification for the choice of the attachment and individuation dimensions (and corresponding fears) and social control and intimacy functions, as opposed to other dimensions, fears, and functions operative in interactions. Additionally, justification for placing social control and intimacy drives at opposite ends of a single continuum is necessary. By placing these functions along a continuum, Markus-Kaplan and Kaplan fail to recognize that a person may be driven by both motives simultaneously.

Second, although this model allows for different interaction patterns to result, depending on the types of people interacting, it implicitly assumes that people remain invariant in the approach or avoidance motives causing them to behave. In other words, patterns of reciprocity and compensation are determined by interactants' individual traits. The authors admit that situational and relational factors indicative of long-term relationships may moderate the predictions they have made, but suggestions as to how this might occur are not offered. The BM therefore cannot account for an individual approaching one person and avoiding another (e.g., approaching a friend and avoiding a stranger).

### Summary

The BM highlights that people have stable behavioral tendencies in interactions, rooted in personality, that extend across situations and people. The bidimensional view of interpersonal distancing suggests that if people are primarily driven by either social control or intimacy needs, noncontingent responses of avoidance or approach, respectively, are expected. However, BM ignores situational factors and the possibility of adaptation during interaction and hence cannot account for the dynamics of interaction.

### DISCREPANCY-AROUSAL THEORY

Another alternative to the ALM is Cappella and Greene's (1982, 1984) modification of D. Stern's (1977) Discrepancy-Arousal Theory (DAT), which was propelled by their extensive analysis of research on infant–adult and adult–adult interaction and the inability of other models to account for the observed patterns. Their model was intended to rectify some of the shortcomings of previous models, among them:

1. Many theories appear to be too "cognitive" to account for the rapid adjustments that take place in dyadic interaction. For example, Communication Accommodation Theory (to be discussed in Chapter 4), despite its claim that adaptation occurs automatically, implies significant cognitive work and is thus more applicable to deliberate choices than to automatic adaptation.
2. Previous theories suffer from scope problems. ACT and other drive-based models do not account for matching responses and are inapplicable to speech- and involvement-related behaviors, such as pauses, loudness, and illustrative ("illustrator") gestures. ALT, in particular,

is too restrictive in focusing only on affiliative behaviors. And most of the theories are inapplicable to infant–adult interaction and unable to account for intermittent cycling between reciprocity and compensation by the same dyad.

3. Many of the theories appear to be tautological or nonfalsifiable. For example, invoking approach–avoidance forces is problematic. The theories do not predict a priori when approach versus avoidance forces will prevail, and the evidence cited for the existence of approach–avoidance behaviors is often the same affiliative behaviors to be predicted, resulting in a tautology. ALT similarly fails to specify the particular conditions producing positive versus negative labeling, which may make the theory tautological and nonfalsifiable (because any outcome can be justified in terms of the unseen labeling process). Patterson's (1982, 1983) Sequential-Functional Model (SFM, presented in Chapter 5) is difficult to test because one possible outcome of a partner's involvement change is a functional reassessment with no concomitant change in behavior. There is also no evidence that functional reassessments take place.

4. Arousal-based models such as ALT and Expectancy Violations Theory (EVT, presented in Chapter 5) purportedly place inordinate emphasis on cognitive processes and labeling to the neglect of arousal processes. DAT was designed to eliminate this "unnecessary cognitive baggage."

DAT proposes the following causal linkages, each of which is explicated in turn:

*Norms,* → *expectations* → *discrepancy* → *arousal* → *affect* → *behavioral*
*preferences,* *response*
*experiences*

### Norms, preferences, and experiences to expectations to discrepancies

Cappella and Greene (1982, 1984) assume that individuals have well-established expectations for the expressive (involvement) behavior of others that are derived from their own present and past personal experiences, social norms attending the particular situation, and personal preferences. These expectations encompass a *range* of behaviors (rather than exact behaviors) that define an acceptance region. The width of the acceptance region varies by individual, by relationship, and by situation. For example, factors such as attraction and relationship stage may influence the width of the acceptance region; the acceptance region may be much wider for liked than disliked others (a principle similar to the concept of reward valence in EVT in Chapter 5) and relational intimates may have a wider acceptance region for their involvement behavior than strangers.

### Discrepancies to arousal to affect

[When another's enacted behavior exceeds or falls short of expectations, a discrepancy exists. Discrepancies are posited to elicit arousal change, with the degree of arousal change monotonically related to the magnitude of the discrepancy.] Thus, small discrepancies should have little impact on arousal; large discrepancies should activate large changes. For Cappella and Greene (1982), "arousal is conceptualized as cognitive activation, that is as neural excitation of the cortex, reticular activating system, and possibly the limbic system" (p. 98). Cognitive activation (as measured by electroencephalograms or average evoked responses) is assumed to precede autonomic activation, so presumably it is the physiological activation (reflected in such measures as heart rate, blood pressure, and galvanic skin response) that controls ultimate behavioral responses.

[Discrepancies within the acceptance range are posited to trigger moderate arousal changes. Because moderate arousal change is supposed to be pleasurable, it should be accompanied by positive affect. Discrepancies outside the acceptance range are posited to trigger large arousal changes, which are said to be aversive and accompanied by negative affect.] The result is a nonmonotonic relationship between arousal and affect that forms an inverted-U shape as one deviates in either direction from the expected level of expressiveness. These relationships are depicted in Figure 3.2. Because the link between arousal and affect is assumed to be direct and automatic, there is no need to interpose a cognitive labeling process (in contrast to ALT).]

*or inconsequential*

### Affect to behavioral response

The last link in the model is from emotional reaction to actual communicative behavior. As shown in Figure 3.2, positive affect is posited to elicit approach responses, and negative affect to elicit avoidance responses. [This means that deviations within the acceptance region, which are supposed to trigger moderate arousal change and positive affect, should produce reciprocation when the partner increases involvement, and compensation when the partner decreases involvement.] (Conversely, deviations outside the acceptance region should trigger large arousal change, negative affect, and concomitant compensation of increased involvement and reciprocity of decreased involvement.)

The actual degree of reciprocity or compensation depends on the degree to which both participants' acceptance regions overlap, given that both people may be making moment-to-moment adjustments in their interaction behavior.[Reciprocity should be most common when both individuals are predicted to show approach behavior; that is, there is an approach–approach pairing. Compensation becomes more likely when people's acceptance regions do not overlap, producing approach–avoidance combinations](Although Cappella and Greene also mention avoidance–avoidance combinations as cases of compensation, both people exhibiting avoidance would actually yield a reciprocal pattern.) Elsewhere in their writings, Cappella and Greene occasionally lapse into equating reciprocity with approach and compensation with avoidance and their own figures imply the same, but in the majority of their writing it seems clear that their true intent is to predict the patterns shown in Figure 3.2.

One last element not depicted in the figure is self-regulatory change ☀ in behavior. Although the model is designed to account for reactions to another's change in expressive behaviors, it is acknowledged that individuals also make intrapersonal adjustments, just as posited in ACT, as well as maintain a fair degree of consistency in their behavior over time. Thus, stability (or autocorrelation) is an important source of influence on individual behavior that must be taken into account when predicting reciprocity and compensation.

### Empirical support

Summaries of previous empirical research adduced to support the various linkages in DAT appear in Cappella (1983) and Cappella and Greene (1982).[Supportive evidence includes findings that people hold expectations for the expressive behavior of others, that deviations from expectations produce cognitive activation and orienting to discrepant stimuli, that certain nonverbal behaviors elicit arousal, that individuals vary in their tolerance for arousal (i.e., have different acceptance regions), and that unfamiliar stimuli produce both arousal and varying

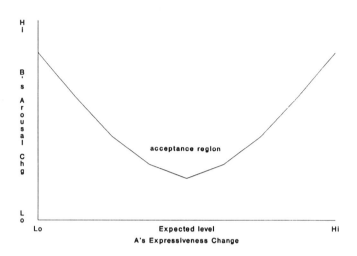

a. Relationship of A's Discrepancy to
B's Arousal Change

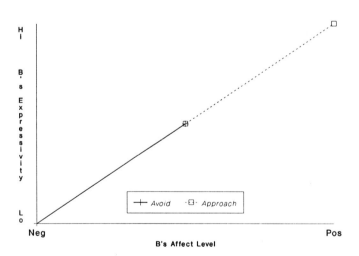

c. Relationship of B's Affect
to B's Behavioral Response

**b. Relationship of B's Arousal
Change to B's Affect**

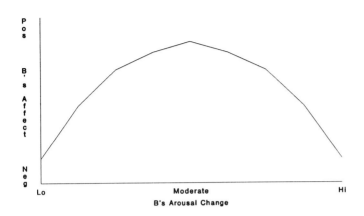

**d. Relationship of A's Behavioral
Change to B's Behavioral Change**

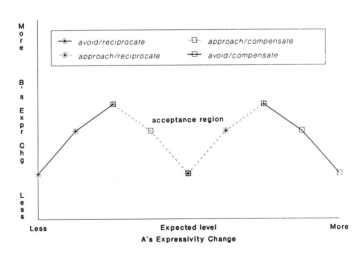

Figure 3.2   Relationships posited in Discrepancy-Arousal Theory.

affective reactions⌡ Previous theories postulating an inverted-U relationship between arousal and hedonic tone (positivity of affect) are also invoked to support the predicted relationship between arousal change and affect.

In the first direct test of the theory, Cappella and Greene (1984) examined one individual difference factor assumed to affect arousability – sensation seeking – and experimentally varied whether a confederate adopted a close or normal interaction distance. (There was no far distance condition.) They then measured partner's behavioral responses on four nonverbal composites (composed of several kinesic, proxemic, and vocalic variables). They predicted that high sensation seekers should reciprocate increased immediacy, while low sensation seekers should compensate for it.

Results failed to produce the hypothesized interaction between sensation seeking and distance. Only when state sensation seekers were combined with trait sensation seekers did results show any effects and then, only on an affiliation index. High sensation seekers compensated less at the close distance than did low sensation seekers; both exhibited more immediacy at the normal distance (contrary to predictions). No tests were reported on effects of discrepancy on arousal change, or the link between arousal and affect, or between affect and behavioral response. Thus, the study provided very little support for the theory.

The only other experiment to test DAT directly was conducted nearly a decade later by Le Poire and Burgoon (1993), who attempted to pit DAT against EVT. The results are presented in more detail in Chapter 5, where EVT is described. However, several aspects of the results that are particularly germane to DAT are presented here.

In brief, confederates, purported to be medical students, conducted medical interviews with naive participants during which the confederates increased or decreased involvement from a baseline level to create four degrees of involvement violations (very high, moderately high, moderately low, very low). During the interviews, physiological measures of arousal were taken on participants, permitting assessment of arousal change following the change in involvement level. After the interaction, participants reported on their affective state during the interaction.

⌞Results revealed that degree of involvement change (i.e., the discrepancy) was not monotonically related to arousal change, as DAT would predict. Instead, all of the violations produced arousal change, with the greatest arousal occurring in the low involvement condition. In turn, arousal change was not directly related to degree of positive or negative affect, and affective response did not predict behavioral response.

These results reveal that violations are capable of stimulating arousal change, but arousal per se does not mediate interaction patterns. Put another way, arousal is a *consequence* of violations but not a *cause* of interaction patterns. Le Poire and Burgoon (1993) concluded that DAT could achieve greater parsimony by dispensing with arousal, given that arousal change did not determine interaction patterns. This recommendation was bolstered by the fact that discrepancy size *did* directly influence affective reactions, and affective reactions partly related to interaction patterns in the manner specified by DAT. The most negative emotional reactions occurred in the same condition with the greatest discrepancy, the very low involvement condition. Also, the moderate discrepancy in the very high involvement condition produced a reciprocal increase in involvement (approach) and the large discrepancies in the two low involvement conditions also produced reciprocal decreases in involvement (avoidance), as DAT would predict. (The high involvement condition was not a change from baseline and therefore no discrepancy occurred.)

Whether this pattern of responses was due to the size of the discrepancies or the valences associated with them is unclear inasmuch as discrepancy was conflated with violation valence: The moderate discrepancy occurred in the positive condition and the large discrepancy, in the negative condition. What would be needed to untangle these factors is another experiment crossing moderate and large discrepancies with positive and negative valence. Of course, the investigation attempted to create just such combinations, but the actual discrepancies, as measured by trained coders, did not conform to the design plans.

## Summary

DAT was developed to improve upon previous arousal-based theories by better explaining how rapid adjustments are made to partner micro-level behaviors. The theory incorporates many of the same components as other models – expectancies, deviations or discrepancies, arousal change, and affect or valence – but attempts to combine them in ways that account for both reciprocal and compensatory patterns. In that respect, it shares many commonalities with EVT. Further discussion of DAT is therefore deferred until EVT is introduced so that the two can be compared.

## DIALECTICAL MODELS

In Chapter 2, evidence was presented that synchronous behavioral patterns are cyclical. Further evidence suggests that in some situations, both reciprocity and compensation may occur and do so simultaneously or concatenously within an individual or between two interactants. Given that prior models cannot account for these patterns, because they were largely rooted in stable predispositions and interaction patterns (e.g., ACT and BM) or affective-arousal responses (e.g., ALM and DAT), dialectical models were advanced as an alternative approach to viewing interactions and relationships.

Although a dialectical approach to interpersonal communication is relatively recent, dialectical principles have existed in the literature for quite some time. These basic principles remain constant across contexts, whether applied at a macrolevel, such as class struggles, or at the microlevel, such as an individual's psychological and physical strains. When dialectical tensions are applied to communication, such as to explain differences in interaction patterns of physical and psychological distance, they are cast at the individual or dyadic level.

In 1981, Altman, Vinsel, and Brown presented a model in which dialectic oppositions were proposed to be the source of changes in interpersonal distance. Instead of examining self-disclosure as a cumulative and linear process, as postulated in Altman and Taylor's (1973) Social Penetration Theory, dialectics provides a framework by which temporary increases and decreases in the breadth and depth of self-disclosure are possible. That is, dialectics offers a viable explanation for periods of openness and closedness within a relationship or interaction as well as for seemingly contradictory interaction patterns.

### Assumptions

A dialectic approach embraces an assumption of constant change, caused by the oscillation of forces between two ends of a bipolar opposition. These oppositional forces are presumed to arise from everyday interaction with others and from cyclical fluctuations in needs, rather than being biologically based such as the theories discussed in Chapter 2. Additionally, dialectical tension is viewed as neither good nor bad, and a steady state or balance between tensions (i.e., equilibrium) is unnecessary (Altman, 1993; Montgomery, 1993).

The primary polarities identified in the literature are autonomy–connection, openness–closedness, and novelty–predictability (Altman, 1993; Altman et al., 1981; Baxter, 1988, 1989; Montgomery, 1992). Others include independence–dependence, and affection–instrumentality (Rawlins, 1983, 1992). The autonomy–connection dialectic stems from the competing needs for privacy and for communion with others (Altman et al., 1981) and can be characterized as reflecting tensions between centripetal and centrifugal forces (Baxter, 1992). The openness–closedness dimension, also labeled the dialectic of expressiveness, relates most obviously to tensions between being verbally disclosive and "vulnerable" or nondisclosive and "protected," although nonverbal openness–closedness may also be implicated. The novelty–predictability dialectic concerns competing desires for variety and newness versus sameness and familiarity.

Drawing from Social Penetration Theory, which explains the closeness or communion aspect, and from privacy regulation principles, Altman et al. (1981) suggest that when people are satiated with closeness with another, they naturally seek its opposite – privacy. After a period of solitary time, however, a natural gravitation toward communion with others ensues, continuing the cyclical approach–avoidance pattern. In moving toward one extreme of a dialectic tension and its satiation, the opposite force becomes more salient and causes a pull in the opposite direction. The two oppositional forces are coexistent but alternate in governing behavior at any given time, propelling individuals and dyads into constant movement and cycling along the dialectic continuum (or seeking ways to manage the tensions).

Although the interpersonal dialectical models have implications for interaction adaptation in that they predict individuals will exhibit considerable fluctuations in behavior as their needs change, the greater applicability of the dialectic models is in their predictions for dyadic (rather than individual) approach–avoidance behavior. In Altman et al.'s (1981) original conceptualization, the "congruence" between two people's dialectic cycles is proposed to be a sign of the viability and stability of their relationship. For example, congruence can be translated as a form of reciprocity, or at least matching, of expressive behaviors if both people are being pulled toward openness and communion. However, instability may be hypothesized to result from mismatching cycles wherein one partner (Person A) seeks closeness while the other (Person B) seeks privacy. In this example, A's desire for closeness will propel A to approach B, while at the same time, B will enact avoidance behaviors in an effort to be alone, producing a compensatory pattern.

The main principles of dialectic approaches can be summarized as follows:

1. *Oppositional forces exist concurrently along a continuum.* One end of the continuum is dominant at a given time, until the person's need is satisfied (or satiated), in which case the alternative force exerts its pull.
2. *People do not inherently seek a balance of these oppositional forces* (contrary to ACT), but instead, cycle back and forth along the continuum between them (although they may pursue strategies to manage or minimize these tensions within their relationships).
3. *On a dyadic level, cyclical matching is posited to lead to stable relationships* (and, implicitly, partner satisfaction).

### Empirical support

Baxter and Wilmot (1983) were among the first to test several of Altman et al.'s (1981) hypotheses about dialectics. While they found evidence of cyclical patterns of openness and closedness, their method of obtaining self-report data from only one partner of a dyad prevented them from examining the (dis)synchrony of cyclical behavior. VanLear (1987) subsequently conducted a longitudinal study, which included data from both partners, to assess cyclical patterns. He found evidence of sequential reciprocity; that is, subjects in his study were observed disclosing information to one another at three levels of depth in a lagged sequential fashion. In addition, the type of disclosure made a difference such that more self-disclosure occurred at moderate depth (semiprivate) than at very personal and very impersonal levels. Sequential analyses of the data indicated that "fluctuations in reciprocity across time tended to occur concurrently across the levels of disclosure such that the zeniths . . . tended to occur together as did the nadirs" (VanLear, 1987, p. 313). However, because of a small sample, the sequential analysis results are tenuous.

In a subsequent two-part longitudinal study, VanLear (1991) pursued the issue of congruence in patterns of openness and closedness. The behavioral data from this study (as opposed to self-reports in his prior study) indicated that relationship partners tended to match their partner's openness both in duration and amplitude of self-disclosure. This behavior was evident both within and across conversations. Using a different set of subjects, VanLear (1991) obtained perceptual data in which subjects reported matching their self-disclosure to that of their partners. He concluded that self-disclosure matching occurs (i.e., people reciprocate periods of openness and closedness), and that partners perceive congruence in the timing of their own and their partners' disclosures. Additionally, those who perceived matching cyclical openness were more satisfied in their relationships than those who did not perceive congruence.

## Contributions

The literature examining other facets of a dialectic approach to personal relationships is diverse, and Altman (1993) notes that dialectic tensions operate intrapersonally, dyadically, and on larger scales, such as between smaller and larger social units (e.g., a couple and their respective families or friends).

VanLear (1991) suggests that there may be a dialectic tension between reciprocity and compensation as much as between openness and closedness. Depending on the circumstances of the relationship, it is not always appropriate to reciprocate self-disclosure, and his data provide evidence that reciprocity did not occur in every case. Further, he indicates that "the complexity of cycles . . . suggests that there may be a variety of regular factors, activities, and constraints that entrain people's periodic openness behavior" (VanLear, 1991, p. 356). He does not elaborate specifically on what these factors or circumstances might be. The issue of moderating factors is an area deserving greater attention. For example, dyad sex combination and relationship length may have differential effects on interaction patterns and cyclicity. While Van-Lear's (1991) conclusions should be accepted with caution, they raise a number of interesting questions about potential underlying mechanisms of reciprocal and compensatory patterns.

## Criticisms

A number of criticisms might be lodged against dialectical approaches, one being theoretical imprecision. Dialectic models cannot by themselves lead to clear predictions of when dyads will compensate or reciprocate. Neither can they account for how relationships escalate or deescalate intimacy. They do not specify when or how exogenous factors cause a reversal in direction in openness–closedness or approach–avoidance within or across interactions.

Also problematic is whether people actually recognize these dialectical forces. VanLear (1991) tried to demonstrate that perhaps people do perceive the tensions. However, because he used two different subject pools, one for self-disclosure measures and another for perceptual measures, it is unclear whether those exhibiting behavioral reciprocity actually perceived it or if those who perceived cyclical reciprocity exhibited it behaviorally.

Finally, the models have yet to generate much in the way of empirical testing. Only a few studies have tested Altman et al.'s (1981) original claim of congruence as an indication of relationship stability and, apart from VanLear's (1987, 1991) interactional studies, dialectic predictions have not been tested during actual interaction.

### Summary

This review of the dialectical perspective of reciprocity and compensation is sparse in part because the dialectical perspective is fairly new and has not yet generated a corpus of literature and empirical evidence. Obviously, the issues of congruence, matching, and reciprocity and whether there is a dialectic opposition between reciprocity and compensation are ripe for exploration. The main contributions of the dialectical perspective are the acknowledgment that needs and behaviors are cyclical and no single pattern may predominate consistently. Additionally, the dialectical perspective challenges the notion of an equilibrium level; instead of attempting to balance opposing forces, people may be compelled to satisfy the internal needs represented by one end of the dialectical opposition before reversing their behaviors and satisfying opposite needs. Indeed, people are free to experience a wide range of behaviors along the continuum (Altman, 1993).

### CONCLUSION

In this chapter, we have reviewed theories and models that share a common focus on arousal or psychological needs as the impetus for interpersonal adaptation. The assumptions and propositional relationships in several of these models are based on general notions of human spatial behavior. As such, they tend to emphasize compensation over reciprocity, though some include explanations for both compensation and reciprocity. Affiliative Conflict Theory and the Bidimensional Model assume participants' predispositions and preferences for stable interaction patterns guide the need for adjustment to one another. Arousal-Labeling Theory and Discrepancy-Arousal Theory posit that arousal change results from a partner's behavior changes and deviations from expected behavior. Arousal change in these theories leads to positively or negatively labeled affect, which produces behavioral adjustment designed to reduce arousal and achieve homeostasis. The dialectic models presume there is no strain toward stability or balance, but instead, people adapt to one another to achieve alternating opposing desires.

The underlying theme of all the theories and models presented in this chapter is that people have internal drive states that impact their emotional state. Moreover, discrepancies from normative or expected behaviors produce arousal. This results in behavioral adjustments, in some cases mediated by affect, though tests of these theories and models have not borne out specific predictions. In spite of this shortcoming, several assumptions have carried through to more recent models. Notions of the coexistence of compensation and reciprocity and recognition that individuals are driven by internal cognitive and affective states along with behavioral predispositions are useful. Finally, allusions to the environment and partner characteristics as factors influencing interaction are useful.

# 4

## Social norm approaches

We now shift away from a focus on individuals, their biological drives, and the affect–arousal link, to larger group processes, such as social and cultural norms and social exchange principles, as the guiding forces in dyadic interaction. We begin at the macroscopic level with Gouldner's (1960) norm of reciprocity, conceptualized as a societal mechanism that preserves order. This is followed by consideration of exchange theories as applied to reciprocal exchanges within relationships, and to models and research applied specifically to dyadic reciprocity within interactions. We conclude with Communication Accommodation Theory, which relies on social and cultural norms in its explanatory calculus, and incorporates a dyadic focus on communication and interaction processes.

As preface, we note that the concept of reciprocity has been in the scholarly literature for quite some time. Although some scholars trace it back to Jourard (1959) and Gouldner (1960), others credit George Herbert Mead (1934, 1964) with first directing attention to mutual adaptation processes. Mead's interest in adaptive responses, and specifically the ability to take another's perspective (which allows one to anticipate and adjust to another's behavior), can be seen to reflect an assumption about the mutuality of human interaction that resonates through much contemporary writing about shared understandings and other-directedness in human discourse (Foppa, in press; Linell, in press; Rommetveit, 1974). The concept of mutual other-directedness as foundational to communication implies a reciprocal orienting and attention that may be a prerequisite to all forms of social exchange.

### THE NORM OF RECIPROCITY

The "norm of reciprocity" so often appearing in the interpersonal interaction literature derives specifically from Gouldner's (1960) principle stating that "people should help those who have helped them, and people should not injure those who have helped them" (p. 171). Gouldner conceptualized reciprocity as a process of exchanges operating at the societal level in order to maintain harmonious and stable relations.[1] This conceptualization implicitly treats such exchanges as beneficial: People are obliged to help others and avoid doing others harm, in return for the same kind of treatment. Thus, in Gouldner's usage, reciprocity does not encompass negative or detrimental cycles of reciprocity. Additionally, the norm of reciprocity structures role relations by imposing rights and duties upon each person.[2] A violation of reciprocity, therefore, is considered a violation of values and basic social functioning; widespread continuing violations are hypothesized to lead to societal instability.

Gouldner (1960) cast reciprocity as a fundamental and universal principle underlying every interaction that functions to preserve social order. Cialdini (1984) subsequently endorsed its pervasiveness, asserting that it is an overpowering principle permeating all social exchanges: "Indeed, it may well be that a developed system of indebtedness flowing from the rule of reciprocation is a unique property of human culture" (p. 30).

Although Gouldner (1960) did not put forward a full-fledged theory of dyadic interaction, many of his thoughts undergird present work. First, he attempted to clarify the definition of reciprocity, which in the sociological literature had been widely and variously utilized without clear definition (much as definitional confusions continue to plague adaptation research to this day). As part of his definition, he advanced a view of reciprocity as contingent – that is, one person's behaviors are dependent upon the other's – and transactional – that is, as part of an exchange process between two people. This is a view to which we and many others subscribe (see Chapter 6).

Second, Gouldner incorporated reciprocity into sociological theory (functionalism) as one of the basic building blocks of human interaction. In the more than thirty years since Gouldner's piece, reciprocity has been utilized both theoretically (e.g., in social penetration theory and the various intimacy theories discussed in this text) and atheoretically (e.g., self-disclosure reciprocity studies) and, regardless of its theoretical role, is held as a persistent feature of human interaction.

Third, Gouldner argued that moderating variables, such as power differences, may contribute to nonreciprocal patterns. For example, the touch literature is replete with instances of nonreciprocal touch as the appropriate pattern of behavior between superior and subordinate. Similarly, Roloff (1987) and Derlega, Metts, Petronio, and Margulis (1993) identify several factors that influence timing of reciprocation (immediate or delayed) as well as type of reciprocity (a review of Roloff, 1987, follows shortly).

Fourth, Gouldner recognized that reciprocity occurs by *degrees:* "Reciprocity is not merely present or absent but is, instead, quantitatively variable – or may be treated as such" (p. 164). Varying degrees of reciprocity (same, greater, or lesser) pose a dilemma – how much reciprocation must be present in order to "count" as reciprocity as opposed to being considered nonaccommodation? Additionally, do differing amounts of reciprocation function similarly?[3] Some of these issues are considered within this text.

Fifth, Gouldner acknowledged that benefits exchanged may be either identical or equal. Roloff (1987) later referred to these as homeomorphic reciprocity (identical exchanges) and heteromorphic reciprocity (not identical, but similarly valued exchanges). Reciprocity in the form of similarly valued resource exchanges provides the necessary bridge to communication and to a functional approach in studying reciprocal *message,* rather than identical behavior, exchanges.

Last, Gouldner, in his discussion of exploitation, noted that some scholars conceptualized reciprocity as a strategic maneuver, whereas he and others envisioned it as operating at the societal level (such as politeness rules and rituals) below conscious awareness. Today, both types of reciprocity are recognized as operating within interactions, with context often determining the extent to which reciprocal routines are enacted below conscious intent or are purposeful (e.g., reciprocal concessions in negotiations).

As one can see, Gouldner's (1960) discussion of the norm of reciprocity is richly inlaid with a variety of assumptions, many of which we uphold to this day. His notion of reciprocity as "exchange" is one aspect of particular significance. Recent work by communication scholars, rather than taking such a broad and global view of human relations, has narrowed this notion of societal exchange down to resource exchange within relationships (Foa & Foa, 1972; Roloff, 1987). Reciprocity, in addition to preserving societal order, is seen to play an important role in relationship development and maintenance.

### Empirical support

It bears mentioning that no empirical support has accompanied Gouldner's norm of reciprocity. He explicated his conceptualization of the reciprocal nature of societal obligations. Because he did not propose a testable theory, no empirical tests have been conducted. However, the empirical evidence we report at the end of this chapter does speak implicitly to the pervasiveness of the norm of reciprocity.

## SOCIAL EXCHANGE THEORY AND RESOURCE EXCHANGE THEORY

Social Exchange Theory, originally introduced as a sociological parallel to Economic Exchange Theory, viewed human relations as a pattern of behavioral exchanges. Although originally posited for societal and larger group functioning, social exchange principles and the norm of reciprocity have proven fruitful at the interpersonal level. Roloff and Campion (1985) argue that social exchange principles and the norm of reciprocity govern interactions as people incur and meet social obligations through the give and take of different resources. Foa and Foa (1972) suggest the currency of dyadic interaction is money, material possessions (goods), information, status, love, and services. Communication, both verbal and nonverbal, becomes important within intangible resource exchanges, particularly those of love, status, and information.

### Reciprocal resource exchange

Roloff (1987) is but one scholar who identifies how relational acquaintance may impact reciprocity. A quick recap of his eight components of exchange and corresponding hypotheses follows:

1. *Resource exchanges may be homeomorphic (similar in form) or heteromorphic (similar value, but not identical resources).* The appropriateness of homeomorphic or heteromorphic reciprocity depends on situational and relational factors. For example, at times, reciprocal self-disclosure is appropriate (homeomorphic reciprocity), while at other times, listening and asking questions in response to a partner's disclosure (heteromorphic reciprocity) is necessary. Acquaintances and intimates alike must be flexible and perceptive of the situational demands to know which is warranted. Both relational intimates and acquaintances utilize homeomorphic and heteromorphic reciprocity. However, nonintimates may engage in more homeomorphic exchange, whereas intimates use more heteromorphic reciprocity. That is, intimate partners have the flexibility to

reciprocate with many different types of resources. For example, strangers typically reciprocate with similar "goods" such as self-disclosure reciprocity, whereas intimates may touch or embrace each other in response to a personal self-disclosure (Berg & Clark, 1986). It may be that *nonverbal* messages of intimacy and concern take on greater significance in developed relationships, thus necessitating a closer look at their manifestations.

2. *The time lag between when a debt is incurred and when it is repaid varies.* Timing of exchange may be predicated on the nature of the resource being exchanged. Some exchanges require immediate returns (e.g., students who exchange lecture notes for an upcoming exam), while others may allow for delayed returns (e.g., compliments or favors). Additionally, relational familiarity may affect exchange timing. Strangers may feel compelled to complete an exchange within a single interaction because they may not meet again, whereas intimate partners have many opportunities to reciprocate in future interactions (Derlega et al., 1976). Therefore, as degree of relational intimacy increases, the time allowed to complete the exchange process should increase.

3. *The degree to which reciprocity entails a resource of exact versus "rough equivalence" may vary.* As relational intimacy grows, approximate equivalence (or parity) becomes increasingly appropriate, as compared to exact equivalence. In established intimate relationships, discrepancies between resource exchanges are allowed if the "indebted" partner does not have the means to complete an equivalent exchange.

4. *Exchanges vary in whether contingency between resource exchanges and thus a fulfilled transaction, is clear* (i.e., there is a definite link between the initial and returned resource). It may be more appropriate in intimate relationships to give and take resources without keeping track of how balanced the exchange is. That is, noncontingent exchanges increase as intimacy increases.

5. *The resources used in exchanges vary in degrees of appropriateness.* Those in role relationships, such as doctor–patient and teacher-student relations, are bound to exchanging resources appropriate for their role. On the other hand, those in less restricted relationships have more variety in resource exchange. Additionally, within interpersonal relationships, those with greater relational intimacy should have a greater variety of (appropriate) resources to exchange.

6. *Exchange obligations may be transferred to another individual in some situations;* in others, the obligation is specifically tied to a particular individual. Transferability is posited to increase with increasing intimacy. For example, with a close friend or relative, a child may fulfill a parent's obligation to reciprocate a neighbor's previous help with yardwork or housework.
7. *People's feelings of obligation to conduct exchanges may vary.* The willingness to incur and meet obligations may be seen as one way to maintain trust and show participation in the relationship. Thus, as relational intimacy increases, the obligation to initiate exchanges should increase.
8. *The degree to which people tolerate as well as invoke sanctions against inequitable exchanges varies.* This proposition is similar to the delayed versus immediate reciprocation proposition; people who have an enduring relationship may trust that all the exchanges will balance in the end. Therefore, as relational intimacy increases, tolerance of inequitable exchange is posited to increase.

In summary, Roloff (1987) emphasizes that degree of relational acquaintance affects not only *when,* but with *what* behaviors one reciprocates. Once again, strangers are more compelled to return similar behaviors within a relatively short time span, whereas relational intimates return a wider array of behaviors with a greater degree of latitude in the timing of reciprocation. Also, relational partners do not match behaviors as closely as strangers, as they have more opportunities for exchange that will eventually "balance the account" over the course of their relationship.

### Empirical support

As in the case of Gouldner's reciprocity norm, Roloff's (1987) propositions of resource exchange in relationships have not been confirmed empirically. Whereas some of them are intuitively appealing, others, such as transferability of exchange obligations and obligations to initiate exchanges may be held more tentatively. Many of Roloff's propositions may be incorporated into current views of reciprocity, but empirical validation is necessary before we embrace them wholeheartedly.

## COUPLE INTERACTION AND THE "DYADIC EFFECT"

Also tacitly building upon a norm of reciprocity have been two highly visible research directions related to communication patterns within and across interactions. One, initiated by Jourard (1959), focuses on self-disclosure reciprocity and what he dubbed the "dyadic effect." The other represents a loose amalgamation of investigations, primarily descriptive in nature, exploring the extent to which couples adapt to each other's general interaction styles during single interactions and across a span of time within their relationship.

Writing at the same time as Gouldner, Jourard (1959) took a microscopic approach to reciprocity, envisioning it as an interpersonal phenomenon operating within personal relationships. Driven by a belief that the willingness to become "transparent" to others and to share risky information about self builds personal relationships, he initiated research on *self-disclosure*. Self-disclosure refers to the degree to which one divulges personal information or evaluations related to self or the relationship. He labeled the pattern in which a person reciprocates a partner's disclosure with one of equal intimacy the "dyadic effect." Jourard's writings ignited a flurry of studies that swept across the allied fields studying interpersonal relationships and communication.

At about the same time, a convergence of interests in marriage and the family among sociologists, family therapists, and psychologists (see Gottman, 1979) burgeoned into investigations of couples' interaction patterns. Often guided by systems or developmental views of interaction patterns, a common assumption in this research was and continues to be that members of couples and families influence and are influenced by one another. Although not grounded in a reciprocity norm per se, empirical evidence soon began to demonstrate strong reciprocal tendencies (although not always in the direction that Jourard had imagined). This body of research does not represent a particular theoretical position but does seem to be most congruent with the notion of a dyadic effect, hence our inclusion of it here.

### Empirical evidence

Early and more recent self-disclosure research has generally demonstrated the pervasiveness of reciprocal self-disclosure (Davis & Skinner, 1974; Derlega, Wilson, & Chaiken, 1976; Ehrlich & Graeven, 1971;

Hosman & Tardy, 1980; Savicki, 1972; Won-Doornick, 1985; Worthy, Gary, & Kahn, 1969). For any given self-disclosure, partners typically reciprocate a similar level of intimacy in their subsequent self-disclosures, or at least reciprocate the degree of disclosure they perceive from their partner (Pearce, Sharp, Wright, & Slama, 1974). Reciprocal exchange of self-disclosure purportedly promotes liking and creates trust, leading to more personal self-disclosures and propelling partners toward greater relational intimacy (Altman & Taylor, 1973; Derlega et al., 1976, 1993; Worthy et al., 1969).

Verbal self-disclosure is not the only behavior to be matched or reciprocated. Research on nonverbal behavior exchange and other verbal patterns has also provided extensive evidence of matching and reciprocity. Numerous investigations have found that interviewers and interviewees tend to match such speech phenomena as switch pauses, response latencies, pause length, utterance length, loudness, interruptions, body orientation, and gazes (e.g., Gregory, 1990; Honeycutt, 1991; Street & Buller, 1988; Street & Murphy, 1987; see Cappella, 1981, 1985, 1991a, for summaries). Investigations of involvement and immediacy behaviors have similarly found reciprocity and matching (Thompson & Aiello, 1988). Guerrero and Andersen (1994) found that romantic partners matched touch, with marrieds showing more matching than serious daters, who matched more than casual daters. D. A. Gilbert (1993) observed that nurses reciprocated involvement behaviors of clients and that the reciprocity included both immediate and delayed matching of functionally related (but not identical) behaviors. And Manusov (1994), in an experiment employing discussions among romantic couples, found a predominance of matching on numerous kinesic, proxemic, and vocalic variables during baseline interactions. Moreover, partners' behaviors continued to be positively associated when one partner shifted to a more immediate and positive interaction style, but the degree of association weakened somewhat when the same partner shifted to a more negative interaction style.

In contrast to this latter finding of less matching in response to negative behavior, much of the marital interaction literature has found strong patterns of reciprocity for both negative and positive affect. This research has tended to focus on the "darker" side of interactions, examining how couples manage conflict and disagreements. A prime exemplar is Gottman's (1979) program of research contrasting distressed couples (those seeking help for marital problems) with nondistressed couples (those relatively satisfied with their marriages). Gottman consistently found that partners in both types of couples reciprocated verbal disagreements and nonverbal affect, especially negative affect. Interestingly, Gottman found that reciprocation of negative affect was more pronounced among distressed couples than nondistressed couples (as well as in couples' communication at home) but he found little difference between distressed and nondistressed couples' reciprocation of positive affect. Whereas a negative affect comment or complaint was predictive of a subsequent negative affect comment or complaint, a positive comment was not predictive of a subsequent positive comment. However, when distressed couples reciprocated positive affect, it was more delayed than for the nondistressed couples.

Others (e.g., Billings, 1979; Burggraf & Sillars, 1987; Jacobsen, Follette, & McDonald, 1982; Pike & Sillars, 1985; Sabourin, Infante, & Rudd, 1993; Schaap, 1984) have replicated the prevalence of reciprocity and the finding of heightened reciprocation of negative affect among distressed and violent couples. Burggraf and Sillars (1987), in fact, found that marital conflict styles were so strongly reciprocal that they overshadowed individual style differences. Husbands' and wives' proportions of different conflict strategies were closely matched, and antecedent acts were highly likely to be reciprocated. Even though confrontation was an infrequent strategy, when one partner used it, there was a strong probability that the partner would follow suit, leading to "chaining out" of longer confrontational sequences. Later research by Sabourin et al. (1993) suggested that verbally aggressive acts may be more prevalent than previously thought and that reciprocal verbal abuse often escalates to physical abuse. Of course, positive behaviors are also sometimes reciprocated. Newton and Burgoon (1990) found that during disagreements, husbands and wives were likely to reciprocate the positively valenced strategies of content validation and other-support as well as the negatively valenced strategies of content invalidation and other-accusations. However, partners tended to use positive strategies only in the absence of the partner's use of negative strategies.

Other research has examined sequences and patterns over more extended periods of time. For example, in a two-year longitudinal study, Huston and Vangelisti (1991) found evidence of wives reciprocating husbands' earlier expressions of affection and negativity.

In summary, the cumulative evidence from these and other studies offers compelling evidence that homeomorphic strategies and "global" affect are frequently reciprocated in couples' interaction, both during individual interchanges and across the course of their relationship.

However, there are exceptions. Among the more notable ones, Kaplan, Firestone, Klein, and Sodikoff (1983) found that interactants only reciprocated an overall measure of intimacy from attractive others; when it was initiated by unattractive others, they compensated for it. Also, as behaviors under examination become more heteromorphic, matching and reciprocity become less common and consistent.

Several factors may also moderate the degree to which reciprocity occurs. Among them are relational goals, attributions and resultant valencing of received disclosures, relational stage or intimacy level, and opportunity to disclose (Derlega et al., 1993). Finally, the relationship between verbal and nonverbal intimacy may not be reciprocal. Several investigations have found increased verbal intimacy to produce compensation on latencies, gaze, smiling, proximity, and speech duration; conversely, close proximity has been found to reduce disclosure (e.g., Mahl, 1987; see Cappella, 1981, and Firestone, 1977, for summaries). Thus, reciprocity is by no means a universal response.

### Criticisms

For our current purposes, the greatest shortcoming of this body of research is its lack of an overarching theoretical framework guiding the research. It is therefore unclear just which theories or theoretical assumptions would be embraced by the various researchers studying these interaction patterns. Nor is it evident how they would account for the evidence of compensation.

A related problem is the degree to which dyadic effects are assumed to stem from intimacy or empathy motives and the extent to which they merely reflect normative behavior. For example, the reciprocity of conversation topics could just as easily be explained by Grice's (1989) theory of conversational coherence. By following conversational maxims for quantity, relation, and manner, interactants might feel compelled to contribute utterances on similar topics with similar linguistic detail and style, regardless of any desire to create a more intimate relationship.

Additional problems surround the research on self-disclosure. When one examines this body of evidence, one is struck by the variety of findings encapsulated by the term "reciprocal self-disclosure." For example, reciprocity of questioning a partner, rather than revealing information about oneself, has been labeled as self-disclosure reciprocity, although no actual self-disclosure took place. (The finding that both questioning and revealing information are reciprocated, however, does at least offer evidence that there is a strong tendency to reciprocate.) Problems with conceptual definitions, prior experimental methods, and subject pools offer a convincing basis to reconsider whether the claim for a preponderance of reciprocal self-disclosure has been reified prematurely.

Conceptually, although self-disclosure is defined as "revealing something about oneself that otherwise would not be known," this definition masks the complexity that underlies the process of sharing ourselves with others. Derlega et al. (1993) distinguish between descriptive (facts) and evaluative (expressions of personal feelings, judgments, etc.) self-disclosure, with evaluative disclosures being more personal or intimate, and thus more risky, than descriptive disclosures. They also distinguish between personal (self) and relational ("the relationship") disclosures. Similarly, several decades of research (e.g., Derlega et al., 1993; S. Gilbert, 1976) have identified several dimensions of self-disclosure: its topical breadth and depth, its duration or length, its relevance, whether it is positive or negative, the voluntary nature of the information disclosed, the reward value of receiving the disclosure (recipient's perception), the informativeness of the disclosure (i.e., how much information is provided), and the reasons and attributions made for disclosing. Are all of these forms and facets of self-disclosure to be treated similarly, or is there reason to treat them as qualitatively distinct?

Past research indicates that self-disclosure dimensions should be treated as distinct. For example, Ehrlich and Graeven (1971) found reciprocity of partner intimacy level, but not of the topic. This is but one illustration of how certain dimensions may be reciprocated more than others. More than just identifying dimensions, however, we need to start taking a functional approach toward self-disclosure. Including both verbal and nonverbal elements may help us to focus on messages rather than "dimensions."

This brings us to additional methodological problems. First, most studies have utilized strangers who get together for a one-time experiment on self-disclosure and who do not expect to interact with their experimental partner again. Just as inappropriate amounts of self-disclosure are found in the "stranger on the train" phenomenon, where people divulge highly personal information to complete strangers, strangers paired for these discussions in laboratories may abide by different norms of interaction appropriate to that context (Shaffer, Ogden, & Wu, 1987).

Second, self-disclosure studies often utilize unnatural experimental designs. In some instances, subjects pass notes back and forth, sometimes underneath a partition, to another subject, confederate, or hypothetical confederate (e.g., Derlega et al., 1976; Lynn, 1978; Worthy et al., 1969). These note-passing, get-acquainted sessions bear little resemblance to relational interactions other than how one might interact with a pen pal. Other designs have people interact via microphone and headset while sitting in separate cubicles (e.g., Savicki, 1972) or ask subjects to assess pairs of reciprocal or nonreciprocal responses (e.g., Hosman, 1987; Hosman & Tardy, 1980). These studies may capture the nature of self-disclosure norms among noninteracting (and at times, nonvisible or hypothetical) strangers. Future research is needed among people in continuing relationships because relationship and interaction factors may affect the nature of reciprocity (Derlega et al., 1993; Gilbert & Whitehead, 1976; Roloff, 1987). As one example, Won-Doornick (1985) found a curvilinear pattern between intimacy of self-disclosure reciprocity and relational stage. Reciprocity of highly intimate disclosures was found in the middle stages of relational development, whereas advanced relationships were characterized by reciprocity of moderately intimate self-disclosure. The highest amount of nonintimate disclosure was found in the early stages of relationships.

The dynamic nature of conversations and self-disclosure also may be particularly influenced by the nonverbal behavior and physical proximity of conversational partners (Mahl, 1987). Argyle and associates (1965, 1972, 1976) have alerted us to the interplay between verbal and nonverbal intimacy cues and the likelihood of compensation as the primary mode of interaction when conversations and interactions become too intimate. Compensatory processes are largely ignored when we focus on verbal behaviors (self-disclosure) without attention to nonverbal behaviors. Thus, many manifestations of reciprocity (and compensation) must be taken into account. And, instead of simply assessing self-disclosure, a more functional approach toward communication may be warranted – that of reciprocity and compensation of global messages (such as intimacy) rather than discrete behaviors.

## Summary

Like the norm of reciprocity, the dyadic effect implies that reciprocity is omnipresent. Even strangers and newly acquainted individuals tend to reciprocate self-disclosures, almost in a tit-for-tat fashion, within a single interaction. But unlike the presumption underlying the social norm that reciprocity prevails because it preserves societal harmony, the dyadic effect may include harmful as well as beneficial forms of reciprocity. The research on marital conflict and couple interaction highlights the pervasiveness of both positive and negative reciprocity cycles.

## COMMUNICATION ACCOMMODATION THEORY

Communication Accommodation Theory (CAT) began as Speech Accommodation Theory, a sociopsychological model conceived to explain why people's accents often converge during interviews (Giles, 1973). From its early narrow focus on language features, the theory has since grown into a more broad-based theory applicable to a wide range of macroscopic and microscopic linguistic, prosodic, and nonverbal phenomena such as language formality, code switching, utterance length, speech rate, pauses, gaze, and smiling (e.g., Gallois & Callan, 1988; Giles & Powesland, 1975; Giles, Taylor, & Bourhis, 1973). It is now being touted as a multidisciplinary approach to understanding a wide range of communicative motives, processes, and consequences.

### The original theory

Arising at a time when sociolinguists gave primacy to context in governing speaker moves during interaction, CAT aimed to direct attention to other factors such as language itself, speaker motivations, and receiver characteristics as influences on interaction processes and outcomes. The focal interaction patterns were, and continue to be, speech convergence and divergence.

*Convergence* is a strategy whereby one or both interactional partners adapt their linguistic and nonverbal styles to become more similar to one another. *Divergence* involves two people accentuating dissimilarities in their communication styles. These two accommodation patterns may be asymmetrical or symmetrical. When adaptation is unilateral (asymmetrical) such that only one partner adapts to the other, convergence appears reciprocal and divergence appears compensatory. When adaptation is mutual (symmetrical), however, convergence and divergence appear compensatory because their behaviors are going in opposite directions. For example, Person A begins an interaction by speaking loudly. Person B responds to this "inappropriate" volume by speaking softer. If Person A becomes frustrated with B's move to quiet the conversation by whispering, and adapts by speaking even louder, mutual divergence and compensation have occurred.

Convergence and divergence also may be complete or partial. For example, if Person A speaks at a rate of 100 words per minute (wpm), Person B could increase speech rate from 50 to 75 wpm (partial convergence) or from 50 to 100 wpm (complete convergence). Or, Person B could speed up to the point of exceeding Person A's rate, resulting in hyperaccommodation. Additionally, adaptation may be manifested in a single modality (e.g., accent) or in multiple modalities (e.g., gaze, smiling, and tempo). Because adaptation need not be restricted to a single modality, convergence may occur on some behaviors while divergence or nonaccommodation simultaneously occurs on others, resulting again in only partial adaptation (see Giles, Coupland, & Coupland, 1991a; Giles, Mulac, Bradac, & Johnson, 1987).

Many of CAT's propositions specify the motivations and conditions for converging or diverging. The cornerstone proposition states that people are *"motivated to adjust (or accommodate) their speech styles as a strategy for gaining one or more of the following goals: evoking listeners' social approval, attaining communication efficiency between interactants, and maintaining positive social identities"* (Giles et al., 1987, p. 15). Convergence thus becomes a means for conversants to express similar attitudes and values, to facilitate smooth and clear communication, to foster attraction, and to reinforce identification with an ingroup or positively regarded other.

Typically, convergence is "upward" toward the more "prestigious" or positively valued style. However, when perceived costs associated with convergence outweigh perceived rewards or when social norms and power differentials dictate complementary speech styles, convergence is not expected to occur. Convergence will also be limited by individual repertoires and abilities (Giles et al., 1991a).

Street and Giles (1982) stressed that convergence is toward (or divergence is away from) one's *perception* of a partner's speech style. Thus, perceptions and expectations are potentially more important than objective, observable behavior. Equally important are the meanings ascribed to convergent and divergent behavior. Just as interactants have multiple goals and interactions have multiple functions, convergent and divergent patterns have multiple interpretations. Convergence toward a nonstandard dialect, for example, may promote solidarity while simultaneously undermining evaluations of a speaker's competence.

Additional CAT propositions specify conditions leading to convergence or divergence and the consequences of such acts. The extent of convergent or divergent adaptation is limited by the abilities of the participants to alter their behaviors. Convergence also depends on the personal and environmental conditions that affect one or both participants' needs for social approval or communication efficiency or both, as well as social norms that may dictate alternative communication strategies. Divergence, on the other hand, is proposed to occur when participants (a) want to express their identification with a group while distinguishing themselves from others outside of the group, (b) desire dissociation from an interactional partner in an interpersonal context, (c) wish to influence a partner's speech behaviors so as to bring the involvement level of the interaction to a comfortable and acceptable level, or (d) wish to signal dislike for the other. These goals need not always be achieved through divergence; maintenance of a particular speech style will sometimes suffice.

Remaining CAT propositions address the consequences of convergence and divergence. Most specify positive evaluations of convergence. This underscores an implicit assumption that convergence leads to similarity, which is inherently positive. In general, positive evaluations of convergence result from the perception of a positive behavior, decreased cognitive load on the part of the receiver, and an attribution of positive intent. Negative evaluations of divergence and maintenance are proposed to result from behaviors that are seen as psychologically divergent. However, there are exceptions. If, for instance, one defines a situation in intergroup terms and shares a positive identity with a speaker who is perceived as diverging from others outside the group, a positive evaluation is posited.

It should be emphasized that complete convergence or divergence is not always desirable. Instead, interactants may have a *tolerance range of acceptable behaviors* (Giles, 1980), similar to that found in Cappella and Greene's (1982) Discrepancy-Arousal Theory. In other words, there is a potential for too much or too little convergence or divergence that may lead to a negative evaluation.

## Later modifications of CAT

CAT has undergone multiple incarnations and modifications in attempting to explain the circumstances and reasons for people adopting similar or dissimilar communication styles (see Gallois, Giles, Jones, Cargile, & Ota, 1995; Giles et al., 1991a,b). It has been applied to such diverse contexts as second-language learning, intergenerational communication, intergroup and intercultural interactions, medical consultations, courtroom proceedings, radio broadcasts, and organizational interactions (Giles et al., 1991b). It has also been extended beyond its original emphasis on linguistic and vocalic features to apply to a greater range of nonverbal behaviors. Gallois and colleagues (Gallois & Callan, 1988, 1991; Gallois et al., 1995), for example, have examined gaze, smiling, vocal pleasantness, response latencies, and pauses in intercultural interactions. And the interaction patterns have routinely been linked to outcomes (to be discussed in Chapter 12).

Recent articulations (e.g., Coupland, Coupland, Giles, & Henwood, 1988; Giles et al., 1987, 1991a) have further refined the theory's propositions. They have also distinguished between *approximation strategies* (convergence, divergence, and maintenance) and nonapproximation or *attuning strategies*. The latter are ones speakers may use to attend to the needs and abilities of the interaction partners. To adapt to the partner's communication competence, they may use *interpretability strategies* – speaking more slowly, using simpler language, checking often that the listener understands, and selecting topics of common interest. This may be especially common in interethnic and intergenerational interactions where speakers doubt listeners' linguistic proficiency or hearing ability. Speakers may also adopt *discourse management* and *interpersonal control strategies* – the former to facilitate the partner's conversational participation and repair problems or face threats, the latter to reinforce or alter role relationships (e.g., through forms of address and offering up the floor). This extension of the theory, which is similar to the functional perspective discussed in the next chapter, recognizes that all conversational moves are not designed to increase or decrease similarity in speech patterns. The latest revision of the theory (Gallois et al., 1995) places accommodative or nonaccommodative orientations within a sociohistorical context (i.e., social and cultural norms), takes into account intrapersonal and intergroup factors in predicting initial orientation, but also includes immediate situational factors such as interactant goals, behavioral repertoires, and attributions in determining actual interaction behavior.

### Empirical support

Because a number of review articles detail the widespread support CAT has enjoyed (see Giles et al., 1991a, 1987), only a sampling of typical lines of research is offered here.

Much of the research can be organized according to the goals or motives postulated to guide the decision to converge or diverge. Many studies focusing on the motive of expressing similarity have demonstrated that interactants who perceived themselves to be attitudinally or psychologically similar converged within turn and switch pauses and vocal intensity levels more often than those who saw themselves as dissimilar or who were randomly paired (Welkowitz & Feldstein, 1969, 1970; Welkowitz, Feldstein, Finkelstein, & Aylesworth, 1972). Giles et al. (1987) proposed that the effort to appear similar reflects a desire for social approval. Indeed, many studies have shown that convergence in communication styles is associated with a partner's perceived attractiveness, predictability, intelligibility, and involvement (Berger & Bradac, 1982; Coupland, 1984; Dabbs, 1969; LaFrance, 1979; Putman & Street, 1984; Triandis, 1960).

Another set of studies has demonstrated how minority subgroups tend to adopt the dialect or language of a larger group, perhaps one to which the subgroup has immigrated (Bourhis & Giles, 1977; Fishman, 1966; Taylor, Simard, & Papineau, 1978). This adaptation not only reflects a need for social approval but also implies that often those in a less powerful position will adapt to become more similar to those with more power. This pattern of unilateral convergence has been found, for example, among Chicano 6-year-olds adapting to the language of Anglo-American children (Aboud, 1976; Day, 1982; Giles et al. 1973) and among Mexican-American women adapting to the language-switching styles of men (Valdes-Fallis, 1977). Thus, convergence not only conveys a need for social approval but also can signify which groups are more valued and powerful.

Following Tajfel and Turner's (1979) social identity theory of intergroup relations, a number of studies have demonstrated that divergence is employed strategically to establish one's identity as an ingroup member. Thus, when gender was made salient, Hogg (1985) found that males were judged more masculine in interactions with females than when gender was not highlighted. Other studies have shown that ethnic groups often maintain or diverge on characteristics such as language, dialect, slang, phonology, and language structure to establish their ingroup identity with one another (Giles, Bourhis, & Taylor, 1977; LaFrance, 1985).

Another motive posited for divergence is to bring an interaction partner's behavior to an acceptable level of involvement or activity. For example, therapists may talk less or slow the rate of talk in order to encourage patients to talk more and faster (Matarazzo, Weins, Matarazzo, & Saslow, 1968; Street, Street, & VanKleeck, 1983). Divergence may also be dictated by social norms, under which circumstances it is judged positively rather than negatively (see, e.g., Matarazzo & Weins, 1972; Miller & Steinberg, 1975; Putman & Street, 1984). A less powerful person's divergence from the speech pattern of a more powerful one is deemed acceptable, appropriate, and even expected.

This cursory sampling is part of a large body of evidence supporting many CAT predictions and explanations. Overall, the evidence points to people tending to converge more than they diverge, although there are numerous factors moderating the interaction patterns and producing highly complex relationships. Convergence appears to be a fairly automatic process, though it can be used strategically to present a particular image. While divergence may also occur tacitly, this process appears to be used more often with intentional forethought in the service of signaling ingroup and outgroup identity. Further, that attributions and evaluations are made based on these processes elevates them beyond mere indicative behaviors to the status of communication.

### Criticisms

Some of the criticisms applicable to CAT are also applicable to other theories. The first three concern its scope. CAT best fits circumstances where it can be assumed that people are conscious of, and deliberate about, their communicative behavior. This strategic view of communication may be appropriate for interactions among strangers and status-unequals but appears questionable when applied to routine conversations among acquaintances and to task-oriented interactions. CAT attempts to evade this problem by assuming that, consciousness notwithstanding, much of the adaptation process occurs automatically by drawing upon procedural information in memory to make behavioral adjustments. Yet Cappella (1985) criticizes CAT as accounting poorly for automatic adjustments, stating that the theory "works well in situations in which individuals are making relatively deliberate choices but not so well in situations in which individuals are making relatively automatic reactions" (p. 422). Thus, CAT is limited implicitly to highly intentional forms of adaptation. Like all of the adaptation theories, it must come to grips with the degree to which adaptation processes engage conscious deliberation prior to or during their enactment. Theories attempting to broaden their scope by incorporating both strategic and nonstrategic forms of adaptation must delineate under which conditions each will emerge and why.

A second scope problem afflicting CAT is its relevance to only a few communication functions. By making identity and relationship management functions paramount, CAT is most applicable where these goals are important and less adequate in explaining interactions in which other communication goals or functions take precedence. For instance, CAT is unable to account for reciprocal spirals of positive or negative affect associated with the emotion management functions or for complementary dominance and submission patterns associated with the relational communication function.

Third, recent revisions of CAT intended to broaden its scope have been a mixed blessing. By including nonverbal behaviors beyond those linked to speech and by acknowledging that some adaptation strategies may be directed not toward approximating another's communication style but toward adjusting to an interlocutor's needs and abilities, CAT has increased its validity. The addition of attunement and interpretability strategies probably better reflects the reality of the multipronged nature of adaptation. But it has come at the cost of reduced parsimony and increased nonfalsifiability because there is yet no clear designation of which behaviors and patterns are linked to which strategies. If convergence is performed in the service of some functions, divergence satisfies others, and yet other behaviors reflect attunement rather than accommodation, indeterminacies arise as to which behaviors should exhibit which patterns. Indeed, the complexity of past findings showing a mix of convergence, divergence, and attunement-related behaviors calls into question the theory's ability to make precise a priori predictions. This criticism of course is not unique to CAT. It applies to all of the theories that attempt a more comprehensive depiction of contextualized interaction processes.

### Summary

CAT is a well-articulated and well-supported theory that has developed systematically over the past two decades from a simple explanation of speech accent convergence into a detailed model and set of propositional statements. The theory has proved useful in specifying the conditions for interactional adaptation and the outcomes resulting from those adaptations. It makes an original contribution, relative to preceding theories, by emphasizing the capacity of interaction behaviors to be used strategically to meet individual and group goals, by identifying key motivations for interpersonal adaptation, and by recognizing constraints such as individual competencies, roles, and cultural norms on adaptation. Further, it highlights the multifunctionality of interaction behaviors and the multiplicity of behaviors that may serve a particular goal. It underscores the importance of the evaluations and attributions associated with interaction behaviors. Finally, nonaccommodation is shown to sometimes function as divergence or compensation.

## CONCLUSION

This chapter includes explanations for interaction adaptation patterns based on sociological principles as dominant forces causing behavioral adjustments. The first three theories or models suggest that most adaptations are reciprocal because of a pervasive social norm dictating that exchanges be similar in form, function, and value. This norm of reciprocity and the social exchange principles associated with it are seen as applying not only to broad societal phenomena but also to interpersonal interactions. Resource exchange principles emphasize that reciprocation within relationships is essential, but depending on the level of acquaintance, reciprocity may manifest itself in a variety of verbal and nonverbal forms and with different lag times. Still, within individual interactions, the dyadic effect is common. Couples reciprocate not only self-disclosures but other facets of verbal and nonverbal communication. Thus, reciprocity is posited to occur at all levels, from the individual to societal, implying that this principle is a powerful influence in social interactions.

Because of its recognition that multiple functions interact with social norms to guide behavioral adaptation, CAT, the last theory covered in this chapter, helps us bridge the gap between the earlier social norm models and the upcoming communication-based theories of adaptation patterns. We chose to include CAT in this chapter because of its acknowledgment of the strong impact of sociocultural and psychological factors on interactional patterns. The theories covered in the next chapter build upon the preceding ones by incorporating many of the same factors but focus primarily on the functional message value of behavior changes and adaptations.

**NOTES**

[1] While the norm of reciprocity may be claimed as a universal organizing principle of human behavior, its practice may differ across cultures. In Western and individualistic cultures, the norm typically implies *equity* in the receipt of rewards (i.e., rewards are proportional to inputs) whereas in collectivist cultures it implies *equality* of rewards exchanged (Ting-Toomey, 1986).

[2] For those familiar with Gouldner's (1960) article, it is important to note that his discussion of complementarity bears no resemblance to our conceptualization of it. Gouldner frames complementarity in four different ways, all centering around the notion that the rights of one person are complemented by the corresponding "duties" of another. We use complementarity as a pattern similar to compensation, but without evidence of contingency or influence.

[3] Gouldner conceived of reciprocity as functioning to ensure smooth interactions between people. Coming from a sociological-functionalist perspective, he did not address other interpersonal functions such as managing impressions, emotions, or intimacy, although he noted that some scholars conceptualized reciprocity as a strategic maneuver used to achieve one's purposes.

# 5

## Communication and cognitive approaches

Many of the theories discussed so far implicate a strong biological influence. Several theories also add psychological and sociological components in the form of affect, needs, expectations, and norms. What sets these theories apart from the preceding ones is the increasing emphasis on behavior as communication and on the functions and meanings that such behaviors entail. Functional and meaning-centered perspectives permeate many contemporary approaches to the study of interpersonal and nonverbal communication generally. We therefore review the more salient critical attributes of these perspectives before examining particular theories.

### A FUNCTIONAL PERSPECTIVE

A functional approach to interaction adaptation acknowledges that interactions are multifunctional: Interactants bring multiple goals, objectives, needs, and wishes to be accomplished through communication. Among the "functions" that communication serves are message production and processing (also labeled information exchange or message transmission), identification and identity management, impression formation and management, relational communication and relationship management, emotion expression and management, conversation structuring and management, social influence and control, and personal resource management (see, e.g., Argyle, 1972; Burgoon, 1994; Burgoon & Saine, 1978; Dillard, Segrin, & Harden, 1989; Ekman & Friesen, 1969b; Goffman, 1959; Graham, Argyle, & Furnham, 1980; Patterson, 1983, 1990, 1991). Interactants must encode comprehensible messages (the message production function) and attend to, interpret, and evaluate the partner's messages (the message processing function) in the process of conducting a conversation. At the same time, they must manage their verbal and nonverbal communication to project who they think they are (the identity function), who they want others to think they are (the impression function), what kind of relationship they perceive they have with the partner (the relational communication function), and their definition of the situation in which they find themselves (the structuring function). They must also monitor and control their emotional displays (the emotion management function), regulate and coordinate the flow of conversation (the conversation management function), and, on occasion, alter the partner's attitudes or behavior (the influence function) while securing their own safety, pleasure, and access to desired resources (the personal resources function).

Individual goals operate within these large functional categories while also incorporating personal priorities and situational constraints (see Cronkhite & Liska, 1980). A person's foremost interaction goal in a first encounter with a stranger, for example, may be to seek information about the other or merely to "get along," that is, create a smooth interaction (Snyder, 1992; Snyder & Haugen, 1994); other functions such as managing emotions are less likely to be salient in such situations. In a compliance-gaining situation, an individual may need to balance self-interest goals (e.g., winning or maximizing personal rewards) with relationship goals (e.g., saving face for the other) and interaction goals (e.g., maintaining equanimity and minimizing conflict).

The presence of multiple, sometimes competing, communication goals can explain why reciprocity occurs under one circumstance and compensation under another or why both patterns may materialize within the same context. A quick reflection offers numerous illustrations. In public and formal situations that demand adherence to politeness norms, people may eschew reciprocation of hostility and instead show compensatory appeasement in response to public displays of annoyance. But in private or intimate situations where such constraints are relaxed or ignored, they may easily be swept up in a spiraling contagion of verbal and physical aggression. People may choose to reciprocate another's profanity and humor so as to create a sense of solidarity (a relational communication function) but compensate another's personal, embarrassing self-disclosures with impersonal ones so as to preserve an unblemished reputation (an identity management function). They may reciprocate another's smiling to express affiliation but compensate gaze to lessen emotional arousal (a pattern found by Kendon, 1990).

A functional approach grounds interaction adaptation predictions in the communication functions and goals that are likely to be operative in a given situation, as well as any constraints that might prevent goal attainment or limit behavioral options. Just as interpersonal interaction entails multiple concurrent functions, each of which may be accomplished through multiple verbal and nonverbal behaviors, interaction behaviors themselves are multifunctional; that is, they are enlisted to satisfy more than one function simultaneously or in quick succession. Argyle and Dean (1965) and Abele (1986), for example, proposed that gaze not only regulates intimacy and defines interpersonal relationships, it also manages conversations, identities, and emotions through information seeking, monitoring, and revealing or concealing one's inner states. As an intimacy regulator, gaze can increase or decrease the experienced level of intimacy in a dyad by how long, how frequently, and how directly two people engage in mutual eye contact. But a certain amount of gaze may also be mandated, regardless of how much intimacy one desires to communicate, to achieve adequate surveillance of an unfamiliar partner. This greatly complicates the task of designating when gaze is acting as a communicative cue as opposed to functioning in an information-seeking capacity. But identification of the likely functions present in a situation can at least restrict the range of interpretations or purposes imputed to a given behavior.

## EMPHASIS ON MEANING AND INTERPRETATION

Communication and cognitive perspectives also place emphasis on the meanings that interaction behaviors convey and/or the inferences that are drawn from them. Recognition that a behavior's meaning will influence the response to it is not original with the models to be discussed. Apart from this being a basic assumption of all communication, Patterson's (1976) ALT first introduced explicitly the importance of the "label" or meaning assigned to the behaviors of others. But in Patterson's model, the label referred to one's own hedonic response to a stimulus rather than to any inherent communicative value in it. By contrast, communication-based models make more direct claims about the "message value" of another's behavior. That is, actions are treated as symbolic and part of a shared vocabulary among members of a given speech community. The communicative meanings of behaviors are featured prominently. As part of this "meaning analysis," cognitive models additionally invoke attributional processes in their explanations; that is, they consider the motivations and possible causes for people's behavior. Both the communicationally oriented and cognitively oriented models imply more "cognitive work." The models that follow, although disparate, share these features. In them, communication takes center stage.

## PATTERSON'S SEQUENTIAL-FUNCTIONAL MODEL

Patterson's (1983) Sequential-Functional Model (SFM) was introduced as a "new and improved" model to ALT, the latter failing to receive empirical, as well as theoretical, support (see, e.g., Ickes et al., 1982; Patterson et al., 1981; Patterson, Roth, & Schenk, 1979). The SFM was designed to account for both automatic and planned reactions as well as for actor motivations within an interaction. Additionally, the SFM was constructed to correct for the limited attention paid to the role of antecedent factors in influencing outcomes. Although prior theories acknowledged the potential influence of factors such as age, gender, and personality, Patterson found they were "not classified in any consistent fashion and their relationships to central processes are left indeterminate" (Patterson, 1983, p. 19). These concerns led Patterson to propose a more comprehensive model to (a) address multiple functions, (b) include both nonverbal and verbal expressions of involvement, and (c) attend more carefully to the effects of antecedent factors and preinteraction mediators than previous explanations. It should be noted that this model focuses exclusively on involvement and not other aspects of interpersonal exchange.

### The original theory

The primary components in Patterson's (1982, 1983) original conceptualization of the SFM include antecedent factors (brought to the interaction by the participants), preinteraction mediators (influencing expectancies about the current interaction), and the interaction phase. (For a thorough discussion of these, see Patterson, 1983.) A key assumption underlying the SFM is that all humans strive for stable interaction patterns. However, a number of factors, including the unique combination of characteristics brought to the conversation by interactants, present challenges to a smooth and stable exchange.

#### Antecedent factors

Three types of factors are included under antecedent factors: personal, experiential, and relational-situational. *Personal factors* comprise sociocultural, gender, age, and personality features. Cultural norms and standards generate large differences between cultures (Hall, 1966). For example, people from Latin American, Arab, and southern Mediterranean cultures exhibit more nonverbal involvement than people from northern European and North American cultures. Morris et al. (1979) also report diversity in the extent, types, and meanings of gestures employed across 25 countries in western and southern Europe and the Mediterranean. Involvement may also differ by social class, occupation, and religion (Patterson, 1983).

Gender and age also affect interaction behavior (e.g., Aiello & Aiello, 1974; Burgess, 1983; Dabbs et al., 1980; Hall & Veccia, 1990; S. E. Jones, 1986; Jourard, 1966; LaFrance & Mayo, 1979; Mayo & Henley, 1981; Mosby, cited in Burgoon, Buller, & Woodall, 1989). For example, females routinely display more involvement than males. As children grow older, they require more space, perhaps due to learning the appropriate spatial norms. Touch is more likely to be initiated by the male if the dyad is younger but by the female if the dyad is older. Additionally, personality characteristics such as internal–external locus of control, self-monitoring, field dependence–independence, and social approach–avoidance are associated with differential patterns of behavioral involvement (Patterson, 1982, 1983).

*Experiential factors* include recent events, situations, or interactions that are similar to or relate to the current exchange. Patterson (1983) explains that experiential factors influence interactions according to one of two perspectives. The first, a learning-reinforcement perspective, suggests that individuals are rewarded or punished for particular levels of involvement they previously exhibited. Those levels for which they were rewarded (or witnessed others being rewarded) are more likely to be displayed in subsequent interactions than levels of involvement that were punished or sanctioned. The second perspective, the regulation of sensory stimulation levels, is based on the notion that people seek an optimum level (e.g., an equilibrium) of sensory stimulation (Altman, 1975; Milgram, 1970). Given too much stimulation, people will withdraw for a period to avoid activity; with too little stimulation, they will become more involved with others to increase the level of stimulation. Regardless of the underlying mechanisms, Patterson (1983) posits that experiential factors affect responses in social interactions.

*Relational-situational* factors are grouped together because they are posited to interact with one another in influencing nonverbal involvement patterns. Relational factors refer to dyadically defined variables such as degree of familiarity. For example, strangers stand farther apart than friends or close acquaintances. Situational factors are similar to contextual factors. Patterson (1982) contends that in more formal environments, characteristics of the situation take precedence, causing interactants to behave in predictable normative patterns. In less formal environments, however, relational characteristics are posited to have a greater impact on interaction patterns, leading to more variable and relationally negotiated interaction patterns.

These antecedents have a pervasive influence on elements in the next stage.

### Preinteraction mediators

This second set of elements includes behavioral predispositions, potential arousal change, and cognitive assessment, all of which affect participant expectations. These characteristics are proposed to have more proximal impact on behavioral patterns than antecedent factors and to evoke automatic rather than intentional responses.

*Behavioral predispositions* are habituated patterns of behavior that tend to occur automatically without much cognitive activity. Patterson (1983) suggests they are tied integrally to the personal factors discussed earlier. Although behavioral predispositions are typically automatic, should participants actively think about an interaction, attentional focus shifts toward situational influences and away from predispositions or personal factors (E. E. Jones & Nisbett, 1971).

Another mediator of involvement exchange is *potential arousal change.* Although the relationship between arousal, cognition, and behavior is not as clear cut as once thought (e.g., Schachter & Singer, 1962), Patterson (1983) argues that potential arousal change is still a mediating source, either by affecting behavioral adjustments directly or activating cognitive activity.

*Cognitive-affective assessments* include affective reactions, which are largely subconscious and automatic responses to (primarily) nonverbal cues, and complex cognitive responses, which together create expectancies and mediate interactions. These may occur prior to and during interactions. For example, a friend might suggest you attend church with her next weekend. Before you actually attend the service, you might experience a "gut-level" affective response to it. You might also think about the last time you attended such an event, which might call into action certain scripts or schemata you have. The affective and cognitive expectancies that are formed will then affect how you behave during the event. All of this activity may transpire without your awareness of specific thoughts or plans.

In review, in this second stage partners form conscious or tacit interaction expectancies that may be revised as the interaction unfolds. These expectancies, in combination with arousal level and behavioral predispositions, set the stage for actual interaction and the types of dyadic patterns that should emerge.

### Interaction phase

This last phase entails actual involvement level, perceived communication functions, arousal change, and cognitive-affective assessment. In any interaction, SFM assumes the participants send meaningful messages (with or without awareness) to one another through their behaviors; each, in turn, infers the intended meaning. For each meaning, there is a corresponding set of appropriate, normative, and expected behaviors. These meanings represent the various *functions* of nonverbal behaviors. Patterson (1983, 1987, 1991) notes that often multiple functions are served by the same set of behaviors and multiple behaviors may accomplish a single function. The SFM proposes that, within the constraints set by the environment and situation, interactants use involvement behaviors to provide information, regulate interaction, express intimacy, exercise social control, facilitate service or task goals, and manage self-presentations and affect. Because so many of the antecedent factors and preinteraction mediators are expressed primarily via nonverbal signals or are based on observing nonverbal signals, Patterson focuses on nonverbal rather than verbal indices of involvement.

Interactants observe their partner's nonverbal involvement behavior (and infer the function). Overly intense behavior and behavior that violates expectancies is posited to cause *arousal change* in the observer. When arousal change is minimal, Patterson (1982) claims stable, reciprocal exchange takes place. Stable exchange may also arise due to interactants abiding by similar scripts or being subjected to the same environmental and situational constraints (such as behaving formally). Unstable exchanges, by contrast, are characterized by discrepancies between participants' behaviors, functional intents, or expectations. These result in compensatory adjustments: "A disparity between the functional expectancies of the interactants should also create instability and increase the likelihood of compensatory behavior" (Patterson,

1983, p. 31). Like DAT, SFM predicts that large arousal increases, caused by discrepancies between expected and actual involvement, are evaluated negatively and lead to compensation. Additionally, the greater the difference in personal characteristics of the interactants, the greater the likelihood of unstable exchange and compensatory responses occurring, presumably because of differential expectations and perceived functions.

Once participants have responded to an unstable situation with compensatory adjustments, Patterson (1983) claims they will engage in a second round of *cognitive-affective assessment* of the partner's behavior. The assessment may lead to further behavioral adjustments or to a more elaborate assessment of the interaction function. Patterson (1982) adds that "should an interaction continue to be unstable and unaffected by the adjustments of one or both parties, an earlier than normal termination would be expected" (p. 241). Whenever an interaction terminates, whether preceded by stable or unstable exchange, a remnant of the cognitive-affective activity becomes part of the antecedent factors for the next interaction.

In summary, Patterson's assumptions may be outlined as follows:

1. *Interactional behavior is guided by factors brought to the interaction by each individual as well as by emergent features of the actual interaction.*
2. *Multiple functions may be operating in a given interaction.* Behaviors are also multifunctional.
3. *People develop behavioral expectancies and interpret behaviors according to the function they assign to them.*
4. *Certain functions elicit primarily strategic behaviors, and others, primarily nonstrategic behaviors.* Both may occur during interactions.
5. *When both partners behave according to similar preferences, expectancies, or norms, a pattern of reciprocal exchange, or "stable exchange" results.*
6. *Discrepancies between expected and actual involvement behavior initiate compensatory patterns – "unstable exchanges" – or lead to termination of the interaction.*

### Recent modifications of SFM

Reflecting some of his own dissatisfaction with the original model, Patterson (1991, 1994) has since modified and expanded the SFM. One new version, shown in Figure 5.1, now includes *genetic and environmental determinants* of the antecedents of culture, biology, personality, and gender. Genetics control encoding and decoding abilities, affect the ability to learn patterns of behaviors, influence basic universal expressions and needs (e.g., bonding and the need to form social relationships), and underlie the predisposition to attend to others in one's environment. Physical environment factors (e.g., temperature, climate, and terrain) influence social roles, family structure, and child-rearing practices. Social environment factors frame and structure social situations. Patterson (1991) argues there are nonrecursive relationships between genetic and environmental determinants and between determinants and antecedent factors. Genetic determinants, along with social situation and relationship factors, also may influence preinteraction factors directly.

Within *preinteraction mediators,* Patterson (1991) has changed cognitive-affective assessments to cognitive-affective expectancies. (The 1994 version further modifies these elements by labeling them as cognitive-affective mediators composed of expectancies, goals, affect, and dispositions, all of which influence cognitive resources.) The *interaction phase* now includes action schemas and attentional focus (in the 1994 version). As before, if participants have similar interaction goals and perceptions, there is greater likelihood that the interaction will be stable and predictable. If another's behavior is not facilitative of an actor's goals, it may lead to behavioral and/or cognitive adjustment or termination of the interaction. Other factors influencing the behavioral pattern are cognitive resources and affect. If behavior management requires significant cognitive effort and cognitive resources are overtaxed, actors may be less likely to accommodate to their partner. But behavior that is primarily the product of interpersonal affect may be largely spontaneous and require little cognitive effort for behavior management. Under such circumstances, positive affect associated with increased immediacy and involvement is predicted to yield reciprocity and negative affect, to yield compensation (Patterson, 1994).

### Empirical support

Because the SFM consists of a great number of steps or stages and many of them are affective and cognitive, the model has not been tested in its entirety. Rather, particular stages or processes have been examined individually, and it is argued that results of several studies in combina-

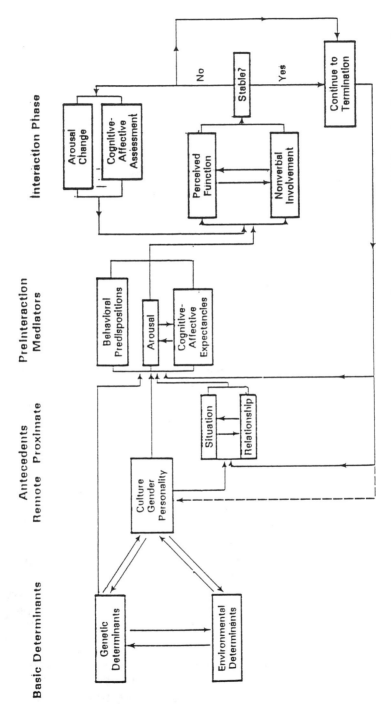

Figure 5.1 Patterson's Sequential-Functional Model. Reprinted with permission from M. L. Patterson (1991), A functional approach to nonverbal exchange, in R. S. Feldman & B. Rimé (Eds.), *Fundamentals of nonverbal behavior* (pp. 458–495), Cambridge: Cambridge University Press.

tion provide evidence that this model is predictive of nonverbal involvement patterns (Patterson, 1991).

In a test of ALT, Patterson et al. (1981) found that a lean-and-touch manipulation designed to increase arousal actually did so only when it occurred in the middle rather than at the outset of interactions. Patterson (1982) contends this result is compatible with SFM predictions if one considers that the same behaviors serve different functions depending on their placement in an interaction; for example, lean–touch combinations at the beginning of interactions may manage interaction, whereas this combination enacted later might serve as social control, and hence produce different interpretations and reactions.

Three experiments that examined effects of expectancies on involvement changes have been interpreted as supporting SFM. Coutts et al. (1980) created negative and positive expectancy conditions by having confederates disagree or agree with subjects during an initial interaction phase. In the negative expectancy condition, confederates' increased involvement led to reciprocal increases by subjects. Coutts et al. (1980) argue that this adjustment supports the SFM's social control function because subjects saw the confederate's increased involvement as a return to normative interaction and subjects responded in order to encourage that involvement level. Yet, increased immediacy by agreeable confederates increased subjects' arousal but did not lead to the compensatory adjustments SFM predicts.

Experiments by Ickes et al. (1982) and Honeycutt (1991) led subjects to expect to interact with a positive or negative target interactant. (Those in a control group received no such expectancy inductions.) Results showed that subjects increased involvement with positive and negative targets more than with control subjects. According to an SFM explanation, increased involvement with a positive target could be attributed to subjects feeling attracted to the target, suggesting the intimacy function was operant. Increased involvement with the negative target could be attributed to subjects attempting social control of the target's behavior. However, these are post hoc speculations; no information was obtained regarding subjects' goals.

Two other studies (Baumeister, Hutton, & Tice, 1989; D. T. Gilbert, Krull, & Pelham, 1988) offer tangential support by shedding light on how the social control function differs from the intimacy one. Subjects who had to ingratiate a disliked partner or create a "modest" as opposed to favorable presentation for a naive partner (both of which would qualify as socially controlled presentations) had more memory and judgment errors than those ingratiating a liked partner or enacting a presentation representative of their true self. The presumption is that the managed impressions were more cognitively demanding and the greater cognitive load caused the errors. Patterson (1991) argues that when managed routines become habituated, cognitive activity decreases, enhancing one's ability to label a partner's disposition and recall interaction details accurately.

These experiments provide modest support for SFM's predictions about effects of the cognitive-affective assessments on involvement outcomes. However, as noted previously, a full-scale test incorporating all the components of the model has yet to be conducted.

### Contributions

A major contribution of the SFM is identification of multiple factors that influence interaction patterns: individual styles and preferences, expectations based on social norms and past experience, and situationally immediate behaviors that occur during interaction. Additionally, Patterson recognizes the multifunctionality of behaviors, including, but not limited to, conveying intimacy. Though this model has been criticized for its lack of parsimony, Burgoon (1984) writes: "the ultimate value . . . is not the specific sequential model that is proposed, but . . . the heuristic utility of the model components and functions that have been identified" (p. 493).

In his attempt to segregate communicative from indicative behaviors, Patterson draws attention to the reality that some behavioral patterns involve reactions and adaptations directed toward a partner while others are internally triggered and nonadaptive. Because indicative behaviors are generally norm- or script-governed, similar behavioral patterns may result that are not truly adaptive, hence not reciprocal, though they may appear so. Thus, one is likely to witness similar but nonadaptive patterns in more formal situations that are governed by social norms.

### Criticisms

Perhaps the greatest concern with SFM is its apparent lack of falsifiability. The lack of a comprehensive test of the model exacerbates this criticism. Many tests of the SFM have focused on the effects of expectancies on functional and behavioral outcomes. Very few have examined how antecedent factors feed into preinteraction mediators. Further, little control has been exercised a priori over an interaction's function. Instead, Patterson examines the results of studies testing models other than SFM and claims post hoc that a particular function was operant. For example, in studies where subjects responded to preinteraction expectancies with increased immediacy behaviors, Patterson claimed the same behavior pattern constituted social control when a negative expectancy was induced but intimacy expression when a positive expectancy was induced. A true test of the expectancy-function-outcome relationship requires advance determination of the functions that should be operative.

Conceptually, Patterson includes only purposeful and mindful behaviors as communication. Thus, habituated, reactive, and automatic responses are relegated to the noncommunicative, indicative category. Yet, many habituated, mindless responses should be considered communicative because they influence a partner's response pattern. Moreover, many may have been consciously enacted at one time, and as such, they continue to represent goal-driven behavior. For example, greeting rituals generally occur habitually – yet they serve a purpose, and without them, interactions would seem incomplete or awkward. Regardless of intent, it is assumed that people make judgments about the presence or absence of certain routine behavioral patterns that conform to social norms.

## Summary

Overall, the SFM provides a comprehensive picture of interaction patterns explaining both compensatory and reciprocal adjustments and incorporating cognitive, affective, behavioral, and contextual components. The model also provides an explanation for both intentionally invoked partner-directed adaptations as well as automatic personal adjustments, both of which appear similar behaviorally. Further, SFM uses multiple functions to explain interaction patterns and acknowledges that multiple behaviors are enacted to fulfill these functions. The most recent explications of the model (Patterson, 1991, 1994) clarify many issues raised when it was initially introduced and offer an appealing discussion of how cognitive and affective factors may relate to strategic and nonstrategic interaction. Yet in further subdividing factors and incorporating additional linkages among the components, the model has become more complex and still lacks specification of which elements take precedence under which conditions, thereby limiting its potential testability. Patterson (1991) himself acknowledges this limitation but adds that the systemlike approach taken should outweigh this disadvantage.

## EXPECTANCY VIOLATIONS THEORY

Expectancy Violations Theory (EVT) originally aimed to explain effects of proxemic violations (Burgoon, 1978, 1983; Burgoon & Jones, 1976). Subsequently, it was expanded to include other kinds of nonverbal and verbal communication violations (e.g., Buller & Burgoon, 1986; Burgoon, Coker, & Coker, 1986; Burgoon & Hale, 1988; Burgoon, Newton, Walther, & Baesler, 1989), hence the name change from Nonverbal Expectancy Violations Theory. Of interest here is the extension of the theory, not to interaction *outcomes* but to the interaction *process* itself, first articulated by Hale and Burgoon (1984).

### Assumptions, propositions, and hypotheses

Like Discrepancy-Arousal Theory (DAT), which EVT predates, EVT begins with the assumption that people have numerous deeply ingrained expectations about the ways others will communicate. Communication expectancies are "cognitions about the anticipated communication behavior of specific others, as embedded within and shaped by social norms for the contemporaneous roles, relationships, and context" (Burgoon & Walther, 1990, p. 236). These expectancies derive from cultural and social knowledge and, in the case of familiar others, known individuating factors (Burgoon, 1978; Burgoon & Walther, 1990). For example, the expectations for interacting with strangers in North America include adopting distances in the personal to social distance zone (rather than intimate or public; see Hall, 1959), refraining from touch except ritualized forms such as in the greeting handshake (Burgoon & Walther, 1990), following certain well-scripted patterns for initiating conversation topics and information seeking (Kellermann, 1986, 1991), and engaging in polite, pleasant, and moderately involved conversation (Burgoon & Le Poire, 1993; Hilton & Darley, 1985; Honeycutt, 1989; Kellermann, 1986). In other cultures, expectations may exist for identifying one's social status (say, through the exchange of business cards), signaling initial hostility or openness through choice of greeting rituals, and avoiding personal inquiries (see, e.g., Gudykunst & Kim, 1992). These expectations, learned and reinforced within one's culture since birth, operate outside conscious awareness and produce habituated, automated behavior patterns.

When an interactant's communication pattern deviates from expectations sufficiently to surpass some perceptual limen or threshold, EVT posits that it is arousing and distracting. In this respect, EVT is similar to DAT, which labels the difference between expected and enacted behavior *discrepancies,* and Patterson's (1983) SFM, which labels changes from an expected level of involvement *unstable exchanges.* EVT, however, depends more on an attentional shift resulting from violations than from some form of physiological arousal, especially in light of many types of violations having little probable physiological impact (see Burgoon, 1992; Le Poire & Burgoon, 1994). This perspective is consonant with findings in literature on information processing and impression formation showing that changes from a stimulus pattern invoke more fine-grained information processing and more extreme judgments of deviants (Langer & Imber, 1980; Newtson, 1973). EVT posits that this attentional shift heightens attention to sender and message characteristics.

Another major feature of EVT is *communicator reward valence.* According to EVT, and congruent with social exchange theory principles, interactants are inherently inclined to make evaluations of one another. Based on assessing the costs and rewards associated with such preinteraction features as physical attractiveness, status, gender, age, and acquaintanceship and such interactional factors as task knowledge, use of humor, type of feedback, and conversational style, interactants place each other on a valence continuum ranging from positive to negative. Communicator valence represents a net assessment of how favorably regarded the other is at that point in time. Although the features contributing to reward valence are complex, the process by which communicators weigh the various factors need not concern us here. What is relevant is that interactants are assumed to arrive at some net assessment of the other that defines the other's reward valence for a particular interaction.

Although reward valence is conceptualized as a continuum and all references to it should be understood as such, for simplicity we will compare those at the favorable end of the continuum to those at the unfavorable end. In general, more favorable communication outcomes are presumed to accrue to positively regarded others than to negatively regarded ones. Applied to interaction predictions, positively valenced communicators should also elicit more approach behavior from partners than should negatively valenced ones.]If the model stopped here, it would duplicate the attraction mediation alternative identified by Kaplan et al. (1983). However, reward valence is predicted to have additional effects apart from its direct, "main effect" ones. Violations are posited to trigger a dual interpretation-evaluation process.[Recipients of the violation are said to attempt to interpret the violation act and to evaluate its desirability.]This appraisal process acknowledges that violations during communicative interaction may carry symbolic or relational meaning. Thus, receivers may first attempt to determine what the act "means." Is a prolonged touch intended to convey liking and approval or is it a patronizing gesture? At the same time, an affective judgment must be made as to whether this act is desirable or not. Actions conveying approval may be considered appealing; actions conveying superiority and disdain are unlikely to evoke such positive evaluations.[The result of this interpretation-evaluation process, coupled with the valence attached to the source of the violation, will determine whether the violation itself is *positively or negatively valenced.*]

Reward valence may influence this appraisal process in two ways. First, although many verbal and nonverbal behaviors have unambiguous meaning (see, e.g., Burgoon et al., 1986; Burgoon & Newton, 1991), many others are subject to multiple interpretations. For example, an arm around the shoulder could communicate dominance or con-  gratulations[Reward valence is posited to moderate choice of interpretations *when there is ambiguity* such that more socially desirable, appropriate, or preferred interpretations are attributed to the positive-valence than the negative-valence communicator.]Second, even when the same interpretation is assigned to both positively and negatively valenced violators (as might be the case with increased involvement; see Burgoon, Newton, et al., 1989), evaluations may differ according to reward valence.[An intimate overture, for instance, may be welcomed from a positively valenced violator but not from a negatively valenced one.]

The interpretation-evaluation process results in the valencing of a violation as positive or negative. For example, frequent use of touch by a disliked other might be interpreted as attempted ingratiation and evaluated negatively because of one's distaste for such transparent efforts to foster attraction. The act would therefore constitute a negative violation. Relative to expectancy confirmation, negative violations are postulated to produce more unfavorable communication patterns and outcomes and positive violations, to produce more favorable ones.

The resultant propositions can be summarized as follows (also see Burgoon, 1978, 1992; Burgoon & Hale, 1988):

1. *Interactants develop expectations about the verbal and nonverbal communication of others.*
2. *Violations of communication expectations are arousing and distracting, causing an attentional shift to communicator, relationship, and violation characteristics and meanings.*
3. *Communicator reward valence moderates the interpretation of ambiguous or polysemous communicative behaviors.*
4. *Communicator reward valence moderates evaluation of communicative behaviors.*
5. *Violation valences are a function of (a) the evaluation of the enacted behavior, (b) the direction of the discrepancy between the expected and enacted behavior toward a more favorably or unfavorably valued position, and (c) the magnitude of the discrepancy. Enacted behaviors that are more favorably evaluated than expected behaviors constitute positive violations; enacted behaviors that are less favorably evaluated than expected are negative violations.*
6. *Positive violations produce more favorable outcomes and negative violations produce more unfavorable ones relative to expectancy confirmation.*

### Application to reciprocity and compensation

⌈The application of EVT to interaction patterns themselves parallels the predictions for interaction outcomes in taking into account both the *who* and the *what* of the interaction, that is, the reward valence of the communicator initiating the behavior and the valence of the act itself⌋ Together, these determine the end state the recipient is likely to prefer. (In this respect, the theory parallels Kaplan et al.'s, 1983 attraction transformation hypothesis, but the ultimate predictions differ.⌡⌈Positive-valence acts by positive-valence communicators should elicit reciprocity because reciprocity results in more of a desired behavior⌡⌊Negative-valence acts by positive-valence communicators should elicit compensation to achieve a more desirable interaction pattern⌋ Thus, increased detachment should be compensated with increased involvement so as to restore the interaction to the previous level of involvement, on the assumption that people would prefer greater rather than lesser involvement with highly regarded others.⌈These predictions apply to both

expectancy-confirming and expectancy-violating acts, the main difference being that violations should generate more intensified reactions
(Burgoon & Le Poire, 1993).⅃

⌈Conversely, negative-valence acts by negative-valence communicators (e.g., intimate touch) should prompt compensation because nonintimacy is the desired state⌡ Positive-valence acts by negative-valence
communicators could yield either reciprocity or compensation, depending on whether the valence of the act or the valence of the communicator is more salient. In the case of the communicator reducing intimacy,
the result should be a reciprocal decrease because the desired state
would be nonintimacy. Thus, the receiver would have no motivation to
restore the interaction to a more intimate level. These predictions are
illustrated in Figure 5.2.

Because initial applications of EVT to reciprocity and compensation
patterns (Burgoon, Le Poire, & Rosenthal, 1992; Burgoon et al., 1987;
Hale & Burgoon, 1984) were all based on predicting reactions to
changes in immediacy or involvement, the aforementioned predictions
all seem rather straightforward. However, extension of the theory to
other forms of violations creates some indeterminacies. For example, a
positive violation by a negative-valence communicator – such as increased deference – might produce a reciprocal response, if an interaction based on mutual respect and equality were the desired state. But
would increased dominance by a positive-valence interactant produce
reciprocal assertions of dominance or compensatory submission? It
seems that more is needed to make predictions. If the communicator's
increased dominance is deemed desirable, perhaps as a show of power
and expertise, then a compensatory submissive response might be likely
as a show of deference. But if increased dominance is deemed an
inappropriate, aggressive move, then reciprocal dominance (also called
competitive symmetry) might be expected, producing the classic power
struggle. We defer further comment on the model's predictions until the
findings have been discussed.

### Empirical support

The preceding chapters all offered evidence that both reciprocity and
compensation patterns are commonplace, but under differing conditions. Cappella's 1981 review of available empirical evidence on reciprocal or compensatory patterns for response latencies, pauses, verbal
disclosure, proximity, and gaze, stated:

## Expectancy Violations Theory
## Applied to Immediacy Changes

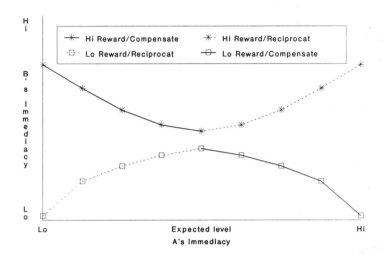

Figure 5.2 Expectancy Violations Theory applied to involvement changes.

＼All these explanations are building toward a view of compensation and matching in which a person's response is dependent on the expected and preferred level of involvement and the other's behavior relative to that expectation. When the other's behavior is outside the expected range, compensation results; when it is inside the expected range, matching results. ＼(p. 112)

Although the conclusion did not parallel EVT predictions, the data did affirm several features of EVT, to wit: the central role of expectancies and deviations, predictions of both reciprocity and compensation, and predictions related to both increases and decreases in involvement. ﹂Moreover,° Cappella noted earlier that "an adequate demonstration of reciprocity requires evidence of matching responses to both increases and decreases" (p. 102) in affiliative behavior, something absent from most studies to that time.﹂Tests of EVT's application to interaction patterns were designed to rectify that shortcoming.

The first direct test came in 1984. Hale and Burgoon hypothesized that reciprocity and compensation of immediacy changes would parallel the U and inverted-U pattern predictions for the effects of expectancy violations on communication outcomes by positive-valence and negative-valence communicators respectively. Applied to interaction behavior, in which the horizontal axis represents immediacy changes by Person A and the vertical axis represents degree of approach by Person B (see Figure 5.1)＼this translates into recipients reciprocating increased immediacy and compensating decreased immediacy by a high-valence communicator (the U pattern) and doing the reverse (an inverted-U pattern) with a negative-valence communicator.) Participants in their experiment engaged in dyadic discussions of some social-moral dilemmas for which they had to arrive at a consensual solution. During the discussions, one person became a confederate who greatly increased or decreased immediacy (or maintained normal immediacy) shortly after the discussion commenced. After the interactions, participants rated each other on perceived relational messages (e.g., affection, dominance, immediacy) present in their nonverbal and verbal behavior, untrained observers made similar ratings from the videotaped interactions, and trained coders rated specific verbal and nonverbal measures.

The results, summarized in Table 5.1, show a mix of reciprocity and compensation, but with reciprocity prevailing. In no case did communicator reward valence moderate results. (Compensation only occurred on measures related to arousal and immediacy – gaze, body orientation, and perceived arousal – and some of that compensation appeared to prevent the interaction from becoming too nonimmediate early in the discussion.) Later, overly high levels of gaze were compensated, while decreases in gaze were reciprocated, perhaps reflecting participants' willingness to reduce the overall level of sensory engagement. Speculatively, the compensation of body orientation worked to maintain an equilibrium level of distance. Also noteworthy, confederate and subject perceptions of each other's level of relational intimacy and detachment were reciprocal and confirmed by observers' ratings.

These results are consistent with the motivation underlying EVT and some of the other arousal-based theories – namely, that both compensation and reciprocity are likely to occur. Especially important is that both patterns were found within the same data set, something that seldom happened in previous research because so few measures were included. But it is also clear that none of the theories received unqualified support from the combined results. Although coded and observed arousal did change in response to violations as EVT and other arousal-based theories would predict, the results were neither consistent across measures nor across time. Moreover, the nonimmediacy violation tended to elicit more activation and less composure than high immediacy, a pattern contrary to the assumed physiologically arousing potential of high immediacy. Hale and Burgoon (1984) concluded,

> the preponderance of linear reciprocity effects in the current data set, especially on those measures indicative of positive or negative evaluations, indicates that the reciprocity model may best account for the affective tone of an interaction. However, compensatory reactions,

Table 5.1. *Results from the Hale and Burgoon (1984) experiment testing Expectancy Violations Theory*

| Independent variable | Dependent variable | Pattern |
|---|---|---|
| C experimentally manipulated nonverbal immediacy | S global involvement, TIme 1 (coded) | Reciprocity |
| | S intimacy, rated by C | Reciprocity |
| | S intimacy, rated by O | Reciprocity |
| | S detachment, rated by C | Reciprocity |
| | S arousal/receptivity, rated by O | Reciprocity |
| | S arousal/receptivity, rated by C | Reciprocity of High Immediacy, Compensation of Nonimmediacy |
| | S verbal immediacy (coded) | Reciprocity of High Immediacy, Compensation of Nonimmediacy |
| | S eye contact, Time 1 (coded) | Reciprocity of High Immediacy, Compensation of Nonimmediacy |
| | S eye contact, Time 2 (coded) | Compensation of High Immediacy, Reciprocity of Nonimmediacy |
| C verbal immediacy (coded) | S verbal immediacy (coded) | Reciprocity |
| C intimacy and detachment, rated by S | S intimacy, rated by C | Reciprocity |
| | S detachment, rated by C | Reciprocity |
| | S global involvement, Time 2 (coded) | Reciprocity |
| | S facial pleasantness, Time 2 (coded) | Reciprocity |
| | Directness of orientation (coded) | Compensation |

*Note:* C = confederate, S = subject, O = untrained observer. The following measures did not produce significant results in response to C nonverbal immediacy: O rating of S detachment, facial pleasantness, directness of orientation, lean, and two subcategories of S verbal immediacy (implicit, modified).

particularly on those behaviors related to sensory stimulation and comfort, insure that an interaction will not escalate too abruptly to an intimate level or, conversely, deescalate in an unchecked fashion to total withdrawal. In other words, there are some elements of equilibrium built into the system that will retard and smooth changes in the overall level of intimacy and immediacy in an encounter. (p. 310)

The next investigation to test the model directly (Burgoon et al., 1987) had participants conduct mock job interviews. One participant in each dyad was randomly chosen to be a confederate and instructed to either greatly increase or decrease conversational involvement in a second interview session. Trained coders subsequently rated participants' nonverbal involvement at five time intervals. Scores within dyads were compared to determine if they constituted reciprocity, compensation, or nonaccommodation. Interviewers exhibiting any change less than .3 (out of a range of .03 to 2.43 on a 7-point scale) were classified as showing nonaccommodation. Those whose involvement changed greater than .3 and in the same direction as the confederate were classified as reciprocal, while those changing in the opposite direction were classified as compensatory.

[ Results showed that women primarily compensated increased involvement and reciprocated decreased involvement, whereas most men showed nonaccommodation of increased involvement and compensated decreased involvement.] Partner's reward level also influenced responses somewhat such that there was greater nonaccommodation with negative-valence confederates. Although these results were interpreted cautiously, they suggested that people may be more likely to show responsivity to attractive than unattractive partners.>

This investigation was undertaken to determine predictors of interaction patterns, and especially the role of communicator reward in moderating them and so did not address the actual extent of each pattern. Rather, an arbitrary criterion was used to define reciprocity and compensation in advance. Because the videotaped interactions offered an excellent venue for examining dyadic interaction patterns in more detail and because this first pass through the interaction behaviors had included only a single nonverbal measure, we undertook a much more extensive analysis of this data set at a later time, the results of which are reported in Chapter 9. A similar, large-scale analysis was subsequently undertaken on another multivariate data set and is reported in Chapter 10. (In both of these investigations, we were mindful of Hale and Burgoon's (1984) urgings that future replications employ multiple dependent measures (both objective coder measures and self-report measures), to obtain a more complete picture of the totality of adaptation, and multiple time periods, to test the conjecture that compensatory strategies might give way to reciprocal ones if interactants subjected to nonimmediacy continued to be rebuffed in their efforts to reestablish a more intimate interaction.)

Meantime, Le Poire and Burgoon (1993) conducted another test of EVT and contrasted it with DAT. Under the ruse of a physician–patient medical interview, confederate medical students increased or decreased involvement after a 3-minute baseline of moderately involved interaction. The involvement changes were intended to create two types of positive violations – high and very high involvement – and two types of negative violations – low and very low involvement. The male and female confederates, who were introduced as advanced medical students, were presumed to be highly rewarding (an assumption borne out by manipulation checks).(Based on the theory's predictions for involvement violations by positive-valence communicators, both increases and decreases in involvement were hypothesized to generate "approach" tendencies, resulting in reciprocation of high and very high involvement violations and compensation of low and very low involvement violations.) Because the investigation was designed to pit EVT against DAT, physiological arousal and affect were also measured. Additionally, trained coders rated confederate and participant involvement over twelve 30-second time periods, six prior to the violation manipulation and six following it.

Contrary to predictions, all violation conditions showed reciprocity when tested with repeated measures analysis of variance. Intraclass correlations, though weaker and nonsignificant in three conditions, also supported a predominance of reciprocity (very low $r_I = .36$, low $r_I = .24$, high $r_I = -.05$, very high $r_I = .17$; see Le Poire, 1991). Additionally, all types of violations produced arousal changes, regardless of the direction or magnitude of the violation. Surprisingly, arousal was most evident, not in the high or very high conditions (which should have elevated sensory engagement), but rather in the low involvement condition. Yet it was the very low involvement violation that generated the most negative or least positive affective responses.(Thus, contrary to the hypothesis, negative violations generated a reciprocal (avoidant) response rather than a compensatory (approach) one.

Le Poire and Burgoon noted that EVT predictions were imprecise under circumstances like the current one in which communicator valence and violation valence were at odds with one another. The results suggested that with these types of violations, at least, violation valence might outweigh communicator valence in determining outcomes. Thus, the negative violation valence would predict an avoidant response, rather than the positive communicator valence predicting an approach one. Nevertheless, the brevity of the interactions and the absence of a low reward condition relegated the findings to a tentative status.

## Summary

The three investigations produced a mixed pattern of results (excluding those to be reported in Chapters 9 and 10) that failed to offer unequivocal support for any of the theories. Together, they warranted the following conclusions:

1. *Support for equilibrium theory is meager at best.* In light of the large number of behaviors analyzed, the equilibrium model may only apply to a small subset of immediacy behaviors, possibly those related to physical comfort (proximity, lean, orientation, gaze).
2. *Reciprocity is prevalent, especially for gestalt-type measures (e.g., involvement) and ones reflecting some degree of positive or negative affect.* People may therefore be most likely to reciprocate the general positive or negative affective tone of the interaction.
3. *There is some evidence, albeit mixed, that violations cause arousal.* Nonimmediacy in particular appears to generate negative psychological arousal.
4. *The results fail to support DAT, no matter how construed.* DAT does not provide criteria for determining what constitutes moderate versus high arousal. In the investigations by Hale and Burgoon (1984) and Burgoon et al. (1987), if arousal change in the violation conditions were interpreted as moderate, affect should have been positive and reciprocity should have obtained at all times; it did not. If arousal change were instead regarded as high, negative affect should have obtained under both types of violations and compensation should have obtained at all times; it did not. Even if the nonimmediacy condition were regarded as more arousing and negative, DAT would have predicted compensation, yet reciprocity was the more typical pattern. The proposed relationships among discrepancy magnitude, arousal, and affect also failed to hold in the Le Poire and Burgoon (1993) experiment.

5. *Results can be viewed as partly supporting ALT or EVT if all the interactions are treated as positive-valence ones on the basis of communicator reward valence.* Determination of support for these theories depends on (a) how communicator reward valence is interpreted and (b) whether labeling is the result of environmental factors rather than meanings intrinsic to the immediacy adjustment itself. In the Hale and Burgoon, 1984, experiment, the reward valence factor consisted of comparing friends to strangers. Although it did produce some main effects, strangers received evaluations high enough to challenge treating them as having negative valence. If the results are viewed as only pertaining to the positive-valence condition, then the dependent measures showing straight reciprocity fit ALT but not EVT; conversely, the measures showing the reciprocity of high immediacy and compensation of nonimmediacy fit EVT but not ALT. However, if the meaning of the violation itself is factored into the labeling process, then nonimmediacy should have been labeled negatively and routinely elicited compensation but did not.

Further conclusions about EVT are offered in Chapter 11, based on the findings from the investigations reported in Chapters 9 and 10.

## COGNITIVE-VALENCE THEORY

Andersen's (1983, 1984) Arousal-Valence Theory, relabeled Cognitive-Valence Theory (CVT) in its most recent reincarnation (Andersen, 1992), builds upon ALT, DAT, and implicitly, EVT. Focusing on effects of increased immediacy and intimacy, CVT is based on intimacy behavior change leading to arousal and, depending on the magnitude of the arousal change, a valencing process leading to reciprocity or compensation. The elements of the theory are depicted in Figure 5.3.

### Assumptions, Propositions, and Hypotheses

CVT assumes that there is a level of intimacy display between interactants that is comfortable and expected. When conversational partners engage in intimacy behaviors within this range, their arousal level is stable. Andersen (1984) argues that when change in intimacy by one partner is *perceived* by the other, arousal is induced. The magnitude of arousal change then determines the valence attached to the arousal, and consequently, the response.

According to Andersen (1983, 1992), small changes in immediacy either are not perceived (and thus do not induce arousal), are perceived

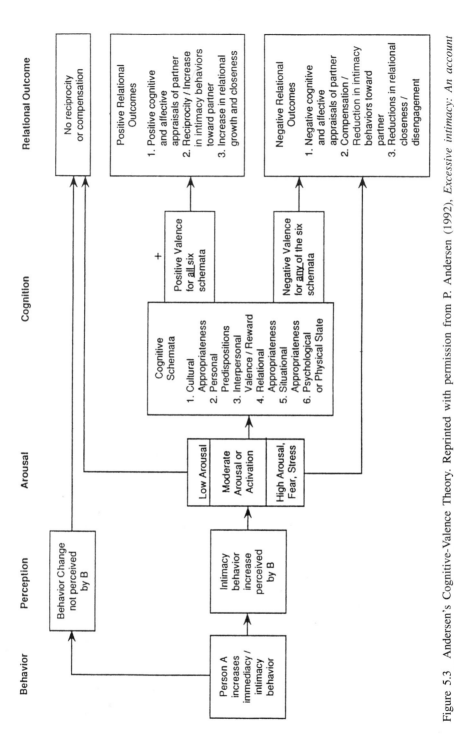

Figure 5.3 Andersen's Cognitive-Valence Theory. Reprinted with permission from P. Andersen (1992), *Excessive intimacy: An account analysis of behaviors, cognitive schema, and relational outcomes.* Paper presented at the annual conference of the International Society of Personal Relationships, Orono, ME.

but do not induce arousal, or lead to very small changes in arousal. Because small fluctuations in immediacy and arousal are normal within the course of interactions, no *reaction* to the partner is made (i.e., nonaccommodation). These basic propositions are congruent with ALT.]

If a large intimacy increase is perceived, however, large arousal change may result. Large arousal change is "unpleasant and aversive. Such highly aroused individuals are likely to become startled, fearful, or disoriented and engage in flight or fight response. The behavioral consequence is withdrawal, compensation, and reduction of immediacy behaviors" (Andersen, 1984, p. 334; 1992). Large arousal changes lead to automatic, or reactive, responses that bypass active cognitive processing; responses are relatively mindless due to "survival" instincts that kick in. This prediction mirrors DAT.]

Active cognitive valencing occurs when immediacy and arousal changes are moderate. With moderate arousal, both reciprocity and compensation may result; if the arousal is valenced positively, CVT predicts a reciprocal response, and if valenced negatively, CVT predicts a compensatory response. In the moderate arousal condition, the *valencing* process is critical and so resembles EVT.]

Valencing is dependent upon six valencers (Andersen, 1983) or in its most current form, six cognitive schemata (Andersen, 1992):

1. *Cultural schemata* encompass the cultural and social norms that dictate the appropriateness of interaction behavior. Immediacy behaviors that violate norms are posited to be negatively valenced.
2. *Relational schemata* encompass the relational history between interactants as well as expectations of behaviors appropriate for the stage of the relationship. Past negative interactions (such as recurrent conflict) taint further interactions, such that increased immediacy may be perceived as a threat, and valenced negatively. Increased, yet appropriate, immediacy from a partner in "good standing" may be valenced positively.
3. *Interpersonal schemata* include perceptions of reward valence of the communicator (Andersen, 1992). Three judgments that influence arousal valencing are credibility, attraction, and homophily. Andersen argues that we negatively valence increased immediacy by those communicators that we do not like or trust. This is consonant with EVT premises.
4. *Situational schemata* include the environmental context and the appropriateness of immediacy displays within that context. For example, immediacy displays between lovers (such as extended touch and

gaze) that may be welcomed in private may not be welcomed in public situations, and thus valenced negatively. Additionally, unfamiliar or threatening contexts may cue people to valence immediacy displays more negatively when they are interpreted as aggressive or threatening.

5. *State schemata* are factors that affect people's psychological and physiological well-being (e.g., their mood, headaches) as well as temporary situational conditions they are experiencing (e.g., stressful work or home situation, positive events such as getting a raise).

6. *Individual schemata* refer to one's personality traits. For example, Andersen suggests that people with high affiliation needs (such as extroverts) may valence increased immediacy positively, whereas those with low affiliation needs (such as introverts) may valence immediacy displays negatively.

Andersen (1992) argues that moderate arousal is positively valenced if *all six* of the valencers yield positive valences. Positively valenced arousal leads to reciprocity – or increased immediacy. If a *single negative* valence occurs during the valencing process (such as five positive valences and one negative valence), then the overall valence of the arousal is negative. Thus, negative valencing carries more weight than positive valencing. The negatively valenced arousal leads to compensation and withdrawal.

## Contributions

Andersen's CVT is an improvement upon ALT and DAT. First, the factors that influence the valencing process are outlined. Second, Andersen (1983) argues that very small and very large arousal increases bypass cognitive processing, thus allowing for quick reactive responses, in contrast to ALT. Third, the attempt to identify how the six valencers yield an overall valence for arousal change, and especially the explicit connection between cognitive factors and resultant moderate levels of arousal due to immediacy changes, is also an improvement upon not only ALT and DAT but also the SFM.

## Empirical support

To date, no full empirical test of CVT has been conducted. However, segments of CVT are being tested. One investigation (Andersen, 1992), attempting to validate the factors that affect the valencing process of unwanted intimacy, found that relational schemata were most often utilized (about half of the reasons for unwanted intimacy were relationship oriented), followed by individual and interpersonal schemata. Another investigation in progress is pitting CVT, EVT, and DAT against one another (Andersen, Guerrero, Jorgensen, & Buller, 1995).

## Criticisms

Apart from the absence of any published empirical tests, CVT is limited by its exclusive focus on increased immediacy displays, to the exclusion of decreased immediacy displays. Will the theory's predictions hold if applied to decreased immediacy? We think not. It is argued that high arousal change is aversive and necessarily leads to compensation. But the argument is really predicated on the assumption that it leads to avoidance. If high arousal change results instead from *decreased immediacy,* is the prediction still one of compensation (which would mean approach) or avoidance (which would mean reciprocity)? The model's predictions are indeterminate when one moves out of the realm of immediacy increases.

Additionally, the theory is at odds with literature showing that high positive arousal can lead to approach and reciprocity; that is, not all large arousal changes are negatively valenced and not all of them result in compensation. In this regard, many of the criticisms of ALT and DAT in predicting that large arousal changes lead to compensation are applicable here.

## MOTOR MIMICRY REVISITED

Motor mimicry is defined by Bavelas, Black, Lemery, MacInnis, and Mullett (1986) as behavior by an observer that is appropriate to the situation of another person (e.g., wincing while witnessing another's pain). As noted in Chapter 2 of this text, traditional theories view this behavior as an indicator of a vicarious cognitive or empathic experience. That is, one takes on the role of the other in the situation. Regardless of the cognitive or affective explanation, Bavelas, Black, Lemery, and Mullett (1986) argue that because mimicry is outwardly displayed via verbal and nonverbal behaviors, it serves a social function. In other words, mimicry is conceived as a message directed toward another indicating "I know how you feel" rather than a mere emotional response indicating one's own internal state. It is not necessarily the case that the observer vicariously experiences the internal state of another individual, but instead, the observer displays a representation of that state to another person. Hence, mimicry functions to signal a relational message of similarity or rapport between the observer and the observed.

## Empirical support for communicative motor mimicry

In pitting three explanations for mimicry against one another, Bavelas, Black, Chovil, Lemery, and Mullett (1988) concluded that *(a) mimicry represents a nonverbal message of similarity, (b) mimicry is enacted by mirroring the behavior of the partner,* and *(c) cognitive and empathic explanations are overridden by a communicative explanation for this particular response pattern.* In a two-part study, Bavelas, Black, Lemery, and Mullett (1986) found that mimetic facial expressions occurred during the observation of painful experiences. This held true regardless of the presence of eye contact between the observer and observed, but was more likely to occur in the presence of eye contact. Decoders' ratings of mimicry indicated that the expressions were interpreted as messages of caring and knowing. The researchers in this study concluded that motor mimicry is both informative and communicative, and it is the communicative situation that determines the overt response.

Ploog (in press) provides evidence of comparable mimetic responses among squirrel monkeys. A ritual observed among these monkeys occurs when one rolls over on its back, eliciting an approach response from other nearby monkeys. Ploog argues that while the back-rolling ritual could result from an innate response to external stimuli, and the subsequent approach response may be just as automatic, an alternative explanation is that habitual performance of this ritual may be learned. In other words, the monkeys may strategically engage in the back-rolling ritual, hence eliciting the approach of others. Ploog notes, "Whatever the mechanism may be, the result is observable mutual approaches by the intruder and the group members" (p. 3).

## Contributions and criticisms

This conceptualization of motor mimicry acknowledges that our tendency to synchronize and adapt to conversational partners originates as a fairly automatic instinctive response, but can be used to signal messages of rapport and understanding to others. In addition, this approach demonstrates that expressions of empathy have a communicative aspect and that reciprocity or matching is the overriding response pattern employed to express this message. Further, because of its biological basis, mimicry in the form of matched or reciprocal behaviors may provide us with an explanation for evidence of cross-cultural universal behaviors. One limitation of this perspective is its focus on empathy; there are numerous additional instinctual responses, such as fear, joy, and surprise, that can be enacted in a more deliberate fashion to signal "appropriate" but not felt responses to a partner. For our purposes, approaching motor mimicry as communicative provides us with an explanation for a predominant pattern of reciprocity while cautioning us to consider that what may appear on the surface as an automatic instinctual response could be in reality an encoded message signaling similarity, rapport, or understanding.

### Summary

The stance that Bavelas and her colleagues adopt is that motor mimicry represents a response *to* another individual rather than expressions of internal cognitive or affective states of the individual. This view of mimicry, sometimes manifested as mirroring, implies that behaviors are contingent on and directed toward an interactional partner. Communicative motor mimicry is grounded in a biological predisposition to mirror another's behavior, based on empathic responses appropriate to another's situation. As people begin to recognize the effects their automatic mimicry has on others, they learn to manipulate it. That is, they begin to consciously use mimicry to signal messages of similarity and rapport. Because communicative motor mimicry has biological underpinnings, this adaptation pattern may prove especially useful in situations where interactants cannot understand one another's language. Further, communicative motor mimicry provides a viable explanation for universal behaviors and behavioral patterns one observes even in the presence of cross-cultural differences. As Bavelas, Black, Lemery, and Mullett (1986) note, when a researcher wants to distinguish indicative (or biological) motor mimicry from its communicative counterpart, it is necessary to look "beyond the individual to the immediate interpersonal context in which the behavior occurs" (p. 328). Perhaps, then, one can distinguish that which is a response to internal conditions from that which is directed toward others to achieve some purpose.

### CONCLUSION

The theories explaining interactional adaptation patterns in this chapter are distinct in that the primary focus and impetus for reciprocal and compensatory responses is the message value or perceived function of a partner's behavior. The SFM incorporates antecedent factors and preinteraction mediators as determinants of an arousal labeling process that ultimately leads to adaptation to a partner. Among preinteraction mediators are attributions about a partner's meaning and expectations about what behavior is appropriate for that function. EVT is similar in that it posits expectancies mediated by impressions of a partner's reward valence and the perceived function of an interaction. When expectations are violated, attention is drawn away from the topic to the partner, and behavioral adjustments are made to restore the interaction to a comfortable and expected level of involvement. Similarly, CVT posits that deviations from expected behaviors lead to arousal change which determines the response. Low arousal change leads to no behavioral changes, high arousal change is said to always produce compensation, and moderate arousal change leads to either reciprocity or compensation, depending on whether it is labeled positively or negatively according to six valencers or cognitive schema. Finally, a communicative view of motor mimicry is presented in which seemingly automatic empathic responses have been demonstrated to be produced with communicative intent, signaling messages of similarity, rapport, and understanding.

Because of their complexity, many of these theories have not been examined with great detail empirically. The exception is EVT. In general, tests of EVT demonstrate that reciprocity tends to be a more prevalent pattern than compensation, and when we do see evidence of compensation, it tends to occur as a response to discomfort with a partner's immediacy signals. Further, although there is some evidence that violations of expected and normative behavior produce arousal change, the evidence of an arousal-to-behavior link is more tenuous.

In all, the theories examined in this chapter have at their core a concentrated focus on the exchange and interpretation of meanings and functions via verbal and nonverbal signals. Moreover, these theories incorporate aspects of the communicators and their immediate and past situations as mediators in assigned meanings. Thus, the evolution from attention to individual needs and emotions to an examination of cultural and societal principles as factors guiding interaction patterns culminates in the theories reviewed here.

*Part III*

Issues in studying interaction adaptation

# 6

## Reconceptualizing interaction adaptation patterns

The vast amount of research we have reviewed in the last four chapters has spawned a proliferation of terms to describe adaptation patterns in interpersonal interaction. The lack of consensus on how terms are being used has made it extremely difficult to determine where research findings are similar or different and where theorists are making the same or different predictions. Our objective in this chapter is to sort through this morass of labels for patterns, identifying what we consider as the crucial features associated with each pattern, and to propose some definitions that we hope will become standard usage in the future. Because we are especially interested in those interaction patterns where people are actually adapting to one another, our focal point for drawing distinctions will be the accommodation patterns of reciprocity, convergence, compensation, and divergence.

But first, we should answer the question, why should we care about definitions? There are at least three reasons: (1) If students of interpersonal interaction are to talk with one another, we must have a common vocabulary. We must be able to assume that if we use the term "reciprocity," for example, we share the same understanding of all that is implied by it. (2) We need greater precision in describing how people actually behave. To deduce what evidence exists for each of the patterns, we have to be sure that we have been connecting the right observations to the right patterns. Before we adduce evidence that people actually adapt to one another, we need to be sure that what we have been labeling in the past as an adaptation pattern really does involve people influencing one another; we need separate labels for those cases where

Portions of this chapter have been adapted from Judee K. Burgoon, Leesa Dillman, and Lesa A. Stern (1993), Adaptation in dyadic interaction: Defining and operationalizing patterns of reciprocity and compensation, *Communication Theory, 4,* 293–316, with permission of Guilford Publications, Inc.

people's behavior looks the same (or different) but only coincidentally so. This in turn affects which theories we think are supported and which are not. (3) From a practical standpoint, if we are to design communication and intervention strategies that work, we need to identify accurately the circumstances under which people are susceptible, or impervious, to influence from others and whether one person's behaviors elicit the same or an opposite response.

### PREVIOUS DEFINITIONS AND CONCEPTUALIZATIONS

In Chapter 1, we defined the most commonly recognized interaction patterns: reciprocity, compensation, matching, mirroring, complementarity, motor mimicry, convergence, divergence, synchrony, and dissynchrony. As should now be evident from our review of the theories and empirical evidence, a major problem is that these terms have often been used interchangeably and without formal definition. Consider Hinde's (1979) definition: "A reciprocal interaction is one in which the partners show similar behaviour, either simultaneously or alternately" (p. 79). This definition could actually fit reciprocity, matching, mirroring, convergence, or synchrony. Although more detailed, Street and Cappella's (1985) definition suffers from the same problem: "Reciprocity occurs when participants produce similar behaviours, adapt behaviours in similar directions, or respond to partner's behaviours with behaviours of comparable functional value (such as when one romantic partner signals intimacy with a smile and the other responds with touch)" (p. 244). Likewise, Hinde's (1979) and Street's (1991) definitions of complementarity are indistinguishable from definitions of compensation.

In an effort to increase clarity, Ross et al. (1988) proposed four types of reciprocity: individual, dyadic, temporal, and relational. Individual reciprocity, which refers to a balance between an individual's own give and take, is actually an intrapersonal rather than an interpersonal concept and so is not within the domain of our current interests. Dyadic reciprocity, which is defined as "the symmetry of behavior given and received within dyads" (Ross et al., 1988, p. 146), appears to correspond to matching. Temporal reciprocity, following Gottman's (1982) earlier conceptualization, is said to occur when a socially directed act of one person increases the likelihood of a response in kind by a partner. This seems to best approximate what many others mean by reciprocity. By contrast, relational reciprocity appears to be synonymous with Kenny and La Voie's (1984) dyadic reciprocity and refers to reciprocal patterns that are unique to a given dyad or relationship.

Bernieri and Rosenthal (1991) have also attempted to bring some clarity to the interrelationship among patterns by subsuming all of the interaction adaptation patterns under the label of "interpersonal coordination" and dividing them into two subcategories of behavioral matching and interactional synchrony. While these subcategories are helpful in distinguishing similarity due to the form of behaviors from similarity due to their pacing or timing, they ignore all patterns that entail some form of dissimilarity. They also group many disparate forms of similarity together.

We believe a more productive approach to arriving at definitions is to consider what attributes distinguish the patterns from one another. With rare exceptions (notably, Ross et al., 1988), most definitions offered to date fail to answer some crucial questions: Must one person's behaviors be contingent on, or directed toward, the other? Must both people change their behavior for us to conclude that adaptation is occurring? And, if change is a prerequisite, must the magnitude of change be the same for both people or is it enough that they both change in the same direction? Are opposite or merely dissimilar behaviors sufficient to count as compensation? What should we call it if two people maintain their initial interaction styles? And, if one person fails to respond to a partner's increase in intimacy, is that nonaccommodation or is it a compensatory "drag" on intimacy escalation? How similar or dissimilar do the respective individuals' behaviors have to be? What role does timing play in these patterns? Finally, do people have to know they are making these changes?

These questions guided our own analysis of interaction adaptation patterns. What follows is our assessment of how attributes such as contingency, change, rhythmicity, intentionality, and functional equivalence figure into the definitions. We conclude with what we hope are some sensible definitions that distinguish the patterns from one another in useful ways.

## CRITERIA FOR DISTINGUISHING ADAPTATION PATTERNS

### Directedness and behavioral contingency

Two interrelated characteristics that set convergence, reciprocity, motor mimicry, divergence, and compensation patterns apart from such patterns as matching, imitation, and complementarity are that one person's behavior is *contingent upon* and *directed toward* the other. The underlying common thread between these two criteria is that they link Person A's behavior to Person B's behavior. The contingency principle specifies that one person's behavior is the proximate cause of the other person's behavior. In keeping with Gouldner's (1960) description that Person A reciprocates services provided by B, A's return to B depends on B's behaviors toward A. Thus, the return behavior(s) must be contingent upon the "initial" behaviors of the partner (Ross et al., 1988; Street & Cappella, 1985). That is, reciprocity entails conditional probabilistic change (Gottman, 1979) where the probability of one person's behavior is changed from its baserate following the presentation of partner's behavior. For example, if Person A's normal rate of gaze is 50% prior to interacting with Person B and now increases to 80% following Person B's frequent use of gaze, then Person A's gaze rate can be said to be contingent upon Person B's gaze rate and therefore reciprocal. The same principle would apply to compensation: Person A's decrease in gaze would have to be a function of Person B's increase in gaze.

The directedness criterion concerns whether a communicator's behavior can plausibly be regarded as aimed at the other interactant. According to Ross et al. (1988), reciprocity "requires that similar actions of two participants be *directed* to one another such that the action of B to A would return or requite the action of A to B" (p. 144). This same principle of directedness is echoed in Motley's (1990a,b) four postulates of communication, one of which is that communication entails behaviors that are "consciously or unconsciously *other-directed, or 'intended' to be interpreted by a receiver*" (Motley, 1990b, p. 3). Such behaviors can be distinguished from reflex or autonomic behaviors in that they are "performed *for* others; that is, to influence, affect, be interpreted by, be 'received' by, or have 'meaning' for others" (Motley, 1990b, pp. 5–6). Thus, reciprocity (and by implication, compensation) encompasses "communicative" behaviors in the sense that there is an identifiable recipient for whom the behaviors are performed. A good illustration of other-directed behavior is motor mimicry. Bavelas and colleagues' (Bavelas et al., 1988; Bavelas, Black, Lemery, & Mullett, 1986) experiments confirmed that motor mimicry most often occurs in the presence of others and is a communicative response rather than an instinctive gesture.

By contrast, matching and complementarity need not be contingent or other-directed. Such patterns may be in response to or directed toward factors internal to the individual (e.g., one's own mood state) or external to the interacting pair (e.g., the presence of a third party or social norms). The mere co-occurrence of similar behaviors doesn't demonstrate contingency or directedness because the similarity may be an artifact of the two individuals having separate but similar internal states or goals (e.g., both displaying anxiety about being videotaped), of responding to a common external stimulus (e.g., seating constraints imposed by the physical environment), or of orienting to the same social norms and expectations for the particular type of interaction taking place (e.g., the requirement that people be politely attentive during initial encounters). In all these latter instances, the apparent contingency between the two people's behavior is spurious: Neither person "caused" the other's behavior; rather, both people's behavior was "caused" by something else. And in the case of the anxiety cues or the chosen seating position, the behaviors were probably not intended to be received or interpreted as a message by the other person.

The directedness and contingency criteria help to separate true adaptation patterns from nonadaptive ones. Based on these criteria, we propose that the terms "reciprocity" and "compensation" be reserved for clear instances of partner influence and that the terms "matching" and "complementarity" be used when the behaviors are neither contingent nor directed toward one another or when contingency and directedness are indeterminate.[1]

Two patterns we have not mentioned so far are synchrony–dissynchrony and mirroring. These patterns appear to be contingent, in that the probability of one person's behavior is altered by the other person's behavior. They fall into a gray area on directedness because the rhythmic entrainment or behavioral similarity that is manifested could be due either to the partner or to other internal and external stimuli. For example, people's own biological cycles may be responsible for the interaction rhythms they follow. Similarly, the environment contains many *zeitgebers,* or time givers, that can set the pace for both interactants. The same is true with postural mirroring (adopting identical postures, trunk, or limb positions), which can be artificially induced by the shape of furniture that people occupy. In all these cases, something other than the partner is causing the behavioral similarity. In other cases, though, the evidence is compelling that interactants are reacting and adapting to one another. Thus, the processes of synchrony and mirroring do not in and of themselves imply that the behavior is directed and contingent. However, when independent evidence is available that the behavior is contingent and/or directed, these patterns qualify as adaptation. For example, if a person intent on showing liking for another adopts the partner's posture and pacing, we may claim that adaptation occurred.

### Mutual versus unidirectional influence

The principles of contingency and directedness imply that adaptation patterns such as reciprocity and compensation involve one or both parties influencing each other. An unanswered question is whether that influence must be bidirectional or whether it can be unidirectional. When reciprocity is the focus of investigation, many researchers emphasize *mutual* influence (Argyle & Ingham, 1972; Dindia, 1982; Ross et al., 1988; Street & Cappella, 1985). When compensation is the focus, however, *unidirectional* influence seems to be sufficient.

Operationally, many compensation studies entail one person (often a confederate) adjusting behavior and examining whether the partner compensates. Conceptually, it is also easy to imagine numerous situations where influence is a one-way street. Davis and Skinner (1974) observed that often a leader emerges in an interaction, such that one partner follows the other's lead. Similarly, work on behavioral synchrony and entrainment shows that one individual may set the interactional pace and rhythm that others follow (see Bernieri & Rosenthal, 1991).

On these grounds, we think it most prudent to include both unidirectional and mutual influence as part of interaction adaptation. With this approach, mirroring and motor mimicry (displaying empathic, often identical behaviors in response to another's plight) both qualify as adaptive even if only one person is adjusting behavior toward the other.

### Change versus maintenance

One feature that should be evident from the adaptation pattern descriptions we have offered so far is that they involve an exchange between two interactants. Change must occur in order to assess whether adaptation takes place and is linked to the other interactant. Change is thus a necessary but not sufficient condition to declare that adaptation is taking place.

When two parties' behaviors are similar but unchanging, their behavior can be said to match but not reciprocate one another. Conversely, when two parties maintain opposite behaviors (A sustains low intimacy throughout and B sustains high intimacy), they are showing complementarity but not compensation. And if they both change but in such a way that they are marching to their own separate drummers, the change criterion is satisfied but the contingent and directed criteria are not, so again, there is no adaptation.

Conceptually, change may be manifested in several ways. The most obvious is when one or both individuals exhibit change over time within the same interaction. For example, one individual escalates the amount of self-disclosure and the partner follows suit, producing an acceleration in disclosure rate for the dyad.

A second, less obvious way is where change is inferred relative to a person's behavior prior to interacting with the particular partner. For example, two individuals may show modest similarity in vocal tension at the outset of an interaction. Then, after one person is given a difficult encoding task that elevates vocal tension, the co-interactant becomes much more tense vocally, producing a strong association between their two vocal patterns. The relevant change here is between the initial level of matching and the subsequent level of reciprocity after one person's tension changes.

A third, more tenuous form of change is an implied comparison to social norms or expectations. For example, if the normal trajectory for a dyad is decreased involvement over time, but a dyad instead exhibits sustained high involvement, this persistence might reflect a "change" from the implied control condition – the social norm – and hence, reciprocity. Such persistence would reflect a conditional response in that the probability of reducing involvement is altered by the presence of the partner's high level of involvement. A more obvious case is the circumstance where behavior within the dyad is abnormally high or low compared to the social norm, as might be the case if both members of a dyad avoid all eye contact or start laughing uncontrollably. In these cases, we might conclude that this departure from "normal" behavior is due to partner influence if it is atypical and not attributable to other situational factors. Similarly, change may take the form of presenting an unexpected behavior (e.g., an intimate touch) or omitting an expected one (e.g., a handshake) such that the behavioral pattern again deviates from the typical one. Thus, change may be exhibited through the presence or absence of a behavior as well as change in the degree of an existing behavior.

A final way in which change can be demonstrated is alterations in patterns across interactions. For example, Person A may have a history of being fairly detached and rebuffing intimate overtures from Person B. If A now begins an interaction by being very affectionate toward B, we may regard this as reciprocation of B's previous intimacy. This kind of longitudinal analysis is especially appropriate for exchanges such as gift giving or helping behaviors that are unlikely to be contiguous in time. However, declaring such exchanges as reciprocal becomes increasingly tenuous as the acts become more removed in time because it is unclear whether they are truly linked to one another.

The concept of change does not carry implications about the rapidity of such change. One can "test the waters" with a partner by slowly disclosing intimate feelings or "plunge in" by revealing one's innermost thoughts immediately. Both are acceptable forms of change that may evoke adaptation by the partner, but the more slowly change occurs, the more difficult it is to detect.

Although requiring behavioral change as a criterion for interaction adaptation makes analysis more complex, it leads to greater terminological clarity. Where change does not occur or is indecipherable, the terms "matching" and "complementarity" are most appropriate.

## Magnitude versus direction of change

The issue at stake here is whether change by one interactant must be matched with a change of equal size by the other or whether it is sufficient that both be changing in the same direction. On behalf of the "equal magnitude" position, Ross et al. (1988) contend that reciprocity "denotes a quantitative symmetry in qualitatively similar socially directed actions" (p. 145), and *symmetry* occurs "when social agents make equal contributions to social exchanges whether they be reciprocal or complementary" (p. 145). On this view, reciprocity entails not only an exchange of behaviors of like kind (e.g., a gaze for a gaze), but also like degree (i.e., equal frequency, duration, intensity, or tempo). Presumably, compensation would only be distinguished from reciprocity in that the behaviors would be dissimilar rather than similar (e.g., gaze avoidance in response to a stare); the magnitudes of change would still be symmetrical.

The difficulty with this approach is that it may be overly restrictive. Often, people adjust to another but to a lesser degree, either because they are unable or unwilling to change as quickly or as much as their co-interactants. One relevant consideration here is people's own individual style, which has been shown to be highly consistent within and across interactions (Cappella, 1984). If individuals have a certain range of behavior within which they are accustomed to interacting, they may be uncomfortable departing radically from their own norm and/or they may be incapable of adapting to a highly different style. For example, inexpressive individuals may not have the skill or experience to enact a highly animated gestural or vocal style. A modest change in the partner's direction may be all they can muster. Yet, in such cases, influence still has occurred.

As a consequence, Burgoon et al. (1987) proposed emphasizing direction rather than magnitude of change as the primary consideration in declaring the presence of adaptation. We concur with this position, although we recognize it is not free of problems. A very small change may be equivalent to no change in both its intent (e.g., a person wishes to adhere to her own dialect rather than to accommodate to another's) and its impact (e.g., a slight increase in speaking tempo may effectively serve as a "drag" on another's rapid speech rather than as a reciprocation and reinforcement of it). Because of these possibilities, we believe size of change must play a role, albeit a secondary one, in distinguishing accommodation from nonaccommodation. We take up the issue of how to take magnitude into account in the next chapter.

### Timing and rhythmicity

So far, we have dealt with the temporal qualities of behaviors only tacitly. The concepts of change and contingency imply that one person's behavior must precede the other's; that is, the behaviors must be lagged if we are to infer causality. Indeed, the ability to infer causality in science depends on temporal ordering of phenomena. Given these criteria, all synchrony patterns might technically have to be nonsimultaneous to qualify as adaptation.

However, the presence of interaction rhythms may vitiate this requirement. Chapple (1970) claimed that "all communication is endowed with rhythmic properties" (p. 39). Others have similarly argued that the behavior of all organisms is temporally organized and controlled by central rhythmic patterns (McGrath, 1988). Sometimes the rhythmic pattern is established by one individual in an interaction, a leader to whom others entrain their interaction. To the extent that two or more interactants coordinate their behavior with each other and synchronize it to the same rhythmic pattern, they will be able to engage in simultaneous actions (e.g., changes in head positions at the same time) while still qualifying as accommodating to one another.

Consider the frequently used analogy of musicians:

> A particular rhythm, once adopted by a group of musicians, becomes the supporting structure of the music. The rhythm sets the tempo and style in which the others must play. . . . In jazz, the elements of the music are highly synchronized in that individual notes from the different instruments tend to occur precisely at the same instant. There is a downbeat with which all instruments synchronize. Notes from individual musicians tend to begin and end simultaneously. In fact, a band's ability to hit a note simultaneously, sometimes referred to as its *tightness,* is an important criterion of their quality and skill. (Bernieri & Rosenthal, 1991, p. 403)

Interactants may likewise match each other's tempo and thus enact behaviors at the same time. If they also are able to interweave their actions with one another in a way that does not disrupt the tempo or flow of the interaction, then simultaneous and synchronized activities may qualify as adaptation because both participants are pacing and meshing their interaction according to the same rhythm.

## Intentionality

In the last section we introduced the issue of intentionality. Is intent a factor that separates accommodative from nonaccommodative patterns?

It is widely accepted that many interaction adaptation patterns often operate outside conscious awareness. The norm of reciprocity can be understood as a generic and deeply habituated script guiding many of our daily interaction routines without benefit of deliberation. Compensation processes similarly may represent highly automatic adjustments (Argyle & Dean, 1965). And we have seen that synchrony is often regarded as a biologically governed process not subject to conscious intervention. Thus, these patterns may function in a relatively mindless fashion unless and until expectations are violated (Burgoon, 1978; Burgoon & Hale, 1988; Patterson, 1983). Even then, adjustments may occur so rapidly that conscious thought is not likely to have preceded them (Cappella & Greene, 1982).

At other times, adaptation may be deliberate and goal-directed. Parents, for example, may slow down their speaking tempo and exaggerate their articulation when trying to encourage toddlers to talk. A friend may increase smiling with the intent of evoking similar amounts of smiling – and a happier mood – from a despondent friend. A politician's vocabulary may converge toward that of her constituents to create an impression of similarity. Under these circumstances, at least one person's adaptation results from communicative intent (although it may occur without much forethought). The concept of adaptation as an exchange process also seems to imply that it is an intentional one.

One resolution between these apparently conflicting positions – that adaptation often reflects highly automated behaviors yet as a communicative event implies some level of intent – lies in Kellermann's (1992) argument that communication is inherently strategic (intentional) but also automatic (unconscious). Bargh (1989) contends that plans or goals are intentional strategies but the tactical subroutines used to instantiate them are fairly automatic, resulting in "intended goal-dependent automaticity." This is consistent with similar distinctions others have made between broad plans and strategies on the one hand and specific tactics and behavioral routines on the other (Seibold, Cantrill, & Meyers, 1985; Waldron, 1990).

If we accept this view, then accommodation patterns are not differentiated from nonaccommodation ones on the basis of intent. Rather, both types of patterns can be arrayed along a continuum of intentionality. Interactants may deliberately choose to maintain their own style or to converge toward or diverge from another's. They may also do these things unconsciously, with or without intent. A more useful consideration than intent per se might be to distinguish strategic from nonstrategic patterns (see Buller & Burgoon, 1994). *Strategic* patterns would be ones that are intentional and goal-directed, including consciously diverging from another's argot to reinforce respective ingroup and outgroup identities or unconsciously adopting another's accent to create a sense of solidarity. *Nonstrategic* patterns would include indicative or informative but noncommunicative patterns (see Ekman & Friesen, 1969a; Patterson, 1983; Wiener, Devoe, Rubinow, & Geller, 1972), including adjustments due to discomfort. We therefore would count as reciprocity and compensation those behaviors falling closer to the strategic end of the continuum.

### Behavioral equivalence

Another feature that may separate adaptation patterns from each other and from nonadaptation is the equivalence of behaviors being examined. Matching and mirroring have been understood to mean that Persons A and B are displaying identical behaviors. Convergence and divergence typically have implied that the movement toward or away from another was on the same behavior. By contrast, synchrony originally meant that two individuals coordinated their behaviors to the same rhythm or changed directions at the same juncture (see Bernieri & Rosenthal, 1991; Condon & Ogston, 1967; Condon & Sander, 1974), not that the behaviors were the same. As we noted in Chapter 3, Argyle and Cook (1976) revised Affiliative Conflict Theory to allow for compensation among nonidentical behaviors.

Most conceptualizations of reciprocity and compensation in fact have hewn to a middle ground, defining them as exchanges of roughly equivalent but not necessarily identical behaviors. For example, according to Roloff and Campion (1985), reciprocity occurs when "the recipient of a resource is obligated to and at some time will return to the giver a resource roughly equivalent to that which was received" (p. 174). If this approach is taken, however, a new question must be answered: What constitutes equivalence?

Street and Cappella (1985) defined reciprocity as behaviors that are qualitatively similar or "of comparable functional value" (p. 244). At the most abstract and macroscopic level, behaviors can be grouped according to the broad communicative function they perform, such as relational communication, conversational management, emotional expression, or social influence.

One molar function that seems particularly relevant is relational communication. Because many of the patterns of interest have relational message implications, behaviors might be grouped according to the implicit relational messages that are being exchanged, such as involvement, intimacy, trust, dominance, similarity, formality, and composure (see Burgoon & Hale, 1984, 1987). If messages are understood as collections of interrelated verbal and/or nonverbal behaviors that form gestalts (Andersen, 1985), then functional equivalents become all those verbal and nonverbal behaviors and tactics that fit a larger message class, strategy, or function. For example, all the linguistic and nonverbal behaviors that signal similarity would be considered functionally equivalent. Analysis of homeomorphic classes of behavior can be facilitated by application of Foa and Foa's (1972) Resource Exchange Model, which places broad categories of resources that can be exchanged – love, status, goods, services, information, money – in a circle based upon underlying dimensions of particularism and concreteness. Those resources closest to one another are considered the most equivalent or similar for exchange purposes. Thus, one might reciprocate self-disclosure (information) with affection (love) rather than with self-disclosure.

At a more microscopic level, individual behaviors and utterances can be analyzed according to the specific communicative role they fulfill in shorter conversational segments or even single turns at talk. As conversational analysts, we might ask what speech acts or nonverbal behaviors have the same import or can serve as "fillers" in the same conversational "slot" (see Schegloff, 1993; Tiersma, 1993). For example, backchannel behaviors that continue a speaker's turn (e.g., head nods, "uh huhs") serve a different function than those that disrupt it by signalling misunderstanding (e.g., "huh?" or "what?"). Or we might consider what collections of behaviors accomplish the same regulatory effects. Cappella and Palmer's (1990) finding that gaze, talk time, amount of vocalization relative to pausing, and illustrator gestures covary as a "package" of cues implies that they serve a related function – possibly to control who has the floor and to suppress turn requests by auditors.

Embracing a functional perspective obviously makes matters more complicated. The more that the exchanged behaviors are removed from each other, the less clear it is that reciprocity is occurring. If behaviors are classified according to their functions or meanings, then one must know the many different behaviors that fit the same function or meaning to determine what is "equivalent." At the same time, it must be recognized that the same behavior (e.g., nodding) may satisfy different functions (e.g., conversation management, expression of affection, information seeking). Specifying unequivocally a behavior's function at a given point in time can be quite a challenge, as can be determining whether behaviors in service of one function (e.g., dominance) can be said to reciprocate or compensate a partner's behaviors in service of another function (e.g., intimacy).

Nevertheless, even though a functional perspective adds greater complexity to assessing adaptation patterns, failure to utilize such a perspective makes it difficult to say definitively that reciprocity or compensation is taking place. Gaze is an excellent example of how analyzing a single behavior can be misleading. Each party's gaze may be fulfilling different functions. For example, gaze may be an independent (noncontingent) act of surveillance and may serve turn-taking tasks rather than requiting another's gaze. And even if increased gaze by one is met with increased gaze by the other, one or both parties might offset it with greatly increased physical distance, yielding a net reduction in intimacy. We need to know what the entire system of behaviors responsible for construing a particular message or accomplishing a particular function comprises and to take the entire system into account before we can conclude if and what kind of adaptation is taking place. Fortunately, our commonsense understandings, derived from a strong social consensus on the meanings of many behaviors (see Burgoon, 1991; Burgoon, Buller, Hale, & deTurck, 1984; Burgoon & Newton, 1991; Le Poire & Burgoon, 1993) and bolstered by substantial empirical evidence, make this task easier. Knowledge of the functions a collection of verbal and nonverbal behaviors may or may not serve constrains the possible purposes and interpretations assigned to any single behavior, and redundancy among behaviors may lead to a convergence in function or meaning.

## PROPOSED DEFINITIONS

The foregoing considerations form the basis for the constitutive definitions we wish to advocate for accommodative and other related interaction patterns:[2]

1. *Matching:* exhibition of behavioral similarity between two interactants, regardless of etiology, intentionality, or partner influence. This is the most general term and can be applied when intent, directedness, and contingency are indeterminate. It subsumes several other more narrowly defined forms of behavioral similarity.
2. *Mirroring:* behavioral matching in the form of identical, static visual behaviors (e.g., postural asymmetry).
3. *Convergence:* the process of interaction adaptation whereby one adopts behavior that is increasingly similar to that of the partner.
4. *Interactional synchrony:* similarity in rhythmic qualities and enmeshing or coordination of the behavioral patterns of both parties. If the behaviors of interest are speaker–auditor ones that occur at the same time (as might be the case with mutual postural shifts or mutual gaze), then *simultaneous synchrony* exists. If the behaviors of inter-

est instead are part of a sequential speaker–speaker pattern (as might be the case with silences), then *concatenous synchrony* is present.

5. *Reciprocity:* adaptation in which one responds, in a similar direction, to a partner's behaviors with behaviors of comparable functional value. Comparable functional value allows for interchangeable and substitutable behaviors that accomplish the same communication function (such as relational communication, impression management, or conversational management) and/or convey the same gestalt message theme (such as dominance, involvement, composure, or rapport).

6. *Complementarity:* exhibition of dissimilar behavior (e.g., using slang and a dialect when another uses nonaccented and "proper" language), regardless of etiology, intent, or partner behavior. Like matching, this is the most general term and can be appropriately applied when intent, directedness, and contingency are indeterminate. It subsumes other, more narrowly defined patterns that entail behavioral dissimilarity between two interactants.

7. *Divergence:* the process of interaction adaptation whereby one adopts behaviors that are increasingly dissimilar from that of the partner.

8. *Compensation (interpersonal):* adaptation in which one responds with behaviors of comparable functional value but in the opposite direction.

These definitions along with the following examples should clarify the relationships among reciprocity, compensation, divergence, and convergence. Consider the case of Person A initially displaying low involvement and B displaying high involvement. If A increases involvement in response to B, then A has converged *and* reciprocated involvement. If instead the two move toward a state of moderate involvement (i.e., an equilibrium point) by A increasing involvement and B decreasing it, then their styles have converged, but they have also compensated. This is because, in the process of becoming more similar, their behaviors have gone in opposite directions. Thus, unidirectional convergence is reciprocity but mutual convergence need not be; in fact, it may be compensation. Similarly, if parties change in opposite directions (as in adopting submissive behaviors in response to a partner's dominance), it is compensation; if only one person changes, it is divergence. These relationships are illustrated in Figure 6.1.

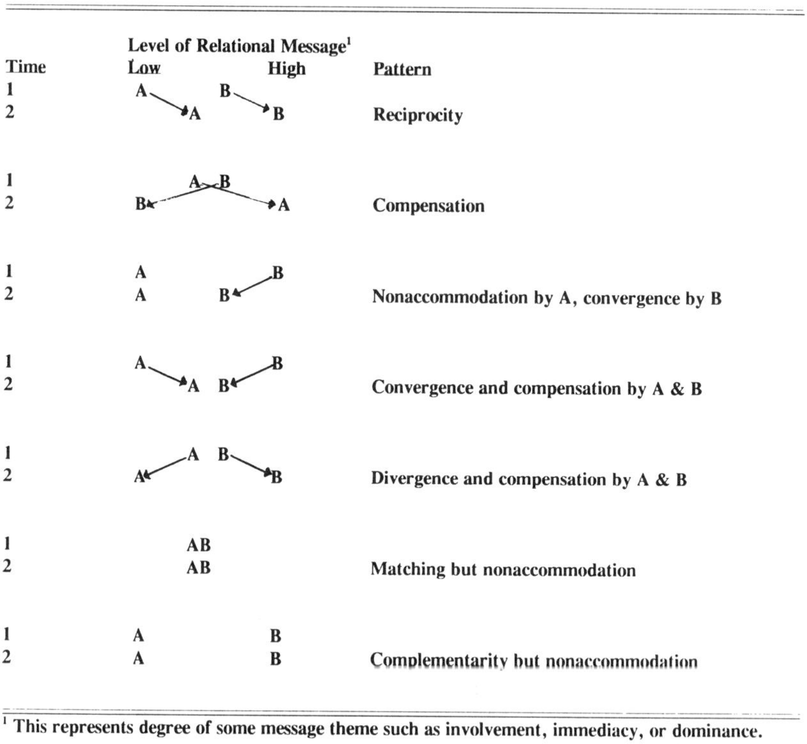

| Time | Level of Relational Message[1] Low          High | Pattern |
|------|--------------------------------------------------|---------|
| 1 | A↘      B↘ | |
| 2 | ↘A        ↘B | Reciprocity |
| 1 |        A↘B | |
| 2 | B↤          ↘A | Compensation |
| 1 | A                  B | |
| 2 | A        B↤ | Nonaccommodation by A, convergence by B |
| 1 | A↘               B | |
| 2 | ↘A  B↤ | Convergence and compensation by A & B |
| 1 |      A  B↘ | |
| 2 | A↤          ↘B | Divergence and compensation by A & B |
| 1 |      AB | |
| 2 |      AB | Matching but nonaccommodation |
| 1 | A           B | |
| 2 | A           B | Complementarity but nonaccommodation |

[1] This represents degree of some message theme such as involvement, immediacy, or dominance.

Figure 6.1    Illustration of different interaction patterns and their associated definitions.

## CONCLUSION

In this chapter, we have attempted to identify key issues involved in conceptually defining interaction adaptation patterns. We have proposed that the following criteria be used to distinguish patterns from one another: (a) contingency, (b) directedness, (c) unidirectional versus bidirectional influence, (d) change versus maintenance of behavior, (e) magnitude and size of behavioral change, (f) timing and rhythmicity, (g) intentionality, and (h) behavioral equivalence. These critical attributes separate interaction adaptation patterns of reciprocity, convergence, compensation, divergence, matching, mirroring, complementarity, and synchrony from one another. In the next chapter, we consider the ways in which these patterns should be operationalized to be tested fairly.

**NOTES**

[1]  Marital interaction researchers (e.g., Gottman, 1979; Revenstorf, Hahlweg, Schindler, & Kunert, 1984; Schaap, 1984) sometimes distinguish "noncontingent," "simultaneous," or "baserate" reciprocity, in which each pair's concurrent behaviors are compared, from "contingent" reciprocity, in which behaviors are sequentially related from one lag to the next. What they are calling noncontingent or baserate-based reciprocity is the same as what we and others call matching. Only the "contingent" variety fits the definition of reciprocity being put forward here.

[2]  Further distinctions among forms of accommodation (e.g., upward versus downward, partial versus full versus hyper-, unimodal versus multimodal, symmetrical versus asymmetrical) can be found in Giles, Coupland, and Coupland (1991a; also see Chapter 5, this volume). Upward accommodation is convergence toward a more prestigious speech form; downward is toward a less desirable one. Most of the other distinctions duplicate ones we present here and in the next chapter.

# 7

## Operationalizing adaptation patterns

The distinctions among interaction patterns that we offered in Chapter 6 carry attendant operationalization considerations. Here we examine measurement and design implications. In Chapter 8, we tackle statistical analysis issues.

### EXCHANGE PRINCIPLES

#### Directed and contingent responses

Matching and complementarity patterns do not require demonstrating that one person's behavior is directed toward or contingent upon the other. All that is needed is evidence that interactants' behaviors are highly similar or dissimilar. Sometimes this is evident through visual inspection of the data. It may be readily apparent, for example, that interactants are using formal forms of address when talking or that they are eschewing touch except for an initial handshake. Other times, statistical measures of association or comparisons between means are used to confirm empirically that patterns are the same or different.

One peculiar problem that can arise when claiming that matching is due to people orienting to social norms is the absence of a statistical test to verify similarity. If, for example, interactants are expected to show a high degree of pleasantness and politeness during initial interactions with strangers, and if we believe people adhere closely to these norms, then we should expect to see highly similar linguistic and nonverbal patterns within any given pair of people and little variance between

Portions of this chapter have been adapted from Judee K. Burgoon, Leesa Dillman, and Lesa A. Stern (1993), Adaptation in dyadic interaction: Defining and operationalizing patterns of reciprocity and compensation, *Communication Theory, 4,* 293–316, with permission of Guilford Publications, Inc.

pairs of people. This presents a dilemma because the statistical hypothesis to be tested is the null (i.e., no differences), which cannot itself be tested, and other measures of association discussed in Chapter 8 require some variance for any association to be detected. Apart from merely looking at descriptive data, one design solution to this problem is to create or observe different normative conditions and compare them. If similarity is a byproduct of people orienting to situational norms, then there should be matching within each pair but differences between conditions.

The remaining adaptation patterns do presume that at least one party's behavior is conditional – that is, influenced by the other. How, then, should we establish that responses are directed toward the other interactant or contingent on that person's behavior? It will be recalled that Ross et al. (1988) included temporal and relational reciprocity among their four types. Our conceptualization of reciprocity includes both temporal and relational reciprocity (but with more emphasis on the less restrictive case of temporal reciprocity, given our interest in generalizing about communication patterns). Tacit in our definitions and those of Ross et al. (1988) is the assumption that the behaviors in question are reasonable candidates for being partner-directed – that is, they are behaviors that could be interpreted as a response to the interaction partner. Repeated gazing toward a window because of a distracting noise outside would therefore not qualify as gaze avoidance "directed toward" the partner.

There are several ways in which directedness and contingency might be determined, some more practical than others. One method would be to query participants directly about their intent, possibly during a postinteraction session during which interactants reviewed their videotapes. Although self-reports might be viable for discrete and symbolic acts, such as extending a dinner invitation in exchange for a previous one, much of our interactional behavior occurs without conscious awareness (see, e.g., Kellermann, 1992) or self-monitoring. Participants may be unable to describe their own behavior, even when they can state their intent (see Palmer & Simmons, 1993, for evidence of this). And even when they have consciously monitored their own behavior, participants have proved to be inaccurate informants about what they did (Bernard, Killworth, Kronenfeld, & Sailer, 1984; S. E. Jones, 1991). Invoking sender intent as an operational criterion may therefore be too stringent a criterion and one that is exceptionally difficult to verify.

A second possibility is to invoke a plausibility criterion, identifying those behaviors that are conventionally used in interactive exchanges in response to one's partner. There are numerous behaviors that members of the same language/speech community should recognize as communicative signals that are typically directed toward another (see, e.g., Burgoon et al., 1984, 1986; Burgoon & Newton, 1991, for evidence of a social consensus on interpretations of nonverbal behaviors).

A third, related possibility is to have one person systematically alter behavior and observe the response of the other. This approach entails observing changes over time, methods for which are discussed in the next section.

A fourth alternative is to employ Kenny's social relations model (Kenny, 1981, 1994; Kenny & La Voie, 1982, 1984), which combines a round-robin interaction design with specific statistical algorithms to parse unique relationship effects from actor, partner, and situational influences. Such an approach is valuable when one is especially interested in influence patterns that are strictly associated with the given dyad. Kenny and La Voie (1982) were able to show more pronounced reciprocity of attraction by employing this analytic method. However, identifying such components of variation does not ensure that the relationship is truly one of contingency. For example, situational factors such as physical proximity, individual goals, and the like may account for the obtained correlations. Moreover, the round-robin design – in which partners must interact with multiple partners – is laborious to schedule and conduct yet necessary to obtain separate actor and partner estimates. Coupled with the statistical analysis requirements, this approach can be less than practical for mainstream interaction adaptation research.

A final option is to rely on statistical analysis to verify that one person's behaviors are dependent upon another's. According to Gottman and Roy (1990), reciprocity "by its very nature argues for *contingency,* and hence compares conditional probabilities with unconditional probabilities" (p. 6). With categorical behavioral measures, determining whether probabilities have been altered by a partner's behavior requires assessing baserates of behavior and comparing conditional probabilities (i.e., one's contingent behavior) to nonconditional probabilities (Gottman, 1979). We can infer that Person A has influenced Person B only if we know how Person B would have behaved in the absence of A. Lag sequential analyses can then be used to compare conditional and unconditional probabilities. With continuous data, time-series regression models can be used to obtain separate estimates for self-influence (an individual's autocorrelation, reflecting stable interaction patterns) and partner influence. (These methods are discussed in Chapter 8.)

All of these design and analysis approaches enable researchers to differentiate individual nonaccommodative patterns from reciprocal and compensatory ones.

### Change versus maintenance

A necessary although not sufficient condition for establishing adaptation is showing that at least one person's behaviors change over time. Where change is absent, one can only conclude that matching, complementarity, or nonaccommodation is occurring. Sometimes this is the objective, as in the case of showing that matching is a function of people adhering to social norms. In such circumstances, behavior should remain fairly constant.

If, however, the objective is demonstrating behavioral change by at least one party, one means of doing so is to include baseline or baserate data that reveal an interactant's behavioral pattern prior to partner influence (Argyle & Ingham, 1972; Patterson, 1982). For example, in experimental research, a baseline interaction period can be incorporated prior to an experimental manipulation occurring. These baselines could come from the same interaction or even a series of interactions. In such cases, change is a within-individual or within-dyad variable. These kinds of changes may involve specific verbal or nonverbal content (e.g., use of metaphorical language), the frequency with which behaviors are emitted (e.g., increased rate of nonfluencies), or the tempo of the interaction itself (e.g., briefer turns at talk).

Alternatively, the same kind of comparison can occur in a between-dyads design, where some dyads serve as a control group that essentially substitutes for a baseline condition. For example, in an experimental design, if some dyads are left to interact without interference and others have a confederate changing behavior, then the first group of dyads serves as a control group for the second group. Suppose, as has been found in some deception research (Burgoon, Buller, Dillman, & Walther, in press), that the control (no suspicion) group shows a steady increase in vocal relaxation over time while a second group (in which suspicion has been induced) maintains an elevated level of tension. It is possible to treat as "change" the difference in slopes over time between the two groups, even though technically the second group appears to be exhibiting a maintenance pattern. It must be recognized that when changes are examined in aggregate across multiple dyads (as in the case of between-dyad designs or use of multiple dyads in a within-dyads design), this does not mean that each individual dyad has exhibited change, only that on average, dyads are showing change.

Yet a third possibility is to infer change by comparison to pre-established norms for behavior, which serve as the "baseline." As noted previously, change can be inferred if people sustain a high level of involvement in the face of an otherwise normal decrease in involvement, as occurred in Burgoon et al.'s (1987) experiment.

A final means of demonstrating change is to use a longitudinal design in which time is one of the factors. Statistical tests for verifying the amount and form of change are discussed in Chapter 8.

### Concatenous responses

As we noted in Chapter 6, the notion of contingency, in principle, implicates concatenous – sequential – rather than simultaneous behaviors (Gottman & Roy, 1990); that is, the onset of a partner's similar or opposite behavior is lagged somewhat with respect to the onset of the actor's behavior (see also Dindia's 1982 discussion of contiguous behaviors). If distinguishing reciprocity from matching is relevant to one's research question, fine-grained measurement strategies may be required to capture the sequential changes in behavior between actor and partner.

If more macroscopic measurement is used, then lagged adjustments to the partner may appear to be simultaneous (Kendon, 1990). Macroscopic measurement may necessitate treating concurrent behaviors as evidence of convergence/divergence and reciprocity/compensation. We can increase our confidence that true adaptation is occurring by supplementing such analysis with independent confirmation that the partner's behaviors are changing in response to those of the actor. One way to verify that two interactants' behaviors are fluctuating in tandem is to use confederates who initiate changes. Matarazzo, Wiens, and Saslow (1965) used this technique successfully to demonstrate that interviewers' increases then decreases in turn length, nodding, and filled pauses prompted similar adjustments by interviewees.

Comparison of baseline correlations to postmanipulation period correlations or correlations under differing experimental conditions may also permit inference that partner changes are due to actor influence. If there is little association between two people's behavior during a baseline period and a strong association after one person initiates a change, a reasonable conclusion is that the behavior change prompted the other person's adaptation (see, e.g., Burgoon, Dillman, Stern, & Kelley, in press; Burgoon, Kelley, Newton, & Keeley-Dyreson, 1989). However, as noted previously in this chapter, small variances in the baseline or an experimental condition may obscure adaptation patterns statistically. Thus, one must use caution when comparing correlations.

### Contiguous versus lagged responses

One limitation of Gottman's (1982) temporal reciprocity is the requirement of immediate, contiguous responses. Although contingency is more obvious with prompt responses, at times contingent behaviors may be lagged within and across interactions. When reciprocity is not observed immediately but participants report it, researchers must infer that the social cognition (perception) of functional reciprocity has taken place. While lagged reciprocity may be less noticeable than temporal reciprocity, thereby reducing the researcher's ability to determine contingency, its effects must not be discounted. Ross et al. (1988) suggest that lagged reciprocity "is both more subtle and more tolerant with respect to the commodity returned, [and] is taken as a sign of trust within a relationship" (p. 152). In addition to the message of trust, lagged reciprocity may indicate other important relational messages such as receptivity, caring, and depth. Likewise, there are cases where instant reciprocity is unacceptable (such as responding to heartfelt disclosure of personal problems with a lengthy dissertation on one's own problems), and its use may lead to relational discord or the attribution of incompetency. We therefore recommend that both lagged and prompt responses be counted as evidence of reciprocity and compensation.

Alternatives for detecting lagged reciprocity *within* a given interaction include: (a) measuring behaviors over larger time intervals, which may cause lagged behaviors to appear as simultaneous, (b) using questionnaire measures of perceived reciprocity rather than observational measures, and (c) using statistical techniques such as lag sequential analysis to detect patterns involving few lags. Alternatives for detecting lagged reciprocity *across* interactions may include, in addition to the above, (d) the use of diaries for reporting larger reciprocated acts such as gift giving or personal self-disclosures.

## Directionality versus magnitude

We have suggested that reciprocity and compensation be defined primarily by the direction rather than the magnitude of change. However, the magnitude of change must be large enough to qualify realistically as accommodation rather than nonaccommodation. Burgoon et al. (1987) set a criterion of .3 scale unit on a 7-point scale as the minimum change needed to qualify as an accommodative pattern in their experiment. Le Poire (1991) used one standard deviation or greater as a criterion for arousal change. We recommend that other researchers likewise set a criterion threshold for what qualifies as an actual adjustment to the partner. Inspection of the range of changes and standard deviations within a particular sample may be useful to determine what magnitude appears to reflect sensitivity to partner behavior. Regardless of what theoretical or empirical basis is used, it is essential to establish some threshold in order to avoid including all changes as reciprocity and compensation (especially in light of Cappella's 1984 conclusion that individuals show a fair degree of consistency in their own behavior across interactions and partners). Further, it may be that the thresholds vary for different behaviors, although simplicity would argue for using the same threshold within a single study unless the units of measurement differ.

## FUNCTIONAL ORIENTATION AND FUNCTIONAL EQUIVALENCE

A functional approach has implications for whether reciprocity and compensation patterns can best be discerned from molar or molecular cues and cue complexes. The behaviors studied to date have included both, ranging from microlevel nonverbal behaviors such as gaze, proximity, smiling, and silences (e.g., Breed, 1972; Cappella & Greene, 1984; Coutts et al., 1977) and verbal behaviors such as self-disclosure (e.g., Cline, 1989; Davis, 1976; Derlega et al., 1976), to more macrolevel measures such as global intimacy, affect, helping, and "resources" (e.g., Cann, Sherman, & Elkes, 1975; Roloff, 1987), which are typically perceived on the basis of behavioral "clusters" (Roloff & Campion, 1985).

The focus on functional equivalence raises at least three measurement considerations. First, it requires a commitment to multivariate measurement or to use of global measures as surrogates. In behalf of multivariate measurement, it is the case that while a single behavior occasionally may signal a given message, a greater number of cues serves to clarify and intensify a message (Henley & Harmon, 1985). Moreover, two consistent cues may override the interpretation of a single contradictory cue (Burgoon et al., 1984). The complexity and multiplicity of cues that a single relational message may comprise is illustrated by Coker and Burgoon's (1987) analysis of conversational involvement. They identified five dimensions of nonverbal behaviors, qualities, and composites that may express involvement. To analyze whether two interactants are reciprocating or compensating involvement, then, may require examining a large proportion of these behaviors. Otherwise, what appears to be compensation on one behavior may be more than offset by reciprocity on a number of other behaviors.[1]

An alternative to measuring multiple behaviors is to use molar measures (such as a rating of involvement, immediacy, or dominance) at several intervals. Considering the complexity of multivariate measurement, a global approach to the assessment of reciprocity and compensation may be warranted. Such an approach also acknowledges the principle of equifinality – that there are several alternative routes to the same outcome. It is not just the case that several behaviors are substitutable for one another but that different sequences of behavior may also convey the same message. Molar measures may better represent such variations on a theme.

Second, the focus on reciprocity and compensation of relational themes encourages researchers to observe both verbal and nonverbal manifestations of a message (or again, to rely on global measures that encompass all relevant channels). Otherwise, one channel's message may negate or neutralize another's (Burgoon, 1985).

Third, when measuring multiple behaviors, the degree of similarity or dissimilarity must be considered in pronouncing behaviors as qualitatively equivalent or opposite. Roloff (1987) suggests that reciprocation of similarly functioning behaviors, rather than exact behaviors, is often preferred. Making an equally intimate disclosure on a different topic, giving a gift of equal value, or listening empathically to the partner rather than immediately self-disclosing in response, are examples of heteromorphic reciprocity – returning resources different in form but of equal value. Such forms of exchange may be especially appropriate when partners occupy different roles with attendant differences in behavioral repertoires. As illustration, D. A. Gilbert (1993) reasoned that nurses and patients have different sets of functionally equivalent behaviors for showing involvement during a clinical visit. It is acceptable for the nurse to touch the patient but not vice versa. However, the patient is free to display facial pleasantness in response to the touch. Thus, the substitutability of behaviors must be allowed.

In recognition of this principle, Gilbert (1993) adopted a measurement approach of aggregating multiple measures into a summed reciprocity score within each 1-second time interval. A similar tack could be taken in measuring alternative compensatory mechanisms, following Argyle and Cook's (1976) identification of more macrolevel compensatory behaviors. One could treat various behaviors (i.e., increased gaze, forward lean, direct body orientation, touch) as equally valid indicators of a compensatory response to increased physical distance. Yet another approach would be to obtain multidimensional measures that are analyzed simultaneously with multivariate statistics. For example, S. J. Gilbert (1976) and Morton (1978) identified multiple dimensions of self-disclosure that could be scored by coders or participants and utilized in a multivariate analysis of variance or multiple regression. It should be clear that a variety of measurement and design alternatives could be fashioned to take into account the substitutability of behaviors, the overarching principle being that a more comprehensive approach is superior to measuring single behaviors.

## PERCEIVED VERSUS BEHAVIORAL ADAPTATION

So far, our focus has been on behavioral adjustments. However, perceptions of adaptation cannot be ignored. CAT, for one, distinguishes between psychological and linguistic convergence or divergence (Giles, Coupland, & Coupland, 1991a). The former refers to beliefs about adaptation, the latter, to overt behavioral change.

Perceptions are relevant at two levels: actual recognition of a partner's behavioral change and interpretation of that change. The recognition issue parallels the concern that the magnitude of behavioral changes be large enough to be detectable. Several researchers (Bernieri et al., 1988; Dindia, 1982; Roloff & Campion, 1985) contend that an exchange must be perceived in order for adaptation to take place. In support of this position, Pearce et al. (1974) found that perceived reciprocity (measured as the congruence between interactants' actual disclosure and their perception of partner's disclosure) outstripped actual reciprocity (measured as agreement between the partner's actual degree of disclosiveness). As for interpretation, Markman (1984) and Bradac (1991) assert that the perceived intent – the meaning – of an act can be as important as whether the act is actually reciprocal or compensatory. The same act of distancing may be viewed positively (e.g., as polite) or negatively (e.g., as aloof), depending on the intent ascribed to it. Such perceptions may govern choice of subsequent behaviors (Cline, 1989; Gaelick, Bodenhausen, & Wyer, 1985; Roloff & Campion, 1985; but compare Dindia, 1988, who found that in regard to self-disclosure at least, perceptions may fail to predict actual behavior). Street and Cappella (1985) conjecture that it is the individual's perception of the function or reward value of a behavior, relative to a "preference range," that will be reciprocated rather than the specific behaviors per se. Behaviors that fall inside the "preference range" should be valenced positively and reciprocated. The evaluations of behaviors falling outside the preference range are likely to be moderated by a number of other variables.

Given the evidence that perceived reciprocity may exceed real reciprocity, a legitimate question to pose is which is more "valid" – a perceptual measure of *congruency* between one person's perceptions and another's behavior, a perceptual measure of *agreement between both people's perceptions,* or a behavioral measure of *agreement between both people's behaviors.* Ultimately, a deciding factor may be which accounts for more variance in interaction outcomes. Markman's (1984) summary of marital interaction research, for example, underscores the importance of couples' perceptions for predicting future outcomes. People in close relationships process events through cognitive screens that influence significantly what partners anticipate from one another and thus how they will respond to each other's actions.

This argues for research comparing perceptual and behavioral approaches. Bernieri et al. (1988) undertook just such a comparison and found a close correspondence between perceptual and behavioral synchrony. If future efforts produce similar results, research on adaptation patterns could become greatly simplified through use of perceptual rather than observational measures. In the meantime, it seems more sensible to supplement behavioral measures with perceptual ones to ascertain how the two types of measures converge or diverge. Triangulation of observed behaviors with participant perceptions then becomes a knotty but essential issue to address.

In other cases where the behavior of interest is highly sensitive and private (e.g., physical and verbal abuse), perceptual measures may have to supplant behavioral measures. One approach that overcomes some of the immediately obvious pitfalls of self-report measures was developed by Sabourin, Infante, and Rudd (1993) to analyze reciprocal verbal aggression. They conceptualized four types of reciprocity: "*objective* – when the husband said he used a given message and the wife also said she used the same message; *husband claimed* – when the husband said he used a message and claimed the wife also used the message; *wife claimed* – when the wife said she used a message and claimed the husband also used the message; and *inferred* – when the husband said the wife used a message and the wife said the husband used that message" (p. 25). Out of separate husband and wife reports of own and partner verbal aggression, they were therefore able to derive four different measures. Their analysis revealed that all four types discriminated between violent, distressed but nonviolent, and nondistressed couples and when used together, accounted for a significant amount of the variance among couple types. Sabourin et al. concluded that the objective and inferred measures were the best discriminators. Interestingly, these two are the most dyadic in nature in that they are derived from both husband and wife reports and are more akin to observational measures than the "claimed" measures, which come from one person's report. Moreover, conclusions about reciprocity emerge from the presence or absence of correlations between husband and wife reports about what they actually did rather than from either party reporting whether or not they perceived reciprocity. The objective and inferred measures might be used productively in tandem in future research inasmuch as they appear to have face validity, they seem less subject to bias than the "claimed" measures, and collecting data on either measure provides data to compute the other.

## SIZE OF MEASUREMENT UNIT

A related measurement issue is whether behaviors and qualities are measured microscopically or macroscopically (see Burgoon & Baesler, 1991). Microscopic measurement entails frequency or durational measures of single behaviors, measured on an event-by-event basis, or ratings of single behaviors based on very brief time intervals. Measurement becomes increasingly macroscopic as it entails larger and longer samples of single behaviors; repeated occurrences of single behaviors; multiple behaviors, presented simultaneously or serially; or more abstract descriptors for the behaviors or qualities. If microscopic measurement is used, it usually means that there will be multiple observations across time for each dyad member. D. A. Gilbert's (1993) method of combining multiple behaviors into a sum for each second is an exemplar. This measurement strategy permits either separate within-dyad analyses on a dyad-by-dyad basis (see, e.g., Cappella & Planalp, 1981) or pooling data across dyads for combined between- and within-dyad analyses. If macroscopic measurement is used, it often means that very few time periods are represented for each dyad or there may be only a single measurement for each individual or dyad (as in rating global immediacy at the end of an interaction). Thus, macroscopic measurement tends to lend itself to between-dyad analyses. However, macroscopic measurement can just as easily be used with multiple brief time intervals, so that it can also be employed with within-dyad longitudinal designs.

The size of measurement unit may affect significantly the ability to detect patterns of reciprocity and compensation. We have already suggested that molar measurement may be better suited to capturing the functional nature of the behavior or set of behaviors under observation. However, the available empirical data are mixed on this issue. D. A. Gilbert (personal communication, August 1991) reported that she found much more evidence of reciprocity when she used 1-second than 30-second intervals. Arundale (1977), following the Sampling Theorem, likewise recommended that studies of speech and silence phenomena in dialogues use very small sampling intervals: "The sampling interval must be equal to (or shorter than) the shortest time interval for which the variable under study can remain in any one of its states" (p. 261).

Because different behaviors change at different rates, one must consider the most appropriate size of time unit for measurement of each behavior. Yet, based on a review of the literature and his own comparison of three different analysis approaches, Street (1988) concluded, "It appears that the larger the unit, the more likely that evidence of speech matching and compensation emerges" (p. 153). One exception he cited was that evidence of response latency matching decreased as the coding interval increased. Street speculated that coding within brief intervals increased error variance by reflecting perturbations due to extraneous factors such as physiological changes or topic transitions, and that expanding the coding interval served to stabilize this error variance. It may be that the potential superiority of macroscopic measurement holds only when the coding interval is still relatively short (say, 1 or 2 minutes). Certainly this is an empirical question to be pursued.

Larger intervals also threaten to increase error variance by failing to detect dynamic changes within those intervals and by encouraging more gestalt, stereotypic coding judgments that may be imprecise estimates of each dyad member's behavior (Burgoon & Baesler, 1991; Cappella, 1991). Very large intervals also may preclude time-series analyses or may at least force use of discrete-time Markov models (Hewes, 1980). Thus the appropriate unit size will depend on the particular behaviors and communication functions being studied, but it may be that a more molar approach is necessary to detect many reciprocity and compensation patterns.

A correspondent concern to measurement unit size is whether an individual or dyadic measure is used. In the former case, each dyad member's behavior is a separate variate (e.g., each person's domineeringness or response latency). In the latter case, the variate is some jointly defined behavior, such as contiguous pairs of behavior labeled *interacts* (as in relational control sequences of dominance followed by submission). Because interacts represent lagged behavior, they better satisfy the contingency criterion than do acts, which, if measured simultaneously, may or may not represent adjustments to the partner. However, this advantage of interacts has led some to claim that relational interaction processes can only be measured dyadically. This is not the case. For example, one may measure perceived reciprocity by relating each separate person's perception with the other's (see Kenny, 1988). Individual measures are an appropriate choice when studying the effects of confederate behavior on a partner's behavior. Moreover, the use of individual measures in certain statistical designs (e.g., time series) can account for both immediate and lagged compensation and reciprocity. Finally, some features such as language choice do not lend themselves to dyadic measurement.

## OBSERVER VERSUS PARTICIPANT PERSPECTIVE

Another operationalization issue concerns who is best able to serve as the "informant" on whether adaptation has occurred – participant or observer? Poole, Folger, and Hewes (1987) note that participant perceptions are useful for explaining responses made in an interaction. However, participant self-reports tend to be biased and inaccurate (Bernard et al., 1984), due in part to respondents giving stereotypical and socially acceptable responses. In contrast, observers cannot access relational history and subtle immediacy cues that are available only to the participant, nor can the observer account for responses that are due to the participant's perceptions of an event (Burgoon & Newton, 1991; Noller & Guthrie, 1991; Surra & Ridley, 1991). Thus, when the aim is determining perceived adaptation, the cued recall method employed by Roloff and Campion (1985) seems to be best suited. When the aim is determining actual behavioral adjustment, observers may provide more accurate estimates. Of course, one may want to compare observed to perceived patterns, as did Dindia (1982).

## SAMPLE COMPOSITION

A final issue meriting attention is who the participants are. To date, few investigations have explored systematically the possible moderating effects of communicator and relationship characteristics on interaction adaptation patterns. Although numerous sample characteristics potentially influence communication processes, culture, gender, relationship level, and relationship type are among the most influential on the communication patterns enacted. So far, interaction adaptation patterns have seldom been studied interculturally or cross-culturally. Similarly, because of a proclivity to use same-sex subjects (e.g., Argyle & Dean, 1965; Coutts et al., 1977; Jourard & Landsman, 1960; Patterson et al., 1981), few studies of reciprocity have considered gender differences. Much of what we know about interaction patterns can only be generalized to males interacting with males and females with females. Moreover, the vast majority of studies have used strangers as subjects, so their behaviors are likely to reflect culturally normative behaviors typical of unacquainted pairs. Finally, we know very little about the patterns exhibited by partners who share a relational history. Levinger and Snoek (1972) suggest that as individuals develop close relationships, their communication patterns become more idiosyncratic. There are bound to be unique patterns associated with various relationship types (e.g., husband–wife, supervisor–subordinate, teacher–student), in part because of asymmetries associated with some relationship types (e.g., parent–child, interviewer–interviewee) and in part due to different expectations for role-bound behaviors. While numerous studies have contributed to our understanding of the basic processes of reciprocity and compensation, their results are limited because of their restricted samples. We believe that it is imperative to examine the variations across same- and mixed-sex pairs, across varying levels of relationship (stranger, friends, and intimates), and across different relationship types in order to achieve generalizability and to discern the unique patterns emerging in each. Researchers would be well advised to include gender and relationship level at minimum as blocking variables in future studies. Other communicator and relationship characteristics may need to be explored as well. Our general point is that to continue to confine studies of interaction adaptation to highly restricted or homogeneous samples is an egregious error that impairs the ability to draw generalizations. Future investigations need to be more sensitive to these sampling considerations.

## CONCLUSION

In this chapter, we have highlighted some of the most important issues involved in measuring dyadic interaction patterns. If the patterns of interest are matching and complementarity, a variety of methodological approaches may work to verify that such patterns are present. However, if the patterns of interest are reciprocity, compensation, convergence, and divergence, more stringent criteria must be satisfied. Methods must establish that behaviors are contingent and directed. Concatenous rather than simultaneous analyses may be required, with the recognition that increasing numbers of lags, or unevenly distributed lags, between behaviors may make demonstration of contingency difficult. Also important are determinations of the communication functions being served by the behaviors under examination, the functional equivalence among behaviors in fulfilling those functions, and the relative impact of perceived versus actual adaptation. Finally, the size of the measurement unit and sample composition may influence the ability to detect patterns of accommodation or nonaccommodation.

### NOTE

[1] The substitutability of behaviors that may communicate the same relational theme is further evident in the variety of nonverbal behaviors that may signal the same relational message. For example, *dominance* can be communicated by controlling more and better territories (Hall, 1966), using greater personal space and invading another's personal space (Burgoon, 1978), placing oneself where visual access to others is maximal (Sommer, 1971), maintaining indirect body orientation (Mehrabian, 1981), initiating and controlling touch behaviors (Henley, 1977), maintaining a visual dominance ratio (Dovidio & Ellyson, 1982), engaging in an unwavering, direct stare (Rosa & Mazur, 1979), using expansive, relaxed, and dynamic gestures and postures (Henley, 1977; Mehrabian, 1981), and vocally displaying louder volume, lower pitch, moderately fast rate, clearer articulation sans accent, and greater intonation (Apple, Streeter, & Krauss, 1979; Giles, 1973; Mehrabian & Williams, 1969). *Intimacy,* composed of messages of

involvement, trust, depth, inclusion, and affection, and *similarity* may be communicated by close distance, forward lean, direct body orientation, mutual gaze, convergent speech patterns, similar body postures and gestures, and mutual touch (Burgoon et al., 1984; Edinger & Patterson, 1983; Hale & Burgoon, 1984; Mehrabian & Williams, 1969; Scheflen, 1964; Street & Giles, 1982). Indicators of *emotional arousal* include gaze aversion, postural rigidity, postural shifts, random kinesic movements, louder volume, nervous vocalizations, faster tempo, and higher pitch (Burgoon & Koper, 1984; Cappella & Greene, 1984; Ekman & Friesen, 1969; Nesbitt & Steven, 1974). *Composure,* conceptualized as the opposite end of the arousal continuum, is conveyed by such relaxation cues as postural asymmetry, open body position, absence of random movements, and frequent, animated gestures (Burgoon et al., 1984; Mehrabian, 1969; Mehrabian & Ksionzky, 1972). *Informality* and *social orientation* may be expressed by relaxed, asymmetrical postures, smiling, and close distances (Altman & Vinsel, 1977; Burgoon et al., 1989). The multiplicity of cues associated with any one theme underscores the notion that behaviors need not be identical to qualify as reciprocal or compensatory. When verbal behaviors are also taken into account, it becomes evident that researchers need to go beyond single cue analysis to identify functionally what is being communicated.

# 8

## Analyzing adaptation patterns

In Chapters 2–5, we saw that the extensive research on interaction adaptation patterns is replete with seemingly conflicting findings and that few unequivocal generalizations have emerged so far. In Chapters 6 and 7 we saw that part of the difficulty has been the mix of conceptual and operational definitions that have been employed. In this and the next two chapters, we consider the role that statistical analysis plays in confounding the picture. As will be apparent, conclusions about interaction adaptation patterns are tied to the type of statistical analysis procedure used. The problem is not that researchers have been using inappropriate methods but rather, they have often failed to recognize how their choice of analysis influenced conclusions about adaptation. Thus, studies using one method might find "reciprocity" while studies using another might find "compensation." Instead of this being a case of contradictory findings, it may merely reflect two different methods – for example, use of a between-subjects versus within-subjects design.

Our intent in reviewing statistical analysis alternatives, then, is not to identify which methods are inherently "better" but rather to distinguish different methods according to their objectives, the forms of measurement for which they are applicable, the restrictiveness of their assumptions, the kinds of estimates they supply, and so forth, so that results emanating from different analyses can be interpreted properly.

That conclusions are linked to analysis choices is not a new idea. Several past investigations have compared methods in an effort to determine empirically how they differ. Five are illustrative. In all cases, the methods used were appropriate for analyzing adaptation patterns, but led researchers to draw different conclusions about the degree and form of adaptation. Gottman (1979) compared marital partners' metacommunication. His initial cross-sectional analyses failed to detect any relationships, but when he shifted to sequential analysis, he detected differences in interaction patterns between satisfied and dissatisfied couples. VanLear (1983) used Markov analysis and repeated measures multiple regression to analyze relational control patterns among seven dyads. He concluded that the analyses differed not only in their adherence to homogeneity and stationarity (consistency) assumptions but also in the patterns exhibited over time. Street (1988) conducted a similar exercise, analyzing dyadic response latency, speech rate, and turn duration with Pearson product-moment correlations, intraclass correlations, and time-series regressions. While all three approaches showed matching effects on response latency, the results differed in both the magnitude and direction of patterns found for speech rate and turn duration adaptations. In particular, the intraclass correlation yielded a pattern opposite of the Pearson *r* and the time-series regression. Le Poire (1991) included repeated measures analysis of variance and intraclass correlations in an experimental study on conversational involvement. The analysis of variance showed that across four separate conditions entailing increased and decreased involvement, participants reciprocated confederate involvement level over time. Intraclass correlations produced a significant positive relationship in only one condition and a negative (albeit near-zero) correlation in another. Finally, Burgoon, Buller, Dillman, and Walther (in press) used the same two types of analyses in an experiment manipulating interviewee deception and interviewer suspicion. Intraclass correlations produced a predominant matching pattern, but repeated measures analyses of variance produced a mixed pattern of relationships.

These investigations exemplify part of the problem in trying to synthesize empirical findings in the adaptation literature. All of the techniques mentioned have been used with some frequency and all are capable of revealing forms of adaptation, yet they can lead to different conclusions even when applied to the same set of empirical observations. The reason is that the methods are not all testing the same thing. Thus, an essential first step in undertaking an analysis of extant literature or in planning future adaptation research is to examine more closely what each statistical procedure is designed to do, both to better understand how choice of statistical analysis procedure can influence the pattern that is claimed and to encourage more precise descriptions of research findings. In this chapter, we present an overview of several statistical analysis approaches that have been or might be used in analyzing dyadic interaction adaptation patterns. Because excellent resources are available summarizing techniques for analyzing categorical data (see, e.g., Allison & Liker, 1982; Feick & Novak, 1985; Gottman &

Roy, 1990; Morley, 1987; see also Cappella, 1987, for a critique of both categorical and continuous data methods) and because our own research employs interval-level measurement, we will emphasize those techniques that can be used with continuous data. Discussion of some categorical approaches, however, is included. In Chapters 9 and 10, we offer illustrations of how applying several techniques to the same data can produce complementary conclusions about interaction adaptation and demonstrate concretely what can be gained from each approach. Those chapters also present more comprehensive empirical analyses than previous investigations and so offer more insights into adaptation patterns.

Several factors distinguish the techniques from one another, among them whether measurement is discrete or continuous, whether the focus is on within-dyad or between-dyad effects, whether data are cross-sectional or longitudinal, whether the sample size is large or small, whether the data set is univariate or multivariate, and whether the investigation is based on natural observation or experimental manipulation of behaviors. Our review of statistical strategies is organized around these features. We highlight key considerations in the use of each technique and attendant implications for uncovering adaptation patterns.

## LEVEL OF MEASUREMENT

A first feature dictating choice of analysis strategy is whether the behaviors of interest are measured as discrete (categorical) or continuous data. A review of the literature reveals that researchers following one tradition seldom cross over to use the other. Thus, some programs of research have relied almost exclusively on categorical measures, while others have relied on continuous ones. It should be kept in mind that differences in conclusions emerging from these alternative approaches may therefore be due to the measurement strategy itself as well as to the statistical technique used to analyze patterns.

For nonparametric data, in which the dependent behavior of interest is dichotomized (e.g., presence or absence of vocalization) or comprises nominal, qualitative categories (e.g., use of cooperative, competitive, or integrative conflict strategies), a number of discrete-state statistical models are appropriate, most of which have analogues used with parametric data. The nonparametric techniques may be used to analyze individual dyads separately or to aggregate data from multiple dyads. The simplest alternatives include various measures of association such as φ (phi) and the contingency coefficient $C$ that are based on chi-square. Like other correlational procedures to be discussed shortly, these can reveal whether behaviors exhibited by Person(s) A match or complement those exhibited by Person(s) B but cannot confirm conclusively that reciprocity or compensation is occurring.

More complex, stochastic models include logit, log-linear, Markov chain, and lag sequential analyses. For example, log-linear analysis is like conducting an analysis of variance on nominal data. It examines contingency patterns between categorical variables (Reynolds, 1977). Sillars, Pike, Jones, and Redmon (1983) employed it to determine whether a spouse's use of positive, neutral, and negative affect is associated with the immediately preceding use of the same behaviors by the partner.

Another alternative that combines categorical dependent variables with continuous or categorical independent variables is multiple discriminant analysis. Burgoon et al. (1987) used this approach to analyze under what conditions interactants reciprocated, compensated, or did not adjust to their partners. Based on interval-level coder ratings, dyads were classified into categories of reciprocating, compensating, or nonaccommodating. The analysis then addressed whether confederate characteristics (gender, reward value) predicted the interaction pattern exhibited. Although these dyads were classified after the interaction by utilizing nonverbal coding and then applying a statistical criterion, classifications could also be assigned in advance, based on experimental manipulations (e.g., instructing participants to match or not match their partner's behavior).

Reynolds (1977) contends that because of possible distortions, underestimates, and low power associated with nominal-level measurement, interval-level measurement is often preferable. When dependent measures are based on behavioral frequencies (e.g., number of head nods, converted to percentages), durations (e.g., length of utterance), or evaluative ratings (e.g., vocal warmth), additional statistical techniques appropriate for use with continuous data (or measures treated by convention as continuous) become available. The simplest and most frequently employed statistics are the Pearson product-moment correlation ($r$) and the intraclass correlation ($r_I$). Additional parametric techniques that take into account multiple behaviors or multiple time periods are canonical correlation, repeated measures multiple regression or analysis of variance, and a host of longitudinal models (e.g., cross-lagged panel correlation, individual time series, interrupted time series, autoregressive integrated moving average – ARIMA – models) and related methods (e.g., Fourier analysis, spectral analysis). Because we approach these techniques as users rather than statisticians, we will focus here on the most used and "accessible" methods.

## BETWEEN-DYADS VERSUS WITHIN-DYADS ANALYSES

Perhaps the most fundamental distinction in statistical analysis approaches is whether one is making comparisons between dyads or within dyads. The former arrays pairs (or groups) of people and make comparisons among all the dyads or groups. The latter considers how each person within a dyad or group compares to others within it. Each type of analysis has its own advantages and both are often required to obtain a full picture, because within the same data set, the within-dyads pattern can have a relationship opposite that of the between-dyads pattern (Kenny, Kashy, & Bolger, 1985).

An illustration may clarify what can appear to be a logical contradiction. Suppose societies differ in formality of discourse during work-related discussions, such that those from cultures with rigid status hierarchies use more formal language and forms of address than those from more egalitarian societies. Suppose also that within each culture, it is the case that subordinates use more formal language with superiors than vice versa. One can imagine an array of data pairs like that shown in Figure 8.1. If you plot a line through all the pairs, it produces an upward slope indicative of a matching pattern. This is the between-dyads relationship. It says that regardless of how hierarchically organized a society is, there will be some tendency for members from the same culture to match each other's language. Yet if you draw the line between each pair of people, their individual patterns show downward slopes indicative of the two people's behaviors being complementary. These are the within-dyad patterns. Such patterns would fit the case of Persons B (the supervisors in each case) being free to use first names and informal language and Persons A (the subordinates in each pair) being restricted to use of titles and more formal language. Another example, this time of how individual physiological responses relate to facial expressiveness, can be found in Knapp and Hall (1992). These and similar examples reveal how important it is to employ both within- and between-subject analyses in case they show different adaptation patterns.

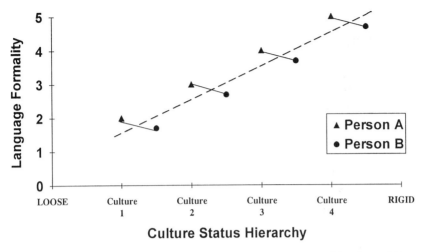

Figure 8.1    Illustration of different adaptation patterns resulting from within-dyad and between-dyad analyses.

Among the most commonly used between-dyads and within-dyads analyses are, respectively, the Pearson product-moment correlation (or some procedure building upon it) and the intraclass correlation.

### Pearson product-moment correlation

Like its nonparametric equivalents $\phi$ and $C$, the Pearson $r$, which is used with parametric data, measures bivariate relationships between two variables, $X$ and $Y$. Among the numerous variants on its formula is the following, which emphasizes that the correlation is the product of the "moments" (distances from the mean) of each of two paired scores:

$$r_{xy} = \frac{\Sigma Z_x Z_y}{N}$$    where $Z_x$ and $Z_y$ are standardized $X$ and $Y$ scores and $N$ is the number of pairs of $X$ and $Y$ scores

In measuring adaptation patterns, $r$ is typically used to assess the degree of association between Person A's behavior and Person B's behavior across multiple dyads. The behavior in question can be two different variables (e.g., A's smiling and B's self-disclosure) or the same behavior for each (e.g., smiling), but in the latter case each person's behavior is treated as a separate variate because it originates from two separate, identifiable people in each dyad. In the first instance, a positive correlation would mean that smilers are more likely to have disclosive partners than are nonsmilers (a result that might be taken as indicative of reciprocating an equivalent message of affection). In the second instance, a positive correlation across multiple dyads would mean that those who smile a lot are more likely to have smiling than nonsmiling partners. This is evidence of matching but does not assure reciprocity, even though researchers have routinely described such patterns as reciprocal. A negative correlation would mean that a complementary relationship exists, but cannot serve as unequivocal evidence of compensation because there is no assurance that one person's behavior is contingent on the other's.

The Pearson $r$ can also be used to correlate A's behavior with B's behavior across time within a single dyad. In this case, one could correlate the same or different behaviors across time (but such correlations would need to be corrected for autocorrelation within Person A and Person B). A positive correlation across time within a dyad would indicate that the two individuals' behaviors covary, again demonstrating matching and implying reciprocity, while negative correlations would indicate complementarity and might imply compensation. Because the Pearson $r$ reveals only the direction of the relationship across sampling units and not similarity between group means or individuals, such correlations do not indicate whether the magnitude of behavior is the same between members of each dyad.

When the correlation is based on the same behavior from both dyad members, the sampling unit should be the dyad and the sample size should be the number of dyads. When the correlation is based on different variates, the ideal is to use the individual as the unit of analysis so that each dyad is represented twice in the data set, once with Person A providing the $X$ estimate and Person B providing the $Y$ estimate, and once with Person A providing the $Y$ estimate and Person B providing the $X$ estimate. However, this introduces a problem of nonindependence (see Kraemer & Jacklin, 1979). Although the problem can be addressed by arbitrarily designating one person as $X$ and the other as $Y$ and using only half the data, an alternative that permits using all information and that doubles the sample size is to remove dyad effects from each person's scores. This is accomplished by subtracting the dyad *mean* for variate $X$ from each person's score on variate $X$ and the dyad mean for variate $Y$ from each person's score on $Y$. Removal of the dyad influence from each person's scores on the *same variate* renders them independent for analysis on the two *different variates*. Residualized scores on $X$

(e.g., smiling) can now be correlated with residualized scores on $Y$ (e.g., self-disclosure) across all dyads.

The problem of nonindependence also appears when data come from a round-robin design in which participants interact with more than one partner. Here the correlations can be obtained through use of the social relations model (Kenny, 1988; Kenny & La Voie, 1984), which identifies separate components of variance associated with actor effects (those behaviors that are consistently associated with a given actor, irrespective of who the partner is), partner effects (those that are consistently elicited by the partner), and relationship effects (those that are the unique product of the particular dyad).

Kenny and La Voie (1984) contend that to measure reciprocity requires partialing out actor–partner effects from the correlation between the two individuals' behaviors so that reciprocity only reflects the unique adaptation of one partner to another. As illustration, Fitzpatrick, Mulac, and Dindia (1994) found that men using masculine language tend to elicit the same from others (actor effect), men conversing with men converge toward a masculine language style and women conversing with women converge toward a feminine style (actor–partner effects), but females reciprocate partner's language more so than males, especially when interacting with husbands (dyadic reciprocity effect). Thus, where the interest is in unique adjustments made within relationships, the advice to partial out actor–partner effects seems sound. However, where the goal is to generalize across relationship characteristics and situations, it may be advisable to include actor–partner effects.

An additional problem with using correlations to assess adaptation is that both the $X$ and $Y$ measure must have adequate variability for a statistically significant relationship to emerge. If there is a restricted range in either or both variates, the correlation will be attenuated. This can occur, ironically, if people are too similar in their behavior. Suppose the expectation in a given culture is to follow very routinized greeting rituals and members of that culture are very homogeneous in adhering to the prescribed ritual. Then even though pairs of people greeting one another from that culture will display nearly identical interaction patterns, a correlational analysis will produce a near-zero correlation because there is too little variance across pairs of people. Under such circumstances, a different strategy is needed to demonstrate similarity (such as the design options identified in Chapter 7 for verifying that people orient to social norms) or one must rely on descriptive data presentations.

Further shortcomings identified by Kenny et al. (1995) are that (a) by using standardized scores, correlations ignore the original metric, which may be more meaningful to interpret; (b) they do not produce information about the mean separate from covariation (as compared to using a regression approach, which calculates both an intercept – the mean – and a slope); and (c) bivariate correlations do not generalize to the multivariate case (i.e., to use of multiple predictor or multiple criterion measures).

### Canonical correlation

Another between-dyads analysis is canonical correlation, which measures patterns of association between sets of related variables. In principle, this analytic approach could be ideal for examining how subsets of behaviors by Persons A relate to subsets of behaviors by Persons B. However, interpretation can become quite complex because several different functions can be extracted and the different sets of coefficients that can be analyzed (structural coefficients and correlations) can lead to different conclusions about which variables are most relevant. Also, a rule of thumb that canonical correlation be used only with very large samples (see Tucker & Chase, 1980) may make it impractical for use in many studies of interpersonal influence patterns, which traditionally have had small sample sizes.

### Intraclass correlation

Although also called a correlation, the intraclass $r_I$ is really not a correlation at all; according to Haggard (1958), the label is an unfortunate misnomer that disguises the fact that the intraclass $r_I$ is a univariate statistic (unlike the Pearson $r$, which is a bivariate statistic). It measures association within groups (in this case, dyads) but when only a single variate (e.g., turn length) is involved. It was originally developed to analyze twins and subsequently extended to other cases of matched members of a given sampling unit, in this case, members of a dyad. It is most appropriate when there is no basis for distinguishing Person A from Person B so that there are no separate $X$ and $Y$ variates, only a $Y$ variate obtained from two or more group members. When some characteristic such as gender distinguishes dyad or group members from one another and is relevant to the issue at hand, then the Pearson $r$ may be used because the two interactants' behaviors can be considered separate variates (e.g., male turn length and female turn length).

Computationally, $r_I$ entails comparing variances within sampling units (in this case, dyads) to variance between sampling units, as indicated by this variant of the formula (McNemar, 1962):

$$r_I = \frac{MS_{\text{between dyads}} - MS_{\text{within dyads}}}{MS_{\text{between dyads}} + (k - 1)MS_{\text{within dyads}}}$$

Sometimes the MS residual is used in place of MS within, in which case systematic variation due to individuals is removed and the within-dyads mean square estimate comes from the individuals by dyads interaction (see Rosenthal, 1984).

The intraclass can be conceptualized as a repeated measures analysis of variance with dyad or group member being the repeated factor. It can also be viewed as a reliability problem, with the focus being on consistency between dyad members. Unlike $r$, $r_I$ considers both similarities in means and the shapes of distributions, but like $r$, it ignores individual differences between partners (Haggard, 1958). Computationally, the numerator for $r_I$ is an estimate of variance across dyad or group means, whereas the numerator for $r$ is an estimate of the covariance between the two variates; the denominator for both statistics estimates the average variance due to individuals. Practically speaking, however, the $r$ and $r_I$ become the same computationally when dyads (rather than larger groups) are being analyzed and the variances are equal. This is perhaps why the two are so often viewed as equivalent, but Haggard (1958) notes that interpretations are not the same because the focus with the intraclass $r_I$ is on similarities or differences within each dyad or group rather than similarities or differences across a collection of dyads or groups.

The intraclass correlation is maximally positive when within-dyad scores are identical and scores differ between dyads. It is maximally negative when dissimilarity within dyads is high (i.e., there is high within-dyad variance) and differences across dyads are small (i.e., there is little variance). Hence, a large, positive $r_I$ may be interpreted as evidence of reciprocity and a large, negative $r_I$ as compensation. However, the latter interpretation is clouded by the fact that $r_I$ is highly sensitive to sources of heterogeneity between dyad members (e.g., sex, age, status, role, or communication competence) that might influence the behavior under examination. Consequently, a negative correlation may be due either to actual adaptation between interactants or to heterogeneity on other variables. It is therefore best reserved for use when dyad members are known to behave similarly prior to the interaction (i.e., their baseline behaviors are nearly the same) or when "investigators assume that reciprocal and compensatory interaction patterns are contingent upon similarities and differences among behavioral *levels*" (Street, 1988, p. 152) and investigators wish to document that the between-subjects factors account for the patterns. For example, Street (1988) found that a negative relationship between adult and child speaking tempo was due to their differential ability to encode speech rapidly rather than to adults adapting to the children's tempos or vice versa. Street and Buller (1987) likewise found negative intraclass correlations between physicians and patients on turn duration and pause-to-turn duration ratio that were due to each producing different levels of these behaviors rather than to patients or physicians compensating for the other. These examples illustrate the potential for misinterpreting negative $r_I$ as complementarity or compensation when it is in fact due to between-dyad heterogeneity.

## CROSS-SECTIONAL VERSUS LONGITUDINAL AND SERIAL DATA

A second fundamental distinction is between cross-sectional and longitudinal analyses. Data for statistical analysis can take one of two basic forms:

> (1) *cross-sectional* data, in which the researcher has observations on a set of variables at a given point in time across many . . . units of analysis; or
> (2) *time-series* data, in which one has a set of observations on some variables for the same unit of analysis . . . over a series of time points.
> (Ostrom, 1978, p. 5)

The previously discussed measures of association such as $\phi$, $r$, and $r_I$ are all cross-sectional analyses. Such analyses are advantageous in providing summary statements about interactions *in general*. They may also be useful in capturing patterns that occur across rather than within interactions, as in the case of reciprocal helping behavior over the course of a relationship, or that involve differential lags between events within each interaction, as in the case of divulging highly personal and embarrassing information. Critical events (e.g., aggressive touch) that occur infrequently also may be especially well-suited to between-dyads rather than within-dyads analyses because of the inordinate and uneven amount of time elapsing between events.

However, cross-sectional analyses are incapable of reflecting time ordering or directionality of influence and do not differentiate spurious from real accommodation patterns. For example, a chi-square showing association between male partners' distributional use of conflict management strategies and female partners' use of the same does not reveal whose behavior is contingent upon whom, or even whether one partner's behavior "caused" the other's. Nor can it reveal whether a spiral of reciprocal conflict strategies is present or not. Similarly, a high correlation between two interactants' gaze patterns may be no more than a demonstration of matching, not reciprocity, particularly if the task is one that requires mutual visual surveillance. The $r$ only permits comparisons between dyads with high versus low gazing members, not comparisons within dyads that reveal whether one member influences or is influenced by the other.

In short, while cross-sectional approaches may be the only viable alternative for analyzing certain kinds of events or behaviors, they fail to distinguish true reciprocity and compensation patterns from nonadaptive matching patterns in which dyadic partners are merely maintaining their own consistent, but similar, styles or exhibiting behaviors which fall within the socially normative range. They also do not identify who is influencing whom or detect cycles and dynamic patterns of behavior.

Another drawback of cross-sectional approaches is that if some individual dyads reciprocate while others compensate, the average effect may be nil, leading to the false conclusion that no mutual adaptation is taking place. Cappella (1979; Cappella & Planalp, 1981; Street & Cappella, 1989) provides convincing evidence that patterns of reciprocity, compensation, and nonaccommodation may all be displayed by different dyads within the same situation. Thus, dyad-by-dyad analysis may be mandated if we are to detect these interaction patterns and the circumstances under which they are manifested. When multiple patterns are present in the same data set, cross-sectional chi-squares and Pearson correlations may be relatively uninformative statistics if used in isolation. They do not reveal anything about the *frequency distribution* of a given pattern (reciprocity or compensation) across the set of dyads and the multiple patterns may cancel each other out, attenuating the estimate of the *magnitude* of the relationship among those dyads exhibiting any particular pattern.

An alternative approach, if the objective is to discern contingent and persistent patterns of behavior, is to adopt some form of Markovian or time-series analysis so as to capture the processual nature of human interaction. The remaining procedures to be reviewed all assess temporal or sequential behavioral changes. As already noted, these analyses are less likely to detect reciprocal or compensatory behaviors that are noncontiguous and temporally distal, that is, ones that are separated by numerous lags (as might occur with the reciprocation of unilateral touch over the course of an interaction) or by unevenly spaced lags (as might occur with statements of positive support). However, they are well-suited for distinguishing the degree to which frequently occurring behaviors and behaviors separated by few lags are reciprocated or compensated.

### Markov chains and lag sequential analysis

Two popular techniques used with nominal data are Markov chain and lag sequential models, both of which look at behavioral contingencies and sequential structure between interactants' behaviors (Gottman & Roy, 1990; Hewes, 1980). Markov chain analysis in particular has gained wide popularity in part because it works with some of the most frequently used coding schemes for analyzing dyadic and group interaction, which happen to be categorical systems. It is capable of discerning relationships among behaviors – e.g., if one conflict style is likely to be followed by another one. As illustration, Markov tests have been used to examine how strongly one person's use of one-up strategies is linked to the other's use of one-down strategies across an interaction (VanLear & Zeitlow, 1990), whether one negotiator's use of an integrative bargaining strategy is reciprocated by another's, and how long such reciprocity persists (Putnam & Jones, 1982). Because these latter analyses look at contingencies based on probabilities, they are capable of satisfying the definitional criterion that reciprocity entail contingent behavior on the part of at least one member of the dyad. They also focus attention on the message behavior itself, rather than the individuals who are producing the behavior, and they identify temporal sequencing of such behavior (Hewes, 1979), both properties that are consistent with the objective of uncovering reciprocal or compensatory message patterns.

One disadvantage of Markov analysis is that the unit of analysis is not individual or group scores but rather probabilities associated with categories of behaviors, making the individual acts nonindependent. The result is that when observations are pooled from several dyads, within-dyad variation becomes confounded with between-dyad variation and more weight is given to those dyads that generate more instances of behavior (VanLear & Zeitlow, 1990, p. 217). Another disadvantage is that important information – about the individuals, their characteristics, and their relationship – that may account for pattern differences is lost (Hewes, 1980). And, variations within a particular category may go unnoticed because they are "swamped" by consistencies among other categories (Fisher, 1978).

### Time-series models

Included here is a class of statistical techniques for examining longitudinal recursive and nonrecursive relationships. Time-series data entail observations on the same unit of analysis (e.g., dyads) over a series of time points (Ostrom, 1978). The Box-Jenkins time-series model (Davis & Lee, 1980; Hibbs, 1973/1974; Ostrom, 1978), widely employed in dyadic interaction research, has few sampling units (in the case of dyadic interaction, usually the single dyad) and a large number of time intervals (usually at least 50). Using a regression model in which one individual's behavior is the criterion, these models can identify simultaneously (a) how much consistency is present in that person's behavior (based on the extent to which self's same behavior in preceding time periods predicts behavior in the subsequent time period), (b) how much the partner's behavior is influencing the individual (based on the degree to which the behavior in a given time period is correlated with partner behavior in previous time periods), (c) whether the influence pattern is one of reciprocity or compensation (based on the sign of the beta weight – positive for reciprocity and negative for compensation), (d) whether any matching is also occurring (based on the degree to which behavior in a given time period is correlated with partner's behavior *for the same time period*), and (e) whether influence is primarily in contiguous time periods or is more lagged. Whether the influence pattern is mutual or unidirectional can also be determined by comparing the resultant regression equations for each participant to see if each person's behavior is contingent on the other's. An example of this approach can be found in Honeycutt (1991), where he counted the numbers of dyads exhibiting mutual influence, unidirectional influence, and nonadaptation, based on individual time series for each dyad.

In principle, these regression models can be expanded to include multiple partner behaviors as predictors (although this can become exceedingly complex). Moreover, data can be subjected to further sophisticated analyses to determine nonlinear patterns, cycles, their amplitudes, periodicity, and frequency with Fourier analysis, and to test mutual influence by correlating dyad members' frequencies and amplitudes with spectral analysis or analyzing "purified" cross-correlations between partners from ARIMA models. Thus, these models are highly robust in their ability to examine several patterns (consistency, multivariate influence, and matching) simultaneously.

Among the disadvantages of time-series models is the complexity of the analysis. For starters, there is the problem of nonindependence among observations at each time period – observations at Time 1 are correlated with those at Time 2 and so on. This necessitates estimating which of five different models of serial dependency (autoregressive and/or moving average) is present in a data set and controlling for the autocorrelation in the analysis (see Judd & Kenny, 1981). Moreover, all the models must meet the assumption of stationarity – the autocorrelation pattern must remain stable throughout the data set. (This assumption also must be met in lag sequential analysis.) Thus, the analyses require sophisticated statistical techniques and knowledge to conduct and interpret them properly.

A second disadvantage is that, although time-series analyses can be conducted on aggregated data, they are typically computed as individual time series (i.e., on individual dyads) and the results across dyads must be pooled before general conclusions are drawn. Analyzing each dyad separately can become extremely burdensome when one has a large number of dyads. Not only is the analysis task itself far more effortful, but the integration of complex findings into parsimonious generalizations may be difficult (see, e.g., VanLear, 1983) and may discourage further attempts to uncover systematic patterns. Nevertheless, it is possible to report average weighted correlations, their range, and the number of dyads exhibiting reciprocal versus compensatory patterns to provide summary analyses of the data as in the Honeycutt (1991) example. Or results can be pooled through standard meta-analytic procedures. Using this kind of approach, Street and Cappella (1989) were able to document which of several interaction behaviors yielded the most evidence of adaptation between children and adults and to reveal that a sizable minority of dyads compensated, despite the more prevalent observation of reciprocity.

A third potential problem is that interaction studies often employ far fewer time periods than those recommended for the standard time-series approach. A simple alternative that can address the problems of the multiple dyads and few time periods is to compute correlations between members of each dyad across time then pool the correlations and test the average $r$ against zero (D. Kenny, personal communication, October 1992). Again, standard meta-analytic procedures can be used for pooling, with $r$ to $z$ transformations used to test the pooled coefficients (see Rosenthal, 1984).

### Interrupted time-series models

These are a subclass of time-series models designed to examine the effects of some kind of intervention that interrupts a trendline over time (Judd & Kenny, 1981). In dyadic interaction research, a common intervention is an experimentally manipulated behavioral change by one dyad member. The analysis uses dummy coding to represent the "before" and "after" time periods and compares how intercepts and slopes from the time-series regression differ prior to and following the intervention.

One main advantage of interrupted time series when the interruption is attributable to a known factor such as one interactant's behavior change is the ability to assess causality directly. By comparison, cross-lagged panel analysis, another alternative discussed below that can be used with nonexperimental data, requires more inferences to draw conclusions about causality. A second potential advantage is the availability of procedures that pool data across dyads and that work with a small number of time periods. One method developed by Simonton (1977) is designed expressly for the circumstance where the number of sampling units (dyads) is large and the number of time intervals is small. His approach expands the dummy coding procedure to take into account experimental manipulations separate from the time-based interruption. The analysis includes terms representing estimates of (a) the mean level of behavior prior to the interruption, (b) the change in the mean behavior from pre- to post-interruption (i.e., the change in intercepts due to the intervention), (c) the rate of change in the behavior prior to the interruption (i.e., the effect of time), (d) the change in rate from pre- to postinterruption (i.e., the change in slopes due to the interruption), and (e) any history effects, based on comparison to a control group.

This is perhaps easiest visualized by looking at Figure 8.2, which shows two different trendlines over time, one for a control group and one for a group receiving the experimental treatment. Suppose, for

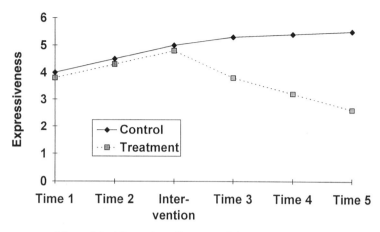

Figure 8.2    Illustration of interrupted time-series regression line on criterion of expressiveness.

example, that the treatment – the "interruption" – takes the form of a confederate in each pair greatly decreasing expressiveness between Time 2 and Time 3. Figure 8.2 shows both groups increasing expressiveness initially, with no noticeable difference between them until the confederate shifts to a pattern of decreasing expressiveness. Now the treatment group members also show a reciprocal decline in expressiveness. More abbreviated models can be used when comparisons are not being made to a control group or when conducting analyses within several experimental conditions.

Among the advantages of interrupted time series, in addition to its applicability to both individual and aggregated data, are that it can rule out rival hypotheses such as history effects, it provides separate estimates of level and rate of change, and it identifies effects for time apart from partner influence. Inasmuch as Burgoon et al. (1987) detected elevated involvement at the beginning of an interaction and a general lessening of involvement over time regardless of whether confederates were increasing or decreasing involvement, such time effects need to be parsed out from changes due to partner adjustments.

One disadvantage of Simonton's (1977) approach is that the dummy-coded vectors are highly correlated with one another, making order of entry into the model an important consideration if hierarchical entry is used. Alternative coding procedures (e.g., effect coding) sacrifice the ability to make comparisons to a control group and become practically indistinguishable from the repeated measures analysis of variance. Among additional disadvantages are that interrupted time-series analysis is only appropriate for use when there is an identifiable interruption; the a priori code assignment must specify whether the anticipated behavioral changes following the interruption are assumed to be transient, decaying, or permanent; the analysis can only examine a single criterion measure at a time; and the analysis itself is both complex to conduct (requiring estimates of autoregressive correlation for each dyad) and difficult to interpret.

### Cross-lagged panel correlation

Another, simpler method for inferring causal relationships over time is to use a quasi-experimental design called cross-lagged panel correlation (Campbell & Stanley, 1963). By comparing correlations between two variables, $X$ and $Y$, measured at two or more time periods, it is possible to infer from the differences between them whether $X$ is more likely to be causing $Y$ or vice versa (see Kenny, 1979). Correlations across (usually numerous) sampling units are obtained at different waves. Because causality is presumed to be indicated by nonspurious relationships, one purpose of the model is to correct for spurious correlations. But the model may also be adapted to test other facets of interaction adaptation, such as stability of behavior within and between partners (which may actually indicate nonresponsiveness to the partner), consistency of one person's behavior from one time lag to another, and rigidity of patterning between partners from one time lag to another. Examples of these various uses appear in Revenstorf, Hahlweg, Schindler, and Kunert (1984), which examines couples' self-reported talking, joint activities, togetherness, and feelings over time.

As with other time series, certain assumptions must be met before this approach can be used. The synchronous correlations (i.e., those from the same time period) are assumed to be stationary, i.e., that the causal structure underlying the variables remains the same over time. Autocorrelations ($X$ correlated with itself at different time periods and $Y$ correlated with itself at different times) are assumed to represent a first-order autoregressive model. If the stationarity and first-order autoregressive model assumptions are met, the cross-lagged correlations ($X_1 Y_2$ and $X_2 Y_1$) are compared to test for "spuriousness," i.e., to see if one person's behavior at Time 1 appears to influence the other's at Time 2. This actually may be the test of interest in dyadic interaction research. For example, if $X$ is his gaze and $Y$ is her smiling, then a stronger $X_1Y_2$ correlation than $X_2Y_1$ correlation would be suggestive of his gaze causing her smiling rather than her smiling causing his gaze.

If there is no assumption that one person's Time 1 behavior is the cause of another's Time 2 behavior but rather that two people's behaviors are covarying simultaneously (as might be the case when testing for synchrony across macroscopic time intervals), then the cross-lagged procedure is probably no longer justified. However, a variation on the Pearson-Filon test can still be used to compare synchronous correlations, i.e., to see if the relationship between $X$ and $Y$ is different at Time 1 than at Time 2 (Raghunathan, Rosenthal, & Rubin, 1993; also see Meng, Rosenthal, & Rubin, 1992, for a simple procedure for comparing correlated correlation coefficients). For example, if the correlation between two people's arousal measures is weak at Time 1 but much stronger at Time 2, it might be possible to infer that one person's arousal has "infected" the other, creating what Hatfield et al. (1994) refer to as emotional contagion.

Kenny (1979) cautions that cross-lagged panel analysis is ill-advised unless the sample size is moderate to large (75 to 300), the variables themselves are likely to change over time, correlations are at least in the moderate range (.3 or better), and measurement is reliable. Ideally, such analyses should also be replicated multiple times across different time lags, different populations, and different operationalizations of the same construct before firm conclusions about causality are drawn. These caveats place significant limitations on the use of the method. However, others have proposed modifications that may at least make this analytic strategy more appropriate for small samples (see, e.g., Dunn & Clark, 1969; Raghunathan et al., 1993).

### Repeated measures analysis of variance

The final analytic approach, repeated measures analysis, can be conducted through multiple regression and multivariate analysis of variance computer programs as well as through standard analysis of variance programs. It is an alternative to interrupted time series in examining the effects of manipulated behavioral changes over a relatively short time-span. When data are based on individual behaviors, the design entails two repeated factors: dyad membership and time. When data form a dyadic measure (perhaps based on interacts), the design reduces to the repeated factor of time. Such analyses partition variance into a between-dyads component (the pooled variance across dyads) and a within-dyads component. Additionally, these analyses can accommodate such between-dyads factors as the experimental manipulation of one partner's behavior.

In experimental studies that lack a baseline, the main effect for the manipulated factor is the direct test of mutual influence patterns. With experiments that include a baseline, an interaction between time and the manipulated factor may be the appropriate test. When statistical interactions obtain, they yield separate trendlines within each condition. With nonexperimental studies (e.g., measuring the frequency of a given type of interact as in VanLear, 1983), a main effect for time reveals whether the pattern persists over time, a main effect for dyads reveals whether different dyads display different degrees of the pattern under examination, and an interaction between dyads and time reveals whether patterns play themselves out differently across time for different dyads.

One drawback of repeated measures analyses is that they are missing the actual sequencing of behavior between individual partners over time, so that one cannot determine, for example, whether dyads initially engage in nonaccommodation and then shift into compensation or reciprocity (although means for a particular measure can be plotted for each time period and partner, allowing a visual determination of whether partners are moving in the same or opposite direction).

## UNIVARIATE OR MULTIVARIATE DATA

We have said that reciprocity and compensation are best understood by examining collections of behaviors that work in concert to convey a broad relational message such as involvement or dominance or to accomplish some other communication function such as persuasion. This implies employing designs that are multivariate in nature. Univariate analyses can be seriously misleading because reciprocation of one or more variables may be completely neutralized by compensation on others. Unfortunately, very few of the statistical techniques reviewed here can handle multiple behavioral measures simultaneously, and those that can become exceedingly complex to analyze. For example, an expanded time-series model that includes the influence of several of A's behaviors on B must include terms representing simultaneous and lagged influences for each of the behaviors of interest. Moreover, the analysis must still focus on a single criterion measure for B (unless one resorts to multivariate multiple regression, which becomes exceptionally difficult to interpret).

At this stage, we see three alternatives. One is to analyze several behaviors singly, then attempt some summary statement of the overall pattern. A detailed behavioral profile analysis might even be conducted on each dyad to uncover the alternative means by which different dyads accomplish the same resultant pattern. For example, all dyads displaying a predominantly reciprocal pattern could be scrutinized for which behaviors are most often implicated in the pattern. Such an analysis recognizes that dyadic variability can exist within the same overarching adaptation pattern.

A second alternative is to measure multiple behaviors initially then reduce them to a few behavioral composites through the use of factor analysis or reliability analysis. This would further simplify analysis and clarify what specific behaviors are associated with various adaptation patterns.

A final alternative is to replace individual behavioral measures with single global ratings. One could rate involvement, intimacy, formality, composure, or dominance in this fashion. It would then be possible to measure the individual behaviors and correlate them with the global measure so as to determine which behaviors are most responsible for the global perceptions. A limitation of these last two alternatives is that they may obscure inconsistent behaviors within a more global pattern.

## SINGLE VERSUS MULTIPLE STATISTICAL APPROACHES

Based on all of the considerations we have outlined, one choice is to employ multiple methods. This may be boon or bane, depending on one's perspective, because as we noted at the outset, each may produce different insights and lead to conflicting conclusions about whether interactants are adapting or not and in what manner. This leaves the researcher in a quandary as to which method or methods to employ.

One way to understand how statistical techniques compare is to examine empirically how the methods vary in their sensitivity to different patterns, the magnitudes of relationships they detect, their ability to detect temporal changes, and differences produced by between-dyad versus within-dyad analyses. To gain firsthand insight into our own data sets, we undertook such comparisons, reported in the next two chapters.

Based on those findings, we offer some statistical analysis recommendations at the end of Chapter 10.

## CONCLUSION

In this chapter, we have reviewed issues involved in the selection of statistical analysis methods. One factor dictating a researcher's choice is level of measurement. Different methods are available for nominal-level versus interval-level measurement. Given our own reliance on interval-level data, we have emphasized continuous data options over the categorical ones, but have noted some of the more prominent categorical procedures. The second and third distinctions are whether analyses focus on comparisons between dyads/groups or within dyads/groups and whether data are cross-sectional or longitudinal. We reviewed the most frequently used methods for conducting each of these kinds of analyses, considering along the way the advantages and disadvantages of employing Pearson product-moment correlations, intraclass correlations, canonical correlations, time-series and interrupted time-series models, cross-lagged panel analysis, and repeated measures analysis of variance. Given the complexities of interpersonal adaptation, we believe that multiple methods and multiple measures are desirable. That conclusion is bolstered by the analyses and findings presented in the next two chapters.

# Part IV

# Multimethod tests of reciprocity and compensation

# 9

## A first illustration

In Chapter 8, we noted that studies employing different statistical techniques had often produced inconsistent results, even within the same data set. Such findings raise the specter of conclusions about the presence and form of interaction adaptation patterns being tied to method. Faced with the dilemma in our own research of choosing the most appropriate and informative design and statistical analysis options, we decided to compare several methods empirically to see concretely just how much results might differ when applied to real interaction data.[1] Our conceptual comparisons led us to anticipate that rather than producing contradictory results, different methods applied to the same data set would produce complementary results but might vary in the unique insights they offered. In this chapter and the next, we report several such comparisons conducted on data from experiments employing actual dyadic interaction. We chose these data sets because of our substantive interest in the patterns that might be uncovered as well as our methodological interest in what the different statistical analyses might yield.

For our first analysis, we selected a data set from an experiment expressly featuring changes in conversational involvement and conducted within an interview context. We considered this data set a viable one for a first set of comparisons because its sample size (104 interactants, 52 dyads) was large enough to achieve adequate power for statistical tests (unlike many dyadic studies, which employ very small samples) and because its extensive set of nonverbal behaviors or perceptions that had been coded permitted numerous "replications" of the test for adaptation. Additionally, the inclusion of both a baseline period and periods following introduction of experimental manipulations meant that we could test for change and contingency – that is, assess actual reciprocity or compensation rather than just matching or complementarity.[2]

In selecting statistical analyses for comparison, we began by following Street's (1988) lead in including Pearson product-moment and intraclass correlations to assess between-dyad and within-dyad cross-sectional patterns. We also included three types of longitudinal analysis that have been used with some frequency: individual time series (conducted on each dyad to examine variability across dyads and behaviors), interrupted time-series regression (conducted on the aggregated dyads), and repeated measures analysis of variance (on the aggregated dyads).

## METHOD

The experiment was an omnibus investigation that had among its multiple objectives (a) assessing how people encode conversational involvement and arousal, (b) testing expectancy violations theory, and (c) conducting a first analysis on reciprocity and compensation (see Burgoon, Kelley et al., 1989; Burgoon, Newton et al., 1989; Burgoon et al., 1987; Coker & Burgoon, 1987). The sample, methods, and measures were summarized briefly in Chapter 5. To recap, previously unacquainted participants were paired to conduct mock interviews. After baseline interviews during which each person alternated the role of interviewer and interviewee, one person was enlisted as a confederate to greatly increase or decrease involvement during the next videotaped interview. Afterward, participants completed postinteraction ratings on their partners' credibility, attraction, and rewardingness, and 10 trained coders, working in pairs, rated confederates or their partners on behavioral subsets comprising 62 kinesic, proxemic, and vocalic percepts and behaviors.

It is the interaction behavior ratings that are the focus of the current analyses. Coders' ratings, which measured objective behaviors (e.g., number of nods, duration of speech) and subjective impressions formed after viewing the behaviors (e.g., warmth, friendliness), were reduced to a manageable set of composites and single-item measures through principal components factor analysis with varimax rotation and reliability analysis (see Table 9.1). Coders rated five 2-minute segments, two segments from the baseline interview and three from the second interview (during which confederates altered involvement level). Coders rating vocal behaviors heard only the audio track of the videotapes; those rating kinesic and proxemic behaviors saw only the video portion.

## MULTIPLE DISCRIMINANT ANALYSIS RESULTS

It may be recalled that the initial analysis of adaptation patterns on these data (Burgoon et al., 1987) classified dyads as exhibiting reciprocity, compensation, or nonaccommodation on the basis of the directionality and size of participants' changes in involvement relative to confederates' changes. Results revealed that confederate involvement level interacted with participant gender such that in the high-involvement condition, most men showed no change, while a plurality of women compensated (i.e., reduced involvement); in the low-involvement condition, most men compensated (i.e., increased involvement), whereas most women reciprocated (i.e., decreased involvement). Overall, women decreased involvement more so than the men. Given that the women began the interactions at a higher level of involvement (female $M = 5.66$, male $M = 5.42$), the patterns in both groups tended to reflect regression toward the mean – that is, toward a moderate level of involvement. This interpretation was bolstered by a near significant main effect for involvement showing that subjects tended to reciprocate decreases and compensate increases in involvement. The conclusion drawn was that moderate levels of involvement are preferable to extreme ones and that men and women will both gravitate toward this norm. Additionally, reward level had some impact on patterns such that those interacting with negative-valence confederates were less inclined to adapt.

Although these results were provocative, in some respects the MDA put the cart before the horse in that the dyads were assigned to one of three interaction patterns based on rather arbitrary criteria rather than first determining empirically which patterns were most evident and would meet statistical significance requirements. Thus, the MDA would have been more appropriate for use after first testing interaction patterns, then using MDA to assess what exogenous factors (such as communicator sex) influence the interaction patterns. Furthermore, only a single criterion of kinesic/proxemic involvement was tested. The remaining analyses to be reported here thus represent not only the more appropriate starting point for assessing adaptation but also a more comprehensive approach.

## PEARSON PRODUCT-MOMENT CORRELATIONS

Pearson product-moment correlations between confederates and partners were computed for the baseline time periods, averaged together, and for the manipulation time periods, averaged together. As a between-dyads analysis, positive correlations indicate that highly involved interactants have highly involved partners and uninvolved interactants have

Table 9.1. Means, Pearson product-moment correlations, intraclass correlations (and standard deviations for each time period) for subject and confederate nonverbal measures during the baseline and manipulation periods

| | Combined baseline | | | | Low involvement | | | | High involvement | | | |
|---|---|---|---|---|---|---|---|---|---|---|---|---|
| | Sub M | Conf M | $r$ | $r_I$ | Sub M | Conf M | $r$ | $r_I$ | Sub M | Conf M | $r$ | $r_I$ |
| **Kinesics/proxemics** | | | | | | | | | | | | |
| Involvement | 5.60 | 5.41 | .37* | .35* | 5.25 | 3.70 | .25 | .20 | 5.30 | 5.86 | −.04 | −.04 |
| | (.72) | (.80) | | | (.62) | (1.14) | | | (.77) | (.83) | | |
| | (.76) | (.87) | | | (.72) | (1.29) | | | (.74) | (.85) | | |
| | | | | | (.77) | (1.33) | | | (.90) | (.96) | | |
| Orientation/ gaze | 5.51 | 5.69 | .29* | .34* | 5.43 | 4.78 | .47* | .36 | 5.59 | 5.99 | .02 | .02 |
| | (.86) | (.88) | | | (.73) | (1.46) | | | (1.05) | (.64) | | |
| | (.96) | (.89) | | | (.75) | (1.75) | | | (1.02) | (.65) | | |
| | | | | | (.87) | (1.60) | | | (.95) | (.66) | | |
| Lean | 3.80 | 4.09 | .07 | .08 | 3.63 | 3.25 | −.14 | −.14 | 3.65 | 4.40 | .18 | .18 |
| | (.99) | (1.16) | | | (.94) | (.98) | | | (1.27) | (1.15) | | |
| | (1.13) | (1.15) | | | (.80) | (.97) | | | (1.33) | (1.29) | | |
| | | | | | (.92) | (1.04) | | | (1.27) | (1.27) | | |
| Facial pleasantness | 5.04 | 4.86 | .12 | .73* | 4.55 | 3.92 | .26 | .26 | 4.62 | 5.15 | .24 | .24 |
| | (.89) | (1.04) | | | (1.11) | (1.19) | | | (.93) | (.94) | | |
| | (.94) | (1.19) | | | (1.05) | (1.17) | | | (1.03) | (1.07) | | |
| | | | | | (1.05) | (1.23) | | | (1.16) | (1.27) | | |

| | | | | | | | | | | | | |
|---|---|---|---|---|---|---|---|---|---|---|---|---|
| Facial animation | 5.10 (.74) (.83) | 4.60 (.92) (.99) | .16 | .16 | 4.69 (.96) (.89) (.96) | 3.47 (.97) (1.27) (1.20) | .36 | .34 | 5.11 (.80) (.85) (1.00) | 5.53 (.94) (1.11) (1.10) | .21 | .21 |
| Gestural animation | 4.01 (1.28) (1.27) | 3.48 (1.40) (1.43) | −.05 | −.05 | 3.76 (1.39) (1.25) (1.18) | 3.20 (1.57) (1.43) (1.66) | .70* | .49* | 3.76 (1.31) (1.43) (1.20) | 4.60 (1.44) (1.37) (1.43) | .69* | .44* |
| Arousal | 5.22 (.78) (.75) | 5.16 (.74) (.86) | .16 | .16 | 4.86 (.65) (.71) (.83) | 4.36 (.96) (1.07) (1.10) | .10 | .09 | 5.11 (.86) (.85) (.89) | 5.53 (.87) (.82) (.86) | .04 | .04 |
| Random movement | 5.36 (1.13) (1.19) | 5.48 (1.24) (1.32) | .10 | .09 | 5.16 (1.20) (.95) (1.15) | 4.28 (1.59) (1.85) (1.72) | .27 | .29 | 5.21 (1.27) (1.39) (1.42) | 5.24 (1.46) (1.37) (1.41) | .26 | .28 |
| Postural relaxation | 3.90 (.78) (.76) | 3.84 (.92) (.90) | .05 | .06 | 4.04 (.80) (.77) (.77) | 4.48 (1.29) (1.36) (1.32) | .32 | .27 | 4.17 (.66) (.67) (.61) | 4.39 (.68) (.58) (.70) | .13 | .13 |
| Self-adaptors | 5.67 (1.36) (1.46) (1.54) | 5.80 (1.46) (1.56) | .05 | .05 | 5.36 (1.68) (1.52) (1.54) | 4.66 (1.80) (1.53) (1.89) | .35 | .35 | 5.10 (1.67) (1.79) (1.74) | 5.33 (1.78) (1.71) (1.69) | .13 | .13 |

Table 9.1, cont'd.

| | Combined baseline | | | | Low involvement | | | | High involvement | | | |
|---|---|---|---|---|---|---|---|---|---|---|---|---|
| | Sub M | Conf M | r | $r_I$ | Sub M | Conf M | r | $r_I$ | Sub M | Conf M | r | $r_I$ |
| Object-adaptors | 5.98<br>(1.25)<br>(1.43) | 6.40<br>(1.36)<br>(1.30) | -.05 | -.05 | 5.46<br>(1.76)<br>(1.72)<br>(1.56) | 6.00<br>(1.26)<br>(1.45)<br>(1.67) | -.26 | -.25 | 5.77<br>(1.62)<br>(1.70)<br>(1.64) | 6.58<br>(1.03)<br>(1.04)<br>(.88) | -.04 | -.03 |
| **Vocalics** | | | | | | | | | | | | |
| Involvement | 4.13<br>(.61)<br>(.60) | 4.12<br>(.48)<br>(.51) | .09 | .12 | 3.89<br>(.63)<br>(.56)<br>(.63) | 3.84<br>(.51)<br>(.50)<br>(.61) | .01 | .00 | 4.04<br>(.54)<br>(.59)<br>(.61) | 4.33<br>(.42)<br>(.34)<br>(.36) | -.17 | -.22 |
| Fluency | 3.99<br>(.84)<br>(.80) | 4.12<br>(.51)<br>(.50) | .11 | .10 | 4.05<br>(.81)<br>(.87)<br>(1.04) | 4.08<br>(.70)<br>(.64)<br>(.72) | -.11 | -.17 | 4.07<br>(.63)<br>(.66)<br>(.90) | 4.16<br>(.67)<br>(.56)<br>(.65) | .10 | .12 |
| Relaxation | 4.54<br>(.42)<br>(.40) | 4.60<br>(.30)<br>(.30) | .04 | .02 | 4.67<br>(.39)<br>(.42)<br>(.38) | 4.56<br>(.31)<br>(.28)<br>(.25) | .01 | -.02 | 4.65<br>(.27)<br>(.32)<br>(.29) | 4.79<br>(.34)<br>(.35)<br>(.33) | .02 | .06 |
| Attentiveness | 4.53<br>(.43)<br>(.49) | 4.54<br>(.38)<br>(.37) | .25* | .24 | 4.47<br>(.35)<br>(.43)<br>(.58) | 4.14<br>(.69)<br>(.71)<br>(.68) | .05 | .07 | 4.47<br>(.46)<br>(.41)<br>(.46) | 4.61<br>(.30)<br>(.41)<br>(.41) | .18 | .28 |

| | | | | | | | | | | | | |
|---|---|---|---|---|---|---|---|---|---|---|---|---|
| Intensity | 3.75 (.86) (.76) | 3.81 (.62) (.61) | −.01 | −.02 | 3.64 (.62) (.61) (.58) | 4.65 (.59) (.53) (.61) | .15 | −.19 | 3.67 (.78) (.79) (.71) | 4.07 (.51) (.50) (.56) | −.10 | −.11 |
| Pauses/ latencies | 3.85 (.57) (.57) | 3.74 (.40) (.36) | .07 | −.06 | 3.73 (.45) (.58) (.49) | 3.64 (.43) (.47) (.52) | .01 | −.07 | 3.74 (.52) (.60) (.58) | 3.90 (.32) (.47) (.43) | .48* | .55* |
| Loudness | 3.67 (.93) (.81) | 3.76 (.85) (.78) | −.07 | −.08 | 3.77 (.87) (.86) (.97) | 3.67 (.87) (.79) (.96) | −.24 | −.27 | 3.59 (.75) (.78) (.71) | 3.77 (.59) (.68) (.89) | −.29 | −.35 |
| Tempo | 3.83 (.77) (.76) | 4.02 (.71) (.77) | −.11 | −.13 | 3.84 (.80) (.92) (.92) | 3.81 (.74) (.82) (.79) | .05 | .08 | 3.69 (.69) (.66) (.69) | 4.07 (.77) (.69) (.55) | −.19 | −.28 |
| Tempo variety | 4.14 (.81) (.72) | 4.24 (.65) (.61) | .09 | .04 | 4.06 (.86) (.88) (.74) | 4.02 (.64) (.63) (.75) | −.14 | −.22 | 4.03 (.64) (.79) (.72) | 4.29 (.59) (.52) (.54) | .10 | .13 |
| Pitch | 4.14 (.69) (.70) | 4.12 (.52) (.53) | −.18 | −.20 | 4.17 (.64) (.73) (.59) | 4.01 (.55) (.58) (.55) | −.14 | −.24 | 4.16 (.74) (.69) (.72) | 4.13 (.49) (.60) (.51) | −.07 | −.07 |

Table 9.1, cont'd.

| | Combined baseline | | | | Low involvement | | | | High involvement | | | |
|---|---|---|---|---|---|---|---|---|---|---|---|---|
| | Sub M | Conf M | r | $r_1$ | Sub M | Conf M | r | $r_1$ | Sub M | Conf M | r | $r_1$ |
| Pitch variety | 4.15 | 4.22 | -.08 | -.09 | 4.07 | 3.93 | .09 | .09 | 4.01 | 4.35 | -.17 | -.22 |
| | (.67) | (.59) | | | (.76) | (.69) | | | (.43) | (.64) | | |
| | (.71) | (.59) | | | (.80) | (.56) | | | (.70) | (.42) | | |
| | | | | | (.76) | (.82) | | | (.65) | (.54) | | |
| Expressivity | 3.98 | 4.11 | -.05 | -.11 | 3.88 | 3.86 | -.24 | -.27 | 3.95 | 4.27 | .12 | .14 |
| | (.70) | (.61) | | | (.80) | (.58) | | | (.74) | (.58) | | |
| | (.71) | (.64) | | | (.79) | (.52) | | | (.70) | (.60) | | |
| | | | | | (.72) | (.49) | | | (.64) | (.55) | | |

*$p < .05$

Note: The means for the baseline are averaged across the first two time periods. The standard deviations for the two time periods appear in parentheses beneath the subject and confederate means. The means for the manipulation period are averaged across the remaining three time periods. Standard deviations, in parentheses beneath the means, are for each of the time periods.

uninvolved partners; negative correlations indicate that involved interactants have uninvolved partners and vice versa.

Although previous literature suggests interactants should begin
adapting to each other very early in an interaction, a conservative interpretation of the baseline correlations is that they reflect the matching or
complementarity that typifies normal conversation, rather than reciprocity or compensation, because of the indeterminacy of who might
be influencing whom and the possibility that initial correlations partly
reflect interactants orienting to the situation rather than adapting to each
other. Given the evidence that adaptation is rapid and fairly automatic,
these initial correlations may indeed reflect true adaptation. Comparatively, however, correlations during the manipulation phase are
even better bets for reflecting influence exerted by confederates on their
partners, inasmuch as confederates initiated changes and then maintained their new involvement level throughout the remainder of the
interaction. Any significant correlations therefore may be more reason-
ably interpreted as reciprocity or compensation. Correlations were computed separately for the low-involvement and high-involvement conditions and compared to baseline correlations to see if increased
involvement by confederates precipitated reciprocity and decreased involvement precipitated compensation (as per EVT predictions for high-
reward confederates).

### Baseline interview results

Table 9.1 shows the product-moment correlations, intraclass correlations, means, and standard deviations. Before looking at the correlations, it is instructive to look at the means and standard deviations
during the baseline interview. The means should be highly similar inasmuch as the confederate role had not yet been assigned. For most
measures, this turns out to be the case – the means are within .2 of each
other on a seven-point scale. In the cases where the standard deviations
are also small – for example, on vocal fluency and vocal relaxation –
there is little likelihood of a significant correlation emerging, despite the
nearly identical means, because of the restricted variability across
dyads. When this kind of data pattern arises – and it is probably common when interactants are governed tightly by situational norms and
constraints – interpreting these low correlations as lack of similarity in
behavior would be erroneous. However, where standard deviations are
much higher, such an interpretation might be justified. This illustrates
one of the anomalies of relying on correlations to verify matching when

behaviors are overly similar and homogeneous. To draw valid conclusions, correlations must be interpreted in light of the means and standard deviations of the associated measures.

With this caveat in mind, let us look at the correlations, skipping those instances where significant correlations could not have obtained because of low variances. We see limited matching and primarily on kinesic/proxemic variables. The "big picture" is best represented by the two global measures. Global kinesic/proxemic involvement shows matching ($r = .35$) but vocalic involvement does not. Among the other kinesic/proxemic variables, correlations range from $-.04$ to $.35$ (average $r = .11$), with significant correlations emerging only for body orientation/gaze. The vocalic measures range from $-.18$ to $.25$ (average $r = .01$), with a significant correlation only for vocalic attentiveness. If it can be assumed that initial interactions are norm governed, these weak and often nonsignificant initial matching patterns may be attributed to participants adhering to polite conversation and interview norms or responding similarly to the unfamiliar setting, presence of audiovisual equipment, and interview task demands. At the same time, we might expect interactants to entrain somewhat to each other's conversation patterns (see Kendon, 1990), resulting in some evidence of matching. This characterization fits the pattern that emerged. Alternatively, the same results could obtain if individuals were highly variable in their interaction styles and nonaccommodative to one another. Against this backdrop, introducing systematic variation by one interactant becomes enlightening. It reveals whether initiated changes by one individual elicit similar changes by the other. If individuals are truly maintaining their own consistent style and not adapting, we should see very little evidence of association – either reciprocal or compensatory – between interactants following one member's change.

### Manipulation interview results

Again, the correlational analyses yielded mostly reciprocal relationships, with stronger effect sizes under low involvement than high involvement and again primarily on kinesic/proxemic rather than vocalic measures. Under low involvement, nearly all correlations were again positive (average kinesic/proxemic $r = .22$, average vocalic $r = -.04$), indicative of matching or reciprocity. Significant relationships emerged on orientation/gaze and gestural animation. Under high involvement, the pattern was weaker (average kinesic/proxemic $r = .16$, vocalic $r =$

.00) and the only significant correlation to emerge was on gestural animation.

The gestural relationships would seem most amenable to a reciprocity interpretation in that the correspondence between partners was not present during the baseline but emerged with the advent of confederate "leadership." These correlations can be compared statistically by modifying the Pearson-Filon test from cross-lagged panel analysis to test the synchronous correlations (see Chapter 8). (Although these correlations in cross-lagged analysis are intended to demonstrate stationarity, in our case, we expect the correlations to change from one time period to the next.) A problem with applying this test is that the small sample sizes within the low- and high-involvement groups mean substantial differences are needed before the comparison reaches conventional levels of statistical significance. As a consequence, almost none of the comparisons are statistically significant, even though the correlations appear to be markedly different.

One exception is the gestural animation correlations. Both gestural animation comparisons were significant, low-involvement $z = 5.14$, $p <$ .05; high-involvement $z = 4.95$, $p < .05$.[3] Thus, it seems legitimate to conclude that some influence is taking place, although we cannot say unequivocally that the influence is all unidirectional (i.e., solely from the confederate to the subject and not from the subject to the confederate). To test the directionality of influence would require comparison of the cross-lagged correlations themselves, but since the assumption of stationarity is violated, the test would not be valid for these data.

Interpreting the orientation/gaze correlation is more complex but also suggestive of adaptation. Matching (and possibly reciprocity) was already present during the baseline and continued through the manipulation period in the low-involvement condition. The fact that it wasn't sustained in the high-involvement condition implies that, by comparison, interviewers were more responsive to interviewee behavior in the low-involvement condition. The means also reveal that confederate interviewees reduced their gaze and direct orientation after introduction of the manipulation and that interviewers did likewise. This offers some corroboration of a reciprocity interpretation. However, the statistical test of differences was not significant.

One final way in which conditions could be compared statistically to draw inferences about adaptation is to compare the high-involvement correlations to the low-involvement ones using $z$-tests to compare $z$-transformed $r$'s. Whereas the comparisons of baseline to manipulation period we have described are between correlated $r$'s, these tests are between independent $r$'s. Although it is evident from a quick perusal of the table that few correlations differed enough to justify a test, two exceptions were orientation/gaze, $z = 1.65$, $p < .05$, one-tailed, and pauses/latencies, $z = 1.73$, $p < .05$, one-tailed. These comparisons indicate that subjects interacting with high-involvement confederates were less likely to reciprocate partners' facing and gaze patterns but more likely to reciprocate their pausing than were those interacting with low-involvement confederates. Perhaps because the baseline was already fairly immediate, it was more difficult to adapt to partner immediacy changes in the high- than the low-involvement condition, but there was room to shorten response latencies to converge toward those of the high-involvement partner. These results are suggestive of the directions of adaptation that are most likely and the invisible boundaries that might limit extremes of adaptation.

## Summary and interpretations

Overall, the results offer anemic evidence of matching and reciprocity. The modest correlations during the baseline might be interpreted as evidence of entrainment effects. The research and theorizing on interactional synchrony and behavioral matching, especially during interviews, leads us to expect some degree of convergence among interactants in their conversational behaviors. To the extent that individuals were in fact orienting to each other's communication, we would have true reciprocity.

However, an equally plausible alternative is that interactants were orienting primarily to social norms for appropriate, polite behavior during initial interactions and interviews. If the assumption, featured in several interaction adaptation theories, is correct that initial interactions are norm governed, then we should expect all interactants to exhibit fairly similar behaviors within the range of acceptable involvement. Such adherence to norms would mean relative invariance within and between dyads, resulting in weak matching or nonsignificant correlations. This is what obtained. Similarly, we might interpret the initial matching on vocal attentiveness behaviors, which tend to be related to anxiety, as due to the influence of the experimental situation and task. This again would be a case of matching being induced by external factors rather than partner influence and would be spurious evidence of reciprocity.

A third alternative is that the weak pattern of findings represents nonaccommodation due to high consistency within individuals (see, e.g., Mahl, 1987) and high variability across individuals in their interaction styles. It is possible, for example, that most vocalic behaviors, apart from those concerned with the pacing of conversation (e.g., pauses), are tied closely to an individual's consistent communication style and not readily adaptable to a partner. Similarly, it could be argued that vocalic cues are less easily monitored and therefore less easily changed in a deliberate fashion. Comparatively, kinesics and proxemics might be more readily manipulated and monitored due to visual primacy (Burgoon, 1985). As a consequence, we might conclude that people do not or cannot readily adjust their vocal patterns to the same extent as they do kinesic and proxemic ones.

These rival interpretations underscore the need to introduce systematic changes in one person's behavior to see if the partner's behavior then follows suit. If individuals or certain nonverbal behaviors are generally resistant to adaptation, then adjustments by a confederate should not elicit correspondent changes by the partner. Moreover, divergence by confederates should weaken any prior associations between confederate and subject behavior that arose due to norm adherence or other contextual cues.

A final alternative is that the results may also have been attenuated by measurement problems, experimental procedures, and low power. Vocalic coding often is less reliable than kinesic coding (see Baesler & Burgoon, 1988). That was certainly the case with these data. Coders had difficulty making fine distinctions among levels of the vocal cues. This may have contributed to the lack of significant relationships on vocal behaviors.

The use of an interview format also may have confounded the observed patterns. Participants initially exhibited high levels of kinesic/proxemic involvement (as indicated by the baseline means), a pattern that is common during initial interviews with strangers, especially when being observed by others. This may have created a ceiling effect: Subjects may have been unable to sustain or increase involvement significantly in the high-involvement condition. Any drift toward a more comfortable level of interaction would have resulted in a regression toward the mean. The interview context may have further influenced participants' behavior by conjuring up "interview" scripts that guide behavior. The interview task itself also may have been cognitively demanding, causing subjects to be more focused on their own performance than that of the partner and therefore less attuned to the partner's interaction style.

Finally, the small sample size within the two involvement conditions resulted in underpowered analyses. Of the 46 correlations computed within the involvement conditions, only 5 were statistically significant. Yet several of the obtained correlations were in the .20 to .30 range, thereby qualifying as medium effect sizes. These would have been significant with a larger sample size. The $z$-test comparisons between baseline and manipulation period correlations were afflicted by the same low power. Judging on the basis of effect sizes alone, then, we would have concluded that there is some correspondence between interactants' nonverbal behaviors.

The upshot of this analysis is that the Pearson correlations were suggestive of some adaptation occurring, primarily in the form of matching or reciprocity. The effect sizes were more supportive than were the actual significance tests, a result that might be expected in other studies of a like nature and sample size. However, were we to rely on these correlation analyses alone, we might conclude that adaptation is far less prevalent than previously thought and we would be unable to infer causality or direction of influence between partners where adaptation appears to be present.

## INTRACLASS CORRELATIONS

Recall that intraclass correlations are within-dyad analyses that contrast variance between dyads to variance within dyads. They are interpreted as showing the degree of homogeneity or similarity in dyad members' behaviors. The analysis plan paralleled that for the Pearsons: All dyads were included in the baseline correlations and separate correlations were computed within the two involvement conditions for the manipulation portion of the interviews.

### Baseline interview results

As shown in Table 9.1, many of the intraclass correlations were similar to the Pearson product-moment correlations, a striking exception being facial pleasantness. This similarity can occur when the analysis is based on dyads (rather than larger sampling units such as groups) and means and variances are the same. Under this special circumstance, the Pearson $r$ and $r_I$ become arithmetically identical (Haggard, 1958). Nevertheless, conceptually they are designed to make different kinds of statements. In general, the positive intraclass correlations should be interpreted as indicating greater similarity between partners than between dyads (i.e., the within-dyad variance was less than the between-dyad variance) and the negative ones as showing more variability within dyads than between them. The kinesic/proxemic correlations, ranging from −.03 to .73, fit a modest matching interpretation, whereas the vocalic correlations, ranging from −.20 to .24, show much greater variability and weaker relationships.

### Manipulation interview results

Correlations averaged across the three manipulation time periods likewise produced little evidence of association between subjects' and confederates' kinesic behaviors. Following the manipulation, partners continued to show greater kinesic/proxemic similarity to partners than dyads were to each other, but this pattern was more pronounced in the low-involvement condition (absolute average $r_I = .29$) than in the high-involvement condition (absolute average $r_I = .18$). Vocalic patterns remained highly variable and evidenced more negative relationships than among the kinesic/proxemic variables.

### Summary and interpretations

Overall, only six significant relationships emerged, five of them among the kinesic/proxemic variables (baseline global involvement, baseline body orientation/gaze, baseline facial pleasantness, and manipulation gestural animation in both involvement conditions), and one among vocalic measures (manipulation pauses/latencies). The fact that few behaviors exhibited a dramatic increase in the magnitudes of their correlations from the baseline period to the manipulation period casts doubt on interpreting any of the relationships found in this analysis as exhibiting true conversational adaptation resulting from the confederate's change in behavior. Rather, it would be more appropriate to interpret the few significant findings as evidence of matching. However, it must also be acknowledged that in both these and the Pearson correlation analyses, a lack of between- as well as within-dyads variation may have attenuated relationships. Correlations are often weakened under restricted range conditions. Vocal characteristics tended to have even less variation than kinesics across their respective behaviors (as revealed by the standard deviations in Table 9.1). This low variability, as well as the discrepancy in variability between subjects' and confederates' behavior, may have further confounded analysis and interpretation of the results. Whether this was due to participants enacting a restricted range of behaviors or coders' inability to discriminate among behaviors is unclear. But it signals one difficulty associated with reliance on the Pearson and intraclass correlation analyses.

## INDIVIDUAL TIME-SERIES CORRELATIONS

The individual time-series analyses computed on each dyad were undertaken to demonstrate how decomposing patterns by dyad, channel (visual, auditory), and behavior can reveal important patterns overlooked by other aggregate techniques. Although the most appropriate approach to conducting individual dyad analyses would be to use a time-series regression analysis that adjusts for autocorrelation in the data, the very small number of time periods involved (5) and the resultant low power attending these analyses justified the use of simple Pearson correlations computed within each dyad across the five time periods (D. Kenny, personal communication, 1992). Following the logic of meta-analytic techniques for combining effect sizes (Rosenthal, 1984), the individual $r$s were transformed to $z$-scores using Fisher's $z$-transformation (see Hayes, 1963). These were averaged across dyads within a given condition and tested against zero using the one-sample $z$-test. Absolute correlations are also reported to show the sheer amount of adaptation occurring, regardless of direction, but no statistical tests exist for these. Results appear in Table 9.2.

### Comparisons by dyad and condition

Overall, all dyads exhibited some form of adaptation, but amount and form differed considerably. The only significant correlations were kinesic/proxemic involvement and facial pleasantness and only within the low-involvement condition. The absolute correlations, however, suggest that adaptation took place on all variables under both high and low involvement, with one exception (vocal expressivity under high involvement). The contrast between the absolute correlations and signed correlations may be due to some dyads matching and others complementing, such that evidence of adaptation in the raw correlations is canceled out through averaging positive and negative correlations. This becomes most evident if one looks at Table 9.3, where positive

Table 9.2. *Time-series correlations and Fisher-transformed z-tests on nonverbal measures*

| | Low involvement | | High involvement | |
|---|---|---|---|---|
| | *r* | *z*-test | *r* | *z*-test |
| **I. RAW CORRELATIONS** | | | | |
| **Kinesics/proxemics** | | | | |
| Involvement | .37 | 2.96* | −.03 | .11 |
| Facial orientation/gaze | .09 | .76 | −.10 | −.72 |
| Lean | .02 | .26 | −.07 | −.73 |
| Facial pleasantness | .43 | 3.36* | −.08 | −.60 |
| Facial animation | .28 | 1.91 | .12 | 1.20 |
| Gestural animation | −.07 | −.35 | −.04 | −.33 |
| Arousal | .18 | 1.80 | −.12 | −.77 |
| Random movement | −.02 | −.30 | .25 | 1.72 |
| Postural relaxation | .06 | .36 | .07 | .50 |
| Self-adaptors | .06 | .39 | −.03 | −.07 |
| Object-adaptors | −.08 | .53 | .16 | 1.23 |
| **Vocalics** | | | | |
| Involvement | .28 | 1.67 | .06 | .61 |
| Pitch | .05 | .36 | .04 | .59 |
| Loudness | .20 | 1.39 | −.05 | .57 |
| Relaxation | .09 | .21 | .08 | .23 |
| Attentiveness | .10 | .52 | −.06 | .43 |
| Intensity | .02 | .14 | .11 | 1.60 |
| Pauses/latencies | .12 | 1.22 | .18 | 1.16 |
| Fluency | .09 | .60 | .12 | .76 |
| Expressivity | .10 | .79 | −.04 | .19 |
| **II. ABSOLUTE CORRELATIONS** | | | | |
| **Kinesics/proxemics** | | | | |
| Involvement | .61 | | .55 | |
| Random movement | .55 | | .58 | |
| Facial orientation/gaze | .51 | | .50 | |
| Lean | .49 | | .42 | |
| Facial pleasantness | .63 | | .43 | |
| Facial animation | .53 | | .58 | |
| Gestural animation | .47 | | .46 | |
| Arousal | .52 | | .60 | |
| Postural relaxation | .56 | | .43 | |

Table 9.2, cont'd.

|  | Low involvement | High involvement |
|---|---|---|
|  | r | r |
| Self-adaptors | .49 | .40 |
| Object-adaptors | .51 | .41 |
| **Vocalics** |  |  |
| Involvement | .55 | .47 |
| Pitch | .50 | .39 |
| Loudness | .46 | .50 |
| Relaxation | .40 | .57 |
| Attentiveness | .50 | .49 |
| Intensity | .44 | .58 |
| Pauses/latencies | .46 | .53 |
| Fluency | .41 | .38 |
| Expressivity | .49 | .36 |

$*p < .05$

*Note:* The raw correlations represent the average correlations across dyads, taking direction (sign) into account. The absolute correlations ignore signs and therefore represent overall correlation, negative or positive, between pairs.

correlations of .50 or greater have been designated with a "+" and negative correlations of .50 or greater have been designated with a "–." (The .50 criterion was chosen because it represents a large effect size and serves to focus attention on the strongest patterns of association. In light of the small number of observations per dyad, the sheer number of large effect sizes is remarkable in itself.) The number of positive and negative entries were also summed to form ratios within the high- and low-involvement conditions across dyads, channels, and behaviors. This latter analysis should be treated as a heuristic for demonstrating how decomposing patterns by dyad, behavior, and channel (visual, auditory) can reveal important patterns overlooked by other aggregate techniques. In many respects, this analysis resembles what descriptive researchers might do in the absence of employing statistical analysis.

In overview, the table shows a large number of both positive and negative correlations, indicating that all dyads were adapting to one another but often in opposite ways across behaviors. The net result was nonsignificant raw correlations averaging .28 in the low-involvement condition and .06 in the high-involvement condition but average absolute correlations of .55 and .47 respectively. The global measures indicate that higher proportions of dyads matched than complemented one another except in the high-involvement condition on kinesic/proxemic involvement. If each dyad's proportion of matching to complementary adjustments is considered across all measures, in fact, the majority of dyads (52%, $n = 27$) demonstrated more matching than complementarity. But a sizable minority (31%, $n = 16$) demonstrated more complementarity than matching, indicating that both patterns were present in notable numbers in this sample.[4]

There was evidence of more adaptation occurring in the low-involvement condition (mean number of adjustments = 10.25) than in the high-involvement condition (mean number of adjustments = 9.50). This may have been due to a greater latitude in which to adapt behaviors in the low-involvement than in the high-involvement condition. By channel, 63% of vocalic behaviors had higher proportions of matching, while only 23% produced higher proportions of complementarity. A similar though less marked trend appeared in the kinesic/proxemic channel: Those predominantly matching (52%) outnumbered those predominantly complementing (35%). The remainder displayed an equal amount of both. However, dyads were not uniform in their response. That is, a dyad might match kinesically but complement vocalically or vice versa.

Although it might be tempting to classify dyads as matching or complementary on the basis of a single aggregate measure (e.g., Burgoon et al., 1987), a single behavior (e.g., Cappella & Planalp, 1981), or a subset of behaviors, Table 9.3 reveals the fallacy of this strategy. Consider dyad 24, which exhibited more matching than complementarity (5:3) in the kinesic/proxemic channels but all complementarity in the vocalic channel (0:4). The net result might be to label the dyad as complementary even though the partners demonstrated more matching kinesically and proxemically. Dyad 12 is a similar case: All kinesic/proxemic changes were complementary (0:8), while vocalic adjustments matched more than complemented (2:1). The net result might be to label the dyad as complementary even though the interactants demonstrated more matching in the vocalic channel. Similarly, one might classify a dyad as matching based on mutual silence when the dyad simultaneously compensated on other behaviors such as gaze, self-adaptors, and postural shifts, for a net compensatory effect. These examples illustrate that the

Table 9.3. *Significant compensation and reciprocity patterns in dyad-by-dyad analysis*

| | | | | | | | | | | | | | | | Vocalics | | | | | | | | | | | | | | | |
|---|---|---|---|---|---|---|---|---|---|---|---|---|---|---|---|---|---|---|---|---|---|---|---|---|---|---|---|---|---|---|
| Low involvement | 1 | 2 | 4 | 7 | 9 | 10 | 11 | 15 | 16 | 18 | 22 | 24 | 26 | 27 | 29 | 31 | 33 | 34 | 35 | 36 | 37 | 38 | 40 | 41 | 42 | 46 | 48 | 52 | +/− |
| Global involvement | | + | | | + | | − | | + | + | + | | + | + | − | − | | | + | | − | | − | + | | + | | | 12/5 |
| Pitch | | | | | | | | − | + | + | + | − | | | | | | | + | − | + | + | − | | − | | | + | 6/5 |
| Loudness | + | − | | | + | | | + | + | | | | + | + | | + | | + | + | | + | + | | | | | − | + | 10/3 |
| Relaxation | | | | | + | | | | | | − | | | | | | | | | + | − | + | + | + | | | + | | 6/2 |
| Attentiveness | | + | − | | | − | | + | | | | − | | | + | | | − | | + | − | | + | − | | + | + | + | 7/5 |
| Intensity | | | | − | − | − | − | − | + | | | | + | | + | | | | + | + | + | + | − | | | | | | 6/7 |
| Pauses/latencies | | − | + | + | | − | − | + | − | | − | | | | | | + | | + | + | + | | + | + | − | | + | | 8/6 |
| Fluency | | | − | + | | | | − | | | + | − | + | | + | | − | − | | + | | − | | + | | | | | 5/4 |
| Expressiveness | + | | | | | | | + | + | | + | | | | − | + | − | + | + | + | + | | − | | − | + | + | | 10/4 |
| Total (+/−) | $\frac{3}{0}$ | $\frac{2}{2}$ | $\frac{2}{1}$ | $\frac{1}{1}$ | $\frac{2}{1}$ | $\frac{0}{2}$ | $\frac{0}{3}$ | $\frac{3}{2}$ | $\frac{4}{1}$ | $\frac{4}{1}$ | $\frac{4}{2}$ | $\frac{0}{4}$ | $\frac{4}{0}$ | $\frac{2}{0}$ | $\frac{4}{3}$ | $\frac{2}{1}$ | $\frac{1}{1}$ | $\frac{2}{2}$ | $\frac{4}{0}$ | $\frac{5}{1}$ | $\frac{4}{2}$ | $\frac{3}{1}$ | $\frac{2}{5}$ | $\frac{4}{1}$ | $\frac{0}{2}$ | $\frac{3}{1}$ | $\frac{2}{1}$ | $\frac{3}{0}$ | $\frac{70}{41}$ |

| High involvement | 3 | 5 | 6 | 8 | 12 | 13 | 14 | 17 | 19 | 20 | 21 | 23 | 25 | 28 | 30 | 32 | 39 | 43 | 44 | 45 | 47 | 49 | 50 | 51 | +/− |
|---|---|---|---|---|---|---|---|---|---|---|---|---|---|---|---|---|---|---|---|---|---|---|---|---|---|
| Global involvement | | + | | | | | + | + | − | | | − | − | − | | + | + | | − | | + | | | + | 7/5 |
| Pitch | | | | | | | | | | | | | | | + | | − | | − | | | − | + | | 2/3 |
| Loudness | | | | − | + | − | − | | + | − | | + | + | | | + | | | | | | − | | − | 5/6 |
| Relaxation | | + | + | + | | | + | | | | + | − | + | − | + | − | − | + | | − | | + | − | + | 10/6 |
| Attentiveness | + | | | | | + | | | − | + | | − | | + | − | − | − | | | | | | + | | 5/5 |
| Intensity | + | + | − | | − | | | − | | − | + | | | + | − | + | + | | | − | | + | + | | 8/6 |
| Pauses/latencies | + | + | + | + | + | | | − | | − | | − | | | + | + | | | | − | | | | + | 8/4 |
| Fluency | + | + | | | | | | + | | + | | | | | | | | + | | − | + | − | | | 6/2 |
| Expressiveness | + | | | | | − | | | − | − | | + | | | | | | | | | + | + | | | 4/3 |
| Total (+/−) | 5/0 | 5/0 | 2/1 | 2/1 | 2/1 | 1/2 | 2/1 | 2/2 | 1/3 | 2/4 | 2/0 | 2/4 | 2/1 | 2/2 | 3/2 | 4/2 | 2/3 | 2/0 | 0/2 | 0/4 | 3/0 | 3/3 | 3/1 | 3/1 | 55/40 |

Table 9.3, cont'd.

| | Kinesics/proxemics | | | | | | | | | | | | | | | | | | | | | | | | | | | | |
|---|---|---|---|---|---|---|---|---|---|---|---|---|---|---|---|---|---|---|---|---|---|---|---|---|---|---|---|---|---|
| | 1 | 2 | 4 | 7 | 9 | 10 | 11 | 15 | 16 | 18 | 22 | 24 | 26 | 27 | 29 | 31 | 33 | 34 | 35 | 36 | 37 | 38 | 40 | 41 | 42 | 46 | 48 | 52 | +/− |
| Global involvement | + | − | + | + | + | + | | | + | | | | | + | + | + | + | | | | + | + | + | + | − | | − | + | 14/3 |
| Orientation/gaze | + | | + | − | − | | − | | | | | | | | + | | | − | | | + | | + | + | | | − | + | 6/5 |
| Lean | − | | | + | + | | | | | | − | − | − | + | − | | | | | + | | | + | + | − | | | | 5/6 |
| Facial pleasantness | | + | + | + | + | + | + | + | + | + | + | + | | + | | − | + | + | | | − | + | + | + | + | | + | + | 18/3 |
| Facial animation | | | + | + | | | | | | + | | | + | − | + | + | + | + | − | | + | | + | + | + | + | + | + | 14/2 |
| Gestural animation | + | | | | − | | | | − | − | | − | − | + | + | − | − | − | + | | + | + | + | | | | | | 6/8 |
| Arousal | | + | + | + | − | + | + | − | + | | + | + | − | + | + | + | + | − | + | + | − | | | | | − | | + | 12/6 |
| Random movement | + | + | − | + | + | − | + | | − | | | | + | | − | + | + | − | + | + | + | + | + | | | − | − | | 10/8 |
| Postural relaxation | − | | + | − | | | + | + | + | | + | + | − | + | + | + | | + | | − | + | + | | − | − | − | − | | 10/7 |
| Self-adaptors | | | | | + | − | − | + | − | | + | + | | − | − | − | | + | + | | − | | | | | | + | − | 5/6 |
| Object-adaptors | | + | + | | | | | + | + | | + | + | | | | | | | | | | | + | | + | | | | 6/4 |
| Total (+/−) | 4/1 | 6/2 | 6/2 | 5/2 | 3/4 | 2/1 | 4/2 | 4/1 | 4/3 | 2/1 | 4/2 | 5/3 | 2/4 | 6/2 | 6/4 | 4/3 | 4/1 | 4/4 | 4/1 | 2/2 | 3/4 | 5/0 | 7/0 | 4/1 | 2/2 | 1/2 | 3/4 | 5/1 | 106/58 |

| High involvement | 3 | 5 | 6 | 8 | 12 | 13 | 14 | 17 | 19 | 20 | 21 | 23 | 25 | 28 | 30 | 32 | 39 | 43 | 44 | 45 | 47 | 49 | 50 | 51 | +/− |
|---|---|---|---|---|---|---|---|---|---|---|---|---|---|---|---|---|---|---|---|---|---|---|---|---|---|
| Global involvement | | + | | | − | + | | | − | − | | | | − | − | | − | | + | | + | − | | | 6/7 |
| Orientation/gaze | + | | − | − | − | − | − | − | | − | | + | + | | | | | + | | | | − | + | | 5/7 |
| Lean | + | | | | − | + | | | + | | | − | | | | + | | + | | | | + | + | | 5/3 |
| Facial pleasantness | − | + | | | − | − | − | − | | | + | | − | − | | | | | | + | | + | | | 4/7 |
| Facial animation | | + | + | − | − | − | + | + | | | + | + | − | + | | | + | | − | + | | − | + | + | 9/6 |
| Gestural animation | − | − | | | | | + | | + | | + | + | | − | − | | + | + | + | | | | − | | 6/6 |
| Arousal | | + | − | + | − | − | | | | | | − | + | + | − | | − | | + | − | + | − | + | − | 5/8 |
| Random movement | | + | − | | − | | − | | − | | − | | − | | − | + | − | − | − | | − | | + | − | 4/11 |
| Postural relaxation | − | | − | − | | − | + | − | | | | + | | | − | | | + | + | + | + | | + | | 6/6 |
| Self-adaptors | | | | + | | | − | | | | | + | − | + | | | | − | − | + | − | − | | | 4/5 |
| Object-adaptors | | | | | | | | | | | | − | | | | | | | | + | | − | | | 1/2 |
| Total (+/−) | 2/4 | 5/1 | 1/4 | 2/3 | 0/7 | 2/5 | 3/4 | 1/3 | 2/2 | 0/2 | 3/1 | 5/3 | 2/4 | 3/3 | 0/5 | 2/0 | 2/3 | 3/2 | 3/3 | 5/1 | 2/1 | 1/4 | 5/1 | 1/2 | 55/68 |

Note: Each column represents one of the 52 dyads.

assignment of a dyad as matching or complementary would differ depending on the behavior or channel analyzed.

Another potential problem with this type of analysis is classifying dyads according to adaptation type regardless of how much or how little they adjust to one another. For example, compare dyad 29 to dyad 51. Dyad 29 exhibited a total of 18 adaptations with the net result being a matching classification, while dyad 51 demonstrated only 7 adaptations with the same net result. By classifying dyads based on the aggregation of behavioral changes, dyads are treated as equivalent regardless of the differences in total amounts of behavioral adaptation.

### Analysis by channel

An analysis of reciprocity and compensation patterns by channel generally echoes the dyadic trend toward matching. In both the kinesic/proxemic and vocalic channels, over half of the entries are blank, signifying nonaccommodation, but the majority of instances in which adaptation occurred were in the direction of matching. Further, there was less evidence of complementarity vocalically than kinesically and proxemically. This was particularly true in the high-involvement condition. These patterns imply that subjects either decreased or maintained kinesic involvement when their confederate partners became more involved over time, whereas they predominantly matched the behaviors of partners who became uninvolved.

### Analysis by behavior

This analysis clarifies which specific cue complexes most contributed to reciprocal and compensatory patterns. Among kinesic/proxemic composites, those adapted most were body movement, facial pleasantness, facial animation, and arousal. Facial animation and facial pleasantness showed the most matching, perhaps signaling an impression-management function or the relational expression of similarity, whereas random body movement showed the most complementarity, possibly reflecting some equilibrium level or comfort zone for overall activity in an interaction. This pattern held both within and across involvement conditions, indicating some stability in their use. Object-adaptors were least adapted. Such behaviors may be more idiosyncratic in their manifestation and less subject to interpersonal influence than other behaviors.

Apart from global vocalic involvement, which showed matching, the specific vocalic behaviors or behavioral complexes adapted most across both involvement conditions were pauses/latencies, which also showed matching, and intensity, which showed complementarity. Matched pauses may have contributed to the overall perception of involvement. Less frequent and brief pauses, shown in the high-involvement condition, denote interest, whereas more frequent and longer pauses, shown in the low-involvement condition, denote disinterest or high cognitive load. In addition, similarity in pause length is suggestive of synchronizing a conversation. The complementarity associated with intensity may reflect the politeness norm in that partners were unwilling to compete vocalically with one another. This finding could also be explained as adherence to norms of the interview situation, in which the roles suggest complementarity of behavior; that is, interviewers generally are more dominant than interviewees, who are generally acquiescent. The least adapted behaviors were pitch and fluency. These vocalic qualities may be more idiosyncratic and less subject to social influence. However, they may also be captured in the more global ratings of involvement and intensity, which would argue for the concept of behavioral substitutability.

### Summary and implications

To summarize, the results indicate a fair amount of adaptation. While the common pattern is one of matching or reciprocity, there are also several instances of complementarity. The amount and type of adaptation varies across channel and dyad, with no single behavior being adapted by all dyads. This suggests that researchers consider the equifinality of multiple behaviors and behavioral complexes in fulfilling particular communication or relational functions. This analysis also illuminates the earlier correlation analyses by revealing that multiple instances of nonsignificant findings were due to significant amounts of both matching and complementarity rather than no adaptation at all.

The combined complementing of high involvement and matching of low involvement, however, should not be interpreted as due solely or even primarily to partners adapting to one another. Instead, the patterns partly reflect a general trend toward decreased involvement over time among these subjects. The means reveal that on most behaviors and composites, subjects began at such a high level of involvement that it would have been uncomfortable or unrealistic to increase the behaviors even further. Thus, as the confederate decreased a behavior in low involvement, the naive partner also decreased kinesic involvement, leaving the researcher to conclude that reciprocity occurred. Conversely, as the confederate increased a kinesic behavior in high involvement, the naive partner decreased or maintained involvement, leading to a conclusion of compensatory interaction. These results caution us to take into account separate time effects, something that correlational analyses by themselves do not do.

Nevertheless, the consistent evidence of more vocalic matching than complementarity in both involvement conditions is suggestive of the convergence effect predicted by Communication Accommodation Theory. It is also consistent with involuntary signals of synchrony. The current results do not permit us to choose between these etiologies.

As a methodological approach, individual dyadic correlations share the weaknesses of other correlational methods in that the researcher is not assured that a pattern is actually reciprocal – that it represents a contingent change in behavior rather than just covarying conversational styles. The method employed here also ignores the degree to which dyads are accommodative, treating dyads accommodating on only one or two behaviors as equivalent to dyads accommodating on as many as eight or nine behaviors. It might be preferable to create some kind of continuous measure, much as D. A. Gilbert (1993) did, to better capture the degree of adaptation. The benefit of these individual dyad analyses is the ability to see more clearly the extent of variability among dyads, behaviors, and channels, relative to analyses relying on behavioral means.

## INTERRUPTED TIME SERIES

Simonton's (1977) appoach to interrupted time series, reviewed in Chapter 8, seems on the surface ideally suited for the current analysis because there are few time periods (5), far more dyads than time periods (52), and an experimental manipulation that occurs after a baseline period. The model plots the regression line for the baseline period and compares it to the regression line following introduction of the manipulation. If one uses the full model proposed by Simonton, it would appear as follows for the current data, with "$Y$" representing behavior of the naive participant:

$$Y_t = b_1 + b_2X_t + b_3Z + b_4t + b_5X_tZ + b_6X_tt + b_7Zt + b_8X_tZt$$

where

$X_t$ = *manipulation* (the interruption), coded 0 for prior to the experimental manipulation and 1 for time periods following it

$t$ = *time* (time period), coded 1 to 5 here

$Z$ = *involvement* (the experimental condition), with high involvement coded as the "control" group

$b_1$ = the intercept for the group treated as a control group (high involvement) prior to the manipulation

$b_2$ = the difference between the pre- and postmanipulation intercepts for the low-involvement group

$b_3$ = the difference in premanipulation intercepts for the low- and high-involvement groups (which should be nonsignificant if participants were randomly assigned to groups)

$b_4$ = the slope of the high-involvement group prior to the manipulation

$b_5$ = the difference in intercepts between the two experimental groups after the manipulation – that is, the $M \times I$ interaction

$b_6$ = the change in slope from pre- to postmanipulation for the high-involvement group – that is, the $M \times T$ interaction

$b_7$ = the differences in slope between the two experimental groups prior to the manipulation (which should be nonsignificant if the two groups were in fact equivalent during the baseline) – that is, the $T \times I$ interaction

$b_8$ = the differences between slopes of the two experimental groups after the manipulation – that is, the $M \times T \times I$ interaction

Using this model to test for patterns of reciprocity or compensation, we should expect to see significant effects for $b_2$, if the introduction of confederate changes in behavior makes a difference; $b_4$, if there are changes in behavior across time within the baselines (e.g., everyone becoming more relaxed); $b_5$, if patterns differ in high as opposed to low involvement; $b_6$, if low-involvement participants show a change in involvement level after the manipulation starts; and $b_8$, if the slopes are different in high than in low involvement.

Unfortunately, despite this analysis's benefits, it becomes confounded because the dummy coding introduces serious multicollinearity among vectors. Consequently, the incremental and unique sums of squares associated with a given term hinge on order of entry and presence or absence of other terms in the model. This is illustrated in Table 9.4, where analyses for two dependent measures are presented.

Table 9.4. *Interrupted time-series analysis on kinesic/proxemic involvement and arousal*

| Step | Variables in equation | $b$ | Beta | $t$ | $p$ | $R^2$ | $R^2$ change |
|------|-----------------------|------|-------|-------|-------|-------|--------------|
| Saturated model for involvement | | | | | | | |
| 1 | Manipulation (M) | .60 | .26 | 4.40 | <.001 | .07 | |
| 2 | Manipulation | −.02 | −.01 | −.07 | .944 | | |
|   | Time (T) | .25 | .31 | 2.65 | .009 | .09 | .02 |
| 3 | Manipulation | −.25 | −.11 | −.92 | .359 | | |
|   | Time | .44 | .55 | 4.08 | <.001 | | |
|   | M × T × I | −.43 | −.25 | −3.46 | <.001 | .13 | .04 |
| 4 | Manipulation | −2.02 | −.88 | −4.66 | <.001 | | |
|   | Time | 1.91 | 2.41 | 7.51 | <.001 | | |
|   | Involvement (I) | .48 | .21 | .87 | .384 | | |
|   | M × T | −1.98 | −1.42 | −6.99 | <.001 | | |
|   | M × I | −.31 | −.13 | −.52 | .606 | | |
|   | T × I | .14 | .13 | .39 | .695 | | |
|   | M × T × I | −.34 | −.20 | −.87 | .386 | .40 | .27 |
| Saturated model for arousal | | | | | | | |
| 1 | Manipulation (M) | .61 | .26 | 4.39 | <.001 | .07 | |
| 2 | Manipulation | −.05 | −.02 | −.18 | .855 | | |
|   | Time (T) | .27 | .33 | 2.78 | .005 | .10 | .03 |
| 3 | Manipulation | −.33 | −.14 | −1.19 | .234 | | |
|   | Time | .49 | .61 | 4.55 | <.001 | | |
|   | M × T × I | −.52 | −.30 | −4.11 | <.001 | .15 | .05 |
| 4 | Manipulation | −1.90 | −.81 | −4.11 | <.001 | | |
|   | Time | 1.86 | 2.31 | 6.89 | <.001 | | |
|   | Involvement (I) | .08 | .04 | .15 | .801 | | |
|   | M × T | −1.92 | −1.35 | −6.37 | <.001 | | |
|   | M × I | −.25 | −.10 | −.40 | .690 | | |
|   | T × I | −.02 | −.02 | −.05 | .956 | | |
|   | M × T × I | −.10 | −.06 | −.25 | .801 | .35 | .20 |
| Arousal analysis within high involvement | | | | | | | |
| 1 | Manipulation | .83 | .33 | 3.82 | <.001 | .11 | |
| 2 | Manipulation | .03 | .01 | .88 | .947 | | |
|   | Time | .32 | .37 | 2.16 | .032 | .14 | .03 |
| 3 | Manipulation | −1.90 | −.76 | −3.79 | <.001 | | |
|   | Time | 1.86 | 2.14 | 6.35 | <.001 | | |
|   | M × T | −1.93 | −1.25 | −5.87 | <.001 | .34 | .20 |

Table 9.4, cont'd.

| Step | Variables in equation | b | Beta | t | p | $R^2$ | $R^2$ change |
|---|---|---|---|---|---|---|---|
| | Arousal analysis within low involvement | | | | | | |
| 1 | Manipulation | .43 | .20 | 2.37 | .019 | .04 | |
| 2 | Manipulation | −.12 | −.05 | −.33 | .741 | | |
| | Time | .23 | .29 | 1.76 | .080 | .06 | .02 |
| 3 | Manipulation | −2.15 | −.99 | −5.46 | <.001 | | |
| | Time | 1.84 | 2.46 | 7.99 | <.001 | | |
| | M × T | −2.03 | −1.53 | −7.88 | <.001 | .35 | .29 |

*Note:* Arousal is scored so that a high score represents nonarousal.

The analysis on kinesic/proxemic involvement used generalized least-squares regression (due to moderate autocorrelation: $\rho = .303$). Manipulation, entered at Step 1, was significant, but when Time entered at Step 2, Manipulation became nonsignificant. At Step 3, the Time × Manipulation × Involvement interaction term was significant but became nonsignificant when the remaining Involvement main effect and three two-way interactions were entered, and the Time × Manipulation interaction and Manipulation and Time main effects were again significant. If one lacks a clear a priori basis for proposing an order of entry of variables or for proposing that some terms be omitted from the analysis in advance, proper interpretation becomes difficult. At Step 3, one could conclude that (a) involvement is increasing during the baseline and (b) high involvement and low involvement do in fact yield different results from partners. However, if one moves to Step 4, the conclusions to be drawn are that (a) the mean level of involvement dropped after the manipulation (based on the Manipulation beta weight, which represents the change in intercepts prior to and following the intervention), a pattern reflecting compensation relative to the confederate in high involvement and reciprocity relative to the confederate in low involvement; (b) involvement increased during the baseline (based on the beta weight for Time, which represents the slope prior to the intervention); and (c) participants became less involved during the experimental time periods (based on the beta weight for the interaction), a further confirmation of the compensatory and reciprocal patterns evidenced by the intercepts. Although the conclusions are not radically different, it is unclear whether one can claim that high and low involvement exhibit different patterns.

An alternative is to conduct the time-series analyses within each condition, which reduces some of the artificial multicollinearity introduced by dummy coding. Of course, such an approach loses the capacity to compare high to low involvement directly. This is illustrated in Table 9.4 in analyses conducted on kinesic arousal (again using generalized least-squares regression due to moderate autocorrelation, $\rho$ = .295). The first analysis parallels the preceding one; the latter two are conducted within each involvement condition. In the full saturated model, one might conclude that high involvement and low involvement do in fact yield different results from partners. But in the separate analyses, results appear to be parallel. In both conditions, mean level of composure (nonarousal) dropped immediately after the manipulation, indicating that the manipulation was arousing; composure increased during the baseline, and the slope changed after the manipulation such that subjects became more aroused during the experimental time periods. These results fit a hypothesis that changes in one individual's arousal infect another and that involvement changes in and of themselves increase arousal, regardless of whether they represent increases or decreases.

### Summary and implications

The latter analysis reveals the interpretation morass attending the use of this particular approach to interrupted time series. Although this method seemed ideally suited to our objectives in advance, the multicollinearity problem introduced by the use of dummy coding left us with several rival interpretations of the findings (something upon which unscrupulous researchers might capitalize). Although this problem could be surmounted by a completely specified order of entry in advance, in practice one does not always have a theoretical basis for anticipating which two-way interactions should be significant or even a basis for arguing that the three-way interaction should enter the model ahead of the other interactions and main effects. Consequently, this approach appears to be more useful when one is comparing a single condition to a true control group. With more complex models such as ours (e.g., ones entailing between-dyad factors to be included in the analysis), other methods, such as repeated measures ANOVA with focused contrasts, may be more informative.

## REPEATED MEASURES MANOVAs

Repeated measures MANOVAs, in which the unit of analysis was the dyad, were performed for 22 behaviors and composites across the 52 dyads. The between-dyad factor was involvement (high vs. low), and two within-dyad factors were role (confederate, naive participant) and time (periods 1 to 5). The analyses produced 56 significant effects (see Table 9.5 for significant effects and Table 9.6 for means). Thirteen significant three-way interactions overrode all but four significant two-way interactions and all but three significant main effects. All kinesic behaviors and composites emerged as significant in either two- or three-way interactions, whereas five vocalic behaviors and composites had no significant effects on the dependent measures. The nonsignificant behaviors and composites were fluency, intensity, pauses/latencies, loudness, and tempo.

The omnibus tests, reported in Table 9.5, by including both people's behavior, are powerful tests that not only are useful in detecting conditions under which both the confederate and subject exhibit the same behavior pattern but also are especially capable of detecting interaction effects. However, they do not reveal whether significant effects are due to the confederate's behavior changes, partner's adaptation, or both. Consequently, they must be supplemented with one-degree-of-freedom focused contrasts. Here, we included contrasts to test the same relationships as those tested with interrupted time series, namely whether baseline behavior differed from that during the manipulation time periods and whether any linear or nonlinear trends were present following the onset of the manipulation. The contrast codes comparing the baseline to the manipulation time periods were $-3, -3, 2, 2, 2$. To test for nonlinear trends over time, linear and quadratic orthogonal polynomials were applied to the three manipulation time periods, producing the following sets of codes: $0, 0, -1, 0, 1$ for the linear term and $0, 0, -1, 2, -1$ for the quadratic term. These contrasts were conducted on confederate and subject data separately.

The confederate analyses serve as a manipulation check that confederates actually made the changes they were supposed to and pinpoint the behaviors on which adjustments were most pronounced. The participant

Table 9.5. *F-tests for significant effects in repeated measures MANOVAs*

| | Between Ss | | Within Ss | | | | |
| --- | --- | --- | --- | --- | --- | --- | --- |
| | involvement | Role | Time | $I \times R$ | $I \times T$ | $R \times T$ | $I \times R \times T$ |
| **Kinesics/proxemics** | | | | | | | |
| Involvement | 15.12 | 9.12** | 18.57† | 28.60 | 31.92† | | 25.03† |
| Orientation/gaze | | | | | 13.39† | | 14.12† |
| Lean | | | 4.48***† | | 14.11† | | 7.41† |
| Facial pleasantness | | 7.85† | | 15.58† | | 9.56† | |
| Facial animation | 6.45* | 14.80 | 8.00† | 12.46** | 24.21† | | 10.58† |
| Gestural animation | | | 3.95** | 5.67* | 5.19***† | 3.95*† | 5.26**† |
| Arousal | 9.67** | | 5.93***† | 5.31* | 10.97† | | 5.58***† |
| Random movement | | | 11.48† | | | 3.97*† | |
| Relaxation | | | 17.13† | | | 4.32*† | |
| Object-adaptors | 5.17* | 7.22* | | | | | |
| Self-adaptors | | | 11.94† | | | | |

**Vocalics**

| | | | | | | |
|---|---|---|---|---|---|---|
| Involvement | 5.42* | | | | | |
| Fluency | | 4.52*† | | 6.40***† | | |
| Relaxation | | 10.45† | | 2.88*† | | 3.17*† |
| Attentiveness | | 3.97*† | 6.01* | 3.61*† | | 3.30*† |
| Pauses/latencies | | | | | | |
| Expressiveness | | 2.93* | | | | 7.40 |
| (composed of: | | | | | | |
| Loudness | | | | | | |
| Tempo | | | | | 4.36***† | |
| Tempo Variety | | | | | | |
| Pitch | | | | 5.75† | | |
| Pitch variety | | | | 5.68 | | |
| Expressivity) | | | | 3.65*† | | |

*Note:* *$p$ <.05, **$p$ <.01, all others $p$ <.001; † Used Huynh-Feldt Epsilon corrected degrees of freedom because homogeneity of variance (Box M) and/or Mauchly's sphericity were violated.

Table 9.6. *Means for significant effects in repeated measures MANOVAs*

| Involvement × role × time interactions | | | | |
|---|---|---|---|---|

Kinesic/proxemic involvement $F$ (4,200) = 25.03, $p$ <.001

| Involvement: | Low | | High | |
|---|---|---|---|---|
| Role: | *ER* | *EE* | *ER* | *EE* |
| T1 | 5.69 | 5.50 | 5.47 | 5.25 |
| T2 | 5.74 | 5.46 | 5.47 | 5.41 |
| T3 | 5.44 | 3.82 | 5.30 | 5.83 |
| T4 | 5.27 | 3.78 | 5.44 | 5.96 |
| T5 | 5.03 | 3.50 | 5.15 | 5.80 |

Orientation/gaze $F(4,200)$ = 14.12, $p$ <.001

| Involvement: | Low | | High | |
|---|---|---|---|---|
| Role: | *ER* | *EE* | *ER* | *EE* |
| T1 | 5.32 | 5.86 | 5.75 | 5.44 |
| T2 | 5.53 | 5.92 | 5.48 | 5.47 |
| T3 | 5.53 | 4.68 | 5.61 | 5.99 |
| T4 | 5.44 | 4.80 | 5.66 | 6.02 |
| T5 | 5.31 | 4.86 | 5.51 | 5.96 |

Facial pleasantness $F(4,196)$ = 9.56, $p$ <.001

| Involvement: | Low | | High | |
|---|---|---|---|---|
| Role: | *ER* | *EE* | *ER* | *EE* |
| T1 | 5.05 | 5.20 | 4.78 | 4.53 |
| T2 | 5.26 | 5.03 | 5.01 | 4.57 |
| T3 | 4.69 | 3.97 | 4.57 | 5.13 |
| T4 | 4.48 | 3.93 | 4.75 | 5.11 |
| T5 | 4.48 | 3.85 | 4.62 | 5.07 |

Kinesic/proxemic arousal $F(4,200)$ = 5.58, $p$ <.001

| Involvement: | Low | | High | |
|---|---|---|---|---|
| Role: | *ER* | *EE* | *ER* | *EE* |
| T1 | 5.24 | 5.07 | 5.10 | 5.18 |
| T2 | 5.30 | 5.13 | 5.23 | 5.30 |
| T3 | 4.98 | 4.47 | 5.14 | 5.49 |
| T4 | 4.88 | 4.40 | 5.17 | 5.56 |
| T5 | 4.73 | 4.21 | 5.03 | 5.53 |

Table 9.6, cont'd.

| Involvement × role × time interactions | | | | |
|---|---|---|---|---|

Facial animation $F(4,200) = 10.58$, $p <.001$

| Involvement: | Low | | High | |
|---|---|---|---|---|
| Role: | *ER* | *EE* | *ER* | *EE* |
| T1 | 5.11 | 4.69 | 4.95 | 4.45 |
| T2 | 5.34 | 4.71 | 4.98 | 4.54 |
| T3 | 4.79 | 3.46 | 4.82 | 5.11 |
| T4 | 4.60 | 3.52 | 4.98 | 5.16 |
| T5 | 4.68 | 3.44 | 4.77 | 5.04 |

Gestural animation $F(4,200) = 5.26$, $p <.001$

| Involvement: | Low | | High | |
|---|---|---|---|---|
| Role: | *ER* | *EE* | *ER* | *EE* |
| T1 | 3.84 | 3.42 | 3.81 | 3.22 |
| T2 | 4.21 | 3.63 | 4.20 | 3.65 |
| T3 | 3.95 | 3.12 | 3.77 | 4.57 |
| T4 | 3.70 | 3.03 | 3.74 | 4.77 |
| T5 | 3.64 | 3.46 | 3.78 | 4.45 |

Body lean $F(4,200) = 7.41$, $p <.001$

| Involvement: | Low | | High | |
|---|---|---|---|---|
| Role: | *ER* | *EE* | *ER* | *EE* |
| T1 | 3.98 | 4.34 | 3.75 | 3.90 |
| T2 | 3.80 | 4.23 | 3.63 | 3.83 |
| T3 | 3.61 | 3.43 | 3.58 | 4.46 |
| T4 | 3.75 | 3.27 | 3.77 | 4.46 |
| T5 | 3.52 | 3.05 | 3.58 | 4.29 |

Vocalic relaxation $F(4,200) = 3.17$, $p <.05$

| Involvement: | Low | | High | |
|---|---|---|---|---|
| Role: | *ER* | *EE* | *ER* | *EE* |
| T1 | 4.50 | 4.55 | 4.49 | 4.59 |
| T2 | 4.59 | 4.64 | 4.59 | 4.63 |
| T3 | 4.68 | 4.57 | 4.59 | 4.76 |
| T4 | 4.68 | 4.56 | 4.61 | 4.81 |
| T5 | 4.68 | 4.54 | 4.74 | 4.79 |

Table 9.6, cont'd.

Involvement × role × time interactions

Vocalic attentiveness (vocalics) $F(4,200) = 3.30$, $p <.05$

| Involvement: | Low | | High | |
|---|---|---|---|---|
| Role: | *ER* | *EE* | *ER* | *EE* |
| T1 | 4.53 | 4.45 | 4.55 | 4.62 |
| T2 | 4.51 | 4.55 | 4.55 | 4.55 |
| T3 | 4.60 | 4.13 | 4.43 | 4.58 |
| T4 | 4.44 | 4.11 | 4.57 | 4.62 |
| T5 | 4.38 | 4.18 | 4.42 | 4.64 |

Expressiveness (vocalic composite) $F(4,200) = 7.40$, $p <.001$

| Involvement: | Low | | High | |
|---|---|---|---|---|
| Role: | *ER* | *EE* | *ER* | *EE* |
| T1 | 4.03 | 4.18 | 4.05 | 4.15 |
| T2 | 3.95 | 4.16 | 4.06 | 4.09 |
| T3 | 3.94 | 3.98 | 3.97 | 4.23 |
| T4 | 3.98 | 3.87 | 3.88 | 4.24 |
| T5 | 3.97 | 3.88 | 3.89 | 4.25 |

Tempo (vocalics) $F(4,200) = 4.36$, $p <.01$

| Involvement: | Low | | High | |
|---|---|---|---|---|
| Role: | *ER* | *EE* | *ER* | *EE* |
| T1 | 3.80 | 4.11 | 3.80 | 4.08 |
| T2 | 3.85 | 4.04 | 3.86 | 3.86 |
| T3 | 3.76 | 3.82 | 3.64 | 3.98 |
| T4 | 3.93 | 3.80 | 3.58 | 4.22 |
| T5 | 3.83 | 3.82 | 3.84 | 4.02 |

Pitch variety $F(4,200) = 5.68$, $p <.001$

| Involvement: | Low | | High | |
|---|---|---|---|---|
| Role: | *ER* | *EE* | *ER* | *EE* |
| T1 | 4.17 | 4.19 | 4.28 | 4.18 |
| T2 | 3.98 | 4.32 | 4.20 | 4.18 |
| T3 | 3.93 | 4.04 | 4.08 | 4.34 |
| T4 | 4.20 | 3.89 | 4.08 | 4.36 |
| T5 | 4.09 | 3.87 | 3.86 | 4.34 |

Table 9.6, cont'd.

| Involvement × role × time interactions | | | | |
|---|---|---|---|---|

Expressivity (vocalics) $F(4,200) = 3.65$, $p < .01$

| Involvement: | Low | | High | |
|---|---|---|---|---|
| Role: | *ER* | *EE* | *ER* | *EE* |
| T1 | 3.96 | 4.07 | 3.94 | 4.10 |
| T2 | 3.93 | 4.13 | 4.08 | 4.12 |
| T3 | 3.87 | 3.98 | 4.04 | 4.20 |
| T4 | 3.85 | 3.80 | 3.94 | 4.26 |
| T5 | 3.93 | 3.80 | 3.86 | 4.36 |

| Role × time interactions | | |
|---|---|---|

Random movement $F(4,200) = 3.97$, $p < .01$

| | *ER* | *EE* |
|---|---|---|
| T1 | 5.52 | 5.52 |
| T2 | 5.20 | 5.44 |
| T3 | 5.24 | 4.77 |
| T4 | 5.21 | 4.71 |
| T5 | 5.09 | 4.67 |

Postural relaxation $F(4,200) = 4.32$, $p < .01$

| | *ER* | *EE* |
|---|---|---|
| T1 | 3.83 | 3.81 |
| T2 | 3.96 | 3.87 |
| T3 | 4.09 | 4.37 |
| T4 | 4.14 | 4.43 |
| T5 | 4.08 | 4.52 |

Pitch (vocalics) $F(4,200) = 5.75$, $p < .001$

| | *ER* | *EE* |
|---|---|---|
| T1 | 4.23 | 4.09 |
| T2 | 4.06 | 4.15 |
| T3 | 4.07 | 4.15 |
| T4 | 4.11 | 4.03 |
| T5 | 4.32 | 4.02 |

Table 9.6, cont'd.

| Involvement × time interaction | | |
|---|---|---|
| Involvement/warmth (vocalics) $F(4,200) = 6.40$, $p < .001$ | | |
| | *Hi involv* | *Lo involv* |
| T1 | 4.17 | 4.10 |
| T2 | 4.15 | 4.10 |
| T3 | 4.23 | 3.88 |
| T4 | 4.17 | 3.89 |
| T5 | 4.56 | 3.82 |

| Involvement main effect | | |
|---|---|---|
| Object-adaptors $F(1,50) = 5.17$, $p < .05$ | | |
| | *Hi involve* | *Lo involve* |
| | 6.27 | 5.76 |

| Role main effect | | |
|---|---|---|
| Object-adaptors $F(1,50) = 7.22$, $p < .01$ | | |
| | *EE* | *ER* |
| | 6.32 | 5.75 |

| Time main effect | |
|---|---|
| Self-adaptors $F(4,200) = 11.94$, $p < .001$ | |
| T1 | 5.84 |
| T2 | 5.63 |
| T3 | 5.28 |
| T4 | 5.19 |
| T5 | 4.84 |

analyses reveal the extent to which subject changes are responsive to confederate-manipulated behavior changes.

The patterns of means and contrasts on confederates confirmed that low-involvement and high-involvement confederates reduced or increased overall involvement respectively during the three manipulation time periods, as instructed. Low-involvement confederates exhibited decreased involvement primarily through reductions in directness of orientation, pleasantness, animation, lean, composure, vocal attentiveness, and vocal expressiveness. High-involvement confederates did the opposite (except on vocal attentiveness and expressiveness), and they increased vocal relaxation slightly. For some behaviors (e.g., facial animation, gestural animation, facial pleasantness), the manipulation was not sustained through time period 5. The confederates were also less adept in making some vocalic adjustments (manipulation period means did not differ greatly from baseline ones) and were unable to make some changes (e.g., relaxed vocalics in the low-involvement condition and vocalic attentiveness in the high-involvement condition).

Analyses of participant behavior revealed that low-involvement participants significantly reduced kinesic/proxemic and vocalic involvement after the manipulation began and continued to show a linear decrease in kinesic/proxemic involvement over time, a pattern clearly indicative of reciprocity. High involvement participants, by contrast, showed (a) a mean decrease in kinesic/proxemic involvement during the manipulation period, which might be taken as compensation; (b) a quadratic pattern of increasing then decreasing kinesic/proxemic involvement during the manipulation that paralleled the confederates' pattern and could be interpreted as reciprocity; and (c) no effects on vocal involvement, a possible pattern of nonaccommodation. Participant changes were generally weaker than those shown by the confederates.

Particular behaviors on which low-involvement participants showed the most changes were (a) body orientation/gaze, which became more direct during the baseline then declined linearly after the manipulation began; (b) gestural and (c) facial animation, which increased during the baseline then dropped after the manipulation; (d) facial pleasantness, which was much lower after the manipulation than before; (e) kinesic arousal, which was much higher after the manipulation than before; (f) vocal attentiveness, which declined after the manipulation; and (g) vocal relaxation, which increased throughout. The behaviors on which high-involvement participants showed the most changes were (a) postural relaxation, with a linear increase over time; (b) random movement, which decreased after the manipulation; (c) vocal attentiveness, which showed the same quadratic pattern as kinesic involvement after the manipulation; (d) vocal relaxation, which increased over time; and (e) tempo, with a pattern of convergence consistent with Communication Accommodation Theory. Main effects showed that more object-adaptors were used under high than low involvement and by the confederate than the naive participant; self-adaptors decreased linearly over time. On all of the measures where significant results obtained, the patterns qualified as matching or reciprocation of the confederate's behavior. Among the behaviors that were not adapted were body orientation/gaze (within low involvement) and several vocalic behaviors, including global expressiveness, pitch variety, and expressivity. Orientation may not be subject to a mutual adaptation process, especially in the context of an interview. An interviewer would typically face an interviewee regardless of changes in the interviewee's orientation. We have considered various explanations for the lack of vocalic adaptations in earlier sections.

### Summary and implications

Overall, the patterns are consistent with conclusions drawn from preceding analyses, that more adaptation took the form of matching and reciprocity than complementarity and compensation and that more adaptation occurred in response to decreased than increased involvement. However, these analyses add a new twist under increased involvement in simultaneously demonstrating compensation – in the form of lower mean involvement after the manipulation – and reciprocity – in the form of a curvilinear pattern matching that of the confederate across the three manipulation time periods. The discovery of a nonlinear relationship, besides being important in its own right, raises the possibility that nonsignificant findings in previous analyses may have been due to the high variability in this condition and the inability of those analyses to detect nonlinear patterns. Finally, the number of specific behaviors shown to evidence adaptation exceeds those of the previous analyses and solidifies an emerging impression that many immediacy behaviors, expressiveness, and arousal-related behaviors are more likely to manifest reciprocity than compensation.

### CONCLUSIONS

Substantively, the results from this investigation offer compelling evidence that interactants do adapt to one another; that reciprocity is the more common but not overwhelming pattern; that dyads differ considerably in their degree of adaptation, in the proportion of reciprocal and compensatory responses they show, and in the particular behaviors and channels on which they adapt; that kinesic/proxemic behaviors may be more susceptible to partner influence; and that some adaptations take the form of nonlinear patterns over time.

Methodologically, this exercise reveals that far more information can be gleaned when multiple methods are used. Despite some inconsistencies, the combined methods largely provide complementary rather than conflicting information. The most information can be gained through a combination of between- and within-dyad analyses and cross-sectional and longitudinal analyses. Given our own interests in true adaptation patterns, the methods arsenal also needs to include tests that can demonstrate directedness, contingency, and adapation.

Armed with these tentative conclusions, we decided to conduct similar comparative analyses on new data sets so that we could better assess the generalizability of our results and the possibility of dispensing with some statistical methods because of their insensitivity or redundancy. Chapter 10 reports the results of those additional analyses.

### NOTES

[1] Some have suggested that the best way to answer the question of how methods differ is either to analyze them conceptually (which we did in Chapter 8) or to create a data set with known statistical parameters and to conduct tests on these simulated data. Monte Carlo replications on such data, for example, could be helpful in addressing such issues as the power and Type I errors associated with each method. Our intent was not to determine which approach was the most "valid" but rather what each approach might add to our insights about interaction adaptation. Bolger et al. (1992), among others, created a sample data set that produced evidence of a positive relationship using a between-subjects analysis and evidence of a negative relationship using a within-subjects analysis *on the same data*. Their illustration revealed that the pattern(s) to be uncovered can be predetermined by constructing a data set designed to produce similar or dissimilar conclusions with each type of analysis. We wanted to know instead what patterns would be uncovered when analyzing observations generated from real, interacting people rather than from an artificially created data set. That is, we were as interested in the substantive issue of how people interact as in how well various methods discern those patterns.

[2] See Burgoon, Dillman, Stern, and Kelley (in press) for further discussion of a subset of these analyses.

[3] Here we have used an approximate $z$-test recommended by Raghunathan et al. (1993), who have shown that this test is more accurate than the standard Pearson-Filon test, especially with smaller sample sizes, and simpler than the $z_r$ version of the Pearson-Filon test. However, they do note that when more power is needed, the $z_r$ version may be preferable. Given the illustrative rather than confirmatory nature of our analyses here, we opted for the simpler version.

[4] The remaining 17% ($n = 9$) exhibited equal numbers of positive and negative correlations. Matching was more evident under low involvement: 66% had more positive than negative correlations and 18% had more negative than positive correlations. The pattern reversed under high involvement, with 40% matching more than complementing and 52% complementing more than matching.

# 10

## Further illustrations

Chapter 9 offered a methodological demonstration of how various statistical analysis techniques spotlight different facets of the adaptation process, with some being more enlightening than others. It also offered empirical evidence for a complex set of adaptation patterns. Because no single investigation is definitive, this chapter presents results from additional dyadic interaction studies to (a) illustrate how statistical methods compare on their informativeness and degree of complementarity and (b) present additional empirical evidence about which adaptation patterns are most prevalent in face-to-face interactions. Before firm conclusions can be drawn, interaction patterns found in one context need to be compared and contrasted with patterns found in others to see whether patterns are stable across contexts or applicable only to specific kinds of contexts such as scripted or structured routines like interviews. These investigations therefore also (c) identify possible moderating factors controlling the different patterns and (d) address the generalizability of our conclusions.

We begin with a detailed description of another dyadic interaction experiment, followed by a briefer summary of findings related to reciprocity and compensation taken from two experiments on deception and suspicion.

### A SECOND MULTIMETHOD DYADIC INTERACTION EXPERIMENT

Whereas the investigation reported in Chapter 9 employed an interview task and setting, the current one employed discussions of social and moral dilemmas. An interview context is highly constrained by the prevalence of role-bound behavior. A discussion format, however, allows much more participant freedom; participants are constrained mainly by social norms and "laboratory expectations." The current investigation also utilized a much larger data set (both in sample size and number of behaviors analyzed) than most studies of reciprocity and compensation. Additionally, multiple forms of measurement were used. Some behaviors were measured at the microlevel (behaviors coded at 5-second intervals for their presence or absence), others were measured at the macrolevel (perceptual judgments made after viewing a minute of the interaction), and still other judgments were made at a gestalt or global level (overall impressions of involvement, anxiety, and pleasantness). This permitted comparing the different levels of coding on their sensitivity to adaptation patterns. Moreover, multiple behavioral levels of analysis enable us to have more confidence in our findings, should the patterns emerge at all measurement levels.

Based on the previous investigation, three statistical methods that we thought would be the most illuminating were singled out for comparison: Pearson product-moment correlations, intraclass correlations, and repeated measures ANOVA. These techniques are appropriate for use with data sets like the current one that entail multiple dyads and few time periods.

The investigation tested hypotheses derived from Expectancy Violations Theory, a precursor to our own Interaction Adaptation Theory. It was anticipated that increased pleasantness and involvement would constitute either a positive violation or a positive confirmation, while decreased involvement and pleasantness would constitute a negative violation. Positive violations were predicted to elicit reciprocal increases in pleasantness and involvement; the same prediction was made for confirmatory pleasant behavior. Negative violations by a positive-expectancy communicator were hypothesized to elicit a compensatory increase in pleasantness and involvement while the same violation by a negative-expectancy communicator was predicted to elicit a reciprocal decrease in involvement and pleasantness.

## Method

### Participants, confederates, and observers

The data come from an experiment reported in Burgoon, Le Poire, and Rosenthal (in press). (In that report, only global measures are presented.) Participants (Ps; $N = 162$) were undergraduates who received extra credit for participating in a videotaped study of "problem-solving patterns." Confederate targets (Ts; $N = 4$) were undergraduate communication students (2 males, 2 females) selected for acting abilities and physical similarities on height, build, coloring, and attractiveness. Despite efforts to match confederates physically and behaviorally, previous experiments have found substantial variability among them (e.g., Burgoon & Aho, 1982; Burgoon, Manusov, Mineo, & Hale, 1985). Thus, observers (Os; $N = 98$) who watched the interactions through a one-way mirror completed manipulation checks on the Ts' behavior.

### Independent variables

The independent variables were two types of preinteraction expectancies (only one of which is relevant here) and actual T communication. The expectancy manipulation was intended to create two levels of communicator reward valence. To maximize differences between conditions, half the Ps were led to expect that the person with whom they would be interacting had many positive qualities, was similar to them, was likely to be a rewarding task partner, and might be someone they would pick for a friend. The other half were led to believe the person had less-than-admirable personal qualities and was dissimilar, unrewarding, and unlikely to be a friend. These were identified as the positive-expectancy and negative-expectancy Ts, respectively.

Actual T communication was manipulated by training Ts to enact either a highly involved and pleasant or detached and unpleasant nonverbal interaction style (hereafter referred to as pleasant and unpleasant T communication, respectively) after the first minute of interaction. Pleasantness and involvement were combined because people often express pleasantness by showing interest and involvement. The pleasant, involved style included high immediacy (forward lean, direct body orientation, high gaze), expressiveness (facial animation, vocal expressiveness), good interaction management (high fluency, coordinated movement and speech), altercentrism (kinesic/proxemic attentiveness, vocal warmth/interest), and composure (minimal random movement and adaptor use, vocal relaxation). The unpleasant, detached style was nonimmediate, inexpressive, egocentric, uncomposed, and lacking the fluency and coordination characteristic of smooth conversations.

### Procedure

Ps completed a brief self-assessment questionnaire, reviewed the discussion topics, and received the expectancy induction (which Os overheard). Ps then met Ts and the interaction commenced. A color-coded worksheet cued the T to enact pleasant or unpleasant communication. Ts presented the same positions on the issues across all interactions to ensure that their verbal contributions remained as consistent as possible. After 8 minutes of discussion, Ps and Os completed postmeasures (reported in Burgoon & Le Poire, 1993) and then were debriefed. Subsequently the videotaped interactions were coded by trained raters.

*Manipulation checks*

To verify that Ts enacted the two different communication styles, Ps and Os rated Ts on several relational communication subscales used in previous investigations (Burgoon & Hale, 1987; Burgoon & Hale, 1988; Burgoon et al., 1985; Burgoon, Newton, et al., 1989) plus six scale items used to measure communication behavior evaluation and expectedness.

*Nonverbal dependent measures*

Global estimates of P and T pleasantness and involvement were obtained from a pair of trained coders who rated P and T on all-channel involvement and pleasantness using a Datamyte computerized event recording system while watching and listening to the videotaped interactions. Macro- and microratings were conducted by additional pairs or triads of trained raters ($N = 46$) who rated either kinesic/proxemic behavior or vocalic behavior. Global or macrojudgments were based on one-minute observations during minutes 1, 3, 5, and 7; microbehaviors were coded every 5 seconds for the same minutes. Ratings were subsequently factor analyzed to reduce the nonverbal measures to a smaller subset of composites. Items not fitting any dimension were measured singly. All are listed in Table 10.1 along with their interrater and interitem reliabilities.

## Results

*Manipulation and confederate behavior checks*

The manipulation checks reported in Burgoon et al. (in press) confirmed that the four Ts did not differ among themselves on expectancies, general reward valence, evaluations of their behaviors, or the relational meanings of the behaviors on the dimensions of immediacy, affection,

Table 10.1. *Reliabilities on nonverbal measures*

| Dimension | Items | Interrater reliability | | Scale (interitem) reliability | |
|---|---|---|---|---|---|
| | | Target | Perceiver | Target | Perceiver |
| **Global perceptions** | | | | | |
| All-channel pleasantness | | .90 | .80 | | |
| All-channel involvement | | .75 | .72 | | |
| Kinesic involvement/pleasantness | involved | .94 | .65 | .99 | .93 |
| | detached* | .94 | .46 | | |
| | interested | .96 | .54 | | |
| | pleasant | .95 | .59 | | |
| | warm | .91 | .64 | | |
| | friendly | .96 | .46 | | |
| | expressive | .93 | .73 | | |
| | animated | .92 | .80 | | |
| Vocalic involvement/pleasantness | involved | .86 | .66 | .99 | .97 |
| | detached* | .88 | .62 | | |
| | interested | .90 | .65 | | |
| | pleasant | .80 | .60 | | |
| | warm | .84 | .55 | | |
| | friendly | .83 | .54 | | |
| | expressive | .86 | .68 | | |
| | animated | .87 | .58 | | |
| Kinesic anxiety | nervous | .61 | .50 | .96 | .93 |
| | relaxed* | .63 | .48 | | |

| | | | | |
|---|---|---|---|---|
| Vocalic anxiety | | | .98 | .97 |
| nervous | .67 | .54 | | |
| relaxed* | .75 | .52 | | .46 |
| **Nonverbal composites and behaviors** | | | | |
| Immediacy composite | | | .91 | |
| Individual behaviors: | | | | |
| gaze | .93 | .87 | | |
| illustrators/emblems | .98 | .93 | | |
| orientation | .91 | .95 | | |
| lean | .84 | .88 | | |
| Kinesic relaxation composite | | | .10 | .63 |
| Individual behaviors: | | | | |
| postural relaxation | −.14 | .52 | | |
| random movement* | .16 | .83 | | |
| self-adaptors* | .72 | .80 | | |
| object-adaptors* | .86 | .57 | | |
| Positive affect composite | | | .70 | .59 |
| Individual behaviors: | | | | |
| smiling | .86 | .88 | | |
| relaxed laughter | .59 | .61 | | |
| nods | .59 | .93 | | |
| Vocal expressiveness composite | | | .65 | .72 |
| Individual behaviors: | | | | |
| fluency | .65 | .85 | | |
| rhythm | .36 | .80 | | |
| pitch variety | .74 | .86 | | |
| tempo variety | .50 | .79 | | |
| tempo | .68 | .50 | | |
| resonance | .91 | .86 | | |
| loudness | .46 | .19 | | |

Table 10.1, cont'd.

| Dimension | Items | Interrater reliability | | Scale (interitem) reliability | |
|---|---|---|---|---|---|
| | | Target | Perceiver | Target | Perceiver |
| **Global perceptions** | | | | | |
| Vocal relaxation behaviors | pitch | .72 | .50 | | |
| | nervous laughter | .73 | .74 | | |
| Conversation management composite | | | | .64 | .64 |
| Individual behaviors: | total talk time | .29 | .97 | | |
| | aver. turn length | .91 | .49 | | |
| | turn switches | .44 | .92 | | |

*These items were reverse scored. Due to low reliabilities, nods were omitted from pleasantness for subjects, resonance was omitted from vocal expressiveness for confederates, loudness was omitted from vocal expressiveness for subjects, and kinesic relaxation was omitted from all confederate analyses.

dominance, and formality. The only difference was that one female T was rated as more composed than the other three.

The expectancy manipulation was successful in distinguishing positive-expectancy Ts from negative-expectancy ones: Ts attributed to have positive personal attributes were expected to be more similar, nice, likable, agreeable, pleasant, and attractive ($M = 5.02$) than those attributed to have negative ones ($M = 4.28$). O ratings and trained coder checks on the communication style manipulation also confirmed that Ts enacting the pleasant style expressed more immediacy ($M = 5.57$) and positive affect ($M = 5.53$) than when enacting the unpleasant style (immediacy $M = 3.07$, affection $M = 3.30$). Repeated measures analyses of variance further confirmed that Ts enacted less involvement and pleasantness in the unpleasant condition than in the pleasant condition, they became increasingly pleasant over time in the pleasant communication condition, and they decreased kinesic pleasantness/ involvement over time in the unpleasant condition; vocalic pleasantness/involvement remained stable in the unpleasant condition. Analyses of the other nonverbal behaviors reveal that compared to the pleasant condition, Ts in the unpleasant condition exhibited (a) greater kinesic and vocalic anxiety (including more random movement, self-adaptors, and object-adaptors) but also more postural relaxation, lower pitch, and less nervous laughter; (b) less immediacy (i.e., less gaze, fewer illustrator gestures, more indirect orientation, and backward lean); (c) less positive affect (i.e., less smiling, relaxed laughter, and nodding); and (d) less vocal expressiveness (especially less fluent, quieter, slower, less varied). Ps also rated unpleasant communication as a negative expectancy violation and pleasant communication from a negative-expectancy T as a positive violation.

### Pearson product-moment correlations and intraclass correlations

The correlation analyses, shown in Table 10.2, were conducted within the two different communication conditions because of the differential predicted responses to pleasant and unpleasant communication. We have pointed out repeatedly that correlations in and of themselves do not demonstrate reciprocity or compensation because correlations cannot confirm causality. However, the fact that confederates initiated behavioral changes and these were followed by participant behavioral changes increased our confidence that influence was taking place. Con-

Table 10.2. *Pearson product-moment correlations and intraclass correlations for participant and target (confederate)*

|  | Unpleasant | | Pleasant | |
|---|---|---|---|---|
|  | r | $r_I$ | r | $r_I$ |
| **Global perceptions** | | | | |
| Involvement | −.28* | −.21* | .43** | .42** |
| Pleasantness | −.02 | −.02 | .51** | .52** |
| Kin. pleasantness/ involvement | .16 | .14 | .20 | .17 |
| Voc. pleasantness/ involvement | .35** | .35** | .38** | .34** |
| Kinesic anxiety | −.02 | −.02 | .34** | .34** |
| Vocal anxiety | .28* | .28* | .02 | .02 |
| **NV composites/behaviors** | | | | |
| Immediacy composite | .33** | .28** | .30** | .29** |
| Gaze | .11 | .14 | .37** | .36** |
| Illustrators | .27* | .27* | −.00 | −.01 |
| Orientation | .23* | .24* | .22* | .21* |
| Lean | −.02 | −.02 | .12 | .09 |
| Kinesic relaxation composite | −.06 | −.04 | .09 | .18 |
| Postural relaxation | .02 | .02 | .03 | .03 |
| Random movement | −.10 | −.09 | .04 | .04 |
| Self-adaptors | −.04 | −.00 | .09 | .00 |
| Object-adaptors | .09 | .00 | −.17 | −.00 |
| Positive affect composite | .11 | .10 | .56** | .51** |
| Smiling | .35** | .31** | .60** | .58** |
| Relaxed laughter | −.03 | −.02 | .32** | .29** |
| Nodding | .43** | .40** | .37** | .35** |
| Vocal expressiveness composite | .38** | .29** | .11 | .09 |
| Fluency | −.02 | −.02 | .00 | .00 |
| Rhythm | −.09 | −.08 | .01 | .01 |
| Loudness | .07 | .06 | .07 | .07 |
| Tempo | .21 | .12 | .25* | .22* |
| Tempo variety | .04 | .05 | −.07 | −.05 |
| Pitch variety | .05 | .05 | .12 | .12 |
| Resonance | .13 | .11 | −.03 | −.02 |

Table 10.2, cont'd.

| | Unpleasant | | Pleasant | |
|---|---|---|---|---|
| | r | $r_I$ | r | $r_I$ |
| Vocal relaxation | | | | |
| Pitch | −.01 | −.00 | −.11 | −.13 |
| Nervous vocalizations | −.04 | −.00 | .11 | .09 |
| Conversation management | | | | |
| Total talk time | −.09 | −.11 | −.21 | −.17 |
| Average turn length | .19 | .15 | .16 | .22* |
| Smoothness of turn switches | .15 | .14 | −.09 | −.10 |

$*p < .05, **p < .01$

sequently, although we will describe the patterns as matching or complementary, they may imply reciprocity or compensation. As a caveat, these analyses are based on averaged scores across time periods and therefore ignore changes over time.

The Pearson bivariate correlations show a predominant pattern of matching, based on the large number of positive correlations. However, the negative correlation in the unpleasant condition for all-channel involvement shows complementarity: that is, Ps tended to increase involvement while Ts decreased it. Otherwise, in the unpleasant condition, Ps generally matched Ts' decreases in vocal pleasantness/involvement, vocal anxiety, immediacy, smiling, nodding, and vocal expressiveness. In the pleasant condition, Ps also matched Ts' increases in all-channel involvement, all-channel pleasantness, immediacy, positive affect, and tempo and Ts' decreases in kinesic anxiety. Kinesic pleasantness/involvement did not produce a significant relationship; in light of significant positive relationships for all-channel pleasantness and immediacy, it is unclear why this is the case.

If one compares the two communication conditions, the effect sizes are generally larger in the pleasant condition, suggesting a stronger influence of T behavior on P behavior in that condition. Additionally, there is a tendency for greater matching in the pleasant communication condition on kinesic behaviors related to affect and arousal (see correlations on kinesic anxiety, gaze, and all the positive affect behaviors), and in the unpleasant condition on vocalic behaviors (see correlations on vocal anxiety and vocal expressiveness). However, most of the vocal behaviors show little relationship between the two interactants. Although these patterns might be due to vocal behaviors being fairly stable individual style characteristics that are impervious to a co-interactant's influence, such a conclusion would be contrary to Communication Accommodation Theory and the considerable empirical evidence of matching on speech-related vocal properties.

The intraclass correlations show a very similar pattern. It should be remembered that when data come from dyads rather than larger groups and when variances are equal, intraclass correlations and Pearson product-moment correlations produce the same results. Large differences between dyad members, however, attenuate intraclass correlations. In this case, there are sizable discrepancies between T and P behavior, with Ts going to more extremes than Ps, especially in the unpleasant condition (see means reported below). This resulted in somewhat weaker magnitudes of relationships than produced by the Pearson correlations. In all other respects, the patterns duplicate those revealed by the Pearsons – a prevailing pattern of matching except for complementarity on overall involvement in the unpleasant condition.

*Repeated measures analyses of variance*

To test for differences in patterns over time in response to pleasant and unpleasant T communication, all dependent variables were initially tested with 3 (no/positive/negative personal attribute expectancy) × 2 (pleasant/unpleasant T communication) × 2 (male/female T gender) × 4 (time periods) × 2 (T or P role) repeated measures ANOVAs. T gender was included to control for any sex differences in confederate behavior. Because significant effects could be due primarily to changes by the T and not the P, these analyses were followed by separate analyses for Ts and Ps. The three degrees of freedom associated with time were partitioned into orthogonal polynomials to test for linear, quadratic, and cubic trends (see Snedecor & Cochran, 1967). Where Mauchly's sphericity test produced significant violations of sphericity, the Huynh-Feldt $\varepsilon$ was used to produce adjusted $p$ values. Analyses were conducted on standardized data; however, for ease of interpretation, means are reported in raw score form. Polynomial trend analysis results for Ps are reported in Table 10.3; only linear and quadratic effects are tabled because very few cubic effects emerged and those that did accounted for very small amounts of variance. The communication by time means for both Ts and Ps are reported in Table 10.4. The results for all-channel involvement and pleasantness and for kinesic and vocalic pleasantness/ involvement are reproduced from Burgoon et al. (in press) for comparative purposes.

Before examining the effects on Ps' behavior, it should be recalled that the manipulation check polynomial trend analyses on Ts' behavior (reported earlier) provide the necessary evidence that Ts adjusted their nonverbal behaviors to create pleasant and unpleasant conditions and that pleasant Ts continued to increase pleasantness over time while unpleasant Ts decreased all-channel and kinesic pleasantness over time but maintained stable vocal unpleasantness.

The initial analyses on P behavior consistently produced large effects for T communication, time, and communication by time interactions and no expectancy or T gender effects.[1] The main effects for T communication indicate that substantial matching occurred. The global pleasantness and involvement measures showed, for example, that those interacting with unpleasant Ts were themselves less involved and pleasant on average than those interacting with pleasant Ts. However, Ps in the unpleasant condition did not reduce their levels of involvement and pleasantness to the same extreme that Ts did. Ps interacting with unpleasant Ts also exhibited greater global kinesic and vocalic anxiety, less immediacy (especially on gaze and use of illustrator gestures), more postural relaxation, less positive affect (especially on smiling and nodding), less vocal expressiveness (especially on pitch variety), less laughter/nervous vocalizations, and more awkward turn switches. In all cases except one, these patterns reflected matching of Ts' behavior. In the case of postural relaxation, unpleasant Ts exhibited hyperrelaxation; their partners, by contrast, appeared somewhat tense, resulting in a complementary pattern in the unpleasant communication condition. We have classified these patterns as matching or complementarity rather than reciprocity and compensation because main effects reflect stable behavior and consequently may result from individual consistency in behavior or the influence of constant external factors (e.g., the situational definition) or both rather than from partner influence.

The communication by time interactions, however, offer evidence of partner influence in that T changes were accompanied by P changes. These results revealed that in the pleasant condition, Ps increased their all-channel, kinesic, and vocalic involvement and pleasantness substantially over time and did so at a steeper rate than those in the unpleasant condition. Moreover, where T patterns exhibited some curvilinearity in

Table 10.3. *F-tests for significant communication main effects, trends for time, and communication by time interactions on participant behavior*

| | Communication | Time | | Communication × time |
|---|---|---|---|---|
| **Global perceptions** | | | | |
| All-channel involvement | 30.55** | linear | 96.71** | 34.06** |
| | | quadratic | 11.20** | |
| All-channel pleasantness | 34.17** | linear | 92.89*** | 22.72** |
| | | quadratic | 10.55** | |
| Kinesic pleasantness/involvement | 49.96** | linear | | 25.46** |
| | | quadratic | | 5.02* |
| Vocalic pleasantness/involvement | 39.13** | linear | | 31.98** |
| | | quadratic | | 5.34* |
| Kinesic anxiety | 11.19** | linear | | 4.30* |
| Vocalic anxiety | 21.60** | linear | | 28.57** |
| **Nonverbal composites/behaviors** | | | | |
| Immediacy composite | 45.85** | | | |
| Immediacy behaviors: | | | | |
| Gaze | 25.28** | linear | 4.35* | |
| | | quadratic | 5.56* | |
| Illustrators | 45.52** | linear | 25.33** | 5.25* |
| | | quadratic | 23.09** | 4.81* |
| Orientation | 5.78* | linear | 4.39* | |
| | | quadratic | 8.21** | |
| Lean | | linear | 18.75** | 9.44** |
| | | quadratic | 6.63* | |

| | | | | | |
|---|---|---|---|---|---|
| Kinesic relaxation composite | 4.73* | | | | |
| Kinesic relaxation behaviors: | | | | | |
| Postural relaxation | 5.95* | linear | 4.27* | linear | 5.62* |
| Positive affect composite | 36.14** | | | | |
| Positive affect behaviors: | | | | | |
| Smiling | 55.11** | linear | 20.97** | linear | 16.11** |
| Relaxed laughter | 7.57** | linear | 11.49** | linear | 4.81* |
| Nodding | 77.47** | linear | 56.18** | linear | 23.10** |
| | | quadratic | 35.14** | quadratic | 6.29* |
| Vocal expressiveness Composite | 36.84** | linear | 66.90** | linear | 40.83** |
| | | quadratic | 5.67* | | |
| Vocal expressiveness behaviors: | | | | | |
| Rhythm | | linear | 6.07* | | |
| Tempo variety | | linear | 23.60** | linear | 7.95** |
| | | quadratic | 9.15** | | |
| Pitch variety | 8.13** | linear | 107.35** | linear | 4.16* |
| | | quadratic | 9.10** | | |
| Vocal relaxation behaviors: | | | | | |
| Pitch | | linear | 5.17* | | |
| Nervous laughter/Vocalizations | 4.94* | linear | 9.75** | | |
| | | quadratic | 9.47** | | |
| Conversational management behaviors: | | | | | |
| Smoothness of turn switches | 4.42* | | | | |

$*p < .05$, $**p < .01$

Table 10.4. *Confederate and participant means for significant communication and time effects*

| | | Time 1 | Time 2 | Time 3 | Time 4 |
|---|---|---|---|---|---|
| **Global perceptions** | | | | | |
| All-channel involvement (1 = not at all, 9 = very involved) | | | | | |
| Unpleasant | Confederate | 5.11 | 5.16 | 5.18 | 5.15 |
| | Participant | 6.27 | 6.49 | 6.46 | 6.51 |
| Pleasant | Confederate | 5.83 | 6.78 | 7.01 | 7.14 |
| | Participant | 6.36 | 6.72 | 7.06 | 7.14 |
| All-channel pleasantness (1 = not at all, 9 = very pleasant) | | | | | |
| Unpleasant | Confederate | 5.28 | 5.18 | 5.15 | 5.16 |
| | Participant | 6.15 | 6.36 | 6.36 | 6.42 |
| Pleasant | Confederate | 6.15 | 6.59 | 6.84 | 7.01 |
| | Participant | 6.31 | 6.65 | 6.90 | 7.01 |
| Kinesic pleasantness/involvement (1 = not at all, 9 = very pleasant) | | | | | |
| Unpleasant | Confederate | 3.42 | 3.29 | 3.20 | 3.10 |
| | Participant | 5.39 | 5.26 | 5.17 | 5.17 |
| Pleasant | Confederate | 6.16 | 7.24 | 7.28 | 7.36 |
| | Participant | 5.70 | 5.77 | 5.86 | 5.87 |
| Vocalic pleasantness/involvement (1 = not at all, 9 = very pleasant) | | | | | |
| Unpleasant | Confederate | 4.32 | 4.50 | 4.58 | 4.58 |
| | Participant | 4.86 | 4.84 | 4.88 | 4.91 |
| Pleasant | Confederate | 5.66 | 6.41 | 6.62 | 6.70 |
| | Participant | 5.23 | 5.53 | 5.83 | 5.96 |

| | | Col 1 | Col 2 | Col 3 | Col 4 |
|---|---|---|---|---|---|
| **Kinesic anxiety (1 = not at all, 9 = very nervous)** | | | | | |
| Unpleasant | Confederate | 5.87 | 6.01 | 6.02 | 5.97 |
| | Participant | 5.01 | 4.73 | 4.60 | 4.53 |
| Pleasant | Confederate | 4.51 | 3.90 | 3.96 | 3.78 |
| | Participant | 4.80 | 4.51 | 4.31 | 4.14 |
| **Vocalic anxiety (1 = not at all, 9 = very nervous)** | | | | | |
| Unpleasant | Confederate | 5.63 | 5.18 | 5.05 | 5.00 |
| | Participant | 5.83 | 5.56 | 5.33 | 5.15 |
| Pleasant | Confederate | 4.55 | 3.89 | 3.46 | 3.25 |
| | Participant | 5.64 | 5.05 | 4.52 | 4.23 |
| **Nonverbal composites/behaviors** | | | | | |
| Immediacy composite (z-scored) | | | | | |
| Unpleasant | Confederate | -.55 | -.77 | -.78 | -.77 |
| | Participant | -.22 | -.27 | -.31 | -.25 |
| Pleasant | Confederate | .54 | .77 | .77 | .75 |
| | Participant | .22 | .27 | .32 | .24 |
| Immediacy behaviors: | | | | | |
| Gaze (% present during time period) | | | | | |
| Unpleasant | Confederate | 21% | 11% | 11% | 8% |
| | Participant | 76% | 76% | 73% | 70% |
| Pleasant | Confederate | 70% | 80% | 77% | 76% |
| | Participant | 82% | 88% | 86% | 82% |
| Illustrators (% present during time) | | | | | |
| Unpleasant | Confederate | 5% | 11% | 8% | 8% |
| | Participant | 10% | 15% | 14% | 15% |
| Pleas:nt | Confederate | 13% | 44% | 40% | 40% |
| | Participant | 18% | 26% | 32% | 27% |

Table 10.4, cont'd.

|  |  | Time 1 | Time 2 | Time 3 | Time 4 |
|---|---|---|---|---|---|
| Orientation (1 = indirect, 9 = direct) | | | | | |
| Unpleasant | Confederate | 4.63 | 3.94 | 3.89 | 3.96 |
|  | Participant | 5.53 | 5.57 | 5.68 | 5.73 |
| Pleasant | Confederate | 6.15 | 7.72 | 7.78 | 7.74 |
|  | Participant | 6.00 | 6.24 | 6.33 | 6.10 |
| Lean (1 = backward, 9 = forward) | | | | | |
| Unpleasant | Confederate | 4.94 | 4.94 | 4.93 | 4.93 |
|  | Participant | 5.21 | 5.33 | 5.19 | 5.06 |
| Pleasant | Confederate | 5.92 | 6.36 | 6.44 | 6.46 |
|  | Participant | 5.26 | 5.19 | 5.15 | 4.98 |
| Kinesic relaxation composite (z-scored) | | | | | |
| Unpleasant | Confederate | .14 | .35 | .35 | .41 |
|  | Participant | -.12 | -.13 | -.14 | -.12 |
| Pleasant | Confederate | -.14 | -.35 | -.34 | -.39 |
|  | Participant | .13 | .14 | .15 | .13 |
| Kinesic relaxation behaviors: | | | | | |
| Postural relaxation (1 = not at all, 9 = very relaxed) | | | | | |
| Unpleasant | Confederate | 5.08 | 5.49 | 5.42 | 5.51 |
|  | Participant | 4.58 | 4.64 | 4.63 | 4.68 |
| Pleasant | Confederate | 4.92 | 4.93 | 4.93 | 4.93 |
|  | Participant | 4.83 | 4.87 | 4.94 | 4.90 |

| Positive affect composite (z-scored) | | | | | |
|---|---|---|---|---|---|
| Unpleasant | Confederate | −.35 | −.49 | −.56 | −.55 |
| | Participant | −.18 | −.22 | −.34 | −.32 |
| Pleasant | Confederate | .34 | .47 | .53 | .55 |
| | Participant | .17 | .22 | .33 | .33 |
| **Positive affect behaviors:** | | | | | |
| Smiling (% present) | | | | | |
| Unpleasant | Confederate | 1% | 2% | 2% | 1% |
| | Participant | 3% | 3% | 4% | 3% |
| Pleasant | Confederate | 11% | 15% | 20% | 18% |
| | Participant | 7% | 9% | 14% | 14% |
| Relaxed laughter (% present during time) | | | | | |
| Unpleasant | Confederate | 0% | 0% | 0% | 0% |
| | Participant | 0% | 2% | 1% | 1% |
| Pleasant | Confederate | 1% | 3% | 5% | 6% |
| | Participant | 1% | 4% | 5% | 5% |
| Nodding (% present during time) | | | | | |
| Unpleasant | Confederate | 9% | 9% | 10% | 9% |
| | Participant | 3% | 9% | 7% | 7% |
| Pleasant | Confederate | 17% | 27% | 27% | 26% |
| | Participant | 9% | 25% | 22% | 24% |
| Vocal expressiveness composite (z-scored) | | | | | |
| Unpleasant | Confederate | −.30 | −.37 | −.31 | −.39 |
| | Participant | −.11 | −.13 | −.14 | −.24 |
| Pleasant | Confederate | −.00 | .29 | .23 | .31 |
| | Participant | .05 | .08 | .10 | .13 |

Table 10.4, cont'd.

| | | Time 1 | Time 2 | Time 3 | Time 4 |
|---|---|---|---|---|---|
| **Vocal Expressiveness Behaviors:** | | | | | |
| Rhythm (1 = not at all, 9 = very rhythmic) | | | | | |
| Unpleasant | Confederate | 6.34 | 6.38 | 6.61 | 6.43 |
| | Participant | 5.87 | 5.86 | 5.76 | 5.75 |
| Pleasant | Confederate | 6.34 | 6.31 | 6.19 | 6.14 |
| | Participant | 5.91 | 5.87 | 5.82 | 5.80 |
| Tempo variety (1 = not at all, 9 = very varied) | | | | | |
| Unpleasant | Confederate | 2.49 | 2.97 | 2.89 | 2.75 |
| | Participant | 5.73 | 5.82 | 5.85 | 5.81 |
| Pleasant | Confederate | 2.92 | 3.73 | 4.06 | 4.05 |
| | Participant | 5.70 | 5.81 | 5.93 | 5.97 |
| Pitch variety (1 = not at all, 9 = very varied) | | | | | |
| Unpleasant | Confederate | 2.42 | 2.72 | 2.80 | 2.70 |
| | Participant | 4.92 | 5.19 | 5.32 | 5.45 |
| Pleasant | Confederate | 2.93 | 3.81 | 4.09 | 4.32 |
| | Participant | 5.15 | 5.44 | 5.74 | 5.84 |
| **Vocal Relaxation Behaviors:** | | | | | |
| Pitch (1 = low, 3 = high) | | | | | |
| Unpleasant | Confederate | 1.49 | 1.68 | 1.71 | 1.68 |
| | Participant | 1.79 | 1.76 | 1.77 | 1.57 |
| Pleasant | Confederate | 1.66 | 1.90 | 1.91 | 1.96 |
| | Participant | 1.76 | 1.73 | 1.73 | 1.74 |

| Nervous laughter/vocalizations (% present during time) | | | | |
|---|---|---|---|---|
| Unpleasant | | | | |
| Confederate | 4% | 2% | 2% | 3% |
| Participant | 6% | 7% | 7% | 7% |
| Pleasant | | | | |
| Confederate | 7% | 7% | 8% | 6% |
| Participant | 7% | 11% | 10% | 9% |
| Conversational Management: | | | | |
| Turn switches (1 = not at all, 9 = very smooth) | | | | |
| Unpleasant | | | | |
| Confederate | 7.12 | 6.84 | 6.75 | 6.87 |
| Participant | 5.56 | 5.61 | 5.60 | 5.62 |
| Pleasant | | | | |
| Confederate | 7.30 | 6.69 | 6.70 | 6.36 |
| Participant | 5.72 | 5.90 | 5.87 | 5.84 |

the pleasant condition, so did P patterns, showing even closer correspondence between T and P behavior (see Figure 10.1). Thus, the global
involvement and pleasantness measures demonstrated strong patterns of
reciprocity. Global kinesic and vocalic anxiety did likewise, with Ps
reciprocating Ts' steep declines in anxiety over time.

On immediacy, Ps interacting with pleasant Ts increased gaze, gesturing, and directness of orientation over time then tapered off slightly
in the last time period, closely corresponding to Ts' pattern and yielding
clear reciprocity. However, Ps reduced forward lean over time, producing a compensatory pattern (moving in the opposite direction as the T).
On positive affect, Ps interacting with pleasant Ts showed the same
increases in smiling, relaxed laughter, and nodding as their partners – a
strong reciprocity pattern. On vocal expressiveness, everyone increased
their tempo and pitch variety over time, but pleasant Ts and Ps showed a
much steeper increase than unpleasant ones, to produce stronger reciprocity in the former condition than the latter. On vocal relaxation
behaviors, Ps interacting with pleasant Ts increased nervous laughter
even more than Ts then tapered off over time, similar to their partner, but
did not follow Ts' rise in pitch level. Overall, then, pleasant communication elicited consistent reciprocity except on lean and pitch (see
Figure 10.2).

The patterns in the unpleasant communication condition were far less
consistent. Those interacting with unpleasant Ts exhibited modest increases in all-channel involvement and pleasantness. These patterns are
best characterized as weak compensation (meeting T's decrease with an
increase). However, Ps showed slight decreases in kinesic pleasantness/
involvement and no change in vocalic pleasantness/involvement, patterns that would be characterized as reciprocity and nonadaptation respectively. On global kinesic and vocalic anxiety, Ps showed decreases
in anxiety over time, which matched Ts' decreases in vocal anxiety but
appeared to compensate Ts' sustained kinesic anxiety. (However, on
kinesic anxiety, given that everyone except unpleasant Ts became more
relaxed over time, Ps' behavior is more attributable to the influence of
time than to the influence of the target.) On immediacy, Ps showed an
increase initially then a decrease over time on three of the behaviors,
suggestive of initial compensation, then reciprocity. On positive affect,
Ps matched their partners in maintaining stable unpleasant patterns over
time. On vocal expressiveness, Ps reciprocated Ts' decline in expressiveness. Overall, then, unpleasant communication elicited a wide range
of responses, ranging from compensation to reciprocity or matching to
nonadaptation.

## DISCUSSION

### Substantive conclusions

The current results, like those from the preceding investigation, produced complementary conclusions from the different analyses. The Pearson product-moment correlations and intraclass correlations produced a predominant pattern of matching, with the exception that participants complemented overall involvement in the low-involvement condition by expressing moderate involvement. Increases in a confederate's pleasantness tended to elicit more change in kinesic behaviors, especially those related to affect and arousal, and decreases in pleasantness tended to elicit more change in vocalic behaviors. The repeated measures analyses of variance likewise produced primarily matching and reciprocity patterns. On average, those interacting with pleasant confederates were more involved and pleasant than those interacting with unpleasant ones. In particular, they tended to match immediacy, positive affect, vocal expressiveness, vocal relaxation, nervous laughter/vocalizations, and turn switches. Over time, participants interacting with pleasant confederates also strongly reciprocated increased pleasantness, immediacy (except for some slight compensation on body lean), positive affect behaviors, vocal expressiveness, and vocal relaxation.

However, decreases in pleasantness elicited a mix of patterns ranging from compensation (on all-channel involvement, initial immediacy, and kinesic anxiety) to nonaccommodation (on vocalic pleasantness/ involvement) to reciprocity/matching (on kinesic pleasantness/ involvement, later immediacy, positive affect, vocal relaxation, and vocal expressiveness). It appears that the violative effect of unpleasant communication introduced substantial variability in interaction behavior. Any compensation that occurred was likely to be related to involvement and composure rather than pleasantness and to occur on kinesic/proxemic or verbal rather than vocal behaviors. It was also more likely to occur during early rather than late time periods, perhaps because participants abandoned their failed compensation strategies.

The combined results are highly consistent in showing that participants closely paralleled target nonverbal patterns when targets became more pleasant and involved. They also partially matched target patterns by becoming less immediate, pleasant, expressive, and relaxed when targets reduced involvement and pleasantness, but resisted changing their nonverbal patterns to the same extent targets did. In this respect,

## All-Channel Involvement

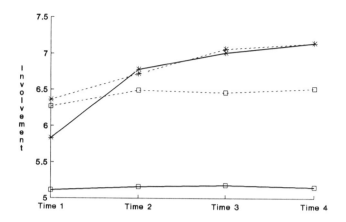

## Kinesic Involvement/Pleasantness

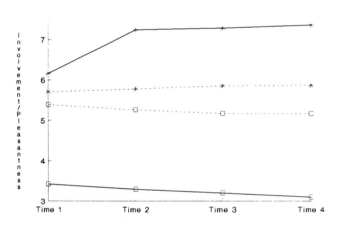

## Global Kinesic Anxiety

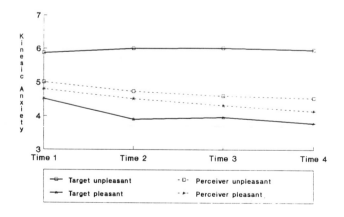

Figure 10.1 Reciprocity/compensation patterns on global nonverbal measures.

## All-Channel Pleasantness

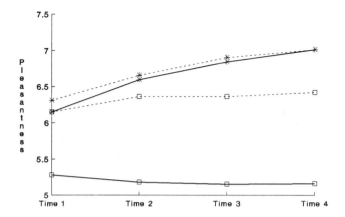

## Vocalic Involvement/Pleasantness

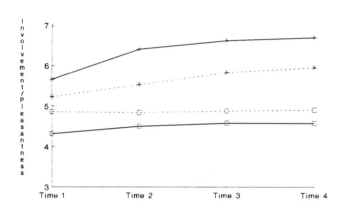

## Global Vocalic Anxiety

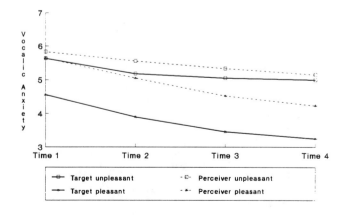

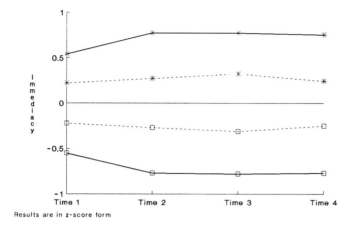

## Immediacy Composite

Results are in z-score form

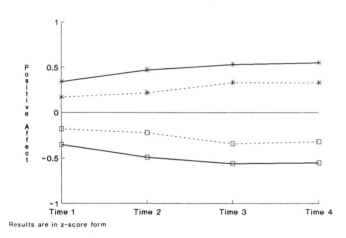

## Positive Affect Composite

Results are in z-score form

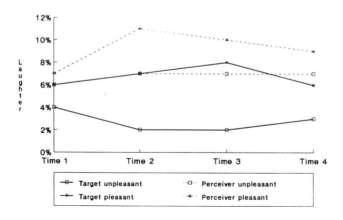

## Laughter (part of Vocal Relaxation)

Figure 10.2 Reciprocity/compensation patterns on composite nonverbal measures. (*Note:* For lean, 1 = backward; for pitch, 1 = low, 3 = high; for the three composite measures: results are in the *z*-score form)

## Lean (part of Immediacy)

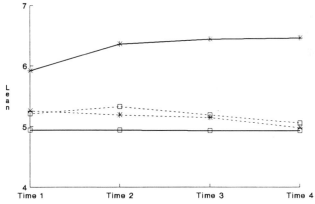

Note: 1 = backward, 9 = forward

## Vocal Expressiveness Composite

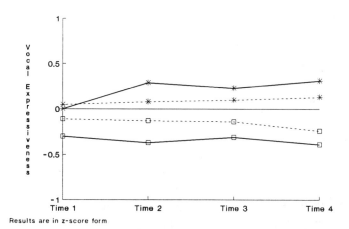

Results are in z-score form

## Pitch (part of Vocal Relaxation)

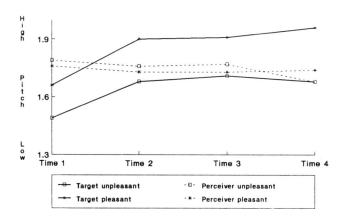

—□— Target unpleasant    -□- Perceiver unpleasant
—*— Target pleasant    -*- Perceiver pleasant

participant behavior served a "braking" or moderating effect on reductions in involvement and pleasantness.

How do these results compare with the preceding study's results? First, in the preceding investigation, the Pearson product-moment and intraclass correlation analyses showed less sensitivity to interaction adaptation than did the repeated measures (or interrupted time-series) analyses. The same was true here but this time the correlations produced more significant relationships.

Second, in the preceding study, the correlations revealed predominantly matching and reciprocity patterns, especially for kinesic/proxemic behaviors under low involvement. In the current study, the patterns were the same except for revealing compensation of overall involvement in the unpleasant condition. These two investigations suggest that the between-dyads correlational analyses may be useful in detecting the extent of similarity between dyad members. With sufficient power they can detect many such relationships and, although they may be more prone to revealing matching or reciprocity than compensation, they are capable of detecting the latter when it is present.

Third, in the preceding study, the repeated measures analyses uncovered a mix of reciprocity and compensation in response to high involvement: Participants showed a mean drop in involvement following the confederate's manipulation of an increase (a compensatory pattern) but then exhibited a nonlinear increase in involvement that paralleled the confederates' own changes (reciprocity). There, it was speculated that participants "put on the brakes" to keep the interaction from escalating too rapidly. Here, the same could be said of the participants' compensatory response to decreased involvement in the correlational analysis. It is as if they were attempting to keep the interaction from sliding too rapidly toward noninvolvement. The repeated measures analyses here likewise imply a braking effect in that participants interacting with unpleasant confederates decreased involvement but not to the same extent as the confederates. They also compensated for too much relaxation in the unpleasant condition and too much forward lean in the pleasant condition. Nevertheless, unlike the preceding investigation, they were willing to reciprocate most increases in pleasantness and involvement, perhaps because they had not already hit an upper threshold of tolerance.

Finally, the preceding investigation implicated immediacy, kinesic/proxemic expressiveness, kinesic positive affect, kinesic/proxemic arousal, vocal attentiveness, and vocal arousal as the behavioral composites most susceptible to influence from the partner's behavior. The same composites emerged here, along with the addition of conversational management behaviors. Thus it appears that most dimensions of conversational involvement and pleasantness play a role in conversational adaptation.

## Methodological implications

The extremely large effect sizes for the global pleasantness and involvement measures reinforce our earlier conclusions that global measures may be an appropriate measurement approach when one wishes to capture large-scale patterns. The measures employed here detected not only stable adaptation patterns that persisted over time but also longitudinal and nonlinear ones.

Nevertheless, there are occasions when more microscopic analysis is warranted, and in any case, it is useful to know which behaviors are most implicated in interaction adaptation. Close inspection of the micro and macro nonverbal analyses pinpoints which behaviors may be particularly susceptible to partner influence. Immediacy behaviors (gaze, orientation, lean, and gestures), for one, showed considerable sensitivity. Participants matched the partner's general level of immediacy, reciprocated increases in three behaviors over time but compensated on a fourth (lean), and initially compensated then reciprocated decreases in immediacy. Such behaviors may therefore serve as a good barometer of transitory changes in involvement and are among the few indicators displaying compensation.

The only other behavior to show any compensation was postural relaxation, with participants being more tense than their overly relaxed targets in the unpleasant communication condition. Relaxation-related cues may therefore be useful to measure. However, only postural relaxation and nervous laughter/vocalizations produced any effects here, the effect sizes were relatively small, and the absence of communication by time interactions on these two measures casts doubt on whether the behaviors were truly sensitive to partner influence.

Positive affect measures (smiling, relaxed laughter, nodding), by contrast, showed very large effects. The presence of main effects for target communication and time as well as communication by time interactions suggests that these measures reflect not only stable individual differences and the influence of time, but also partner influence.

Many of the individual vocal measures did not yield significant effects. However, the several measures that combined to form the vocal expressiveness composite produced substantial effects. It may be that individual vocal cues are too subtle in their adjustments (or too difficult to measure precisely or both) to be useful as single measures but can become very revealing when aggregated. The vocal cues related to conversational management were also generally poor indicators of adaptation, although turn-switch smoothness produced matching. Possibly, improved measurement would lead to more significant effects. Given that many such measures have exhibited matching effects in past research, they should not be discounted.

Because the current results simultaneously uncovered matching/reciprocity and complementarity/compensation patterns within the same data set, they endorse the utility of the particular experimental design employed here. In previous dyadic interaction experiments where target behavior was allowed to vary, this effect was not readily detectable. Manipulating target behavior to achieve two consistent and opposite styles, coupled with the use of a longitudinal design, permitted attributing participant behavior change to the confederate-initiated changes.

Apart from this investigation underscoring the value of multivariate measurement of reciprocity and compensation (or reliance on global measures), it also underscores the value of using multiple statistical methods for analyzing interaction patterns. Kenny et al. (1995) have demonstrated that between-dyad analyses may produce opposite conclusions to those of within-dyad analyses and that both are necessary to fully understand the phenomenon under examination. We agree. Correlational analyses, which are between-dyad analyses, indicate whether people are more like their interaction partners than different. Within-dyad analyses reveal adjustments over time and the extent to which each dyad member is adjusting to the partner. Such a result might be likely on expressiveness. On average, dyads with one highly expressive member are more likely to have another highly expressive member, while those with an inexpressive member are likely to have an inexpressive partner – a matching pattern. But it is also possible that if one member changes expressiveness markedly, the other will compensate to restore the original level. Thus, compensation may occur within dyads even though matching or reciprocity is the norm across dyads. We therefore recommend coupling cross-sectional analyses with within-dyad longitudinal ones such as repeated measures analysis of variance to gain the most complete understanding of these interaction patterns.

The repeated measures approach has the added advantage of permitting inclusion of between-dyad factors that produce more homogeneous groupings of dyads while testing for possible moderators that prompt some dyads to converge or reciprocate and others to diverge or compensate. At the same time, the magnitude and shapes of the reciprocal or compensatory relationships can be assessed. In the current investigation, this analysis not only detected mean differences between experimental conditions but also illustrated how patterns differed over time between conditions. This produced a combination of compensation in terms of mean differences but reciprocity in terms of matching a slope or curve.

A further advantage of repeated measures analysis is that it identifies the influence of time separate from the influence of one's partner. In the case of vocal anxiety, for example, everybody became more relaxed over time. Such changes were not due to partner influence but rather to people becoming more comfortable with the situation. The emergence of independent time effects points out one other important methodological consideration – inclusion of some form of control group. Whether it be a baseline condition or two or more groups or conditions that serve as comparison points, it is necessary to determine whether changes are in fact attributable to one's partner or to external factors. In the case of kinesic anxiety, the unpleasant target sustained a high level of anxiety whereas everyone else became more relaxed. In the absence of a pleasant condition, the pattern in the unpleasant condition looks like one of compensation by the participant. But in reality, the participant was probably just following the natural trend of increased relaxation over time. The presence of the pleasant condition as a comparison group makes this evident.

In turn, this argues for greater use of experimental or quasi-experimental designs where control group comparisons and systematic control of other external factors are inherent features. A combination of experimental and nonexperimental studies is most likely to advance the quest for identifying interaction adaptation patterns.

## DECEPTION/SUSPICION EXPERIMENTS

The findings we were uncovering in our dyadic interaction studies led us to explore whether similar patterns would obtain under conditions of deceit or suspected deceit. Two experiments lent themselves to such an analysis.

The first, reported in Burgoon, Buller, Dillman, and Walther (in press), entailed participants conducting interviews during which one participant, randomly assigned the role of interviewee, either lied or told the truth and the other participant, assigned the role of interviewer, was induced to be moderately or highly suspicious (or not). After the interviews, trained coders rated the participants' nonverbal behavior on multiple dimensions. Analyses included repeated measures analyses of variance testing the effects of interviewer suspicion on interviewee behavior and intraclass correlations between interviewer and interviewee behavior. We chose intraclass correlations over Pearson product-moment correlations because we wanted them to capture heterogeneity, if present, between interviewer and interviewee.

Results showed that as interviewers became more suspicious, they also became more immediate and pleasant. In turn, interviewees encountering high suspicion became more immediate and pleasant (contrary to what the deception literature might have predicted). The result: a pattern of reciprocity. The correlations likewise showed patterns of matching/reciprocity, not just on immediacy but on a host of other nonverbal measures. Specifically, the following related clusters of measures all produced positive correlations, regardless of whether deception and suspicion were present or absent:

1. immediacy composite (comprising four behaviors), $r = .42$
2. kinesic pleasantness, $r = .43$; nods, $r = .29$; vocal pleasantness, $r = .18$
3. kinesic arousal, $r = .20$
4. turn switches/latencies, $r = .49$; fluency, $r = .70$

Only global measures of kinesic and vocalic relaxation failed to produce significant correlations and no compensatory patterns were evident.

To explore whether patterns differed within suspicion and deception conditions, intraclass correlations were calculated within each. While reciprocity continued to prevail, suspicion appeared to produce linear changes in the degree of reciprocity across the three conditions, whereas deception appeared to have little effect. As suspicion increased, reciprocity intensified for kinesic arousal, nods, and vocal pleasantness but became increasingly attenuated for kinesic relaxation, immediacy, and kinesic pleasantness and actually switched to compensation for kinesic relaxation under high suspicion.

The effect of suspicion was even more evident when comparing the condition where neither suspicion nor deception were present (which is most like "normal" interaction) to conditions where both deception and suspicion (moderate or high) were present. The predominant pattern in the "normal" interactions continued to be reciprocity on all but two measures. Comparatively, when deception and suspicion were both present, reciprocity was weaker on immediacy and kinesic and vocalic relaxation but stronger on vocal (un)pleasantness and kinesic arousal. Again, suspicion appeared to exert more influence than deception. These results suggest that introduction of some negative elements in an interaction – such as suspicion – may have the capacity to disrupt the basic reciprocity pattern.

Yet another experiment goes a step further in demonstrating that negatively valenced elements in interaction can actually produce compensation. That experiment, reported in Burgoon, Buller, Ebesu, White, and Rockwell (in press), was similar in employing the interview format and manipulating deception and suspicion. In this case, interviewees told the truth on the first few questions then shifted to one of three types of deception (falsification, equivocation, or concealment) on the remaining questions. Interviewers were or were not induced to be suspicious. A unique feature of this study was that half the sample consisted of laypeople who were presumably novices at deceiving and detecting deceit and the other half consisted of military experts who were trained and experienced in interrogation and interview procedures.

Repeated measures ANOVAs and correlational analyses were again conducted on the nonverbal behaviors coded from the videotaped interactions. The pertinent analyses of variance examined changes from the truthful answers at the beginning of the interview to the later, deceptive ones. (These are the only analyses that show changes in each person's behavior over time, a necessary prerequisite to concluding that reciprocity or compensation occurred.) The between-dyad analyses produced mostly reciprocity but some evidence of compensation also emerged. Following are the behaviors and conditions that produced evidence of adaptation:

| *Reciprocity* | *Compensation* |
|---|---|
| involvement and pleasantness | |
| vocal expressiveness under suspicion (experts only) | vocal expressiveness under non-suspicion |
| kinesic expressiveness (esp. under suspicion) | |

| kinesic tension | vocal tension during equivocation; vocal tension with friends under suspicion |
| formality | |
| fluency | |

The correlations, initially conducted *within* truthful and deceptive answers but across conditions similarly produced reciprocity on pleasantness, formality, kinesic expressiveness, and fluency. However, when participants were separated by suspicion condition and sample, more relationships emerged, including more instances of compensation. For example, interactants reciprocated dominance when suspicion was absent (average $r = .17$) but compensated for it when suspicion was present (average $r = -.28$). Pleasantness correlations were strong and consistent in the no suspicion condition (average $r = .53$) but weaker and variable in the presence of suspicion (range of $r = -.07$ to .51). The full complement of within-dyad analyses can be summarized as follows:

| *Reciprocity* | *Compensation* |
| involvement under nonsuspicion; novice involvement under suspicion | expert involvement under suspicion |
| pleasantness | |
| novice kinesic expressiveness under truth | expert kinesic expressiveness under truth |
| novice vocal expressiveness under nonsuspicion | vocal expressiveness under suspicion and/or deception |
| dominance under nonsuspicion | dominance under suspicion |
| novice formality under nonsuspicion; expert formality under suspicion | |
| novice fluency | |
| novice kinesic tension under suspicion | expert kinesic tension under nonsuspicion; expert vocal tension under suspicion |

Overall, these results offer further indications – albeit in need of further replication – that compensation does occur across a variety of behaviors and channels. Here, it emerged more often under suspicion, deception, and expertise. The implication: Compensation may be more common when interactions depart from "normalcy" – that is, when factors such as suspicion, deception, and differential knowledge and experience with the task are introduced. One reason these elements may evoke compensation is that they create interaction patterns that are outside the desired or expected range, causing interactants to engage in behaviors designed to model desired responses or to "pull" the interaction back to a more typical pattern. If this speculation is valid, then one may expect to see far less evidence of compensation than reciprocity in normal interactions and expect to see compensation only when one interactant engages in "abnormal" behavior. We amplify this idea in the next chapter.

## CONCLUSION

The investigations reported here add further support to a predominant pattern of reciprocity under positively valenced conditions but occasional compensation under negatively valenced or atypical conditions. At the same time, the greater insights gained from using both between-dyad and within-dyad analyses and using multiple dependent measures reaffirms the benefit of adopting a multimethod, multimeasure research strategy.

### NOTE

[1] The significant effects were as follows: (1) for *all-channel involvement,* target communication $F(1,154) = 25.54$, $\eta^2 = .14$, $p < .0001$; time $F(3,462) = 38.16$, $\eta^2 = .20$, $p < .0001$; communication by time $F(3,462) = 10.03$, $\eta^2 = .06$, $p < .0001$; (2) for *all-channel pleasantness,* target communication $F(1,154) = 31.53$, $\eta^2 = .17$, $p < .0001$; time $F(3,462) = 375.10$, $\eta^2 = .20$, adjusted $p < .0001$; communication by time $F(3,462) = 6.88$, $\eta^2 = .04$, adjusted $p < .0001$; (3) for *kinesic pleasantness/involvement,* target communication $F(1,154) = 39.85$, $\eta^2 = .20$, $p < .0001$; communication by time $F(3,462) = 10.17$, $\eta^2 = .06$, adjusted $p < .0001$; for *vocal pleasantness/involvement,* target communication $F(1,154) = 34.15$, $\eta^2 = .19$, $p < .0001$; communication by time $F(3,447) = 17.18$, $\eta^2 = .10$, adjusted $p < .0001$.

*Part V*

Developing a new interpersonal adaptation theory

# 11

## The theories revisited

We are now ready to consider the theories and models that have been forwarded in light of the empirical evidence that we and others have amassed. We begin by briefly recapitulating the main theses of the fifteen or so models and theories that we have examined, then consider the most important conclusions from previous empirical research and from our own investigations reported in Chapters 9 and 10. Against this backdrop, we sketch a new model of interaction adaptation.

### THE EXTANT THEORIES

The biologically based models (e.g., Interactional Synchrony, Motor Mimicry, and Mirroring) largely predict that interacting individuals will exhibit similar patterns to one another – similar in terms of their visual and vocal composition or their temporal properties or both. These adaptation patterns are presumed to have an innate basis, owing perhaps to their survival value and their satisfaction of such basic needs as bonding, safety, and social organization. Consequently, they are presumed to be universal and largely involuntary, although it is recognized that numerous environmental and social factors may facilitate or impede their enactment.

The class of arousal-based and affect-based models includes some of the most well-recognized and tested of the interaction adaptation theories. These theories share in common a belief that internal emotional and arousal states are driving forces in people's decisions to approach or avoid others. Affiliative Conflict Theory (ACT), also known as Equilibrium Theory, posits that interactions are characterized by some comfort level that balances needs for approach and affiliation with needs for avoidance and privacy. When interaction patterns deviate from that "homeostatic" comfort level, ACT postulates that there will be pressure to compensate – either intrapersonally or interpersonally – to restore it.

The Bidimensional Model (BM) works off the same principle of approach and avoidance tendencies but attributes them largely to individual personality traits and attempts to predict conjoint interaction patterns by pairing individual predispositions. A variety of patterns, including both reciprocity and compensation, are predicted by this model.

The Arousal-Labeling Theory (ALT) likewise posits that both compensation and reciprocity may occur, but the focus of this model is on how the undifferentiated arousal engendered by a partner's behavior change is affectively labeled – positive labels producing reciprocity and negative labels producing compensation. Discrepancy-Arousal Theory (DAT) combines arousal and affect with expectancies, predicting that discrepancies from expected behavior patterns produce arousal change, that moderate arousal change is affectively positive and elicits approach (typically reciprocity), and that high arousal change is affectively negative and elicits avoidance (typically compensation). Dialectical models, though not specifically intended to predict adaptation patterns, implicitly argue for a mix of patterns because individual needs and preferences are postulated to wax and wane, causing people's interaction patterns to cycle between poles of approach/openness and avoidance/closedness, among other dialectic tensions (but see Baxter, 1992, for possible response modes other than cycling).

The class of social-norm models elevates the importance of social phenomena as guiding forces and downplays the importance of physiological and psychological factors. The Norm of Reciprocity, which is the simplest theoretical statement favoring reciprocity patterns, predicts that out of felt social obligation, individuals will reciprocate the behaviors they receive from others. It underpins the Dyadic Effect, in which people reciprocate verbal self-disclosure (as well as other interaction behaviors). Other predictions are also derivable from this principle. The interpersonal expectancy literature predicts that interactants may deliberately draw upon this deeply ingrained habit by modeling behavior they desire, in hopes that the target will reciprocate. Other theories, such as Social Exchange and Resource Exchange, rather than directly predicting interaction patterns, amplify the social norms and expectations that would lead others to reciprocate. However, one socially based theory that does explicitly address interaction patterns is Communication Accommodation Theory (CAT). It postulates that interaction convergence and divergence are strategies that will depend, among other factors, on the ingroup or outgroup status of the interactants and on their motivations to identify with one other, to signal affiliation or social distance, and to facilitate or impede smooth interaction and understanding.

Finally, what we have labeled the communication- and cognitive-based models incorporate communication-related cognitions and behaviors in addition to the preceding biological, psychological, and sociological factors. These approaches examine communication functionally; that is, they analyze interaction patterns according to the communicative purposes being served within a given episode and the meanings the behavioral patterns convey.

One model that explicitly calls attention to the multifunctional nature of interaction is the Sequential-Functional Model, which is limited to factors related to involvement changes. SFM identifies multiple preinteractional and interactional factors that determine whether exchanges are stable or unstable and the degree to which interactants accommodate to one another. Among the cognitive elements introduced by this model are cognitive effort related to deliberative, goal-oriented activities and action schemas related to spontaneous, unconscious interaction patterns. Affect and arousal also continue to play a role. When behaviors are affectively charged, the model parallels ALT predictions (i.e., that people reciprocate positively valenced immediacy increases but compensate negatively valenced ones). However, the initial and revised versions still contain indeterminacies as to which circumstances will elicit reciprocity versus compensation.

Another exemplar of work focusing squarely on function and communication is Bavelas and colleagues' reframed view of Motor Mimicry (MM). They found that certain classes of mimetic behaviors are most likely to occur, in full-blown form, in the presence of others who have clear visual access; they demonstrated that ostensibly innate signals are communicative ones designed to convey empathy. What looks like involuntary behavior may actually be deliberate communication. MM predicts matching, but the "matching" is of a functional sort, between a target's state and a perceiver's display of empathy for that state. A perceiver may therefore mimic a target's actual behavior, or, in the case of recalled events, display an empathic response appropriate to the target's situation.

The two remaining theories, Expectancy Violations Theory (EVT) and Cognitive Valence Theory (CVT; formerly Arousal Valence Theory), combine elements of many of the preceding models by including socially based expectations and cognitions, physiological arousal, and affective reactions in the form of communicator and behavior valences. In its most abstract form, EVT requires determining whether one interactant's behavior change qualifies as a positive or negative violation. Within the realm of involvement and immediacy changes, it predicts that (a) unexpected positive behavior by a positively valenced interactant will produce reciprocal behavior, (b) unexpected negative behavior by a positively valenced interactant will produce compensatory behavior, (c) unexpected negative behavior by a negatively valenced interactant will produce reciprocal negative behavior, and (d) unexpected positive behavior by a negatively valenced interactant may produce either reciprocal or compensatory behavior, depending on which is more salient – the valence of the behavior or the valence of the interactant. CVT expands upon the factors (schemata) that influence the valencing process but these factors primarily influence valencing under conditions of moderate arousal change, inasmuch as high levels of arousal change are described as consistently aversive. Positively valenced moderate arousal is predicted to elicit reciprocity, whereas negatively valenced (moderate or high) arousal change is posited to elicit compensation.

CVT, SFM, and MM have restricted domains: The former two are applicable only to immediacy or involvement changes, and CVT applies only to increases. The latter is applicable only to the class of fleeting, mimetic acts likely to emerge in response to some emotionally charged circumstance of the partner. EVT is intended to apply more broadly not only to nonverbal behaviors but also to verbal ones and to communication functions other than the expression of involvement.

This brief summary makes plain that while most theories predict a mix of patterns rather than committing to a single dominant pattern, they conflict over which patterns are likely under a given set of conditions. Like so much else regarding human behavior, the theories' explanatory mechanisms also differ in the extent to which biological, psychological, sociological, or communicological factors are weighted most heavily.

## THE RESEARCH EVIDENCE

Throughout Chapters 2–5, we reported findings related to the foremost models and theories regarding interaction synchronization, adaptation, and nonaccommodation. Much of that evidence has also been summarized elsewhere (e.g., Aiello, 1987; Cappella, 1981, 1983, 1991a;

Giles, Coupland, & Coupland, 1991a; Patterson, 1983). Here, we will not reiterate these findings in fine detail but rather summarize and highlight the major ones.

First, there is strong evidence of synchrony, matching, and convergence occurring. Synchronization begins in infancy and continues into adulthood although many factors can disrupt it. Matching and convergence are especially evident on gaze (if it is not extreme) and on such speech-related behaviors as switch pauses, response latencies, loudness, and talk time. Interactants are more inclined to converge speech styles (including accent, language choice, verbal content, formality) with ingroup members and well-regarded others but to diverge styles with outgroup members and disliked others. There is also solid evidence of reciprocal self-disclosure, especially on intimacy breadth and depth.

But other verbal behavior such as intimate questioning may lead to shorter (compensatory) rather than longer answers. Likewise, increased verbal immediacy may be met with compensatory reductions in nonverbal immediacy (e.g., gaze, proximity) and with longer response latencies. Increased nonverbal immediacy (e.g., close proximity, forward lean, direct body orientation, frequent gaze) may be met with compensatory reductions in nonverbal immediacy, especially when the increased immediacy is "intrusive" or extreme. And, compensation may occur in response to verbal aggression, physical threats, and personal space invasions by strangers. These compensatory reactions may reflect instinctive flight responses.

All of the patterns described may be moderated by such factors as gender, age, personality, interpersonal orientation, individual goals, physical attractiveness, status differences, asymmetrical role relationships, liking for the partner, prospects for future interaction (which is a risk factor related to self-presentation), relational stage, relational definition, relational satisfaction, and attributions about intentions. For example, complementarity is more common in asymmetrical role relationships such as doctor–patient or supervisor–supervisee; reciprocity is more common in the earlier stages of relationships than in later ones. Contextual and situational factors such as purpose of the interaction (social versus task), location and timing of the interaction, and the presence or absence of other parties in the setting are also likely to affect these interaction patterns.

This brings us to our own recent findings. In the investigation reported in Chapter 9, we found that matching and reciprocity were most prevalent, although there was some compensation in the high-involvement condition (a pattern we attributed to the initially high level of involvement being unsustainable over time). In Chapter 10, we reported several further investigations that found a preponderance of matching and reciprocity. However, compensation (and complementarity) tended to occur in response to high degrees of immediacy and assertiveness, to extremely low involvement, or to circumstances likely to engender discomfort.

These recurrent findings led us to conjecture that interactants hold perceptual upper and lower bounds beyond which they are unwilling to let conversational involvement, pleasantness, and dominance drift (at least during brief interactions). Within those boundaries, matching and reciprocity appear to be the default response, possibly due to an almost inexorable pressure to maintain the level of involvement, pleasantness, and equality within that range. The adaptation occurs so effortlessly as to suggest an automatic entrainment process that may be a necessary prerequisite for behavioral coordination, smooth information exchange, and comprehension.

However, when some as-yet-to-be determined boundary is crossed, compensatory actions kick in. Such compensation is typically only partial and may function more to alleviate discomfort and unease – from sensory overload in the case of high immediacy, from fear in the case of an interviewer's assertiveness with a deceiving interviewee, or from uncertainty in the case of decreased pleasantness – than to radically alter the overall level of self or other's involvement. Even when one person decreases pleasantness and involvement, the other tends to maintain a socially polite level of involvement, which appears as nonaccommodation. Nonaccommodation on individual behaviors, which materialized with some frequency, may serve a similar stabilizing function, preventing the interaction dynamic from deviating too far from the norm. Often it is only when behaviors are combined into composites that adaptation patterns emerge, implying that individual behavioral changes are fairly subtle.

## THEORY IMPLICATIONS

How well do the various theories account for these patterns? The combined results are at odds with the predictions from several theories. ACT posits that large changes in one person's behaviors will routinely trigger compensatory responses. The overwhelming degree of reciprocity across investigations makes this position untenable as a general principle. Compensation was operative only under narrowly defined circumstances and for specific behaviors. It may be that many social interactions do not entail deviations large enough to warrant compensation. If so, we should expect only moderate arousal changes, under which circumstances DAT, CVT, and possibly SFM would predict reciprocity. This is what obtained. If, however, we assume for the moment that many of the experiments did indeed produce "large" discrepancies, then several results from the first experiment in Chapter 10 dispute DAT's and CVT's predictions that large deviations from an expected interaction pattern always produce aversion and avoidance. Also contrary to these theories' predictions are (a) the frequent reciprocity of large increases in pleasantness or involvement by pleasant confederates, (b) the initial compensatory (affiliative) response to unpleasant confederates' nonimmediacy, and (c) participants' compensatory decrease in global and vocal anxiety in response to confederates' sustained anxiety. The relative stability of most vocal behaviors in the Chapter 9 and 10 investigations also fail to support CAT's predictions that people adapt vocal patterns to partners. These data instead showed most adaptation occurring in the kinesic or proxemic realm (although we caution readers that problems with vocal cue measurement instead may have been responsible for the weak vocalic patterns we found).

The striking absence of expectancy effects in the first investigation reported in Chapter 10 also calls into question the models positing that communicator valence is a major determinant of response patterns. This includes EVT, expectancy signaling or behavioral confirmation research, DAT, CAT, and possibly CVT (which includes communicator valence as one of six valencers). The failure of communicator valence to make a difference would seem to downgrade the relative importance of personal attributes and to upgrade communication patterns as the most salient cue to interaction *behavior* (in contrast to the significant influence of communicator valence on postinteraction cognitions and affect). In fairness, however, it must be acknowledged that had the interactions been between acquaintances or friends, communicator valence might have exerted more influence. Certainly all the earlier research on reciprocity and compensation documents numerous communicator characteristics that make a difference. And, had the valences been more extreme, perhaps they would have exerted greater influence.

The results *are* consistent with the Norm of Reciprocity except that adaptation seems to be more subconscious, nondeliberative, habitual, and automatic than the reciprocity principle is sometimes conceptualized. In that regard, the results are consonant with biologically based models such as Interactional Synchrony and with the unconscious automatic responses predicted by SFM. At the same time, behaviors that have multiple communication functions tend to be the most labile, consistent with Bavelas and colleagues' MM work showing that behavioral adjustments during dyadic encounters have a distinct communicative purpose.

The results are also consistent with the *premises* of several models: (a) the EVT, DAT, and CAT principle of a threshold, tolerance range, or preference zone outside of which another's behaviors become negatively valenced and prompt different interaction patterns than behaviors falling within it; (b) the EVT, DAT, and CVT principle that the size of discrepancy or violation alters the pattern; and (c) the guiding principle of ACT that some compensatory reactions may be the result of discomfort. Several interpersonal distance models are built around the concept of a "comfort zone" within which matching, convergence, or maintenance are implicitly assumed to prevail; divergence or compensation are only expected to be activated when behaviors fall outside of it. If the concept of discomfort is expanded to include psychological as well as physiological unease and to include atypical events that arouse discomfort, then many of the current findings support this principle and, by implication, many interpersonal adaptation models.

But the scope of these theories extends beyond mere comfort or safety concerns. Our findings, like those from CAT, confirm that divergent and compensatory responses may occur for a wide range of interaction behaviors (e.g., formality, dominance) and functions (e.g., conversation management). If an interaction becomes too informal, divergence may be employed to restore the desired level of formality. If a speaker's response latencies are perceived as too long, an interlocutor may attempt to speed up and "smooth" the interaction by engaging in much shorter turn switches. In this respect, divergence and compensation may come into play whenever a co-interactant's behavior pattern moves outside the required, expected, or desired range for the given set of relationships, setting, and purpose of the interaction.

In short, many theories have been on the right track in assessing motivating factors of behavioral change but have underestimated the strong entrainment effect of another's behavior during normal interactions. Additionally, many theories have focused too narrowly on immediacy and involvement, failing to consider the wide spectrum of behaviors and functions to which they might be applicable.

## REASONS FOR NONISOMORPHISM BETWEEN THEORIES AND EMPIRICAL DATA

Apart from the scope problems just identified, one reason that many past investigations may have failed to detect entrainment is that behaviors have been examined microscopically and piecemeal. Ironically, investigations that examined only a few individual behaviors but measured them precisely (such as at the millisecond level) may have been too fine-grained to capture the subtleties and interconnectedness of most behavioral adaptations or may have been overly strict in expecting to find adaptation on identical rather than functionally equivalent behaviors.

The search for compensation may also have driven researchers to devise studies entailing extremes in immediacy behaviors or to select noninteractive situations such as personal space violations in public facilities. Although such designs may produce compensation, these atypical manipulations are rarely found in daily interactions. Whereas compensatory flight responses may be prevalent in noninteractive situations where people have limited recourse to physical protection and no constraints on their departure, interdependent work and social situations may prevent this kind of compensation, forcing alternative patterns to emerge. Thus, the use of more naturalistic interactional settings, coupled with multivariate data analysis techniques and global measures as benchmarks, has begun to reveal that compensatory moves are in the minority, are confined to particular behaviors, and are more fleeting than reciprocal/matching responses.

These conclusions necessitate our own theoretical model taking into account the predominance of matching and reciprocity as well as the factors that moderate or override this basic and seemingly automatic response pattern.

Relatedly, past investigations may have produced mixed or weak evidence of dyadic adaptation because they failed to consider the communication functions being served by the behaviors in question. Because interactants face multiple tasks and demands to achieve their goals in a competent manner, their communication behavior may originate from and be a reflection of these multiple communication objectives. A common problem has been researchers' treatment of involvement as synonymous with intimacy, leading to confusion about what was actually reciprocated or compensated:

> High nonverbal involvement (including a close interaction distance), for example, may be associated not at all with high intimacy but instead with the managed and purposive function of *social control . . .* or the impersonal function of *service or task.* (Aiello, 1987, p. 407)

Taking a functional perspective – that is, recognizing that multiple interchangeable behaviors may accomplish the same function and that a given behavior may accomplish more than one function – requires knowing in advance what functions are operative and what behaviors accomplish them. Without such knowledge, it is unlikely that precise predictions can be made about which behaviors will be adapted and in which direction. For example, if participants reciprocate behaviors they interpret as functionally appropriate but compensate inappropriate ones, it is necessary to know the salient functions and their behavioral manifestations before determining which behaviors will be adapted. A functional perspective also allows for senders and receivers placing different functional interpretations on a given behavior. Close proximity may be intended to show conversational involvement but interpreted as insistent information seeking. The receiver, who might otherwise match conversational involvement, may compensate proximity in response to perceived overbearing behavior. Predictive precision may therefore require knowledge of participant perceptions as well as behavior.

It also may require knowing what social norms and pressures constrain inclinations to adapt. To illustrate, although interactants might prefer to reduce immediacy to a more distant, comfortable level, they may feel compelled to maintain immediacy out of social propriety or a desire to gain a competitive advantage. A functional perspective obviously makes predicting and explaining adaptation patterns far more complex, but it may better mirror reality and may begin to account for some otherwise anomalous findings.

We have also seen that between-dyad (or between-subject) analyses can produce different conclusions than within-dyad analyses. The same is true of cross-sectional as compared to longitudinal analyses. This is to be expected because each type of analysis answers different questions. But researchers have been fairly cavalier in disregarding these differences when drawing conclusions. The result has been a muddle of conclusions about what patterns are most common, with little attention to the role that choice of design or statistical analysis method played in arriving at a given conclusion. We must be more cautious in the future in using, say, a between-dyads analysis to draw conclusions about within-dyad patterns and must be more careful in describing what kinds of patterns have been uncovered.

## PRINCIPLES GUIDING INTERACTION ADAPTATION THEORY

The foregoing discussion of past theoretical contributions and methodological considerations, coupled with the voluminous empirical evidence from our own and others' investigations, lead us to advance several principles, all of which underpin the new formal model we shall describe shortly:

1. *There may be an innate pressure to adapt interaction patterns,* akin to the pressure to create language. Such adaptation may satisfy survival needs, facilitate information processing and communication, synchronize individual human cycles and activities, and enable group and cultural coordination. Regardless of whether the inclination to adapt is "hard-wired" or arises from its felicitous effects on human social organization, humans are predisposed to mesh their interaction patterns with those of others.

2. *At the biological level, the inherent pressures are toward entrainment and synchrony, with the exception of compensatory adjustments that ensure physical safety and comfort.* Adaptations with biological etiologies should be highly automatic, unconscious, and rapid. (Aiello, 1987, claims this also applies to most compensatory adjustments. Although automatic compensatory adjustments can be used strategically and consciously, more often they are not.) Matching and synchrony patterns should be especially common when both participants are subject to the same external influences. Contexts inducing arousal should elicit increased pitch from both participants, just as situations that heighten cognitive load should elicit increased adaptor use and pauses from both. Similarly, affectively charged situations may drive both people's behavior. To the extent that people's anger and hostility are not under complete self-control, some of the escalation of hostilities that is so prevalent in the literature can be likened to reacting unconsciously to the amount of external negativism present in the "environment." A highly negatively charged situation can become contagious, producing

more an involuntary than a voluntary reaction to the partner. For some, this may take the form of *fight*, for others, *flight*. Positive affect can also be "catching": Yawns and laughter often show a behavioral contagion effect (Hatfield et al., 1994).

Many other compensatory or nonaccommodation patterns may be due to the discomfort of extreme proximity or immediacy. For example, Mahl (1987) found that extreme close and far distances failed to promote more self-disclosure during therapy sessions (as had been expected) and led to less successful therapy because the discrepant distances created anxiety that impaired people's ability to express themselves clearly. Thus, comfort factors are prime suspects when compensatory patterns appear.

3. *Approach or avoidance drives are not fixed or constant but cyclical due to satiation at a given pole.* After one need is satisfied, the gradient of the competing need may become stronger, pulling behavior in the opposite direction. Other kinds of needs and preferences may follow similar dialectical patterns. In other words, rather than predicting matching or complementarity, reciprocity or compensation, and convergence or divergence, theories must determine under which conditions each will occur. Individual differences in how much approach or avoidance partners desire also must be taken into account, as one person may be in an approach phase while the other is in an avoidance phase.

4. *At the social level, the pressure is also toward reciprocity and matching,* at least during normal, socially polite conversation. Communication that is regulated by social norms and expectations may also be highly routinized and unconscious and may restrict tendencies to engage in divergent behavior. For example, the instinct to withdraw under close proximity may be countermanded by the social expectations for displaying moderate conversational involvement. However, if conflict arises and politeness norms are violated, it may be socially appropriate to compensate or even withdraw. Biological and social forces, then, jointly predispose interactants to engage in coordinated interactions with similar interaction styles.

At the same time, some role-related behaviors and structural features of interactions may result in compensatory patterns on particular behaviors. According to Street and Buller (1988), turn duration and gesture rates are compensated in doctor–patient interviews. But these patterns may have been due to the nature of interviews or to status asymmetry present in the physician and patient roles. One can see that during the questioning phase, the patient would be doing more talking and the physician less, and gesturing accompanies longer rather than shorter turns at talk. Later, we might see this pattern reverse when the physician shifts into an instruction- or information-giving phase. In other circumstances, we should expect to see those in high-status roles exhibiting dominance and those in low-status roles exhibiting submissiveness. Such compensation should be understood not as partner-specific adaptation but as a response to role requirements or to the situation. These patterns qualify as adaptations nonetheless and highlight one class of conditions under which compensation should materialize.

In other cases, role relationships themselves may dictate reciprocity. Relationships that are marked by status equality – such as friendships – may dictate and reinforce reciprocity as the norm.

5. *At the communication level, both reciprocity and compensation may occur.* Car salespeople interacting with shoppers may exaggerate reciprocity in an attempt to establish rapport and make a sale. Others may adopt a compensatory, obsequious style to ingratiate themselves to prospective customers. Because interactants may deliberately and strategically manipulate their interaction style to send a relational message, to reinforce a partner's interaction style, or to prompt a change, they may employ either adaptation pattern or even nonaccommodation to achieve their ends. Communication goals such as the desire to create a positive self-image, to process information, or to express interest may override instinctive but socially inappropriate responses. These volitional forms of adaptation may range from convergent to divergent and reciprocal to compensatory. Hence, behaviors *primarily* under the control of biological forces or social norms may follow different patterns than those that are intentionally communicative. For example, interactants may reflexively match the vocal tension and urgency in another's voice. But if they become aware of it, they may attempt to introduce greater calm into the situation, leading to a compensatory display of vocal relaxation and slowed tempo.

The deliberate use of communication patterns need not require a high level of awareness on the part of participants. Palmer and Simmons (1993) showed that interactants who deliberately attempted to increase a partner's affiliation with them were successful in eliciting the intended behaviors but could not identify how they did so. The conclusion: "Even in a situation where intentions and goals are salient, nonverbal behaviors used to increase and decrease interpersonal liking are most likely selected through some covert, automatic process" (Palmer & Simmons, 1993, p. 31). Presumably, the same would be true of adaptation patterns.

6. *Despite predispositions to adapt, the degree of strategic, conscious adaptation present in any situation will be limited due to: (a) individual consistency in behavioral style, (b) internal causes of adjustments, (c) poor self-monitoring or monitoring of the partner, (d) inability to adjust performance, and (e) cultural differences in communication practices and expectations.* Cappella (1984) has pointed out the degree of consistency present in individuals' interaction styles over time and over interactions. The "actor effect" in Kenny's (1988) social relations model also tacitly recognizes the degree of consistency that each individual is likely to exhibit across multiple partners. Other factors that should restrict adaptation are individual mood states and idiosyncratic reactivity to the environment that inhibit coordination with a partner, individuals' own inadequate knowledge of appropriate behavior or inadequate skills, and cultural dictates that require certain types of behavior, regardless of what a co-interactant does. Additionally, once interactants develop an interaction pattern, the pattern is likely to persist. For example, Mahl's (1987) work found that the verbal style of interaction established initially during therapy was sustained through a second interview despite experimental manipulations intended to alter it. Whatever style is adopted and adapted early is likely to show some consistency across the interaction, a conclusion that fits with the predilection toward stable exchanges over time.

7. *The combined biological, psychological, and social forces set up boundaries within which most interaction patterns will oscillate, producing largely matching, synchrony, and reciprocity.* Behavioral changes outside these boundaries will often be met with nonaccommodation, as a means of retarding movement away from the normative range, or with compensation to return interaction to its previous style.

8. *Many variables may be salient moderators of interaction adaptation.* We have already identified several relevant moderators that may exert their influence primarily as exogenous factors affecting the required, expected, or desired level of a given functional set of behaviors. However, it is one's ultimate behavioral predisposition that is the proximate endogenous factor explaining resultant adaptation patterns.

9. *Predictions about functional complexes of behaviors should be more useful and accurate than predictions about particular behaviors viewed in isolation of the function they serve.* In fact, viewed at a more global level, many adjustments may be fleeting and inconsequential. At the same time, some behavioral adjustments may be mistaken for adaptations when in reality they are directed toward accomplishing some other communication function. Individuals make postural and proxemic shifts, for instance, at the junctures of episodes and thematic periods within episodes. Such changes may occur less in response to the partner than to changes in cognitive load or cognitive engagement (although admittedly, such changes are still tied to dyadic communicative activity).

## OUR MODEL: INTERACTION ADAPTATION THEORY

We are now ready to offer a formal statement of our model. For ease of understanding the directionality of each person's behavior, we will often speak in terms such as approach–avoidance and convergence–divergence rather than reciprocity–compensation. But it is implied that the combination of responses by the two parties results in matching, reciprocity, complementarity, compensation, and so forth.

Guided by Ockham's razor, we have aimed for a parsimonious model with the fewest possible terms. We recognize the hazards of such simplification and invite the reader to join us in fleshing out this skeletal model in the future.

There are five key concepts in our model. The first three, which are interrelated, are the *required, expected,* and *desired* level of any given functional set of interaction behaviors. The required behavioral level, $R$, is grounded in an interactant's basic human needs and drives (e.g., survival, safety, comfort, autonomy, affiliation; see Maslow, 1970) and translates into what an individual feels is necessary at that point in time (e.g., physical proximity and touch if one is feeling fearful, nonimmediacy if one needs privacy and autonomy). $R$ is strongly influenced by biological factors. The expectations, $E$, refer to what is anticipated, based on social norms, social prescriptions, or individuated knowledge of the other's behavior, and include the general communication functions or goals operative in the situation (e.g., self-presentation demands, conversational management). $E$ largely reflects social factors. The desired level of the behaviors, $D$, is highly personalized and includes one's personal goals, likes, and dislikes, which often originate from one's basic temperament but may also be shaped by social and cultural influences. *D* captures person-specific factors. *R, E,* and *D* are not independent. For example, desires may be partly influenced by current need states and expectations may frame or constrain personal preferences.

The three classes of *R, E,* and *D* factors combine to predict a fourth factor, a derivative behavioral predisposition we are calling, for lack of a better term, the *interactional position,* or *IP.*[1] The *IP* represents a net assessment of what is needed, anticipated, and preferred as the dyadic interaction pattern in a situation. It may dictate one's own likely initial behavioral choice, when self initiates behavior, or the projected likely behavior of the partner, when partner initiates behavior. For example, if self needs to be included in a group for protection (*R*), the norms are for shows of ingroup solidarity (*E*), and the person by nature enjoys affiliation with the ingroup (*D*), the *IP* is for behavioral displays of inclusion by both self and partner.

The *IP* component has analogues in EVT, which compares expectancies to enacted behavior, and in Altman's (1976) privacy regulation model, which compares desired privacy with achieved privacy. However, we have avoided using the "expectancy" and "desired" labels for the *IP* because we fear they would mislead readers into viewing it as less than we intend it to represent. Some people use "expectation" in the descriptive (i.e., predictive) sense of typical behavior and some use it in the ideal (i.e., prescriptive) sense of what is appropriate and desirable. The former interpretation of "expectation" would incorporate the functional requirements in a situation, the social norms, and knowledge of a co-interactant's idiosyncracies but would omit personal preferences and current need states. We likewise eschewed the "desired" label because of its evaluative connotations that might cause readers to assign preeminent status to personal likes and dislikes. In contrast to the possibly static connotations associated with expectancies, desires, or even terms such as "predispositions" or "dispositions," the *IP* is also intended to imply a current state that is dynamic and subject to change during the interaction itself.

The *IP* is contrasted with the fifth factor, the partner's *actual* performed behavior, *A. IP* and *A* can both be placed on a continuum, the discrepancy between them assessed, and the likely response to the discrepancy predicted. The assessment and behavioral response predictions depend upon *R, E,* and *D,* which together govern (a) the valences associated with the *IP* and *A* and (b) the probable classes of response patterns.

Let us first take up the issue of valence. As in so many previous theories, we assume that behaviors have valences attached to them. In the group solidarity example, shows of inclusiveness and affiliation such as language and accent convergence, symbolic handshakes, physical proximity, matched clothing, and nonverbal tie-signs should be positively valenced because they meet needs, conform to expectations, and satisfy personal desires. If the *IP* is for a high degree of inclusiveness and *A* turns out also to be high, there is no discrepancy. But suppose instead that the *IP* is high but partner's *A* actually turns out to be much lower. Relative to *IP*, *A* is more negatively valenced. If we adopt the convention of always placing the more positively valenced behavior at the right end of the continuum and the more negatively valenced behavior at the left end, we can then describe not only the size of the discrepancy but also the relative valencing such that either $A > IP$ or $IP > A$. It is the latter relationship that will ultimately predict behavioral responses.

The *R*, *E*, and *D* may also proscribe certain response options and enlist others. For instance, a person whose personality is highly timid and fearful will rarely opt for a fight response in the face of a physical threat; such a person is instead predicted to opt for flight. Or cultural dicta may prohibit women from responding to male advances in certain ways or discouraging men from displaying certain emotions in public. Thus, the *R*, *E*, and *D* may also imply what sets of behavioral options out of the total range of possibilities are prescribed or proscribed.

When *R*, *E*, and *D* are congruent, that is, each predicts the same *IP* and valence, then ultimate predictions are the same regardless of whether one relies on *R*, *E*, or *D* information. However, when *R*, *E*, and *D* are discrepant, weights associated with the importance of each of the factors must be considered. *R*, *E*, and *D* should be hierarchically ordered in that the *IP* should be first driven by biologically and psychologically based need states (*R*), followed by socially and communicationally derived expectancies (*E*), and lastly by individual goals and desires (*D*) achieved through communication. When urgent needs have not been satisfied, *R* will be paramount in influencing the *IP*, in accord with Maslow's (1970) hierarchy of needs. Depending on the need, one may be inclined to approach or avoid others; to control or be controlled; and so forth. In other words, drives and needs do not result in a single interaction pattern.

In the absence of pressing needs, $E$ should have the greatest influence on the *IP* because it captures the biological and social pressures toward synchrony, matching, and reciprocity. Meshing one's interaction style with another's and adhering to social norms for reciprocal involvement, formality, and the like, not only are regarded as socially appropriate but also facilitate achievement of such communication functions as information processing and comprehension and smooth conversational management. When $E$ predominates in the equation, the result should be a strong inclination to match and reciprocate another's behavior. One exception is that people may initially make some compensatory adjustments on individual immediacy behaviors while negotiating a comfortable interaction distance and level of sensory engagement. But even here, one's comfort level should be dictated, in large measure, by one's cultural expectations and practices. Another exception is based on findings from the Ickes et al. (1982) studies suggesting that when people anticipate a negatively valenced partner, they may initially compensate for the behavior they "expect" from the partner.

Within the $E$ parameters, $D$ can exert additional influence on the *IP*. For example, one's desire to promote a favorable self-image, to persuade the partner, or to have a brief conversation can affect the *IP* but will be tempered by appropriateness norms. Here again, no single interaction pattern is predicted, but this is one place where compensation may emerge more frequently as a strategic move.

In imagining the relationship among the $R$, $E$, and $D$ factors, it may be useful to borrow a fulcrum analogy from Koch (1993), who compared a reward/cost ratio to needs in predicting when people might initiate interaction with an outgroup member. She proposed that the acceptable costs depend on the strength of the reward/cost ratio (high to low) on one side, relative to the felt needs (strong to weak) on the other. She visualized a fulcrum upon which the decision to interact is balanced such that as needs go up, the level of rewards one expects relative to costs should go down; as needs go down, the reward to cost ratio needed to initiate interaction should go up. If we were to balance our $R$, $E$, and $D$ factors on the same fulcrum, we would probably put requirements on one side of the teeter-totter and expectations and desires on the other. The stronger the required factors, the more the quotient would tilt in their favor, with less influence due to $E$ and $D$; the less pressing the needs, the greater the influence of expectancies, norms, communication functions, and preferences.

In keeping with our preceding assumptions, we also posit that $E$ will carry relatively greater weight during initial encounters and openings to conversations and will recede as interactions and relationships progress, giving way to greater influence by *D*. Models of relationship development and conversational trajectories contend that as familiarity increases or interactions extend over time, interaction patterns become less restrained by cultural norms and biological imperatives (less ritualistic) and more governed by individual psychological differences; that is, they become more idiosyncratic and dyadically negotiated (Berger & Calabrese, 1975; Knapp, 1984; Miller & Steinberg, 1975; Rawlins, 1992). The interaction patterns should therefore show increasing variability over time, reflecting the idiosyncratic and dynamic mix of needs and wants within each relationship. Compensation and complementarity may also surface more often, as people abide less by social constraints or increase strategic activity to achieve their own goals.

To arrive at predictions of actual interaction patterns requires comparing each interactant's *IP* with partner's *A*. Our model predicts that if an interactant's *IP* matches other's *A*, the interactant will be inclined to match or reciprocate the other's behavior. If *IP* equals *A* for both parties, a stable exchange should ensue unless and until *IP* or *A* changes for either party. Such changes may be instigated by external forces (such as entry of a third party to a conversation) or by internal ones (such as the distraction of hunger lowering one's conversational involvement).

Small discrepancies between *IP* and *A* may go undetected or fall within the tolerance range proposed earlier. Large discrepancies between (own) *IP* and (other) *A* should activate (a) behavioral change, (b) cognitive change, or (c) both, with the magnitude of change being monotonically related to the magnitude of the discrepancy.

If behavioral change is probable, the directionality of the adjustment is posited to depend on the relative valences of the *IP* and *A*. The valences attached to the *IP* and *A* should derive from the same *R*, *E*, and *D* elements governing the *IP*. For example, we may expect and desire romantic partners, spouses, and family members to show affection and will hence valence such displays positively. Moreover, if we have been deprived of such affection, our "need state" may intensify the positivity attached to intimacy displays.

The role of valencing is such that any behavioral adaptation should initially move in the direction of whichever is more positively valenced, the *IP* or *A*. If an interactant's own *IP* is more positively valued than other's *A* (i.e., *IP* > *A*), then the discrepancy between them is negative and may even qualify as a negative violation if large enough. This state of affairs initially should propel an interactant away from partner's *A* and toward own *IP* (if the interactant's behavior is not already at that level). The objective is to minimize the gap between *IP* and *A* and align both people's behavior with the *IP* by eliciting a reciprocal response from the partner. Given the deeply ingrained nature of the "Follow the Leader" entrainment principle and the socially based reciprocity principle, we believe the most likely first response should be for the interactant to model desired behavior, expecting a reciprocal response from the partner. (This is the strategic modeling concept introduced by Ickes et al., 1982.) Under this set of conditions, then, the interactant's behavior should appear as nonaccommodative or compensatory relative to the other's.

Now consider the alternative where the discrepancy is *positively* valenced (i.e., *A* > *IP*) and may be a positive violation of expectations. We predict that interactants will be propelled in the direction of *A,* that is, they will converge behavior toward that of the partner, resulting in matching or reciprocity. Such movements have the advantage of shifting own behavior toward a more desired objective and possibly achieving greater behavioral meshing.

Although we have proposed placing the *IP* and *A* on a continuum, with the more negatively valenced element (*IP* or *A*) toward the left end of the continuum and the more positively valenced elements toward the right end of the continuum, we do not wish to imply that the underlying behavioral continuum necessarily reflects a linear increase in positivity. Many behaviors have a curvilinear relationship with evaluation. For example, moderately close distance may be desirable but extreme proximity may surpass a comfort or threat threshold (see Burgoon, 1978) and become negatively valenced. Thus, a moderately close *A* may be more positively valenced than an intermediate distance, but an extremely close *A* may be more negatively valenced. Our predictions should be interpreted as applying only to the range bounded by the *IP* and *A* under consideration. Positions that are outside of that range may reverse polarity and must be analyzed separately for their valence relative to a particular *IP* or *A*.

The basic alternatives are illustrated in Figure 11.1. Although numerous combinations of *R, E,* and *D* are possible, and although these can lead to different *IP*s for self and partner, once an *IP* is specified and valenced relative to partner's *A,* only two main patterns are predicted.

One other remaining possibility is to adjust the *IP.* This may occur within or between interactions. This cognitive transformation may be

### Key Elements of Interaction Adaptation Theory

| | |
|---|---|
| *Required (R)* | biologically based factors governing behavior that incorporate basic human needs and drives, that operate primarily below conscious awareness, and that often take precedence over other components. |
| *Expected (E)* | socially based factors governing behavior that are determined by knowledge of the context, communication functions operative within the context, and knowledge of how the particular partner behaves within that context; *E* components include both predictive (typical, normative) and prescriptive (appropriate) expectations and are strongly influenced by social factors. |
| *Desired (D)* | individually based factors governing behavior that incorporate personality, preferences, moods, and other individual difference variables. |
| *Interaction Position (IP)* | a derivative term combining *R*, *E*, and *D* factors and serving as a valenced behavioral predisposition for own interaction behavior or for what is anticipated (required, expected, and/or desired) from partner. |
| *Actual Behavior (A)* | partner's enacted behavior(s), also valenced, and placed on a behavioral continuum relative to self *IP* or partner *IP*. |

### Predictions from Interaction Adaptation Theory

*IP* and *A*, which are a function of *R*, *E*, and *D*, are placed on a behavioral continuum. Whichever of the two (*IP* or *A*) is more positively valenced will dictate whether and in what manner adaptation will occur.

If IP > A,

diverge/compensate/maintain<br>———————→

Negatively Valenced Behavior_____Positively Valenced Behavior
     (−)                      *A*     *IP*         (+)

If A > IP,

converge/match/reciprocate<br>———————→

Negatively Valenced Behavior_____Positively Valenced Behavior
     (−)                   *IP*     *A*        (+)

### Example

Bob has spent the weekend by himself, taking a solitary hiking trip in the mountains. Come Monday morning, what interaction style might we predict between Bob and a co-worker?

The *IP* includes the *R, E,* and *D,* which may be as follows:

*Required:*    Bob is feeling lonely as well as in need of sensory stimulation after his weekend of isolation. We expect Bob to seek out others (be highly involved) to meet the biological needs for affiliation and sensory stimulation.

*Expected:*    Moderate affiliation with co-workers is generally expected as typical and appropriate, given a work context and task-oriented rather than socially oriented relationships. However, interaction with a close friend may be expected to be more involved; interaction with a disliked co-worker who routinely keeps to a distance may be expected to be more detached.

*Desired:*    Because Bob believes in separation of work and play, he usually prefers a formal, nonaffiliative interaction style during work hours but likes to engage in small talk with friends during social time. He is also generally a shy and private person, which leads him to be somewhat reticent and unlikely to initiate interaction with co-workers. He especially prefers to maintain distance from disliked co-workers.

What *IP* level of involvement do we predict from Bob? If we only consider the required level (*R*), we might predict a highly involved interaction style between Bob and his co-workers. Yet, when we factor in the expected level (*E*), we now predict Bob to be more involved than his personal inclination (relatively uninvolved) would suggest, and with greater predicted involvement and affiliation with a liked co-worker than a disliked one. We also predict more involvement during lunchtime than during work hours. If we then factor in the desired level (*D*), the predictions are further refined. We predict that Bob will be moderately involved with the liked co-worker and moderately uninvolved with the disliked one. Thus, the combined *RED* predicts an *IP* (self and other) of above normal involvement with the liked co-worker but an *IP* of moderate to low involvement with the disliked co-worker.

To predict the interaction pattern between Bob and his co-workers, we must also know the valence for Bob's involvement level relative to the involvement level adopted by the co-worker. Involvement is positively valenced with liked others but negatively valenced with disliked others. If the liked co-worker's actual behavior, *A,* reflects high involvement, *A* will be more positively valenced than *IP.* The model predicts Bob will converge toward and reciprocate that involvement. If the liked co-worker's behavior instead is somewhat low involvement, *IP* will be more positively valenced than *A,* leading to a divergent pattern of compensation or maintenance of Bob's original involvement level in hopes of it eliciting a similar response from the co-worker. If the disliked co-worker's *A* is detached and uninvolved, *A* will be more positively valenced than *IP* and Bob should again reciprocate that but to a lesser degree because of his need for affiliation and sensory stimulation. If the disliked co-worker's *A* is highly involved, *A* will be more negatively valenced than *IP.* Bob should compensate for that with a relatively uninvolved interaction style.

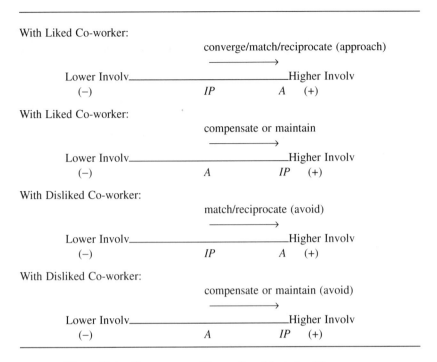

With Liked Co-worker:

converge/match/reciprocate (approach)

————————→

Lower Involv————————————————Higher Involv

(–)          *IP*          *A*    (+)

With Liked Co-worker:

compensate or maintain

————————→

Lower Involv————————————————Higher Involv

(–)          *A*          *IP*    (+)

With Disliked Co-worker:

match/reciprocate (avoid)

————————→

Lower Involv————————————————Higher Involv

(–)          *IP*          *A*    (+)

With Disliked Co-worker:

compensate or maintain (avoid)

————————→

Lower Involv————————————————Higher Involv

(–)          *A*          *IP*    (+)

Figure 11.1    Components of Interaction Adaptation Theory.

more common under the previously noted conditions when nonaccommodation is most prevalent or when interactional constraints preclude or discourage a compensatory behavioral response. It may also transpire when situations become emotionally infused, as when negative emotional states such as anger, fear, or embarrassment erupt or some life-altering event such as death or marriage occurs. Theoretically, it should be possible to specify a priori when behavioral change or cognitive transformation will occur. In the absence of such a priori specification, IAT would suffer the same indeterminacy that has plagued previous functionally oriented theories (e.g., the SFM).

To illustrate how these various factors work together to predict adaptation patterns, we need to consider three alternative scenarios, one where R predominates (depicted *RED*), one where *E* predominates (*rEd*), and one where *D* predominates (*reD*) in determining the *IP*. All of these are cases where R, E, and D are discrepant, since we have already noted that when the R, E, and D each lead to the same *IP*, it does not matter which of the three classes of factors carries the most weight.

### RED examples

The common finding noted in Chapter 4 that marital couples often reciprocate and escalate hostility can be explained if one begins with the assumption that venting anger, protecting one's personhood from verbal abuse and physical violence, and perhaps even punishing those who have injured oneself are biologically rooted needs that result in primitive defense, threat, and fight reflexes. Under such conditions, targets of previous hostility may have self $IP$s of moderately aggressive, affectively unpleasant behavior. Although the $D$ and $E$ for such behavior may be negatively valenced, if $R$ is dominant, and if aggressiveness can be construed as satisfying these basic needs, then this $IP$ may actually have a positive valence associated with it in the sense of satisfying the need, and so may eclipse the valences associated with the $D$ and $E$ factors.

Now suppose partner's actual behavior, $A$, is also one of aggressiveness. If there is little discrepancy between self $IP$ and partner $A$, our theory predicts an entrainment pattern that yields matching. What if, instead, partner's $A$ is more aggressive than the $IP$? If it remains within the same range as $IP$ and increases only incrementally, the entrainment effect should continue to hold, producing a slowly escalating conflict spiral. If, however, $A$ is far more verbally aggressive (and we presume that such behavior is negatively valenced), we might expect the person to instead compensate, because when $IP$ (moderate aggressiveness) is more positively valenced than $A$ (extreme aggressiveness); that is, $IP > A$, the prediction is for movement toward $IP$ and away from $A$. This might take the form of withdrawal – a commonly found part of the demand–withdraw cycle – or at a more extreme level, flight. If partner instead adopts an $A$ of pleasantness and accommodation, such that $A > P$, the situation casts $A$ as more positively valenced than $IP$ and may even qualify as a positive violation. The prediction: convergence toward $A$, that is, a lessening of hostilities.

One exception to the preceding characterization of relational conflict would be the case where personality factors circumscribe the fight option, as might be the case where a person is physically weaker than the aggressor, highly dependent on the aggressor for personal survival, or constitutionally incapable of engaging in physical aggression. This kind of individuated prediction requires having personal knowledge about the range of options actually open to the individual.

The preceding set of predictions can be further refined by considering early moves compared to later ones during an interaction. If self is initially unaware of partner's anger and hostility, initial projected *IP* for the spouse should be one of nonaggression, based primarily on *D* (personal desires) but also on *R* (one's requirements to be safe from threats) and *E* (socially normative expectations for amicable interpersonal relationships, especially with intimates). Such an *IP* would be positively valenced relative to the partner's actual *A* of initiating a fight. Under this circumstance, *IP* > *A*, and our theory would predict an initial divergent move toward appeasement and nonhostile resolution of the argument. But if such efforts were met with resistance, over time the situation would become infused with negative affect, *D* would shrink relative to *R*, and biologically more primitive response patterns like those described above would take over. Thus, the polarities of the aggressive and nonaggressive responses could be transformed over time as the need to express anger and protect self loomed larger.

### RED examples

Expectancies may carry the most weight when situations are strongly influenced by social norms and role relationships. Take the case of an employee interacting with the president of his company. Although the employee may normally prefer an immediate and informal interaction style, he is likely to be attuned to the status differentials and the requirement to behave deferentially and formally in her presence. He may even be intimidated by her commanding demeanor. He should therefore anticipate a businesslike interaction conducted "from afar" rather than "up close and personal" – that is, a partner *IP* for moderately formal, distant interaction. The combination of the professional nature of the relationship, the status-inequality expectation, and task-oriented tone of prior interactions should all cause the *E* factor to override comfort needs, *R*, or personal preferences, *D*.

Suppose now that the employer's actual interaction style, *A*, turns out to be fairly informal and immediate. Given that such an interaction style typically connotes greater equality, familiarity, interest, and solidarity and fits the employee's own personal preferences, the employee may consider the behavior pattern a positive violation (*A* > *IP*) and respond by converging toward it somewhat. However, as noted earlier, social propriety norms should constrain behavior so that the degree of informality and closeness is abbreviated relative to the employer's.

What if instead the employee is highly anxious in the presence of powerful others? *R* may instead overwhelm *E* in dictating self *IP* such that the self *IP* exceeds *A* (i.e., greater formality is preferred and likely). Our theory would predict that the employee's response will be divergence and compensation.

### RED examples

It is common for couples to establish routines in their marriage that reflect their personal preferences for intimacy, autonomy, novelty, and the like. Many traditional and independent couples may develop a pattern of greeting each other warmly and kissing upon arriving home from work. Let us consider a situation where a wife has had a hard day at work and has been criticized by her boss. Tonight, she desires an extra dose of TLC from her husband, making high affection and involvement not only expected (in the sense of one expecting a spouse to supply aid and comfort) but also desired. Such TLC naturally would be positively valenced. If she initiates the interaction, her self *IP* might be more affectionate than normal, while her partner *IP* (what she projects for her husband) should be at the moderately affectionate level.

Now the husband enters the scene. He does not know about her difficult day at work and greets her with only moderate involvement and affection. If his behavior (*A*) falls within her *IP* range for affection and involvement, then IAT predicts she should reciprocate his level, perhaps even being slightly more affectionate and involved than he. However, if his behavior falls outside of her range – that is, *A* is discrepant from the partner IP – then his behavior is toward the negative end of the affection/involvement continuum (*IP > A*) and we would predict her to compensate for his behavior, becoming much more affectionate and involved, to elicit a reciprocal response from him.

Let us take another example, where the same wife had a difficult day at work, but wants to be left alone. In this case, the desire is for less affection and involvement from her husband, making high affection and involvement negatively valenced, in contrast with the earlier example. When the husband greets her with moderately high affection and involvement, his behavior (*A*) may qualify as negative and discrepant from her *IP;* that is, again *IP > A*. In this case, we also would predict compensation for the wife, to pull him toward lower levels of affection and involvement.

Working with this same marital greeting routine, let us now consider the case where the wife's *IP* is for moderately high involvement and affection but the husband is feeling particularly appreciative of his wife (perhaps because his own *IP* is heavily influenced by his desire for showing affection rather than by his *R* or *E*). He therefore greets her at the door with flowers, lots of affection, dinner on the table, and their children at the babysitter's home. If she values lots of affection and attention, his behavior will be more positive than her *IP* for him (*A* > *IP*), something that can occur when our ideal states have given way to more "realistic" expectations and desires over the course of a relationship. Thus, we would predict her to reciprocate his more positively valenced behavior.

Finally, let's consider the case where the husband's actual intimacy level falls far short of what the wife prefers (a fairly common pattern according to the marital literature). Under such circumstances, she is likely to initiate more explicit shows of affection (a divergent, compensatory pattern) in hopes of eliciting reciprocal affection from him. If she succeeds in "pulling" his interaction style up to match her own, she will have accomplished both objectives of satisfying her *IP* and eliminating the discrepancy between *A* and *IP*. However, if he remains unmoved by such initiatives (i.e., shows nonaccommodation, perhaps due to lesser emotional investment in the relationship), her fear of rejection or her frustration with him may override the preference for intimacy, causing a recalibration of her *IP* to a less "risky" level.

Over time, behavioral responses may also change. The rebuffed female may increase avoidant behavior (a convergent or reciprocal pattern) to close the gap between *IP* and *A*. Thus, a pattern, once initiated, need not be sustained; if it fails to meet the objectives, it may be abandoned. And even if the objectives are achieved, the *IP* can change due to a given preference or need being satiated. (Our descriptions should not imply that these behavioral adjustments are highly deliberate, planned moves. More often than not, they should occur at a low level of consciousness, drawing upon cognitive schemata, scripts, and overlearned behavioral routines for their enactments.)

The predictions we have offered so far account for *individual* behavioral inclinations in the absence of any changes by the partner. It is not uncommon for one interactant to maintain a consistent (nondynamic) interaction style, especially if one is highly attuned to social norms or more focused on self than partner. But in cases where both interactants are changing behavior, such as mutual convergence or divergence, we can arrive at *dyadic* patterns through a joint description of their individual predilections. If both people are predicted to approach the other, for example, the resultant approach–approach pattern will take the form of convergence and/or reciprocity. If instead one is predicted to approach and the other to avoid, then a dyadic pattern of compensation should be manifest.

We believe this new model fits not only the data from our own investigations but previous empirical evidence as well. Our model leads to predominant predictions of matching, reciprocity, synchrony, and convergence, except where comfort factors require immediacy adjustments or where interaction style is deliberately manipulated to send a message or to model desired behavior. The bulk of empirical evidence seems to lend itself to this characterization. Synchrony, matching, convergence, and reciprocity are prevalent and especially common with large behavioral gestalts – such as (a) vocalics related to speech production, (b) vocalics and kinesics related to positive and negative affect, and (c) nonverbal and verbal behaviors related to intimacy expression. Compensation, by contrast, has more often emerged on (a) individual immediacy behaviors (e.g., distance, gaze, and body orientation), and compensation and divergence have occurred as strategic moves to (b) offset nonverbal uninvolvement with increased involvement, (c) offset decreased nonverbal intimacy with increased verbal immediacy, or (d) create social distance. While many moderators may affect the intensity with which these patterns are exhibited, in most cases they should not reverse the directionality.

The validity of this model awaits further testing. In Chapter 12, we consider some productive research directions to test predictions generated from this model and to extend it in the natural next direction: linking process to outcomes.

## CONCLUSION

In this chapter, we have reexamined previous theories and models in light of the extant empirical evidence. Out of this analysis we have derived a number of assumptions and sketched a model that derives predictions from juxtaposing an interactant's combined requirements, expectations, and desires (*RED*) – which together form an interaction position (*IP*) – against a partner's actual behavior (*A*). Predictions for interaction adaptation result from valencing the *IP* and *A* and determining which is more positively valenced. Our model predicts that matching and reciprocity will occur when each person's *IP* matches partner's *A* or when discrepancies between the two are small. When discrepancies are large and *A* is more positively valenced than the *IP* (a positive circumstance), the individual inclination will be toward convergence and reciprocity; when the *IP* is more positively valenced than *A* (a negative circumstance), the inclination will be toward nonaccommodation or compensation. Dyadic patterns will depend on the combination of the two individual responses (e.g., approach–approach resulting in reciprocity, approach–avoid resulting in compensation).

These patterns are posited to fluctuate in systematic ways as needs change or are satiated, as a partner's behavior deviates from expected or desired levels, and as a partner rejects or responds to one's strategic initiatives. The relative weights of *RED* elements are also posited to change both within and across interactions. Finally, behavioral adaptation may be supplanted or offset by cognitive changes in the *IP*.

**NOTE**

1 We wish to thank Mike Voloudakis for proposing this label.

# 12

## A research agenda

In the preceding 11 chapters, we have reviewed voluminous research and theorizing on dyadic interaction patterns. In light of the extensive work that has already been completed, one might rightfully ask: Is there more to be done? We think so, and so we propose in this final chapter some future research directions that would test our theory and bring the research full circle to connect interaction patterns with outcomes. As a complement to our selective recommendations here, we direct the reader to Montgomery and Duck's (1991) volume, *Studying Interpersonal Interaction,* which raises a number of additional issues and is full of excellent research suggestions that we will not reiterate here.

### TESTING OUR PROPOSED THEORY

Numerous facets of our proposed model invite empirical testing. The model itself requires assessing interactants' required ($R$), expected ($E$), and desired ($D$) behavior levels and partner's actual ($A$) behavioral level. The $RED$ must be translated into a single Interaction Position ($IP$) value that can be compared to $A$ so that the degree and direction of the discrepancy between $IP$ and $A$ can be determined. The relative valences of the $IP$ and $A$ must also be assessed. Then the actual predicted adaptation patterns can be tested. We address each of these elements below, followed by some discussion of design and statistical analysis considerations.

#### Assessing required, expected, desired, and actual behavior levels

The first step in any analysis applying our model is to infer, measure, or manipulate the $R$, $E$, and $D$ elements associated with the communication function at stake. All of these individual components are discernible through social convention, "objective" observation, or self-report measures.

Consider, first, assessing what each individual "requires" in a situation. In naturalistic settings, it is possible to project what need states might be, based upon firsthand experiences and upon the abundant literature on human needs and wants. For example, we might expect people to be fatigued at the end of a long work week and to have that fatigue translate into low levels of interaction involvement. Similarly, research has shown that invasion of personal space by strangers engenders stress and fear, prompting avoidance behaviors. More direct evidence of needs and other state variables such as mood, anxiety, and stress can be obtained through administration of self-report questionnaires or through observation by trained coders. (Clinicians, for example, may be trained to diagnose arousal and stress.) Apart from inferring or measuring these variables, they can also be induced experimentally. Past psychological experiments have successfully manipulated people's hunger states, emotions, physical comfort, sensory stimulation, and the like.

Assessment of expectancies similarly may rely on known (or observed) social norms and shared cultural knowledge. We can tell by watching, for instance, whether a situation is a task or social one; we may intuit from people's titles whether a status hierarchy is present or not and thus infer the expected attendant behaviors; and so forth. Expectancies can be determined empirically by querying people on what their expectancies are for various communication situations and relationships. Some of this work has already been accomplished in the nonverbal arena (see, e.g., Burgoon, Buller, & Woodall, 1989), but much more empirical verification is needed. In particular, we need to know what expectations are associated with different communication functions. For example, when someone is attempting to persuade us, what behaviors do we anticipate? When someone is expressing affection, how do we expect that to be displayed? As part of a functional assessment, we need to determine the relative salience of different variables in accomplishing these functions. (For example, gaze is heavily implicated in surveillance, information seeking, and conversational management, but is it the primary indicator that these functions are operative?) Alternatively, expectancies can be manipulated experimentally, as has been done in the preinteraction expectancy and expectancy signaling/ behavioral confirmation research.

Individual desires can be inferred, measured, or manipulated in the same manner, but because these are much more idiosyncratic, their role in any given interaction is more difficult to discern. Nevertheless, in principle it is possible to ascertain what they are prior to or following an interaction if they are not controlled experimentally.

The next step is combining these elements. Determining an algorithm for weighting and combining RED components to arrive at the IP quotient is unquestionably quite complicated and something we are not prepared to advance at this stage. However, we can still arrive at some semblance of an IP by holding some elements constant while manipulating others, by measuring some elements and covarying them out of the analysis of other elements, or by measuring several elements and arriving at a statistical weighting. For instance, if we can safely assume that interactants are not in some serious deprivation state and that they expect an interaction with a stranger to be moderately involving, we can then manipulate an interactant's goal (say, to persuade or to ingratiate) and predict their interaction predisposition accordingly.

In the case of nonexperimental research, the *R, E,* and *D* elements must be assessed for both parties; in the case of experimental research where one person's behavior is being held constant or controlled, it may only be necessary to assess *R, E,* and *D* for the partner so that an *IP* can be projected.

The next step is measuring partner's actual behavior. This can be measured objectively by observers or assessed subjectively by co-interactants. Measurement may be microscopic (e.g., number of non-fluencies, degree of physical proximity, utterance length) or macroscopic (e.g., degree of immediacy or formality). Behavioral descriptions pitched at a macroscopic rather than microscopic level can facilitate broad, functional classifications of an interactant's behavior so that predictions can be tied to functions and behavioral valences (e.g., describing one's combined verbal and nonverbal conduct as non-threatening, engaged, and moderately informal).

As part of the *IP* and *A* assessment process, behavior valences must be ascertained so that when *IP* and *A* are placed on the behavioral continuum, we know which end is the most positively valenced. Here again, we can rely on shared social and cultural-level knowledge or on empirically assessed individual preferences.

Based on these assessments, one can predict whether patterns will be synchronous, matched, convergent, divergent, compensatory, reciprocal, or nonaccommodative, and the hypothesized patterns can be tested statistically. Additional predictions can be derived by taking into account temporal interaction and relationship factors such as whether or not the interaction is an initial encounter and whether or not the relationship is a developed one. With initial interactions, $E$ factors are presumed to be most salient; with developed relationships, $R$ and $D$ factors are posited to be most salient.

## An illustration

An excellent illustration of how IAT can be used to predict interaction patterns comes from Guerrero's (1994) application of attachment theory to interaction adaptation. Although IAT was not used a priori to derive predictions, it worked well to account for patterns on a post hoc basis.

In this investigation, participants were selected who fit one of four attachment styles defined by two dimensions: approach versus avoidance orientations and need for external validation. Dismissing Avoidants are people who tend to avoid interactions with others and who have little need for validation from others. Fearful Avoidants also tend to avoid interactions because they have high anxiety but also desire others' approval because they have a negative model of self. Preoccupieds seek high intimacy with others and have great need for others' validation, while Secures also prefer high intimacy but because they are emotionally secure, do not depend on others for validation.

In the experiment, romantic partners of these individuals with different attachment styles either greatly increased or greatly decreased involvement after a baseline interaction period. Consistent with the case we have made for reciprocity being the "default option" in normal interaction, reciprocity was the predominant pattern, but there were some noteworthy differences depending on attachment style that Guerrero was able to explain by invoking IAT. Specifically, Preoccupieds, who desire highly intimate relationships and highly value their partners as a source of personal validation, begin interactions with an $IP$ that is above average on involvement. When partner's actual behavior, $A,$ is even more involved, this should constitute an unexpectedly positive behavior that results in convergence toward higher involvement – that is, reciprocity. Conversely, when partner's $A$ is decreased involvement, Preoccupieds should resist such reductions by compensating because partner's $A$ is more negatively valenced than the $IP.$ These are the patterns that obtained. Preoccupieds showed the greatest reciprocity of increased involvement and the greatest compensation of decreased involvement.

Guerrero had originally predicted that Dismissing Avoidants would actually compensate increased involvement. This did not materialize. Instead, Dismissing Avoidants, like the other types, tended to reciprocate involvement increases. Here again she was able to apply IAT as a possible explanation. She speculated that $R$ factors (such as need for distance and autonomy) might be less relevant for these participants than $E$ factors (expectancies based on context, social norms, and relationship norms). Thus, given the strong pressure toward entrainment in social situations and the receding influence of any counter biological pressures, one might expect the pull toward reciprocity to prevail, and it did.

Finally, by analyzing each dyad's pattern, Guerrero discovered that Fearful Avoidants produced quite a mix of reciprocal, compensatory, and nonaccommodative patterns, while Secures showed greater consistency. These patterns are in keeping with the differential degrees of ambivalence represented by the two attachment styles, with Fearful Avoidants possibly exhibiting behaviorally some of the dialectical tensions between desires for approach and fear of approach that have been ascribed to them. The dyad-by-dyad analysis also reinforced the value of supplementing aggregated data with analysis of each couple's pattern. (A similar demonstration of the importance of looking at individual dyad trendlines and patterns is available in Revenstorf et al., 1984.)

### Measurement considerations in assessing functional equivalence

Our description of *IP* and *A* implies that we know what the salient behaviors are and can identify behaviors that are interchangeable and substitutable. In practice, this is not so simple. Even Argyle and Dean (1965), who described compensation as the joint functioning of several behaviors leading to a macrojudgment, had to modify their conception of what behaviors constitute immediacy (Argyle & Cook, 1976), and consensus is still lacking as to which behaviors should be included in this category. Arriving at the comparability of behaviors that can be placed in the same functional class may in most cases necessitate a molar approach to measurement. Molar labels by definition imply larger collections of behaviors or gestalt impressions. A molar approach may also better match the phenomenological experience and message-processing style of interactants (see, e.g., Burgoon & Baesler, 1991). Global judgments generally and affective ones particularly better fit the perceptual experience of participants than do smaller, discrete behaviors (Stafford, Waldron, & Infield, 1989).

## Use of within-dyads versus between-dyads analyses

The issue of within- versus between-dyads analyses was first addressed in Chapter 7. It is intricately connected to the issue of using cross-sectional data, which come from multiple dyads and are therefore "between" data, versus longitudinal data, which come from within dyads. Because each type of analysis can produce different conclusions about whether reciprocity or compensation is taking place, this entails both design and analysis considerations.

Although we are advocating use of multiple methods, we do not wish to imply that every study include between- and within-dyad elements but rather that researchers strive where possible for designs that permit them to examine patterns both within and between dyads. Ideally, then, dyads should be the sampling unit. Dyad membership or role (e.g., husband, wife) should be one of the "within" factors (unless some kind of dyadic measure is created to replace the individual measures) and a second "within" factor should be time. Such designs and analyses are needed (a) to establish that one person's behavior is contingent on the other's, (b) to identify the persistence and stability of patterns over the course of an interaction or relationship, (c) to uncover cyclic regularities, (d) to assess the effects of irregular, rare, and disruptive "turning point" events on interaction trajectories, (e) to verify causal orderings among behaviors themselves, and (f) to determine the causal paths between interaction patterns and what we believe are consequences but in fact might be antecedents.

One question of particular interest to us, given our proposed theory, is whether patterns reverse themselves over time. If, as we have contended, interactants sometimes adopt compensatory patterns strategically so as to model desired behavior for a co-interactant, how long will they persist in this effort before abandoning it? And what factors might govern their willingness to persist? Only longitudinal designs can answer such questions.

## Identification of moderators

A common direction for putting a basic theoretical principle to a stringent test is to see how well it withstands the effects of various co-present factors, or moderators. The search for moderators so far has centered on what factors influence disclosiveness, proxemic norms, felt comfort, and exhibited affiliation. As noted in Chapter 11, moderators identified so far include gender, age, interpersonal orientation, individual goals, personality, physical attractiveness, evaluations of one's partner, prospects for future interaction (which is a risk factor related to self-presentation), status and role relationships, perceived affiliation, intimacy level of the relationship, and relational satisfaction. Many of these are individual rather than relational variables or they have been measured at the individual rather than the dyadic level.

We would like to encourage greater attention to relationship factors. One that has been found to be relevant is relationship stage or degree of intimacy. Won-Doornink (1985) found more reciprocity of nonintimate disclosures during early stages of a relationship, a curvilinear relationship for intimate disclosure during middle stages, and highest reciprocity of moderately intimate self-disclosure in advanced stages. This raises the question of how relationship stage might affect other interaction adaptation patterns. Another factor that appears to influence interaction patterns is degree of honesty or perceived honesty. Toris and DePaulo (1985) found that interviewees and interviewers matched perceived liking and tension during honest interviews but not deceptive ones. Burgoon, Buller, Dillman, and Walther (in press) found that suspicion altered degree of reciprocity or compensation. It is possible that by making interactions nonrewarding, actual or perceived suspicion and dishonesty trigger discomfort and unconscious avoidance responses. Alternatively, deceivers may compensate strategically to minimize the other's ability to detect deception. Suspicious interactants may do likewise to reduce a deceiver's awareness of their doubts. The presence of ulterior motives and perceptions of trust and honesty therefore may influence interaction patterns significantly.

Another likely moderator, culture, has received negligible attention. Won-Doornink (1985) found that nationality of the participants had only a slight effect in altering disclosure patterns. But much more study of verbal and nonverbal adaptation is needed in intercultural and cross-cultural contexts before we can draw any valid conclusions about the universality or culture-boundedness of the principles we have identified here.

## LINKING INTERACTION PATTERNS TO OUTCOMES

No book on interpersonal adaptation would be complete without considering the consequences of the various interaction patterns we have identified. Like Cappella (1984), we agree that the ultimate interest in these communicative patterns should be in what they *do*. Indeed, one theory – Communication Accommodation Theory (CAT) – includes as a major focus the consequences of different adaptation patterns.

Although the labels sometimes seem to be imbued with positive connotations, reciprocity, matching, synchrony, and convergence do not presuppose smooth, coordinated, or satisfying exchanges any more than compensation, complementarity, and divergence are always associated with negative consequences. As but two examples, a compensatory pattern during conflict episodes may actually reflect much greater dyadic coordination and harmony than a reciprocal pattern. An aggressive move followed by an acquiescent, conciliatory response may promote smoother interaction than a reciprocal dominant response.

Neither should the labels imply that each pattern leads to a different set of outcomes. Rather, equifinality of outcomes is possible: Both reciprocity and matching may lead to liking. In a friendship, whether one is matching, reciprocating, or maintaining intimacy may be inconsequential to the friends themselves, as long as positive relational messages are produced. In short, the pattern itself in no way implies the outcomes associated with it.

Here we consider what we know so far about the consequences of different interaction patterns and where we should go next. At the most basic level, there is the well-founded belief that healthy human functioning depends on the ability to adapt to one's surroundings and to others within those surroundings. If we accept Cappella's (1991a) arguments that adaptation is a defining quality of interpersonal communication and that failure to adapt to others may be a sign of abnormality, then we should expect to find that adaptation has positive consequences. The questions to be answered, then, are which forms of adaptation produce favorable outcomes and how much adaptation is desirable.

The bulk of research and theorizing related to these questions has centered on evaluations of individual communicators, evaluative states of interpersonal relationships, and effects in achieving influence.

## Effects on communicator evaluation

Much of the outcomes research has been undertaken to test CAT tenets. Generally, the research evidence has been supportive of speech convergence producing positive evaluations. Similarities in language, accent, response latencies, speech rates, nonverbal immediacy, and positive affect tend to receive higher ratings than dissimilarities on such outcomes as perceived warmth, communication effectiveness and intelligibility, social attractiveness, involvement, and competence (Berger & Bradac, 1982; Coupland, 1984; Dabbs, 1969; Feldman, 1968; Giles & Smith, 1979; LaFrance, 1979; Putman & Street, 1984; Street, 1984, 1991; Street, Brady, & Putman, 1983; Triandis, 1960; Welkowitz & Kuc, 1973). Stated as a proposition, positive evaluations are most likely to accrue when convergent behavior is perceived to adhere to the communication style of one's ingroup or to a valued communication norm and is attributed to reflect high effort, high choice, and benevolent intent (Gallois, Giles, Jones, Cargile, & Ota, 1995). If a communicator's attempt to converge is seen as an effort to break down cultural barriers, it will be perceived favorably; if it is seen as imposed by external pressures, it will be perceived negatively.

The degree of convergence is not linearly related to positive evaluations. If a behavior falls outside the tolerance range, it may be evaluated negatively (see, e.g., Bradac, Hosman, & Tardy, 1978; Giles & Smith, 1979; Street, 1982). Hyperaccommodation, for example, may be perceived as condescending or ingratiating.

Divergence may also earn positive evaluations – if it is dictated by social norms or role expectations (see, e.g., Matarazzo & Weins, 1972; Miller & Steinberg, 1975; Putman & Street, 1984; Street, 1991). Patients, for instance, prefer physicians to display complementary rather than similar dominance and control behaviors during medical consultations. But divergence by poorly regarded others may instead earn disfavor. When outgroup members diverge, it is evaluated as rude, impolite, or hostile (Deprez & Persoons, 1984; Sandilands & Fleury, 1979), especially if it appears to be intentional and volitional. Consistent with EVT and CAT premises, rewarding communicators are permitted to deviate with impunity while nonrewarding communicators are maligned for it.

In a unique investigation, Kikuchi (1994) tested the hypothesis that listener convergence toward a speaker's baserate of backchanneling behavior (head nods, verbal interjections such as "uh huh") would lead to more positive relational attributions. His hypothesis was confirmed: Greater convergence in backchanneling led speakers to view listeners as more competent and as expressing more relational messages of intimacy, immediacy, composure, and equality. The more positive evaluations of the listener also resulted in speakers increasing speaking tempo and using less "channel-tracking" behavior – questions asking listeners if they understood what was being said. Thus, one simple form of convergence had significant effects not only on communicator evaluations but also on subsequent interaction behavior.

Other research not conducted under CAT auspices has further examined the effects of verbal reciprocity, synchrony, and mirroring on partner evaluations. In one study (Infante, Hartley, Martin, Higgins, Bruning, & Hur, 1992), observers judged the credibility and validity of arguments of two speakers who initiated or reciprocated verbal aggression. Communicators who reciprocated the verbal attacks were seen as more credible than those who did not. The "turn the other cheek" mentality apparently was less image enhancing than returning "an eye for an eye." This finding might account for why hostilities so often escalate: People feel justified and even compelled to respond in kind to explicit or implied criticisms and personal attacks (see Harris, Gergen, & Lannamann, 1986).

Reciprocation of positive verbal behavior is also generally preferable. Research reviewed in Chapter 4 showed that those who reciprocate another's disclosures are evaluated more favorably than those who do not. But accompanying these findings have been several caveats: The disclosure needs to be conversationally relevant, to match the level of riskiness of the original disclosure, and to reflect conversational sensitivity by not demanding "equal floor time" when listening to another's problems. Those who divulge too much too soon or too often are evaluated negatively. Research on marital satisfaction has also shown that moderate rather than high levels of self-disclosures to partners are preferred (see Bochner, 1984), suggesting that maximal reciprocity of disclosure may not be desirable.

Greater synchrony is also better. An investigation testing the effects of self-synchrony on communicator credibility found that speakers whose kinesic actions were well-coordinated to the vocal-verbal stream were judged as more credible and attractive than those whose behavior was dissynchronous (Woodall & Burgoon, 1981). By extension, we should expect that communicators who are interactionally synchronous (as well as self-synchronous) would also garner higher credibility and attraction ratings. Research by Erickson and Shultz (1982) supports this contention. They found that nonmatched interaction patterns led to conversational arrhythmia (dissynchrony) and that such arrhythmia, especially in mixed-culture dyads, led to less positive regard for the other. However, extreme rhythmicity can also be detrimental, perhaps because it indicates inflexibility (Warner et al., 1987). Thus, some moderation is warranted here as well.

Research on mirroring (e.g., Harrigan, Oxman, & Rosenthal, 1985; LaFrance, 1979, 1985) similarly endorses its beneficial consequences. Like synchrony, it is said to connote empathy and promote rapport. Although such findings have doubtless been responsible for the increasing popularity of instructing interviewers and interviewees to mirror each other's behaviors, a recent study of romantic couples' interaction introduces a cautionary note. Manusov (1993) instructed one member in each couple to engage in mirroring. Interactants evaluated their partners more negatively if they believed the mirroring was intentional and manipulative. This suggests that conscious and overt adoption of otherwise positively valenced interaction behaviors such as mirroring may backfire if it is seen as insincere.

The investigations on reciprocity or compensation of *expected* interaction patterns, in addition to examining the patterns themselves, also are relevant here because those investigations obtained partner evaluations. It will be recalled that in the first of the series (Ickes et al., 1982), interactants who were led to expect an unfriendly interaction partner adopted a compensatory pattern that successfully elicited pleasant behavior from the target. Despite that, partners rated them negatively after the interaction. Ickes et al. surmised that perceivers may have been suspicious of the targets' behavior changes and given themselves or the situation "credit" for the improved behavior rather than treating it as indicative of the target's true character. Coutts et al. (1980) similarly found that even though interactants reciprocated increased immediacy from an initially disagreeable partner, they did not evaluate the partner more favorably at the end of the interaction. The conclusion that might be drawn: Interaction patterns may not matter. Negatively evaluated targets remain negatively evaluated, despite what they do.

However, Honeycutt (1991) and Burgoon, Le Poire, and Rosenthal (in press) arrived at the opposite conclusion. Honeycutt, who replicated the Ickes et al. procedure of inducing preinteraction expectancies, correlated behavioral responses in each of the expectancy conditions with subsequent evaluations of the target on sociability, likableness, and kindness. In the unfriendly-expectancy condition, targets who increased affiliative gaze – which would be a compensatory pattern – were rated as more attractive. Honeycutt (1991) concluded that the behaviors were a positive violation of expectations and that they overcame prior expectancies:

The accommodation results lead to the interpretation that unfriendly-expectancy perceivers do not always place a disproportionate emphasis on their expectancy. . . . Rather, these individuals seemed to examine the situation closely and looked for signs of affiliation which fit with interaction preferences for smooth, friendly interaction. . . . When expectancies go against preferences, behavioral signs congruent with the preference may be more salient for the perceiver. (pp. 174–175)

Burgoon et al. (in press) likewise induced positive or negative preinteraction expectancies and examined the interaction styles adopted by participants who interacted with a confederate exhibiting a pleasant/involved or unpleasant/uninvolved interaction pattern. As reported in Chapter 10, interactants tended to reciprocate when partners increased pleasantness/involvement over time, to partially match a partner's reduced level of pleasantness/involvement when the partner decreased it, but also to compensate for that decreased pleasantness/involvement over time. These patterns occurred regardless of the preinteraction expectancies, indicating that interactants were much more responsive to actual communication behavior than to preinteraction expectancies, consistent with Honeycutt (1991).

Just how those interaction patterns relate to postinteraction outcomes can be seen from yoking the interaction patterns associated with pleasant and unpleasant communication to the postinteraction evaluations. As reported in Burgoon and Le Poire (1993), interactants gave the most favorable evaluations to those who (a) were expected to be rewarding and pleasant, (b) actually engaged in pleasant/involved behavior, and/or (c) positively violated expectations. From this, we might infer that reciprocity of positively valenced interaction behavior (pleasantness) was associated with favorable postinteraction evaluations (given that both occurred in the pleasant communication condition) and that compensation of negatively valenced behavior was associated with unfavorable postinteraction evaluations (given that both occurred in the unpleasant communication condition). This would fit Ickes et al.'s (1982) conjecture that if one has to adopt a compensatory strategy to elicit desired behavior from another, one may discount or mistrust the resultant behavior and continue to evaluate the other negatively.

But these implicit correlations between interaction patterns and outcomes are just that – correlations. They do not confirm that the interaction patterns *caused* the evaluations. A direct test connecting the patterns themselves to the outcomes is needed to draw such a conclusion. We illustrate one possible method for doing this momentarily.

Another implication of the foregoing investigations is the effect of deviating from expected interaction patterns. Gain-Loss Theory (Aronson & Linder, 1965) and Expectancy Violations Theory (Burgoon, 1978, 1993) both claim that changes in behavior patterns affect outcomes more strongly than does the persistence of a behavior. For example, people judge partners more favorably if partners begin with a cold interaction style then shift to a warm one than if they maintain a warm style throughout. Thus, the mere act of disrupting a habitual interaction pattern may have felicitous effects. Alternatively, it might be that engaging in a positive violation is more important than whether the resultant interaction pattern is reciprocal or compensatory or even adaptive at all. In fact, refusal to be caught up in a negative conflict spiral – which would mean showing nonaccommodation – might be considered a positive violation in itself and might promote more favorable evaluations of the partner as a consequence. Here again, more research could profitably consider whether it is the violative nature of the behavior, its valence, or both that makes a difference.

### Effects on relationship functioning and satisfaction

Another significant line of research has examined how distressed marital or romantic couples differ from nondistressed couples and how interaction patterns factor into their successful or unsuccessful management of conflict. The prototypical conflict cycle is one in which one person's expression of hostility is generally met with further hostility, leading to an escalating spiral of negative affect and anger. Verbal aggression begets verbal aggression (Infante, 1989), accusations prompt defensiveness and more accusations (Newton & Burgoon, 1990b), and confrontative sequences tend to "chain out" into longer ones, setting up reciprocal negative interaction spirals (Burggraf & Sillars, 1987).

Such reciprocity can lead to severe discord, disfluency, and negative relational consequences, as confirmed by numerous investigations. In seminal work on marital interaction, Gottman (1979) found that couples generally showed a high degree of interaction reciprocity, but that the affective tone (primarily signaled nonverbally) differentiated happy (nondistressed) couples from unhappy (clinical) ones. Although distressed couples did not differ from nondistressed couples in the degree of reciprocated positive affect, happy couples were quicker to provide it, and distressed couples reciprocated more negative affect than nondistressed ones. Pike and Sillars (1985) and Manusov (1994) replicated Gottman's finding that reciprocity was normative, but whereas Pike and Sillars (1985) found that reciprocation of negative affect was more pronounced for distressed couples, Manusov (1994) found that happy couples were more likely to reciprocate partners' positive affect cues. Conversely, Rusbult and colleagues (Rusbult et al., 1991) found that couples were much more satisfied and committed to their relationships when partners compensated for an initial destructive behavior by inhibiting tendencies to react destructively and by engaging in constructive actions.[1]

These findings implicate some cyclical interaction patterns that are intimately tied to couple functioning and satisfaction but do not indicate whether the interaction patterns caused the satisfaction levels or the satisfaction caused the interaction patterns. In an attempt to sort out this chicken and egg problem, Huston and Vangelisti (1991) conducted a longitudinal study in which couples' interaction patterns and evaluations were measured at three different times over the course of two years. Results showed that husbands' early (phase 1) expressions of affection and expressions of negativity were both reciprocated later by wives. Moreover, husbands' negativity predicted wives' satisfaction whereas wives' satisfaction predicted husbands' negativity. This led Huston and Vangelisti (1991) to speculate:

> These asymmetrical patterns are consistent with two possible cycles, one in which husbands' negativity induces dissatisfaction in their wives, which in turn creates an atmosphere that increased the tendency for husbands to behave in ways that increase wives' dissatisfaction. . . . The second interesting pattern suggests that wives' negativity may be indirectly related to husbands' satisfaction in that wives' negativity early in marriage predicted declines in their own satisfaction, and as noted previously, wives' own dissatisfaction may create a climate that encourages their husbands to become more negative. That negativity, in turn, may increase the dissatisfaction of wives later on. (p. 731)

As with all correlational data, this study was unable to determine definitively the ordering between communication patterns and satisfaction. The authors concluded that, regardless of the causal ordering, "spouses' attitudes and behavior operate as a complex, integrated whole. Each spouse both influences and is influenced by the other, either directly or indirectly" (p.731). Although this is an important conclusion, it would be beneficial to determine the extent to which certain interaction patterns breed satisfaction or are themselves a product of that satisfaction.

At this stage, the various studies of marital and couple interaction patterns do support the conclusion that reciprocity is commonplace and that its presence per se is neither boon nor bane to conflict resolution and satisfaction. Rather, what does matter is the valencing of the behaviors that are reciprocated. The more negatively toned reciprocity that occurs, the more deleterious the effects. And the use of compensatory positive behaviors has positive impact.

These conclusions have great import for practitioners and theoreticians alike because they galvanize attention toward communication strategies and affect displays, matters of particular import to communication scholars. At the verbal strategy level, we know that content validation, other-support, concessions, and other integrative conflict strategies are more positively toned (e.g., Newton & Burgoon, 1990b; Rusbult et al., 1991). At the nonverbal affective level, Noller (1984) identified one nonverbal element in this mix with her finding that satisfied couples are more likely to reciprocate positive gaze than are dissatisfied couples, and Newton and Burgoon (1990a) found that other-support and content-validation strategies were often accompanied by nonverbal displays of involvement, submissiveness, and relaxation. We still need to know more, however, about which nonverbal cues are most implicated in these affective displays and which verbal elements (e.g., language intensity, language immediacy, use of humor) contribute significantly to affective tone.

If we combine the conclusion that reciprocation per se is not preferred with the argument that overly rigidified interaction patterns are not healthy for a relationship (see, e.g., Baxter, 1989; Millar & Rogers, 1987), then we can also surmise that excessive reciprocity of any type may be dysfunctional. (The negative evaluations associated with extreme rhythmicity bolster this conclusion.) This may be true of compensation as well. For example, traditional marriages in which the interaction pattern is usually one of male dominance and female submissiveness may be equally problematic. This speculation merits further attention. If a system – be it a dyad, a family, or an entire organization – is too predictable in its interaction patterns, it may become less able to adapt to its environment and to unexpected circumstances. For example, traditional households in which the husband is suddenly stricken with a debilitating illness may lack appropriate inter-action patterns to cope with the new decisions and changes in role relations that are necessitated. Just as the failure to adapt to others may be harmful to individual functioning, hyperadaptation within relation-ships may be harmful to their functioning.

### Social influence effects

In his review of a vast array of persuasion and compliance techniques, Cialdini (1984) identified the principle of reciprocity as one of the most powerful in securing behavioral compliance and concessions during negotiations. One manifestation of this principle appears in the strategy of pregiving. Even people who are ordinarily disliked may be successful in persuading others to comply with a request by doing a small favor first, which elicits a felt obligation to comply with a subsequent request. The same principle works in achieving concessions during negotiations – an offered first concession is likely to trigger reciprocal ones. Interestingly, despite reciprocity resulting in people giving ground to others, Cialdini (1984) claims that reciprocity also engenders more satisfaction with the interaction. Those who achieve settlements as the result of concessions by both parties are more satisfied with the interactions.

One reason that reciprocity is successful as an influence strategy is because attached to it are an obligation to receive and an obligation to repay "gifts" (i.e., it operates on a *debt* principle). The second way in which reciprocity facilitates influence is by *fostering a positive identity* (i.e., a liking principle). Edinger and Patterson (1983) and Cialdini (1984) contend that the reciprocity of involvement behaviors leads a target to like the source, which leads to a greater likelihood of com-pliance. Coker and Burgoon (1987) suggest that by appearing involved in a conversation, the interaction will be perceived as rewarding. When participants feel an interaction is rewarding, they are likely to be more open to persuasive attempts.

Building upon these principles, Dillman (1992) proposed a model of reciprocity as a means of achieving influence. The model is predicated on the assumption that three types of goals guide social interactions: instrumental (which would be achieving the desired persuasive outcome in this case), relational (which would include managing the interper-sonal relationship in a desired way), and identity (which would include promoting a favorable self-image) (Clark & Delia, 1979). Reciprocity is posited to serve each of these goals through its role in expressing in-volvement, equality, homophily, and positive or negative affect. By expressing involvement, equality, similarity, and affection, an interac-tant may simultaneously promote a favorable image and a positive relationship. These messages in turn should make the recipient more receptive to influence, thus satisfying the instrumental objective.

Two strategies for expressing these messages are homeomorphic and heteromorphic exchanges. Verbally, homeomorphic exchanges occur when one partner's self-disclosure elicits disclosure on the same topic and at the same level of intimacy from the other partner. To find out another's age, a person may disclose his or her own age, which is likely to prompt a reciprocal response. On the nonverbal level, touch that elicits reciprocal touch and eye gaze that elicits matching gaze are also homeomorphic exchanges. Those seeking intimate relations with an-other may use this strategy to elicit intimate behaviors. Heteromorphic exchanges occur when, for example, partners offer their time and effort in exchange for another's money (as long as both participants see the exchange as equivalent). Homeless people bearing signs that they will work for food or pay are attempting to influence in this manner. These examples illustrate that similar as well as identical exchanges can be successful influence strategies.

Dillman (1992) has proposed a variety of verbal and nonverbal be-haviors that may serve as reciprocity tactics:

| *Nonverbal* | *Verbal* |
|---|---|
| Close proximity | Making an offer |
| Forward lean | Giving a compliment |
| Direct body and facial orientation | Disclosing personal information |
| Increased direct eye gaze | Agreeing with an opinion |
| Positive head and facial affect signs | Making a concession |
| Postural openness | Discussing mutually interesting topics |
| | |
| Frequent gesturing | |
| Touch | |
| Fast speech rate | |
| Louder speech volume | |
| Lower pitch and pitch variety | |
| Short response latencies | |
| Wearing similar clothing | |

The efficacy of each in eliciting compliance, helping behavior, and attitude change awaits further testing.

Reciprocal interactions may also be used at a more unconscious level to achieve persuasion. For example, Rocissano, Slade, and Lynch (1987) found that toddlers were more compliant when their mothers were able to get into attentional sync with them. Often we forget that the "nuts and bolts" of persuasion may be at the attentional and basic conversational management level; acquiring and retaining another's attention and establishing rapport may promote social influence attempts.

At the same time, there may be occasions where a compensatory pattern is most advantageous. This speculation is fueled by Newton and Burgoon's (1990b) finding that partners who engaged in content validation and other-support strategies and who eschewed content invalidation and other-accusations were seen as most persuasive. Considering the infrequency with which these behaviors occur and the common pattern of disagreements involving escalations of partner reproach, it seems likely that adopting a complementary pattern of responding to antagonistic behavior with affirmations of the partner's arguments or personhood may ultimately lead the partner to be more persuaded by one's own arguments. Earlier, we also raised the possibility that nonaccommodation can be an effective means of preventing an interaction from moving outside the comfort range or preventing relational intimacy from escalating or deescalating too rapidly. Yet Dixson (1992) found in parent–child conversations that failure to accept or adjust to one person's change in the affective tone or purpose of the conversation (i.e., nonreciprocation of verbal behaviors) tended "to lead to negative affective messages and/or conflict" (p. 26). In such cases, nonaccommodation can produce negative results. Clearly, then, we need to know the boundaries for the conditions under which reciprocity induces influence and those under which compensatory or nonaccommodative patterns might be more successful.

One other finding that merits mention is that in addition to promoting credibility, synchronous speaker presentations are more persuasive and better recalled (Woodall & Burgoon, 1981). It is but a small inferential leap to conjecture that interactional synchrony would likewise facilitate message comprehension and acceptance.

## Linking outcomes to patterns: A preliminary assessment

As an illustration of how one might link interaction patterns with outcomes, we provide a preliminary outcome analysis, utilizing the data set from Chapter 9. In addition to coders' ratings of both confederate and subject nonverbal behaviors, we obtained subjects' ratings of the relational message themes they attributed to confederates' behavior (such as receptivity/trust, similarity/depth, composure, dominance) and ratings on the confederates' rewardingness and attraction (task, social, and physical).

To analyze how interaction patterns relate to outcomes, we first computed correlations between subject and confederate ratings on each nonverbal behavior composite. These correlations, which measured the degree to which each dyad exhibited matching/reciprocity or complementarity/compensation, were computed for each dyad across the five time periods. Signed correlations indicated the type of adaption: Positive correlations meant that subjects matched or reciprocated the confederate's behavior; negative correlations meant the subjects complemented or compensated for the confederate's behavior. Absolute correlations measured degree of adaptation, regardless of direction. These signed and unsigned dyadic scores were then correlated with subject perceptions of the confederate after the interaction. Significant relationships, shown in Table 12.1, reflect the degree to which the subject's response to the confederate communication (reciprocal or compensatory and total adaptation) affected subsequent judgments.

Although a quick perusal of Table 12.1 indicates that the patterns and their relationship to outcome measures are anything but clear and unambiguous, some interesting observations are possible. First, adaptation on overall involvement tends to have positive consequences in terms of attraction. When dyads showed greater adaptation to a partner's general level of kinesic/proxemic involvement, especially when the confederate increased involvement, confederates were perceived as more attractive. But too much total adaptation, which included cases of compensation, undermined the appearance of composure. Second, individual involvement behaviors are tied to specific evaluations. For example, matching a partner's lean increased perceived physical attractiveness, as well as sent relational messages of similarity and depth. Matching body orientation created positive evaluations and communicated receptivity. But high amounts of total adaptation, which includes compensation, lowered perceived social attraction. Third, avoiding adaptation appears to be advisable in response to a partner's increase in arousal level. If subjects remained at a low level of anxiety by nonaccommodation or compensation rather than reciprocating the confederate's anxiety, they saw the confederate as more rewarding, task attractive, similar, receptive, and trustworthy. When confederates reduced arousal level and became more relaxed, however, adaptation was desirable.

These results still do not indicate clear directions of causality because it is indeterminate whether adaptations are being made by both parties or not and whether it is the subject's or the confederate's behavior that is ultimately responsible for the postinteraction ratings. Nevertheless, the results do document that patterns can be linked to outcomes, and the method offers one means by which to investigate such linkages. Moreover, the findings suggest that it is not the pattern per se that makes a difference in the outcome but rather the meanings that are imparted through enacting the patterns. This underscores the importance of determining how different interaction patterns are construed. Finally, the results imply that sometimes it is not the particular pattern that matters as much as whether or not some form of adaptation is occurring. It may be that any form of adaptation signals greater activation and responsivity to the partner than does adhering to one's own interaction style. The latter might be construed as egocentrism rather than altercentrism. These kinds of speculations of course warrant further investigation.

## CONCLUSION

These proposed research directions by no means exhaust what is needed. They merely represent what we think would be some particularly productive avenues for the next wave of research. Tests of our proposed theory, along with systematic assessment of the compatibility of previous empirical evidence with our framework, will enable us to better determine the pervasiveness of matching, reciprocal, and synchronous interaction patterns as well as the range of interaction conditions and moderators that attenuate these patterns or elicit compensation. This enterprise will be facilitated by descriptive research identifying communicative expectations and sets of verbal and nonverbal behaviors that represent functional equivalents. It will also be fostered by research designs and analysis plans that incorporate both between- and within-dyad factors and include as part of the within-dyad analyses changes over time. Finally, as we make progress in linking interaction patterns to interaction outcomes, we will be able to offer a more complete causal chain from antecedents to adaptation patterns to consequences.

Table 12.1. *Relationship of subjects' interaction adaptation patterns to their postinteraction ratings of confederates*

For each behavior or composite on the left, the listed adaptation patterns correspond with confederates being seen as more:

| | Rewarding | Physically attractive | Socially attractive | Task attractive |
|---|---|---|---|---|
| Kinesic/proxemic involvement | | adapt to C's increased involvement | adapt to C's increased involvement | reciprocate/adapt to C's increased involvement |
| Lean | | reciprocate C's lean when C increases involvement | | |
| Orientation | reciprocate C's body orientation | | don't adapt to C's body orientation | |
| Facial animation | reciprocate C's facial animation | | adapt to C's facial animation | |
| Arousal | don't adapt to C's arousal change | | | reciprocate or don't adapt to C's arousal when C increases involv. |
| Postural relaxation | adapt to C's relaxation, esp. when C increases involvement | | reciprocate C's relaxation, esp. when C decreases involvement | |

| | Similar | Receptive/trustworthy | Composed | Dominant |
|---|---|---|---|---|
| Random body movement | | adapt to C's random movement, esp. when C increases involv. | | adapt to C's random move., esp. when C decreases involv. |
| Self-adaptors | | | | adapt to C's self-adaptors when C increases involv. |
| Kinesic/proxemic involvement | | | don't adapt to C's involvement | |
| Lean | reciprocate C's lean when C increases involv. | | | |
| Orientation | | reciprocate C's body orientation when C increases involvement | | |
| Arousal | compensate C's arsousal changes | compensate or don't adapt to C's arousal changes | | don't adapt to C's arousal changes |
| Postural relaxation | don't adapt or reciprocate C's relaxation when C decreases involv. | don't adapt or reciprocate C's relaxation when C decreases involv. | adapt to C's relaxation when C decreases involvement | reciprocate C's relaxation |
| Self-adaptors | don't adapt to C's self-adaptor changes | don't adapt to C's self-adaptor changes | compensate or don't adapt to C's self-adaptor changes | don't adapt to C's self-adaptors when C decreases involvement |

**NOTE**

[1] Rusbult et al. have labeled this pattern accommodation, but it is used in the sense of making concessions to one's partner rather than in the more general sense of adaptation as used throughout this volume.

# References

Abele, A. (1986). Functions of gaze in social interaction: Communication and monitoring. *Journal of Nonverbal Behavior, 10,* 83–101.

Aboud, F. E. (1976). Social development aspects of language. *Papers in Linguistics, 9,* 15–37.

Aiello, J. R. (1977a). A further look at equilibrium theory: Visual interaction as a function of interpersonal distance. *Environmental Psychology and Nonverbal Behavior, 1,* 122–140.

Aiello, J. R. (1977b). Visual interaction at extended distances. *Personality and Social Psychology Bulletin, 3,* 83–86.

Aiello, J. R. (1987). Human spatial behavior. In D. Stokols & I. Altman (Eds.), *Handbook of environmental psychology* (Vol. 1, pp. 389–504). New York: John Wiley.

Aiello, J. R., & Aiello, T. D. (1974). The development of personal space: Proxemic behavior of children 6 through 16. *Human Ecology, 2,* 177–189.

Aiello, J. R., & Thompson, D. E. (1980). When compensation fails: Mediating effects of sex and locus of control at extended interaction distances. *Basic and Applied Social Psychology, 1,* 65–82.

Allison, P. D., & Liker, J. K. (1982). Analyzing sequential categorical data in dyadic interaction: A comment on Gottman. *Psychological Bulletin, 91,* 393–403.

Allport, G. W. (1968). The historical background of modern social psychology. In G. Lindzey & E. Aronson (Eds.), *Handbook of social psychology* (2nd ed., Vol. 1, pp. 1–80). Reading, MA: Addison-Wesley.

Als, H., Tronick, E., & Brazelton, T. B. (1979). Analysis of face-to-face interaction in infant–adult dyads. In M. E. Lamb, S. J. Suomi, & G. R. Stephenson (Eds.), *Social interaction analysis* (pp. 33–76). Madison: University of Wisconsin Press.

Altman, I. (1975). *The environment and social behavior.* Monterey, CA: Brooks/Cole.

Altman, I. (1993). Dialectics, physical environments, and personal relationships. *Communication Monographs, 60,* 26–34.

Altman, I., & Taylor, D. A. (1973). *Social penetration: The development of interpersonal relationships.* New York: Holt, Rinehart & Winston.

Altman, I., & Vinsel, A. M. (1977). Personal space: An analysis of E. T. Hall's proxemics framework. In I. Altman & J. F. Wohlwill (Eds.), *Human behavior and environment: Advances in theory and research* (Vol. 2, pp. 181–259). New York: Plenum.

Altman, I., Vinsel, A., & Brown, B. B. (1981). Dialectic conceptions in social psychology: An application to social penetration and privacy regulation. In L. Berkowitz (Ed.), *Advances in experimental social psychology* (Vol. 14, pp. 108–160). New York: Academic Press.

Andersen, P. A. (1983, May). *Nonverbal immediacy in interpersonal communication.* Paper presented to the annual meeting of the International Communication Association, Dallas.

Andersen, P. A. (1984, April). *An arousal-valence model of nonverbal immediacy exchange.* Paper presented to the annual meeting of the Central States Speech Association, Chicago.

Andersen, P. A. (1985). Nonverbal immediacy in interpersonal communication. In A. W. Siegman & S. Feldstein (Eds.), *Multichannel integrations of nonverbal behavior* (pp. 1–36). Hillsdale, NJ: Erlbaum.

Andersen, P. A. (1989, May). *A cognitive valence theory of intimate communication.* Paper presented to the annual conference of the Iowa Network on Personal Relationships, Iowa City.

Andersen, P. A. (1991). When one cannot not communicate: A challenge to Motley's traditional communication postulates. *Communication Studies, 42,* 309–325.

Andersen, P. A. (1992). *Excessive intimacy: An account analysis of behaviors, cognitive schema, and relational outcomes.* Paper presented to the annual conference of the International Society for the Study of Personal Relationships, Orono, ME.

Andersen, P. A., & Andersen, J. F. (1984). The exchange of nonverbal intimacy: A critical review of dyadic models. *Journal of Nonverbal Behavior, 8,* 327–349.

Andersen, P. A, Guerrero, L. K., Jorgensen, P. F., & Buller, D. B. (1995, May). *The immediacy-arousal link: A critical test of three intimacy exchange theories.* Paper presented to the annual meeting of the International Communication Association, Albuquerque.

Apple, W., Streeter, L. A., & Krauss, R. M. (1979). Effects of pitch and speech rate on personal attributions. *Journal of Personality and Social Psychology, 37,* 715–727.

Argyle, M. (1972). Non-verbal communication in human social interaction. In R. A. Hinde (Ed.), *Non-verbal communication* (pp. 243–269). Cambridge: Cambridge University Press.

Argyle, M., & Cook, M. (1976). Gaze as a signal for interpersonal attitudes and emotions. In *Gaze and mutual gaze* (pp. 58–81). Cambridge: Cambridge University Press.

Argyle, M., & Dean, J. (1965). Eye-contact, distance, and affiliation. *Sociometry, 28,* 289–304.

Argyle, M., & Ingham, R. (1972). Gaze, mutual gaze, and proximity. *Semiotica, 6,* 32–49.

Aronson, E., & Linder, D. (1965). Gain and loss of esteem as determinants of interpersonal attractiveness. *Journal of Experimental Social Psychology, 1,* 156–171.

Arundale, R. B. (1977). Sampling across time for communication research: A simulation. In P. M. Hirsch, P. V. Miller, & F. G. Kline (Eds.), *Strategies for communication research* (pp. 257–285). Beverly Hills, CA: Sage.

Baesler, E. J., & Burgoon, J. K. (1988). Measurement and reliability of nonverbal behavior and percepts. *Journal of Nonverbal Behavior, 11,* 205–233.

Bandura, A. (1977). *Social learning theory.* Englewood Cliffs, NJ: Prentice-Hall.

Bargh, J. A. (1989). Conditional automaticity: Varieties of automatic influence in social perception and cognition. In J. S. Uleman & J. A. Bargh (Eds.), *Unintended thought* (pp. 3–51). New York: Guilford.

Baumeister, R. F., Hutton, D. G., & Tice, D. M. (1989). Cognitive processes during deliberate self-presentation: How self-presenters alter and misinterpret the behavior of their interaction partners. *Journal of Experimental Social Psychology, 25,* 59–78.

Bavelas, J. B. (1990). Behaving and communicating: A reply to Motley. *Western Journal of Speech Communication, 54,* 593–602.

Bavelas, J. B., Black, A., Chovil, N., Lemery, C. R., & Mullett, J. (1988). Form and function in motor mimicry: Topographic evidence that the primary function is communicative. *Human Communication Research, 14,* 275–300.

Bavelas, J. B., Black, A., Lemery, C. R., MacInnis, S., & Mullett, J. (1986). Experimental methods for studying "elementary motor mimicry." *Journal of Nonverbal Behavior, 10,* 102–119.

Bavelas, J. B., Black, A., Lemery, C. R., & Mullett, J. (1986). "I *show* how you feel": Motor mimicry as a communicative act. *Journal of Personality and Social Psychology, 50,* 322–329.

Baxter, L. A. (1988). A dialectic perspective on communication strategies in relationship development. In S. Duck (Ed.), *Handbook of personal relationships: Theory, research and interventions* (pp. 257–288). Chichester, UK: John Wiley & Sons.

Baxter, L. A. (1989, May). *On structure and its deconstruction in relationship "texts": Toward a dialectical approach to the study of personal relationships.* Paper presented to the annual meeting of the International Communication Association, San Francisco.

Baxter, L. A. (1992). Forms and functions of intimate play in personal relationships. *Human Communication Research, 18,* 336–363.

Baxter, L. A., & Wilmot, W. (1983). *An investigation of openness–closedness cycling in ongoing relationship interaction.* Paper presented to the annual meeting of the Western Speech Communication Association, Albuquerque.

Beebe, B., Gerstman, L., Carson, B., Dolins, M., Zigman, A., Rosensweig, H., Faughey, K., & Korman, M. (1982). Rhythmic communication in the mother–infant dyad. In M. Davis (Ed.), *Interaction rhythms* (pp. 79–100). New York: Harvkady.

Berg, J. H., & Clark, M. S. (1986). Differences in social exchange between intimate and other relationships: Gradually evolving or quickly apparent? In V. J. Derlega & B. A. Winstead (Eds.), *Friendship and social interaction* (pp. 101–128). New York: Springer-Verlag.

Berger, C. R., & Bradac, J. J. (1982). *Language and social knowledge.* London: Edward Arnold.

Berger, C. R., & Calabrese, R. J. (1975). Some explorations in initial interaction and beyond: Toward a developmental theory of interpersonal communication. *Human Communication Research, 1,* 99–112.

Berger, S. M., & Hadley, S. W. (1975). Some effects of a model's performance on an observer's electromyographic activity. *American Journal of Psychology, 88,* 263–276.

Berghout-Austin, A. M., & Peery, J. C. (1983). Analysis of adult–neonate synchrony during speech and nonspeech. *Perceptual Motor Skills, 57,* 455–459.

Bernard, H. R., Killworth, P., Kronenfeld, D., & Sailer, L. (1984). The problem of informant accuracy: The validity of retrospective data. *Annual Review of Anthropology, 13,* 495–517.

Bernieri, F., Reznick, J. S. & Rosenthal, R. (1988). Synchrony, pseudo-synchrony, and dissynchrony: Measuring the entrainment process in mother–infant interactions. *Journal of Personality and Social Psychology, 54,* 243–253.

Bernieri, F. J., & Rosenthal, R. (1991). Interpersonal coordination: Behavioral matching and interactional synchrony. In R. S. Feldman & B. Rimé (Eds.), *Fundamentals of nonverbal behavior* (pp. 401–432). Cambridge: Cambridge University Press.

Billings, A. (1979). Conflict resolution in distressed and nondistressed married couples. *Journal of Consulting and Clinical Psychology, 47,* 368–376.

Bochner, A. P. (1984). The functions of communication in interpersonal bonding. In C. C. Arnold & J. W. Bowers (Eds.), *Handbook of rhetorical and communication theory* (pp. 544–621). Boston: Allyn & Bacon.

Bolger, N., Kashy, D. A., & Kenny, D. A. (1992, October). *Analyzing diary, log, and experience sampling data: Potentials and pitfalls.* Workshop presented to the annual meeting of the Society for Experimental Psychology, San Antonio, TX.

Bourhis, R. Y., & Giles, H. (1977). The language of intergroup distinctiveness. In H. Giles (Ed.), *Language, ethnicity, and intergroup relations* (pp. 119–135). London: Academic Press.

Bradac, J. (1991, February). *Some issues in accommodation theory: Perceived intentionality.* Paper presented to the annual meeting of the Western States Communication Association, Phoenix.

Bradac, J. J., Hosman, L. A., & Tardy, C. H. (1978). Reciprocal disclosures and language intensity: Attributional consequences. *Communication Monographs, 45,* 1–17.

Brazelton, T. B., Tronick, E., Adamson, L., Als, H., & Wise, S. (1975). Early mother–infant reciprocity. In M. A. Hofer (Ed.), *Parent–infant interaction, Ciba Foundation Symposium 33* (pp. 137–168). Amsterdam: Elsevier.

Breed, G. (1972). The effect of intimacy: Reciprocity or retreat? *British Journal of Social and Clinical Psychology, 11,* 135–142.

Bruneau, T. (1994, July). *Subjective time, social interaction, and personal identity.* Paper presented to the 5th International Conference on Language and Social Psychology, University of Queensland, Brisbane.

Buck, R. (1988). Nonverbal communication: Spontaneous and symbolic aspects. *American Behavioral Scientist, 31,* 341–354.

Buck, R. (1991). Social factors in facial display and communication: A reply to Chovil and others. *Journal of Nonverbal Behavior, 15,* 155–161.

Buller, D. B., & Burgoon, J. K. (1986). The effects of vocalics and nonverbal sensitivity on compliance: A replication and extension. *Human Communication Research, 13,* 126–144.

Buller, D. B., & Burgoon, J. K. (1994). Deception: Strategic and nonstrategic communication. In J. A. Daly & J. M. Wiemann (Eds.), *Strategic interpersonal communication* (pp. 191–223). Hillsdale, NJ: Erlbaum.

Bullowa, M. (1975). When infant and adult communicate, how do they synchronize their behaviors? In A. Kendon, R. M. Harris, & M. R. Key (Eds.), *Organization of behavior in face-to-face interaction* (pp. 95–125). Paris: Mouton.

Burgess, J. W. (1983). Developmental trends in proxemic spacing behavior between surrounding companions and strangers in casual groups. *Journal of Nonverbal Behavior, 7,* 158–169.

Burggraf, C. S., & Sillars, A. L. (1987). A critical examination of sex differences in marital communication. *Communication Monographs, 54,* 276–294.

Burgoon, J. K. (1978). A communication model of personal space violations: Explication and an initial test. *Human Communication Research, 4,* 129–142.

Burgoon, J. K. (1983). Nonverbal violations of expectations. In J. M. Wiemann & R. P. Harrison (Eds.), *Nonverbal interaction* (pp. 11–77). Beverly Hills, CA: Sage.

Burgoon, J. K. (1984). Nonverbal behavior: A functional approach [Review of M. L. Patterson's *Nonverbal behavior: A functional approach*]. *Quarterly Journal of Speech, 70,* 492–493.

Burgoon, J. K. (1985). Nonverbal signals. In M. L. Knapp & G. R. Miller (Eds.), *Handbook of interpersonal communication* (1st ed., pp. 344–390). Beverly Hills, CA: Sage.

Burgoon, J. K. (1991). Relational message interpretations of touch, conversational distance, and posture. *Journal of Nonverbal Behavior, 15,* 233–258.

Burgoon, J. K. (1992). Applying a comparative approach to nonverbal expectancy violations theory. In J. Blumler, K. E. Rosengren, & J. M. McLeod (Eds.), *Comparatively speaking: Communication and culture across space and time* (pp. 53–69). Newbury Park, CA: Sage.

Burgoon, J. K. (1993). Interpersonal expectations, expectancy violations, and emotional communication. *Journal of Language and Social Psychology, 12,* 13–21.

Burgoon, J. K. (1994). Nonverbal signals. In M. L. Knapp & G. R. Miller (Eds.), *Handbook of interpersonal communication* (2nd ed., pp. 229–285). Newbury Park, CA: Sage.

Burgoon, J. K., & Aho, L. (1982). Three field experiments on the effects of violations of conversational distance. *Communication Monographs, 49,* 71–88.

Burgoon, J. K., & Baesler, E. J. (1991). Choosing between micro and macro nonverbal measurement: Application to selected vocalic and kinesic nonverbal indices. *Journal of Nonverbal Behavior, 15,* 57–78.

Burgoon, J. K., Buller, D. B., Dillman, L., & Walther, J. B. (in press). Interpersonal deception: IV. Effects of suspicion on perceived communication and nonverbal behavior dynamics. *Human Communication Research.*

Burgoon, J.K., Buller, D. B., Ebesu, A., White, C., & Rockwell, P. (in press). Interpersonal deception: XI. Effects of suspicion on nonverbal behavior and relational messages. *Communication Theory.*

Burgoon, J. K., Buller, D. B., Hale, J. L., & deTurck, M. A. (1984). Relational messages associated with nonverbal behaviors. *Human Communication Research, 10,* 351–378.

Burgoon, J. K., Buller, D. B., & Woodall, W. G. (1989). *Nonverbal communication: The unspoken dialogue.* New York: HarperCollins.

Burgoon, J. K., Coker, D. A., & Coker, R. A. (1986). Communicative effects of gaze behavior: A test of two contrasting explanations. *Human Communication Research, 12,* 495–524.

Burgoon, J. K., Dillman, L., & Stern, L. A. (1991, May). *Reciprocity and compensation patterns: I. Definitions, operationalizations, and statistical analysis*. Paper presented to the annual meeting of the International Communication Association, Chicago.

Burgoon, J. K., Dillman, L., & Stern, L. A. (1993). Adaptation in dyadic interaction: Defining and operationalizing patterns of reciprocity and compensation, *Communication Theory, 4*, 293–316.

Burgoon, J. K., Dillman, L., Stern, L. A., & Kelley, D. L. (1992, May). *Reciprocity and compensation patterns in dyadic interaction: Statistical analysis*. Paper presented to the annual meeting of the International Communication Association, Miami.

Burgoon, J. K., & Hale, J. L. (1984). The fundamental topoi of relational communication. *Communication Monographs, 51*, 193–214.

Burgoon, J. K., & Hale, J. L. (1987). Validation and measurement of the fundamental themes of relational communication. *Communication Monographs, 54*, 19–41.

Burgoon, J. K., & Hale, J. L. (1988). Nonverbal expectancy violations: Model elaboration and application to immediacy behaviors. *Communication Monographs, 55*, 58–79.

Burgoon, J. K., & Jones, S. B. (1976). Toward a theory of personal space expectations and their violations. *Human Communication Research, 2*, 131–146.

Burgoon, J. K., Kelley, D. L., Newton, D. A., & Keeley-Dyreson, M. P. (1989). The nature of arousal and nonverbal indices. *Human Communication Research, 16*, 217–255.

Burgoon, J. K., & Koper, R. J. (1984). Nonverbal and relational communication associated with reticence. *Human Communication Research, 10*, 601–626.

Burgoon, J. K., & Le Poire, B. A. (1993). Effects of communication expectancies, actual communication, and expectancy disconfirmation on evaluations of communicators and their communication behavior. *Human Communication Research, 20*, 75–107.

Burgoon, J. K., Le Poire, B. A., & Rosenthal, R. (in press). Effects of preinteraction expectancies and target communication on perceiver reciprocity and compensation in dyadic interaction. *Journal of Experimental Social Psychology*.

Burgoon, J. K., Manusov, V., Mineo, P., & Hale, J. L. (1985). Effects of eye gaze on hiring, credibility, attraction and relational message interpretation. *Journal of Nonverbal Behavior, 9*, 133–146.

Burgoon, J. K., & Newton, D. A. (1991). Applying a social meaning model to relational message interpretations of conversational involvement: Comparing observer and participant perspectives. *Southern Communication Journal, 56*, 96–113.

Burgoon, J. K., Newton, D. A., Walther, J. B., & Baesler, E. J. (1989). Nonverbal expectancy violations and conversational involvement. *Journal of Nonverbal Behavior, 13*, 97–120.

Burgoon, J. K., Olney, C. A., & Coker, R. A. (1987). The effects of communicator characteristics on patterns of reciprocity and compensation. *Journal of Nonverbal Behavior, 11,* 146–165.

Burgoon, J. K., & Saine, T. (1978). *The unspoken dialogue: An introduction of nonverbal communication.* Boston: Houghton-Mifflin.

Burgoon, J. K., & Walther, J. B. (1990). Nonverbal expectancies and the evaluative consequences of violations. *Human Communication Research, 17,* 232–265.

Byers, P. (1976). Biological rhythms as information channels in interpersonal communication behavior. In P. O. Bateson & P. H. Klopfer (Eds.), *Perspectives in ethology* (pp. 135–164). New York: Plenum.

Cacioppo, J. T., Tassinary, L. G., & Fridlund, A. J. (1990). Skeletomotor system. In J. T. Cacioppo & L. G. Tassinary (Eds.), *Principles of psychophysiology: Physical, social, and inferential elements* (pp. 325–384). Cambridge: Cambridge University Press.

Campbell, D. T., & Stanley, J. C. (1963). *Experimental and quasi-experimental designs for research.* Chicago: Rand McNally.

Cann, A., Sherman, S. J., & Elkes, R. (1975). Effects of initial request size and timing of a second request on compliance: The foot in the door and the door in the face. *Journal of Personality and Social Psychology, 32,* 774–782.

Cappella, J. N. (1979). Talk and silence sequences in informal social conversations: I. *Human Communication Research, 6,* 3–17.

Cappella, J. N. (1981). Mutual influence in expressive behavior: Adult–adult and infant–adult dyadic interaction. *Psychological Bulletin, 89,* 101–132.

Cappella, J. N. (1983). Conversational involvement: Approaching and avoiding others. In J. M. Wiemann & R. P. Harrison (Eds.), *Nonverbal interaction* (pp. 113–152). Beverly Hills, CA: Sage.

Cappella, J. N. (1984). The relevance of microstructure of interaction to relationship change. *Journal of Social and Personal Relationships, 1,* 239–264.

Cappella, J. N. (1985). The management of conversations. In M. L. Knapp & G. R. Miller (Eds.), *Handbook of interpersonal communication* (1st ed., pp. 393–438). Beverly Hills, CA: Sage.

Cappella, J. N. (1987). Interpersonal communication: Definitions and fundamental questions. In C. R. Berger & S. H. Chaffee (Eds.), *Handbook of communication science* (pp. 184–238). Beverly Hills, CA: Sage.

Cappella, J. N. (1991a). The biological origins of automated patterns of human interaction. *Communication Theory, 1,* 4–35.

Cappella, J. N. (1991b). Mutual adaptation and relativity of measurement. In B. M. Montgomery & S. Duck (Eds.), *Studying interpersonal interaction* (pp. 103–117). New York: Guilford.

Cappella, J. N., & Greene, J. O. (1982). A discrepancy-arousal explanation of mutual influence in expressive behavior for adult and infant–adult interaction. *Communication Monographs, 49,* 89–114.

Cappella, J. N., & Greene, J. O. (1984). The effects of distance and individual differences in arousability on nonverbal involvement: A test of discrepancy-arousal theory. *Journal of Nonverbal Behavior, 8,* 259–286.

Cappella, J. N., & Palmer, M. T. (1990). The structure and organization of verbal and non-verbal behavior: Data for models of production. In H. Giles & W. P. Robinson (Eds.), *Handbook of language and social psychology* (pp. 141–161). Chichester, U.K.: John Wiley & Sons.

Cappella, J. N. & Planalp, S. (1981). Talk and silence sequences in information conversations: III. Interspeaker influence. *Human Communication Research, 7,* 117–32.

Chapple, E. D. (1982). Movement and sound: The musical language of body rhythms in interaction. In M. Davis (Ed.), *Interaction rhythms: Periodicity in communicative behavior* (pp. 31–52). New York: Human Sciences.

Cialdini, R. B. (1984). *Influence: The new psychology of modern persuasion.* New York: Quill.

Clark, R. A., & Delia, J. G. (1979). Topoi and rhetorical competence. *Quarterly Journal of Speech, 65,* 187–206.

Cline, R. J. W. (1989). The politics of intimacy: Costs and benefits determining disclosure intimacy in male–female dyads. *Journal of Social and Personal Relationships, 6,* 5–20.

Coker, D. A., & Burgoon, J. K. (1987). The nature of conversational involvement and nonverbal encoding patterns. *Human Communication Research, 13,* 463–494.

Condon, W. S. (1980). The relation of interactional synchrony to cognitive and emotional processes. In M. E. Key (Ed.), *The relationship of verbal and nonverbal communication* (pp. 49–65). New York: Mouton.

Condon, W. S. (1982). Cultural microrhythms. In M. Davis (Ed.), *Interaction rhythms: Periodicity in communicative behavior* (pp. 53–76). New York: Human Sciences.

Condon, W. S., & Ogston, W. D. (1966). Sound film analysis of normal and pathological behavior patterns. *Journal of Nervous and Mental Diseases, 143,* 338–457.

Condon, W. S., & Ogston, W. D. (1967). A segmentation of behavior. *Journal of Psychiatric Research, 5,* 221–235.

Condon, W. S., & Ogston, W. D. (1971). Speech and body motion synchrony of the speaker–hearer. In D. L. Horton & J. J. Jenkins (Eds.), *Perception of language* (pp. 150–173). Columbus, OH: Charles E. Merrill.

Condon, W. D., & Sander, L. W. (1974). Synchrony demonstrated between movement of the neonate and adult speech. *Child Development, 45,* 456–462.

Coupland, N. (1984). Accommodation at work: Some phonological data and their implications. *International Journal of the Sociology of Language, 46,* 49–70.

Coupland, N., Coupland, J., Giles, H., & Henwood, K. (1988). Accommodating the elderly: Invoking and extending a theory. *Language in Society, 17,* 1–41.

Coutts, L. M., Irvine, M., & Schneider, F. W. (1977). Nonverbal adjustments to changes in gaze and orientation. *Psychology, 14,* 28–32.

Coutts, L. M., Schneider, F. W., & Montgomery, S. (1980). An investigation of the arousal model of interpersonal intimacy. *Journal of Experimental Social Psychology, 16,* 545–561.

Cronkhite, G., & Liska, J. (1980). The judgment of communicator acceptability. In M. E. Roloff & G. R. Miller (Eds.), *Persuasion: New directions in theory and research* (pp. 101–140). Beverly Hills, CA: Sage.

Crowder, M. J., & Hand, D. (1990). *Analysis of repeated measures.* London: Chapman and Hall.

Dabbs, J. M., Jr. (1969). Similarity of gestures and interpersonal influence. *Proceedings of the 77th Annual Convention of the American Psychological Association, 4,* 337–338.

Dabbs, J. M., Jr., Evans, M. S., Hopper, C. H., & Purvis, J. A. (1980). Self-monitors in conversation: What do they monitor? *Journal of Personality and Social Psychology, 39,* 278–284.

Davis, D. R., & Lee, J. (1980). Time-series analysis models for communication research. In P. R. Monge and J. N. Cappella (Eds.), *Multivariate techniques in human communication research* (pp. 429–454). New York: Academic Press.

Davis, J. D. (1976). Self-disclosure in an acquaintance exercise: Responsibility for level of intimacy. *Journal of Personality and Social Psychology, 33,* 787–792.

Davis, J. D., & Skinner, A. E. G. (1974). Reciprocity of self-disclosure in interviews: Modeling or social exchange? *Journal of Personality and Social Psychology, 29,* 779–784.

Davis, M. R. (1985). Perceptual and affective reverberation components. In A. B. Goldstein & G. Y. Michaels (Eds.), *Empathy: Development, training, and consequences* (pp. 62–108). Hillsdale, NJ: Erlbaum.

Day, R. R. (1982). Children's attitudes toward language. In E. B. Ryan & H. Giles (Eds.), *Attitudes toward language variation: Social and applied contexts* (pp. 116–131). London: Edward Arnold.

Deprez, K., & Persoons, K. (1984). On the identity of Flemish high school students in Brussels. *Journal of Language and Social Psychology, 3,* 273–296.

Derlega, V., J., Metts, S., Petronio, S., & Margulis, S. T. (1993). *Self-disclosure.* Newbury Park, CA: Sage.

Derlega, V. J., Wilson, M., & Chaikin, A. L. (1976). Friendship and disclosure reciprocity. *Journal of Personality and Social Psychology, 34,* 378–382.

Dillard, J. P., Segrin, C., & Harden, J. M. (1989). Primary and secondary goals in the production of interpersonal influence messages. *Communication Monographs, 56,* 19–38.

Dillman, L. (1992, October). *Reciprocity as a means of influence in interpersonal interactions.* Paper presented to the annual meeting of the Speech Communication Association, Chicago.

Dindia, K. (1982). Reciprocity of self-disclosure: A sequential analysis. In M. Burgoon (Ed.), *Communication yearbook 6* (pp. 507–528). Beverly Hills, CA: Sage.

Dindia, K. (1988). A comparison of several statistical tests of reciprocity of self-disclosure. *Communication Research, 15,* 726–752.

Dittmann, A. T. (1974). The body movement–speech rhythm relationship as a cue to speech encoding. In S. Weitz (Ed.), *Nonverbal communication* (pp. 168–181). New York: Oxford University Press.

Dittmann, A. T., & Llewellyn, L. G. (1969). Body movement and speech rhythm in social conversation. *Journal of Personality and Social Psychology, 11,* 98–106.

Dixson, M. D. (1992, October). *Reciprocal interaction and positive/negative affect in parent–child communication: How do they do it?* Paper presented to the annual meeting of the Speech Communication Association, Chicago.

Dovidio, J. F., & Ellyson, S. L. (1982). Decoding visual dominance behavior: Attributions of power based on the relative percentages of looking while speaking and looking while listening. *Social Psychology Quarterly, 45,* 106–113.

Dunn, O. J., & Clark, V. A. (1969). Correlation coefficients measured on the same individuals. *Journal of the American Statistical Association, 64,* 366–377.

Edinger, J. A., & Patterson, M. L. (1983). Nonverbal involvement and social control. *Psychological Bulletin, 93,* 30–56.

Ehrlich, H. J., & Graeven, D. B. (1971). Reciprocal self-disclosure in a dyad. *Journal of Experimental Social Psychology, 7,* 389–400.

Ekman, P., & Friesen, W. V. (1969a). Nonverbal leakage and clues to deception. *Psychiatry, 32,* 88–106.

Ekman, P., & Friesen, W. V. (1969b). The repertoire of nonverbal behavior: Categories, origins, usage, and coding. *Semiotica, 1,* 49–98.

Ellsworth, P. C. (1977). *Some questions about the role of arousal in the interpretation of direct gaze.* Paper presented to the annual meeting of the American Psychological Association, San Francisco.

Erickson, F. (1979). Talking down: Some cultural sources of miscommunication in interracial interviews. In A. Wolfgang (Ed.), *Nonverbal behavior:*

*Applications and cultural implications* (pp. 99–126). New York: Academic Press.

Erickson, F., & Shultz, J. (1982). *The counselor as gatekeeper: Social interaction in interviews.* New York: Academic.

Feick, L. F., & Novak, J. A. (1985). Analyzing sequential categorical data on dyadic interaction: Log-linear models exploiting the order in variables. *Psychological Bulletin, 98,* 600–611.

Feldman, R. E. (1968). Response to compatriots and foreigners who seek assistance. *Journal of Personality and Social Psychology, 10,* 202–214.

Firestone, I. J. (1977). Reconciling verbal and nonverbal models of dyadic communication. *Environmental Psychology and Nonverbal Behavior, 2,* 30–43.

Fisher, B. A. (1978). *Current status of interaction research.* Paper presented to the annual meeting of the Western Speech Communication Association, Phoenix.

Fishman, J. A. (1966). *Language loyalty in the United States.* The Hague: Mouton.

Fitzpatrick, M. A., Mulac, A., & Dindia, K. (1994, July). *Convergence and reciprocity in male and female communication patterns in spouse and stranger interaction.* Paper presented to the 5th International Conference on Language and Social Psychology, University of Queensland, Brisbane.

Foa, U. G., & Foa, E. B. (1972). Resource exchange: Toward a structural theory of interpersonal communication. In A. W. Siegman & B. Pope (Eds.), *Studies in dyadic communication* (pp. 291–325). New York: Pergamon.

Foot, H. C., Chapman, A. J., & Smith, J. R. (1977). Friendship and social responsiveness in boys and girls. *Journal of Personality and Social Psychology, 35,* 410–411.

Gaelick, L., Bodenhausen, G. V., & Wyer, R. S., Jr. (1985). Emotional communication in close relationships. *Journal of Personality and Social Psychology, 49,* 1246–1265.

Gallois, C., & Callan, V. J. (1988). Communication accommodation and the prototypical speaker: Predicting evaluations of status and solidarity. *Language and Communication, 8,* 271–284.

Gallois, C., & Callan, V. J. (1991). Interethnic accommodation: The role of norms. In H. Giles, J. Coupland, & N. Coupland (Eds.), *Contexts of accommodation: Developments in applied sociolinguistics* (pp. 245–269). Cambridge: Cambridge University Press.

Gallois, C., Giles, H., Jones, E., Cargile, A., & Ota, H. (1995). Accommodating intercultural encounters. In R. Wiseman (Ed.), *Theories of intercultural communication* (pp. 115–147). Newbury Park, CA: Sage.

Gatewood, J. B., & Rosenwein, R. (1981). Interactional synchrony: Genuine or spurious? A critique of recent research. *Journal of Nonverbal Behavior, 6,* 12–29.

Gilbert, D. A. (1993). Reciprocity of involvement activities in client-nurse interactions. *Western Journal of Nursing Research, 15,* 673–688.

Gilbert, D. T., Krull, D. S., & Pelham, B. W. (1988). Of thoughts unspoken: Social inference and the self-regulation of behavior. *Journal of Personality and Social Psychology, 55,* 658–694.

Gilbert, S. J. (1976). Empirical and theoretical extensions of self-disclosure. In G. R. Miller (Ed.), *Explorations in interpersonal communication* (pp. 197–215). Beverly Hills, CA: Sage.

Giles, H. (1973). Accent mobility: A model and some data. *Anthropological Linguistics, 15,* 87–105.

Giles, H. (1980). Accommodation theory: Some new directions. In S. de Silva (Ed.), *Aspects of linguistic behavior* (pp. 105–136). York: University of York Press.

Giles, H., Bourhis, R. Y., & Taylor, D. M. (1977). Towards a theory of language in ethnic group relations. In H. Giles (Ed.), *Language, ethnicity, and intergroup relations* (pp. 307–348). London: Academic Press.

Giles, H., Coupland, N., & Coupland, J. (1991a). Accommodation theory: Communication, context, and consequence. In H. Giles, J. Coupland, & N. Coupland (Eds.), *Contexts of accommodation: Developments in applied sociolinguistics* (pp. 1–68). Cambridge: Cambridge University Press.

Giles, H., Coupland, J., & Coupland, N. (Eds.) (1991b). *Contexts of accommodation.* Cambridge: Cambridge University Press.

Giles, H., Mulac, A., Bradac, J. J., & Johnson, P. (1987). Speech Accommodation Theory: The first decade and beyond. In M. L. McLaughlin (Ed.), *Communication yearbook 10* (pp. 13–48). Newbury Park, CA: Sage.

Giles, H., & Powesland, P. F. (1975). *Speech style and social evaluation.* London: Academic Press.

Giles, H., & Smith, P. M. (1979). Accommodation theory: Optimal levels of convergence. In H. Giles & R. St. Clair (Eds.), *Language and social psychology* (pp. 45–65). Oxford: Blackwell.

Giles, H., Taylor, D. M., & Bourhis, R. Y. (1973). Towards a theory of interpersonal accommodation through language: Some Canadian data. *Language in Society, 2,* 177–192.

Goffman, E. (1959). *The presentation of self in everyday life.* Garden City, NY: Anchor Books/Doubleday.

Gottman, J. M. (1979). *Marital interaction: Experimental investigations.* New York: Academic Press.

Gottman, J. M. (1982). Temporal form: Toward a new language for describing relationships. *The Counseling Psychologist, 44,* 943–962.

Gottman, J. M., & Roy, A. K. (1990). *Sequential analysis: A guide for behavioral researchers.* Cambridge: Cambridge University Press.

Gouldner, A. W. (1960). The norm of reciprocity: A preliminary statement. *American Sociological Review, 25,* 161–178.

Graham, J. A., Argyle, M., & Furnham, A. (1980). The goal structure of situations. *European Journal of Social Psychology, 10,* 345–366.

Gregory, S. W. (1990). Analysis of fundamental frequency reveals covariation in interview partners' speech. *Journal of Nonverbal Behavior, 14,* 237–251.

Grice, P. (1989). *Studies in the way of words.* Cambridge, MA: Harvard University Press.

Guerrero, L. K. (1994). *An application of attachment theory to relational messages and nonverbal involvement behaviors in romantic relationships.* Unpublished dissertation, University of Arizona.

Guerrero, L. K., & Andersen, P. A. (1994). Patterns of matching and initiation: Touch behavior and touch avoidance across romantic relationship stages. *Journal of Nonverbal Behavior, 18,* 137–153.

Gudykunst, W., & Kim, Y. Y. (1992). *Communicating with strangers: An approach to intercultural communication* (2nd ed.). New York: McGraw-Hill.

Haggard, E. A. (1958). *Intraclass correlation and the analysis of variance.* New York: Dryden.

Haggard, E. A., & Isaacs, K. S. (1966). Micromomentary facial expressions as indicators of ego mechanisms in psychotherapy. In L. A. Gottschalk & A. H. Auerbach (Eds.), *Methods of research in psychotherapy* (pp. 154–165). New York: Appleton-Century-Crofts.

Hale, J. L., & Burgoon, J. K. (1984). Models of reactions to changes in nonverbal immediacy. *Journal of Nonverbal Behavior, 8,* 287–314.

Hall, E. T. (1959). *The silent language.* Garden City, NY: Anchor Books/Doubleday.

Hall, E. T. (1966). *The hidden dimension* (2nd ed.). Garden City, NY: Anchor Books/Doubleday.

Harrigan, J. A, Oxman, T. E., & Rosenthal, R. (1985). Rapport expressed through nonverbal behavior. *Journal of Nonverbal Behavior, 9,* 95–110.

Harris, L. M., Gergen, K. J., & Lannamann, J. W. (1986). Aggression rituals. *Communication Monographs, 53,* 252–265.

Hatfield, E., Cacioppo, J. T., & Rapson, R. (1994). *Emotional contagion.* Cambridge: Cambridge University Press.

Hatfield, E., & Rapson, R. (1990). Emotions: A trinity. In E. A. Bleckman (Ed.), *Emotions and the family: For better or worse* (pp. 11–33). Hillsdale, NJ: Erlbaum.

Haviland, J. M., & Lelwica, M. (1987). The induced affect response: 10-week-old infants' responses to three emotion expressions. *Developmental Psychology, 23,* 97–104.

Hayduk, L. (1983). Personal space: Where we now stand. *Psychological Bulletin, 94,* 293–335.

Hayes, W. L. (1963). *Statistics for psychologists.* New York: Holt, Rinehart & Winston.

Helson, H. (1964). *Adaptation-level theory.* New York: Harper & Row.

Henley, N. M. (1977). *Body politics: Power, sex, and nonverbal communication.* Englewood Cliffs, NJ: Prentice-Hall.

Henley, N. M., & Harmon, S. (1985). The nonverbal semantics of power and gender: A perceptual study. In S. L. Ellyson & J. F. Dovidio (Eds.), *Power, dominance, and nonverbal behavior* (pp. 151–164). New York: Springer-Verlag.

Hewes, D. (1979). The sequential analysis of social interaction. *Quarterly Journal of Speech, 65,* 56–73.

Hewes, D. (1980). Stochastic modeling of communication processes. In P. R. Monge & J. N. Cappella (Eds.), *Multivariate techniques in human communication research* (pp. 393–427). New York: Academic Press.

Hibbs, D. A., Jr. (1973/1974). Problems of statistical estimation and causal inference in time-series regression models. In H. Costner (Ed.), *Sociological methodology* (pp. 252–308). San Francisco: Jossey-Bass.

Hilton, J. L., & Darley, J. M. (1985). Constructing other persons: A limit on the effect. *Journal of Experimental Social Psychology, 21,* 1–18.

Hinde, R. A. (1979). *Towards understanding relationships.* New York: Academic Press.

Hogg, M. (1985). Masculine and feminine speech in dyads and groups: A study of speech style and gender salience. *Journal of Language and Social Psychology, 4,* 99–112.

Honeycutt, J. M. (1989). Effect of preinteraction expectancies on interaction involvement and behavioral responses in initial interaction. *Journal of Nonverbal Behavior, 13,* 25–36.

Honeycutt, J. M. (1991). The role of nonverbal behaviors in modifying expectancies during initial encounters. *Southern Communication Journal, 56,* 161–177.

Hosman, L. A. (1987). The evaluational consequences of topic reciprocity and self-disclosure reciprocity. *Communication Monographs, 54,* 420–435.

Hosman, L. A., & Tardy, C. H. (1980). Self-disclosure and reciprocity in short- and long-term relationships: An experimental study of evaluational and attributional consequences. *Communication Quarterly, 28,* 20–30.

Hsee, C. K., Hatfield, E., Carlson, J. G., & Chemtob, C. (1990). The effect of power on susceptibility to emotional contagion. *Cognition and Emotion, 4,* 327–340.

Hull, C. L. (1933). *Hypnosis and suggestibility.* New York: Appleton-Century.

Huston, T. L., & Vangelisti, A. L. (1991). Socioemotional behavior and satisfaction in marital relationships: A longitudinal study. *Journal of Personality and Social Psychology, 61,* 721–733.

Ickes, W., Patterson, M. L., Rajecki, D. W., & Tanford, S. (1982). Behavioral and cognitive consequences of reciprocal versus compensatory responses to preinteraction expectancies. *Social Cognition, 1,* 160–190.

Iizuka, Y., Mishima, K., & Matsumoto, T. (1989). A study of the arousal model of interpersonal intimacy. *Japanese Psychological Research, 31,* 127–136.

Infante, D. A. (1989). Response to high argumentatives: Message and sex differences. *Southern Communication Journal, 54,* 159–170.

Infante, D. A., Hartley, K. C., Martin, M. M., Higgins, M. A., Bruning, S. D., & Hur, G. (1992). Initiating and reciprocating verbal aggression: Effects on credibility and credited valid arguments. *Communication Studies, 43,* 182–190.

Jacobsen, N. S., Follette, W. C., & McDonald, D. W. (1982). Reactivity to positive and negative behavior in distressed and nondistressed marital couples. *Journal of Consulting and Clinical Psychology, 50,* 706–714.

Jones, E. E. (1986). Interpreting interpersonal behavior: The effects of expectancies. *Science, 234,* 41–46.

Jones, E. E., & Nisbett, R. E. (1971). *The actor and the observer: Divergent perspectives of the causes of behavior.* Morristown, NJ: General Learning Press.

Jones, S. E. (1986). Sex differences in touch communication. *Western Journal of Speech Communication, 50,* 227–241.

Jones, S. E. (1991). Problems of validity in questionnaire studies of nonverbal behavior: Jourard's tactile body-accessibility scale. *Southern Communication Journal, 56,* 83–95.

Jourard, S. M. (1959). Self-disclosure and other cathexis. *Journal of Abnormal Social Psychology, 59,* 428–431.

Jourard, S. M. (1966). An exploratory study of body accessibility. *British Journal of Social and Clinical Psychology, 5,* 221–231.

Jourard, S. M., & Landsman, M. J. (1960). Cognition, cathexis, and the "dyadic effect" in men's self-disclosing behavior. *Merrill-Palmer Quarterly, 6,* 178–186.

Kaplan, K. J. (1977). Structure and process in interpersonal "distancing." *Environmental Psychology and Nonverbal Behavior, 1,* 104–121.

Kaplan, K. J., Firestone, I. J., Klein, K. W., & Sodikoff, C. (1983). Distancing in dyads: A comparison of four models. *Social Psychology Quarterly, 46,* 108–115.

Kellermann, K. (1986). Anticipation of future interaction and information exchange in initial interaction. *Human Communication Research, 13,* 41–75.

Kellermann, K. (1991). The conversational MOP: II. Progressions through scenes in discourse. *Human Communication Research, 17,* 385–414.

Kellermann, K. (1992). Communication: Inherently strategic and primarily automatic. *Communication Monographs, 59,* 288–300.

Kempton, W. (1980). The rhythmic basis of interactional micro-synchrony. In M. R. Key (Ed.), *The relationship of verbal and nonverbal communication* (pp. 67–75). New York: Mouton.

Kendon, A. (1970). Movement coordination in social interaction: Some examples described. *Acta Psychologica, 32,* 1–25.

Kendon, A. (1974). Movement coordination in social interaction: Some examples described. In S. Weitz (Ed.), *Nonverbal communication* (pp. 150–167). New York: Oxford University Press.

Kendon, A. (1990). *Conducting interaction: Patterns of behavior in focused encounters.* Cambridge: Cambridge University Press.

Kenny, D. A. (1979). *Correlation and causality.* New York: Wiley-Interscience.

Kenny, D. A. (1981). Interpersonal perception: A multivariate round robin analysis. In M. Brewer & B. Collins (Eds.), *Knowing and validation: A tribute to Donald Campbell* (pp. 288–309). San Francisco: Jossey-Bass.

Kenny, D. A. (1988). Interpersonal perception: A social relations analysis. *Journal of Social and Personal Relationships, 5,* 247–261.

Kenny, D. A. (1994). *Interpersonal perception: A social relations analysis.* New York: Guilford.

Kenny, D. A., & Judd, C. M. (1981). *Estimating the effects of social interventions.* Cambridge: Cambridge University Press.

Kenny, D. A., & Kashy, D. A. (1991). Analyzing interdependence in dyads. In B. M. Montgomery & S. Duck (Eds.), *Studying interpersonal interaction* (pp. 275–285). New York: Guilford.

Kenny, D. A., Kashy, D. A., & Bolger, N. (1995). *Analysis strategies for multilevel data: An overview and evaluation of approaches.* Manuscript submitted for publication.

Kenny, D. A., & La Voie, L. (1982). Reciprocity of interpersonal attraction: A confirmed hypothesis. *Social Psychology Quarterly, 45,* 54–58.

Kenny, D. A., & La Voie, L. (1984). The social relations model. In L. Berkowitz (Ed.), *Advances in experimental social psychology* (Vol. 18, pp. 141–182). New York: Academic Press.

Kerlinger, F. N., & Pedhazur, E. J. (1973). *Multiple regression in behavioral research.* New York: Holt, Rinehart & Winston.

Kikuchi, T. (1994, July). *Effects of backchannel convergence on a speaker's speech rate and track-checking behavior.* Paper presented to the annual meeting of the International Communication Association, Sydney.

Knapp, M. L. (1984). *Interpersonal communication and human relationships.* Boston: Allyn and Bacon.

Knapp, M. L., & Hall, J. A. (1992). *Nonverbal communication in human interaction* (3rd ed). Fort Worth, TX: Harcourt Brace Jovanovich.

Knowles, E. S. (1980). An affiliative conflict theory of personal and group spatial behavior. In P. B. Paulus (Ed.), *Psychology of group influence* (1st ed., pp. 133–188). Hillsdale, NJ: Erlbaum.

Knowles, E. S. (1989). Spatial behavior of individuals and groups. In P. B. Paulus (Ed.), *Psychology of group influence* (2nd ed., pp. 53–86). Hillsdale, NJ: Erlbaum.

Koch, P. (1993). *Initial interaction choice: A theoretical framework based on need and reward-cost evaluations.* Unpublished paper, University of Arizona.

Kraemer, H. C., & Jacklin, C. N. (1979). Statistical analysis of dyadic social behavior. *Psychological Bulletin, 86,* 217–224.

LaFrance, M. (1979). Nonverbal synchrony and rapport: Analysis by the cross-lag panel technique. *Social Psychology Quarterly, 42,* 66–70.

LaFrance, M. (1982). Posture mirroring and rapport. In M. Davis (Ed.), *Interaction rhythms: Periodicity in communicative behavior* (pp. 279–298). New York: Human Sciences.

LaFrance, M. (1985). Postural mirroring and intergroup relations. *Personality and Social Psychology Bulletin, 11,* 207–217.

LaFrance, M., & Ickes, W. (1981). Posture mirroring and interactional involvement: Sex and sex typing effects. *Journal of Nonverbal Behavior, 5,* 139–154.

LaFrance, M., & Mayo, C. (1979). A review of nonverbal behaviors of women and men. *Western Journal of Speech Communication, 43,* 96–107.

La Gaipa, J. J. (1977). Interpersonal attraction as social exchange. In S. Duck (Ed.), *Theory and practice in interpersonal attraction* (pp. 129–164). London: Academic Press.

Langer, E., & Imber, L. (1980). Role of mindlessness in perception of deviance. *Journal of Personality and Social Psychology, 39,* 360–367.

Le Poire, B. A. (1991). *Two contrasting explanations of involvement violations: Orientation response or affective reaction?* Unpublished dissertation, University of Arizona.

Le Poire, B. A, & Burgoon, J. K. (1993). *Participant and observer perceptions of relational message interpretations associated with nonverbal involvement and pleasantness.* Manuscript submitted for publication.

Le Poire, B. A., & Burgoon, J. K. (1994). Two contrasting explanations of involvement violations: Nonverbal expectancy violations theory versus discrepancy arousal theory. *Human Communication Research, 20,* 560–591.

Levinger, G., & Snoek, J. D. (1972). *Attraction in relationship: A new look at interpersonal attraction.* Morristown, NJ: General Learning Press.

Lewin, K. (1951). *Field theory in social science.* New York: Harper.

Liska, J. (1987). Variations in the arbitrariness of ASL: An assessment of the symbolicity in simian signs. *Human Evolution, 2,* 205–212.

Liska, J. (1993a). Bee dances, bird songs, monkey calls, and cetacean sonar: Is speech unique? *Western Journal of Communication, 57,* 1–26.

Liska, J. (1993b). The role of rhetoric in semiogenesis: A response to Professor Kennedy. *Philosophy and Rhetoric, 26*, 31–38.

Liska, J. (1993c). Signs of the apes, songs of the whales: Comparing signs across species. *European Journal of Cognitive Systems, 3/4*, 381–397.

Lynn, S. J. (1978). Three theories of self-disclosure exchange. *Journal of Experimental Social Psychology, 14*, 466–479.

Mahl, G. F. (1987). *Explorations in nonverbal and vocal behavior.* Hillsdale, NJ: Erlbaum.

Manusov, V. (1993). "It depends on your perspective": Effects of stance and beliefs about intent on person perception. *Western Journal of Communication, 57*, 27–41.

Manusov, V. (1994). *Reacting to changes in nonverbal behaviors: Relational satisfaction and adaptation patterns in romantic dyads.* Paper presented to the Western States Communication Association, San Jose.

Markman, H. J. (1984). The longitudinal study of couples' interactions: Implications for understanding and predicting the development of marital distress. In K. Hahlweg & N. S. Jacobson (Eds.), *Marital interaction: Analysis and modification* (pp. 253–281). New York: Guilford.

Markus-Kaplan, M., & Kaplan, K. J. (1984). A bidimensional view of distancing: Reciprocity versus compensation, intimacy versus social control. *Journal of Nonverbal Behavior, 8*, 315–326.

Maslow, A. H. (1970). *Motivation and personality* (2nd ed.). New York: Harper & Row.

Matarazzo, J. D., Weitman, M., Saslow, G., & Wiens, A. N. (1963). Interviewer influence on durations of interviewee speech. *Journal of Verbal Learning and Verbal Behavior, 1*, 451–458.

Matarazzo, J. D., & Wiens, A. N. (1972). *The interview: Research on its anatomy and structure.* Chicago: Aldine-Atherton.

Matarazzo, J. D., Wiens, A. N., Matarazzo, R. G., & Saslow, G. (1968). Speech and silence behavior in clinical psychotherapy and its laboratory correlates. In J. Schlier, J. D. Matarazzo, & C. Savage (Eds.), *Research in psychotherapy* (Vol. 3, pp. 347–394). Washington, DC: American Psychological Association.

Matarazzo, J. D., Wiens, A. N., & Saslow, G. (1965). Studies in interviewer speech behavior. In L. Krasner & L. P. Ullmann (Eds.), *Research in behavior modification: New developments and implications* (pp. 179–210). New York: Holt, Rinehart & Winston.

Mayo, C., & Henley, N. (Eds.) (1981). *Gender and nonverbal behavior.* New York: Springer-Verlag.

McDowall, J. J. (1978a). Interactional synchrony: A reappraisal. *Journal of Personality and Social Psychology, 36*, 963–975.

McDowall, J. J. (1978b). Microanalysis of filmed movement: The reliability of boundary detection by observers. *Environmental Psychology and Nonverbal Behavior, 3,* 77–88.

McGrath, J. E. (1988). Time and social psychology. In J. E. McGrath (Ed.), *The social psychology of time* (pp. 255–267). Beverly Hills, CA: Sage.

McNemar, Q. (1962). *Psychological statistics.* New York: John Wiley.

Mead, G. H. (1934). *Mind, self, and society* (C. M. Morris, Ed.). Chicago: University of Chicago Press.

Mead, G. H. (1964). Social consciousness and the consciousness of meaning. In A. J. Reck (Ed.), *Selected writings* (pp. 123–133). New York: Bobbs-Merrill.

Mehrabian, A. (1969). Significance of posture and position in the communication of attitude and status relationships. *Psychological Bulletin, 71,* 359–372.

Mehrabian, A. (1976). *Public places and private spaces.* New York: Basic Books.

Mehrabian, A. (1981). *Silent messages: Implicit communication of emotions and attitudes* (2nd ed.). Belmont, CA: Wadsworth.

Mehrabian, A., & Ksionzky, S. (1972). Categories of social behavior. *Group Studies, 3,* 425–436.

Mehrabian, A., & Williams, M. (1969). Nonverbal concomitants of perceived and intended persuasiveness. *Journal of Personality and Social Psychology, 13,* 37–58.

Meng, X.-L., Rosenthal, R., & Rubin, D. B. (1992). Comparing correlated correlation coefficients. *Psychological Bulletin, 111,* 172–175.

Milgram, S. (1970). The experience of living in cities. *Science, 167,* 1461–1468.

Millar, F. E., & Rogers, L. E. (1987). Relational dimensions in interpersonal dynamics. In R. E. Roloff & G. R. Miller (Eds.), *Interpersonal processes: New directions in communication research* (pp. 117–139). Beverly Hills, CA: Sage.

Miller, G. R., & Steinberg, M. (1975). *Between people: A new analysis of interpersonal communication.* Chicago: Science Research Associates.

Montgomery, B. M. (1992). Communication as the interface between couples and culture. In S. A. Deetz (Ed.), *Communication yearbook 15* (pp. 475–507). Newbury Park, CA: Sage.

Montgomery, B. M., & Duck, S. (Eds.) (1991). *Studying interpersonal interaction.* New York: Guilford.

Morley, D. D. (1987). Revised lag sequential analysis. In M. L. McLaughlin (Ed.), *Communication yearbook 10* (pp. 172–182). Newbury Park, CA: Sage.

Morris, D., Collett, P., Marsh, P., & O'Shaughnessy, M. (1979). *Gestures: Their origins and distribution.* New York: Stein and Day.

Morris, W. (Ed.). (1973). *The American Heritage dictionary of the English language*. Boston: Houghton Mifflin.

Morton, T. L. (1978). Intimacy and reciprocity of exchange: A comparison of spouses and strangers. *Journal of Personality and Social Psychology, 36*, 72–81.

Mosby, K. D. (1978). *An analysis of actual and ideal touching behavior as reported on a modified version of the body accessibility questionnaire*. Unpublished doctoral dissertation, Virginia Commonwealth University.

Motley, M. T. (1990a). Communication as interaction: A reply to Beach and Bavelas. *Western Journal of Speech Communication, 54*, 613–623.

Motley, M. T. (1990b). On whether one can(not) communicate: An examination via traditional communication postulates. *Western Journal of Speech Communication, 54*, 1–20.

Motley, M. T. (1991). How one may not communicate: A reply to Andersen. *Communication Studies, 42*, 326–339.

Mulac, A., Studley, L. B., Wiemann, J. W., & Bradac, J. J. (1987). Male/female gaze in same-sex and mixed-sex dyads: Gender-linked differences and mutual influence. *Human Communication Research, 13*, 323–344.

Nesbitt, P. D., & Steven, G. (1974). Personal space and stimulus intensity at a southern California amusement park. *Sociometry, 37*, 105–115.

Newton, D. A., & Burgoon, J. K. (1990a). Nonverbal conflict behaviors: Functions, strategies, and tactics. In D. A. Cahn (Ed.), *Intimates in conflict: A communication perspective* (pp. 77–104). Hillsdale, NJ: Erlbaum.

Newton, D. A., & Burgoon, J. K. (1990b). The use and consequences of verbal influence strategies during interpersonal disagreements. *Human Communication Research, 16*, 477–518.

Newtson, D. (1973). Attribution and the unit of perception in ongoing behavior. *Journal of Personality and Social Psychology, 28*, 28–31.

Noller, P. (1984). *Nonverbal communication and marital interaction*. Oxford: Pergamon.

Noller, P., & Guthrie, D. (1991). Studying communication in marriage: An integration and critical evaluation. *Advances in Personal Relationships, 3*, 37–73.

O'Connor, B. P., & Gifford, R. (1988). A test among models of nonverbal immediacy reactions: Arousal-labeling, discrepancy-arousal and social cognition. *Journal of Nonverbal Behavior, 12*, 6–33.

Ostrom, C. W., Jr. (1978). *Time series analysis: Regression techniques*. Beverly Hills, CA: Sage.

O'Toole, R., & Dubin, R. (1968). Baby feeding and body sway: An experiment in George Herbert Mead's "taking the role of the other." *Journal of Personality and Social Psychology, 10*, 59–65.

Palmer, M. T., & Simmons, K. B. (1993, November). *Interpersonal intentions, nonverbal behaviors and judgments of liking: Encoding, decoding and consciousness.* Paper presented to the annual meeting of the Speech Communication Association, Miami.

Papousek, M. (in press). Origins of reciprocity and mutuality in prelinguistic parent–infant "dialogues." In I. Marková, C. F. Graumann, & K. Foppa (Eds.), *Mutualities in dialogue.* Cambridge: Cambridge University Press.

Patterson, M. L. (1973). Compensation in nonverbal immediacy behaviors: A review. *Sociometry, 36,* 237–252.

Patterson, M. L. (1976). An arousal model of interpersonal intimacy. *Psychological Review, 83,* 235–245.

Patterson, M. L. (1982). A sequential functional model of nonverbal exchange. *Psychological Review, 89,* 231–249.

Patterson, M. L. (1983). *Nonverbal behavior: A functional perspective.* New York: Springer-Verlag.

Patterson, M. L. (1985). The evolution of a functional model of nonverbal exchange: A personal perspective. In R. L. Street, Jr. & J. N. Cappella (Eds.), *Sequence and pattern in communicative behaviour* (pp. 190–205). London: Edward Arnold.

Patterson, M. L. (1987). Presentational and affect-management functions of nonverbal involvement. *Journal of Nonverbal Behavior, 11,* 110–122.

Patterson, M. L. (1990). Functions of non-verbal behavior in social interaction. In H. Giles & W. P. Robinson (Eds.), *Handbook of Language and Social Psychology* (pp. 101–120). Chichester, UK: John Wiley & Sons.

Patterson, M. L. (1991). A functional approach to nonverbal exchange. In R. S. Feldman & B. Rime (Eds.), *Fundamentals of nonverbal behavior* (pp. 458–495). Cambridge: Cambridge University Press.

Patterson, M. L. (1994). *Toward an integrative model of nonverbal communication.* Manuscript submitted for publication.

Patterson, M. L., Jordan, A., Hogan, M. B., & Frerker, D. (1981). Effects of nonverbal intimacy on arousal and behavioral adjustment. *Journal of Nonverbal Behavior, 5,* 184–198.

Patterson, M. L., Roth, C. P., & Schenk, C. (1979). Seating arrangement, activity, and sex differences in small group crowding. *Personality and Social Psychology Bulletin, 5,* 100–103.

Patterson, M. L., & Schaeffer, R. E. (1977). Effects of size and sex composition on interaction distance, participation, and satisfaction in small groups. *Small Group Behavior, 8,* 433–442.

Pearce, W. B., Sharp, S. M., Wright, P. M., & Slama, K. M. (1974). Affection and reciprocity in self-disclosing communication. *Human Communication Research, 1,* 5–14.

Pike, G. R., & Sillars, A. L. (1985). Reciprocity of marital communication. *Journal of Social and Personal Relationships, 2,* 303–324.

Ploog, D. W. (in press). Mutuality and dialogue in nonhuman primate communication. In I. Marková, C. F. Graumann, & K. Foppa (Eds.), *Mutualities in dialogue*. Cambridge: Cambridge University Press.

Poole, M. S., Folger, J. P., & Hewes, D. E. (1987). Analyzing interpersonal interaction. In M. E. Roloff & G. R. Miller (Eds.), *Interpersonal processes: New directions in communication research* (pp. 220–256). Beverly Hills, CA: Sage.

Putman, W., & Street, R. (1984). The conception and perception of noncontent speech performance: Implications for speech accommodation theory. *International Journal of the Sociology of Language, 46,* 97–114.

Putnam, L. L., & Jones, T. S. (1982). Reciprocity in negotiations: An analysis of bargaining interaction. *Communication Monographs, 49,* 171–191.

Raghunathan, T. E., Rosenthal, R., & Rubin, D. B. (1993). *A simple new method for comparing cross-lagged correlations.* Manuscript submitted for publication.

Rawlins, W. K. (1983). Negotiating close friendship: The dialectic of conjunctive freedoms. *Human Communication Research, 9,* 255–266.

Rawlins, W. K. (1992). *Friendship matters: Communication, dialectics, and the life course.* New York: Aldine de Gruyter.

Reissland, N. (1988). Neonatal imitation in the first hour of life: Observations in rural Nepal. *Developmental Psychology, 24,* 464–469.

Revenstorf, D., Hahlweg, K., Schindler, L., & Kunert, H. (1984). The use of time series analysis in marriage counseling. In K. Hahlweg & N. S. Jacobson (Eds.), *Marital interaction: Analysis and modification* (pp. 199–231). New York: Guilford.

Reynolds, H. T. (1977). *Analysis of nominal data.* Beverly Hills, CA: Sage.

Rocissano, L., Slade, A., & Lynch, V. (1987). Dyadic synchrony and toddler compliance. *Developmental Psychology. 23,* 698–704.

Roloff, M. E. (1987). Communication and reciprocity within intimate relationships. In R. E. Roloff & G. R. Miller (Eds.), *Interpersonal processes: New directions in communication research* (pp. 11–38). Beverly Hills, CA: Sage.

Roloff, M. E., & Campion, D. E. (1985). Conversational profit-seeking: Interaction as social exchange. In R. L. Street, Jr. & J. N. Cappella (Eds.), *Sequence and pattern in communicative behaviour* (pp. 161–189). London: Edward Arnold.

Rommetveit, R. (1974). *On message structure: A framework for the study of language and communication.* New York: Wiley.

Rosa, E., & Mazur, A. (1979). Incipient status in small groups. *Social Forces, 58,* 18–37.

Rosenfeld, H. M. (1982). Measurement of body motion and orientation. In K. R. Scherer & P. Ekman (Eds.), *Handbook of methods in nonverbal behavior research* (pp. 199–286). Cambridge: Cambridge University Press.

Rosenfeld, H. M. (1987). Conversational control functions of nonverbal behavior. In A. W. Siegman & S. Feldstein (Eds.), *Nonverbal behavior and communication* (2nd ed., pp. 563–601). Hillsdale, NJ: Erlbaum.

Rosenthal, R. (1984). *Meta-analytic procedures for social research.* Beverly Hills, CA: Sage.

Rosenthal, R., & Rosnow, R. L. (1984). *Essentials of behavioral research: Methods and data analysis.* New York: McGraw-Hill.

Ross, H. S., Cheyne, J. A., & Lollis, S. P. (1988). Defining and studying reciprocity in young children. In S. W. Duck (Ed.), *Handbook of personal relationships* (pp. 143–160). New York: John Wiley & Sons.

Rubin, L. B. (1983). *Intimate strangers: Men and women together.* New York: Harper & Row.

Rusbult, C. E., Verette, J., Whitney, G. A., Slovik, L. F., & Lipkus, I. (1991). Accommodation processes in close relationships: Theory and preliminary empirical evidence. *Journal of Personality and Social Psychology, 60,* 53–78.

Sabourin, T. C., Infante, D. A., & Rudd, J. E. (1993). Verbal aggression in marriages: A comparison of violent, distressed but nonviolent, and non-distressed couples. *Human Communication Research, 20,* 245–267.

Sandilands, M. L., & Fleury, N. C. (1979). Unilinguals en des milieux bilingues: Une analyse des attributions. *Canadian Journal of Behavioral Science, 11,* 164–168.

Savicki, V. (1972). Outcomes of nonreciprocal self-disclosure strategies. *Journal of Personality and Social Psychology, 23,* 271–276.

Schaap, C. (1984). A comparison of the interaction of distressed and non-distressed married couples in a laboratory situation: Literature survey, methodological issues, and an empirical investigation. In K. Hahlweg & N. S. Jacobson (Eds.), *Marital interaction: Analysis and modification* (pp. 133–158). New York: Guilford.

Schachter, S., & Singer, J. E. (1962). Cognitive, social, and physiological determinants of emotional state. *Psychological Review, 69,* 379–399.

Scheflen, A. E. (1964). The significance of posture in communication systems. *Psychiatry, 27,* 316–331.

Schegloff, E. A. (1993). Reflections on quantification in the study of conversation. *Research on Language in Social Interaction, 26,* 99–128.

Seibold, D. R., Cantrill, J. G., & Meyers, R. A. (1985). Communication and interpersonal influence. In M. L. Knapp & G. R. Miller (Eds.), *Handbook of interpersonal communication* (1st ed., pp. 551–611). Beverly Hills, CA: Sage.

Shaffer, D. R., Ogden, J. K., & Wu, C. (1987). Effects of self-monitoring and prospect of future interaction on self-disclosure reciprocity during the acquaintance process. *Journal of Personality, 55,* 75–96.

Shaffer, D. R., & Tomarelli, M. M. (1989). When public and private self-foci clash: Self-consciousness and self-disclosure during the acquaintance process. *Journal of Personality and Social Psychology, 56,* 765–776.

Sillars, A. L., Pike, G. R., Jones, T. J., & Redmon, K. (1983). Communication and conflict in marriage. In R. N. Bostrom (Ed.), *Communication year-book 7* (pp. 414–429). Beverly Hills, CA: Sage.

Simner, M. L. (1971). Newborn's response to the cry of another infant. *Developmental Psychology, 5,* 136–150.

Simonton, D. K. (1977). Cross-sectional time-series experiments: Some suggested statistical analyses. *Psychological Bulletin, 84,* 489–502.

Snedecor, G. W., & Cochran, W. G. (1967). *Statistical methods* (6th ed.). Ames: Iowa State University Press.

Snyder, M. (1992). Motivational foundations of behavioral confirmation. In M. P. Zanna (Ed.), *Advances in experimental social psychology* (Vol. 25, pp. 67–114). New York: Academic.

Snyder, M., & Haugen, J. A. (1994). Why does behavioral confirmation occur? A functional perspective on the role of the perceiver. *Journal of Experimental Social Psychology, 30,* 218–246.

Sommer, R. (1971). Spatial parameters in naturalistic research. In A. H. Esser (Ed.), *Behavior and environment: The use of space in animals* (pp. 281–290). New York: Plenum.

Stafford, L., Waldron, V. R., & Infield, L. L. (1989). Actor–observer differences in conversational memory. *Human Communication Research, 15,* 590–611.

Stern, D. (1977). *A first relationship: Mother and infant.* Cambridge, MA: Harvard University Press.

Street, R. L., Jr. (1982). Evaluation of noncontent speech accommodation. *Language and Communication, 2,* 13–31.

Street, R. L., Jr. (1984). Speech convergence and speech evaluation in fact-finding interviews. *Human Communication Research, 11,* 139–169.

Street, R. L., Jr. (1988). Communication style: Considerations for measuring consistency, reciprocity, and compensation. In C. H. Tardy (Ed.), *A handbook for the study of human communication: Methods and instruments for observing, measuring, and assessing communication processes* (pp. 139–161). Norwood, NJ: Ablex.

Street, R. L., Jr. (1990). The communicative functions of paralanguage and prosody. In H. Giles & W. P. Robinson (Eds.), *Handbook of language and social psychology* (pp. 121–140). Chichester, UK: John Wiley & Sons.

Street, R. L., Jr. (1991). Accommodation in medical consultations. In H. Giles, N. Coupland, & J. Coupland (Eds.), *Contexts of accommodation: Developments in applied sociolinguistics* (pp. 131–156). Cambridge: Cambridge University Press.

Street, R. L., Jr., Brady, R. M., & Putman, W. B. (1983). The influence of speech rate stereotypes and rate similarity on listeners' evaluations of speakers. *Journal of Language and Social Psychology, 2,* 37–56.

Street, R. L., Jr., & Buller, D. B. (1987). Nonverbal response patterns in physician–patient interactions: A functional analysis. *Journal of Nonverbal Behavior, 11,* 234–253.

Street, R. L., Jr., & Buller, D. B. (1988). Patients' characteristics affecting physician–patient nonverbal communication. *Human Communication Research, 15,* 60–90.

Street, R. L., Jr., & Cappella, J. N. (1985). Sequence and pattern in communication behaviour: A model and commentary. In R. L. Street, Jr. & J. N. Cappella (Eds.), *Sequence and pattern in communicative behaviour* (pp. 243–276). London: Edward Arnold.

Street, R. L., Jr., & Cappella, J. N. (1989). Social and linguistic factors influencing adaptation in children's speech. *Journal of Psycholinguistic Research, 18,* 497–519.

Street, R. L., Jr., & Giles, H. (1982). Speech Accommodation Theory: A social cognitive approach to language and speech behavior. In M. E. Roloff & C. R. Berger (Eds.), *Social cognition and communication* (pp. 193–226). Beverly Hills, CA: Sage.

Street, R. L, Jr., Street, N. J., & VanKleeck, A. (1983). Speech convergence among talkative and reticent three-year-olds. *Language Sciences, 5,* 79–86.

Surra, C. A., & Ridley, C. A. (1991). Multiple perspectives on interaction: Participants, peers, and observers. In B. M. Montgomery & S. Duck (Eds.), *Studying interpersonal interaction* (pp. 35–55). New York: Guilford.

Tajfel, H., & Turner, J. C. (1979). An integrative theory of intergroup conflict. In W. G. Austin & S. Worchel (Eds.), *The social psychology of intergroup relations* (pp. 33–47). Monterey, CA: Brooks/Cole.

Taylor, D. M., Simard, L. M., & Papineau, D. (1978). Perceptions of cultural differences and language use: A field study in a bilingual environment. *Canadian Journal of Behavioral Science, 10,* 181–191.

Termine, N. T., & Izard, C. E. (1988). Infants' response to their mother's expressions of joy and sadness. *Developmental Psychology, 24,* 223–229.

Tiersma, P. M. (1993). Nonverbal communication and the freedom of "speech." *Wisconsin Law Review, 6,* 1535–1589.

Ting-Toomey, S. (1986). Interpersonal ties in intergroup communication. In W. Gudykunst (Ed.), *Intergroup communication* (pp. 114–126). London: Edward Arnold.

Toris, C., & DePaulo, B. M. (1985). Effects of actual deception and suspiciousness of deception on interpersonal perceptions. *Journal of Personality and Social Psychology, 47,* 1063–1073.

Triandis, H. C. (1960). Cognitive similarity and communication in a dyad. *Human Relations, 13,* 175–183.

Tronick, E. D., Als, H., & Brazelton, T. B. (1977). Mutuality in mother–infant interaction. *Journal of Communication, 27,* 74–79.

Trout, D. L., & Rosenfeld, H. M. (1980). The effect of postural lean and body congruence on the judgment of psychotherapeutic rapport. *Journal of Nonverbal Behavior, 4,* 176–190.

Tucker, R. K., & Chase, L. J. (1980). Canonical correlation. In P. R. Monge & J. N. Cappella (Eds.), *Multivariate techniques in human communication research* (pp. 205–228). New York: Academic Press.

Valdes-Fallis, G. (1977). Code switching among bilingual Mexican-American women: Towards an understanding of sex-related language alternation. *International Journal of the Sociology of Language, 17,* 65–72.

VanLear, C. A., Jr. (1983). Analysis of interaction data. In R. N. Bostrom (Ed.), *Communication yearbook 7* (pp. 282–303). Beverly Hills, CA: Sage.

VanLear, C. A., Jr. (1987). The formation of social relationships: A longitudinal study of social penetration. *Human Communication Research, 13,* 299–322.

VanLear, C. A., Jr. (1991). Testing a cyclical model of communicative openness in relationship development: Two longitudinal studies. *Communication Monographs, 58,* 337–361.

VanLear, C. A., Jr., & Zeitlow, P. H. (1990). Toward a contingency approach to marital interaction: An empirical integration of three approaches. *Communication Monographs, 57,* 202–218.

Wallbott, H. G. (in press). Congruence, contagion, and motor mimicry: Mutualities in nonverbal exchange. In I. Marková, C. F. Graumann, & K. Foppa (Eds.), *Mutualities in dialogue.* Cambridge: Cambridge University Press.

Waldron, V. R. (1990). Constrained rationality: Situational influences on information acquisition plans and tactics. *Communication Monographs, 57,* 184–201.

Warner, R. M., Malloy, D., Schneider, K., Knoth, R., & Wilder, B. (1987). Rhythmic organization of social interaction and observer ratings of positive affect and involvement. *Journal of Nonverbal Behavior, 11,* 57–74.

Webb, J. T. (1972). Interview synchrony: An investigation of two speech rate measures in an automated standardized interview. In B. Pope & A. W. Siegman (Eds.), *Studies in dyadic communication* (pp. 115–133). New York: Pergamon.

Welkowitz, J., & Feldstein, S. (1969). Dyadic interaction and induced differences in perceived similarity. *Proceedings of the 77th Annual Convention of the American Psychological Association, 4,* 343–344.

Welkowitz, J., & Feldstein, S. (1970). Relation of experimentally manipulated interpersonal perception and psychological differentiation to the temporal patterning of conversation. *Proceedings of the 78th Annual Convention of the American Psychological Association, 5,* 387–388.

Welkowitz, J., Feldstein, S., Finkelstein, M., & Aylesworth, L. (1972). Changes in vocal intensity as a function of interspeaker influence. *Perceptual and Motor Skills, 35,* 715–718.

Welkowitz, J., & Kuc, M. (1973). Inter-relationships among warmth, genuineness, empathy and temporal speech patterns in interpersonal attraction. *Journal of Consulting and Clinical Psychology, 41,* 472–473.

Wiener, M., Devoe, S., Rubinow, S., & Geller, J. (1972). Nonverbal behavior and nonverbal communication. *Psychological Review, 79,* 185–214.

Won-Doornink, M. J. (1985). Self-disclosure and reciprocity in conversation: A cross-national study. *Social Psychology Quarterly, 48,* 97–107.

Woodall, W. G., & Burgoon, J. K. (1981). The effects of nonverbal synchrony on message comprehension and persuasiveness. *Journal of Nonverbal Behavior, 5,* 207–223.

Worthy, M., Gary, A. L., & Kahn, G. M. (1969). Self-disclosure as an exchange process. *Journal of Personality and Social Psychology, 13,* 59–63.

Wylie, L. (1985). Language learning and communication. *French Review, 53,* 777–785.

# Index

acceptance range (or region) 47–49
affect (or emotion) 12, 19, 24–28, 30,
   48–52, 67–68, 80–81, 86–87, 103–
   104, 109, 126, 151, 166, 219, 221–
   223, 225, 227, 231, 234–235, 241,
   251–254, 262, 292–294
affective labeling (also cognitive-
   affective labeling or assessments)
   38–43, 86–88, 92
affiliation, need for 32, 251, 265, 265,
   272
Affiliative Conflict Theory (ACT) 11–
   12, 30–38, 46, 54, 251, 256, 258
antecedent factors 84–86
approach/avoidance
   gradients 36–37
   mutual 44–45
   needs for 6, 30–32, 46
arousal
   change 38–43, 48–53, 86–88, 103–
      109, 252–254, 300–301
   level of 30, 39–43, 48–51, 87–88,
      103–109, 252–254
Arousal-Labeling Theory (ALT) 38–43,
   252–253
Arousal-Valence Theory (see Cognitive-
   Valence Theory)
attachment 44–47
attraction mediation 9
attraction transformation 9, 97
autonomy, need for 30–32, 55

behavior
   appropriateness of 61, 63–64, 70, 77,
      85, 87, 107, 109, 111
   change vs. maintenance 120–122,
      135–136
   communicative vs. indicative 92–93,
      111, 125
   equivalence (see multifunctional na-
      ture of behaviors)
   magnitude vs. direction of change
      122–123, 138
behavioral meshing 20
Bidimensional Model (BM) 43–46, 252
body orientation (see immediacy)
bonding/rapport, need for 23–26, 29

cognitive schemata or valencers 107–
   108, 112
Cognitive-Valence Theory (CVT) 105–
   109, 253–254, 257–258
comfort, need for 23, 25
Communication Accommodation Theory
   (CAT) 72–79, 198, 211, 224, 252–
   253, 257–258, 287–289
communication efficiency 73–74
communication functions
   conversation management (interaction
      regulation) 81–82, 91, 126–127
   emotional communication and emo-
      tion management (affect manage-
      ment) 81–82, 126
   identity management 81–82
   impression formation and manage-
      ment 81–82, 129, 196
   information processing (speech pro-
      cessing) 25, 29, 81–82
   relational communication and rela-
      tionship management 81–82, 126,
      129
   social influence (social control) 44,
      81–82, 91, 126
compensation
   interpersonal 5, 31, 44, 116–126, 129
   intrapersonal 31–49
complementarity 5, 116, 119, 129, 132,
   135

concatenous behavioral changes or patterns 21, 136–137
conflict (management) 67–68, 262, 274–275, 292–294
contingent behavioral patterns 132–135, 137
convergence 72–79, 128, 255
cultural influences 7, 23, 80, 85, 94–95, 107, 111, 261, 264, 266–269, 286

deindividuation 44–45
design issues
  between- vs. within-dyads (or within-subjects) designs 135–136, 143, 152–158, 173, 175, 212–213, 240, 242, 260, 285
  longitudinal vs. cross-sectional analyses 122, 136, 143, 151–152, 158–167, 174, 242
  use of confederates 120, 135–136, 164, 181, 185, 199, 242
detachment 44–45
Dialectical Model 54–58, 252
directedness of behaviors 117–120, 132–135
discrepancies, magnitude of 48, 52–53
Discrepancy-Arousal Theory (DAT) 46–53, 94, 252
divergence 5, 72–79, 129
dominance 96, 98–99, 126, 144, 146–147, 246, 256, 263
"dyadic effect" (*see also* self-disclosure) 66, 69, 71–72, 79, 252
dissynchrony 5, 23–24, 119

embedded structure 45
empathy (empathic processes) 26–28, 69, 110–111
entrainment 20, 256
environmental influences 20, 32, 36, 74, 86–87, 89, 105, 107, 261, 264
Equilibrium Theory (*see* Affiliative Conflict Theory)
expectancies
  communication 49, 84, 86–88, 91–93, 94, 97, 99
  deviations from 87–88, 95, 99
Expectancy Violations Theory (EVT) 94–105, 215, 253–254
eye gaze (or eye contact; *see* immediacy)

Field theory 36–37
functional equivalence of behaviors (*see* communication functions, multifunctional nature of behaviors)

gender, effects of 34, 76, 84–85, 175

immediacy 30, 33–34, 67, 91, 93, 98–102, 104–109, 212, 216, 221, 235, 240–241, 244, 255, 262, 278, 284
individuation 44–45
ingroup/outgroup identity 73, 76–77
intention (-al, -ality) 124–125, 132
Interaction Adaptation Theory (IAT) 215, 265–278, 283–284
interpersonal coordination 20–21, 23, 117
interpersonal influence, mutual vs. unidirectional 4, 120
intimacy 6, 8–10, 20, 30–32, 34–35, 37–46, 57, 64–67, 69–71, 80, 83, 87, 91–92, 100, 102, 105–107, 109, 126, 128, 147, 260, 277–278, 286
involvement 24, 67, 74, 76, 84–88, 91, 96–99, 102–104, 126, 139–140, 149, 164, 174, 216, 225, 240, 256, 260, 278

lagged sequential analyses (*see also* statistical analysis) 134, 151, 160–162
longitudinal analyses (*see also* design issues) 122, 136, 143, 151–152, 158–167, 174, 242

matching 4, 117, 119, 128, 132–133, 135–136, 255
measurement issues
  aggregating (or averaging) data 136, 140, 150, 162, 164, 188, 191, 242
  baseline behavioral measures 135–137, 158, 167, 173, 198, 243
  categorical vs. continuous measures (or nominal- vs. interval-level measures) 134–135, 149–152, 160–161, 198
  criterion threshold for measuring change 138
  individual vs. dyadic measures 144, 166

micro- vs. macroscopic measurement (or molar vs. molecular) 136–137, 139, 142–144, 166, 284
multivariate vs. single behavior measures 138–140, 166–168, 191, 242
nonindependence of observations or data 154–155, 160, 162
observer vs. participant ratings 144–145
perceptual vs. behavioral measures (or subjective self-report vs. objective coder ratings) 137, 140–142, 144–145
qualitative data (e.g., diaries, interviews) 137
sequential (or concatenous) measures 136–137
validity 142, 182, 213
mirroring 4, 120, 128, 251
modeling 26
motor mimicry 4, 19, 25–29, 109–111, 118, 120, 251, 253
multifunctional nature of
behaviors 83, 87–88, 92, 126–128, 138–140
interactions 81, 83, 88

nonaccommodation 123, 135, 256, 262, 292
nonverbal communication 30, 33–34, 38, 49, 63–64, 67, 71, 75, 81, 83–84, 86–87, 91, 94, 97, 109–110
Nonverbal Expectancy Violations Theory (*see* Expectancy Violations Theory)
norm of reciprocity 60–63, 252

personal space (*see* immediacy)
personality, effects of
extraversion/introversion 34, 108
locus of control 85
sensation seeking 52
preinteraction mediators 86–87, 89
privacy, need for 31, 55, 251
proximity (or closeness/distance; *see* immediacy; intimacy)
postural congruence 21, 26

reciprocity
definitions of 4, 44, 61–62, 119–120, 129
dyadic 116

heteromorphic vs. homeomorphic 62–63, 296
individual 116
magnitude of 122–123, 138
mature 45
perception of vs. actual 56–57, 137, 140–142
relational 116–117, 133
temporal 116, 133
timing of (immediate vs. lagged) 62, 123–124, 136–137
type of 62, 116–117, 142
rejection-intrusion pattern 45
Resource Exchange Model 127, 252
reward valence of the communicator 95–97, 100, 105, 107, 254
round robin design (*see* social relations model)
rhythmicity (or rhythm) 20–25, 123–124

sampling issues
sample composition 145–146
sampling units (and intervals) 142–144, 154, 161, 163
safety/survival, need for 23, 25
satisfaction, partner/relationship 56, 255, 286, 289, 292–295
self-disclosure
descriptive vs. evaluative 70
dimensions of 70
personal vs. relational 70
Sequential Functional Model (SFM) 84–94, 253–254
similarity, expression of 24, 29, 76, 110–111, 125–126, 147, 187, 196
simultaneous behavior (or movement) 20–21, 124, 136
social approval, need for 72–74, 76, 79
Social Exchange Theory 63–65, 95, 252
social norms 73, 77, 92–94, 107, 260
social organization 12
Social Penetration Theory 55, 61
social relations model 134, 155
Speech Accommodation Theory (*see* Communication Accommodation Theory)
stable exchange 84, 87–88
statistical analysis
autoregressive integrated moving average model (ARIMA) 152, 162
canonical correlation analysis 151, 155

statistical analysis (*cont.*)
  chi-square analysis 151, 159
  contingency coefficient 151
  cross-lagged panel correlation analysis 151, 163, 165–166, 183
  Fourier analysis 152, 162
  individual time series analysis 151, 161–163, 188–198
  interrupted time series analysis 151, 163–165, 198–203, 240
  intraclass correlation 149, 151, 156–158, 186–188, 221–224, 240
  lag sequential analysis 134, 151, 160–162
  logit analysis 151
  log-linear analysis 151
  Markov chain analysis 144, 149, 151, 160–161
  multiple discriminant analysis 151, 174–175
  Pearson product-moment correlation 149, 151, 153–156, 159, 175–186, 221–224, 240
  phi 150–151
  repeated measures (multi- and uni-variate) analysis of variance 149, 151, 166–167, 203–212, 224–234, 240
  repeated measures multiple regression 134–135, 149, 151, 166
  spectral analysis 152
synchrony
  interpersonal (interactional) 4, 19–25, 117, 119, 128–129, 251, 255
  intrapersonal (self) 20

theoretical issues
  falsifiability 35, 47, 92
  heurism 10, 92
  parsimony 92, 265
  precision 57, 260
  scope 46–47, 258
  tautology 47
touch (*see* immediacy)

verbal communication 33, 38, 55, 63, 71, 81, 83–84, 94, 97, 109, 255
violation valence 97, 104, 254

*zeitgeber* 20, 119